COMMODITY TRADING MANUAL

Commodity Trading Manual
Prepared by the Education and Marketing Services Department of the
Chicago Board of Trade

Executive Editor	Patrick J. Catania Vice President
Managing Director	Nancy Keefer
Senior Manager, *Communications*	Bruce Andrews
Project Editor	Christine Depp Stebbins
Assistant Project Editor	Barbara Z. Kodlubanski
Contributing Editors	Kirstin Daen, Laura Donkel, Mary Catherine Friel, Jerry Mastey
Copy Editors	Dana Kellerman, John Simpson
Manager, *Publication Services*	David Sural
Production Coordinator	Jenny Garcia

EM42-10
© Board of Trade of the City of Chicago 1973, 1976, 1977, 1980, 1982, 1985, 1989.
All rights reserved. Printed in the USA.
1. 91. 9000

We express our appreciation to the following people who generously gave their time and effort in reviewing sections of this publication.

Reviewers:
Jin Choi, DePaul University; Anthony P. Danielak III, Pillsbury Commodity Services, Inc.; Norman R. Ferren, Andrea B. Liebelt, New York Cotton Exchange; Barbara Fitzgerald, Kansas City Board of Trade; Therese Geraghty, Cathy Macrae, Chicago Mercantile Exchange; Gloria Kareken, MidAmerica Commodity Exchange, Chicago Rice & Cotton Exchange; Mary Ann Matlock, New York Mercantile Exchange; Thomas V. Mauro, Cargill Investor Services, Inc.; Marilyn J. McNally, Philadelphia Board of Trade; Laura Oatney, National Futures Association; Richard T. Pombonyo, New York Futures Exchange; Richard S. Rhodie, Minneapolis Grain Exchange; Roger D. Rutz, Dennis Dutterer, Maureen Brehm, Board of Trade Clearing Corporation; Karen L. San Antonio, Coffee, Sugar & Cocoa Exchange, Inc.; Dirk Walvoord, Chicago Board of Trade member

Education Subcommittee of the Chicago Board of Trade:
Anthony P. Danielak III, co-chairman; Lawrence C. Dorf, co-chairman; Pamela R. Rogers, co-chairman; William D. Brown; F. Gregory Deneen; Frank P. DiMaria; Leonard S. Goldstein; Sidney C. Hamper; Leslie H. Herren; James L. Klotz; Edward R. Krajewski, Sr.; Jerome J. Lacey; Joyce Selander; Joseph M. Stewart; Bradford James Tyl; Dirk Walvoord

Chicago Board of Trade Staff Reviewers:
Lisa Austin; Michael Boyle; Pamela Brassel; Patricia Clarke; William M. Cullen; Kim Daifotis; Ted Doukas; Paul Draths; Craig Fujibayashi; Sue Goll; Jeffrey Hersh; Arthur Hitterman; Richard Jelinek; Terrance Livingston; Rita Macellaio; Gregory Monroe; Patricia Mosley; Eugene Mueller; Thomas Parker; Bruce Phelps; Julia Reinert; Greg Samorajski; JoEllen Schroedter; Randall Sheldon; Donald Sternard; Marzalie Stevens; Thomas Thompson

The *Commodity Trading Manual* holds a special niche among futures market literature. It is a comprehensive textbook/reference guide on the futures industry covering topics from the historical development of futures markets to a nuts-and-bolts description of the day-to-day operations of a futures exchange. While some books offer more in-depth explanations of specific aspects of futures trading, the *Commodity Trading Manual* is unique in providing the interested novice with a concise, yet readable, overview of the futures industry.

This feat becomes harder to accomplish with each new edition of the *Commodity Trading Manual,* as new product lines emerge and futures markets expand throughout the world. Ironically, it is also the industry's growth that makes it important that this publication exists. It is through literature like the *Commodity Trading Manual* that the public is made aware of the importance of the futures industry to the economy and learns of our efforts to ensure a vital, responsive marketplace.

In the time span since the previous edition, the complexion of the futures market has changed immensely. The growth of financial instruments has revolutionized the industry and now financial instruments make up more than half the volume of trading in futures. Also, the advances in communications technology have spread the need and uses of our industry to the whole world—making the futures market a truly global marketplace. These latest developments in the futures industry are discussed in this new edition of the *Commodity Trading Manual.*

Innovations in the futures markets are coming rapidly. The advent of electronic trading could mean a whole new chapter in the history of our marketplace and in the *Commodity Trading Manual* as well. Frequent revisions have become a necessity to keep this learning tool viable. It is a challenge the Chicago Board of Trade accepted over 15 years ago, and one we will continue to meet.

Patrick J. Catania
Vice President
Education and Marketing Services

Cover illustration by Mark McMahon. Chicago Board of Trade Agricultural Trading Floor during the summer of 1988, when grain prices and trading activity soared due to drought conditions. Book design by Allen Stebbins.

TABLE OF CONTENTS

Today's futures markets and the principles that underlie commodity futures trading evolved from practices that are centuries old.

Dating to the ancient Greek and Roman markets, formalized trading practices began with a fixed time and place for trading, a central marketplace, common barter and currency systems, as well as a practice of contracting for future delivery. At the height of the Roman Empire, trading centers, called *fora vendalia* (sales markets), served as distribution centers for commodities that the Romans brought from the far corners of the empire. The Forum in Rome was initially established as a trading center, while the Agora in Athens served as a commercial market.

Despite the fall of these civilizations, the basic principles of the central marketplace survived. During the Dark Ages, when the widespread flow of commerce was disrupted, products were bought and sold in scattered local markets. Eventually, the practice of preannouncing markets to be held at specific times and places reemerged in the form of medieval fairs. These regional fairs were organized by merchants, craftsmen, and promoters with the aid of political authorities. *Pieds Poudres,* or *men of dusty feet,* as they were known, traveled from town to town arranging and promoting the fairs.

By the 12th century, the medieval fairs of England and France were quite large and complex. And, as specialization developed, certain fairs became the focus of trading between the English and Flemish, Spanish,

DEVELOPMENT OF THE MARKETPLACE

Medieval Markets to Today

1

1

French, or Italian merchants. During the 13th century, spot (cash) transactions for immediate delivery were most common; but the practice of contracting for later delivery of merchandise, with standards of quality established by samples, had begun.

Among the chief contributions of the medieval fair to modern commerce are the principles of self-regulation and arbitration, and formalized trading practices. In medieval England, a code known as the Law Merchant established standards of conduct acceptable to local authorities. In some cases, the standards were minimal, but they formed a basis for common practices in the use of contracts, bills of sale, freight and warehouse receipts, letters of credit, transfer of deeds, and other bills of exchange. Anyone who violated a provision of the Law Merchant could be prohibited from trading by his fellow merchants. This principle of self-regulation, found in England's Common Law and followed in the American colonies, was later adopted by U.S. commodity exchanges.

To arbitrate disputes between buyers and sellers, the English merchant associations obtained the right from local and national authorities to administer their own rules of conduct. The associations were able to enforce judgments with assessments of penalties and awards of damages by establishing *the courts of the fair*, also known as *the courts of the Pieds Poudres*. By the time these courts were officially recognized by English Common Law courts in the 14th century, their jurisdiction superseded that of the local courts. The regional fairs declined in importance with improved transportation and communication and as modern cities developed. Specialized market centers replaced the fairs in many parts of the world. In Europe, the markets were called by the names *bourse, boerse, beurs,* and *bolsa*. The words come from the surname of an 18th-century innkeeper, Van der Beurs, whose establishment in Bruges, Belgium, became a gathering place for local commerce. Initially, these markets were held outdoors, usually in town squares. They later moved inside to teahouses and inns and, finally, found more permanent locations.

The development of the bourses was not limited to England and Europe. At the same time, similar markets were formed in Japan and the United States. Japan's commodity exchanges date back to the 1700s and preceded Japanese securities markets by nearly a century and a half. This pattern is generally the reverse of that in Europe, England, and the United States, where securities markets usually predated commodity markets. Spot, or cash, trading in rice dates from the early 1700s and "forward contracting" of rice on the Dojima Rice Market was implemented in 1730. Forward contracting is a cash transaction in which a buyer and seller agree upon price, quality, quantity, and a future delivery date for some commodity. Since nothing in the contract is standardized, each contract term must be negotiated between the buyer and seller. In addition to the Dojima market, Japanese markets also were established for edible oils, cotton, and precious metals, but their trading volume was small in comparison with that of rice.

Commodity markets in the United States existed as early as 1752 and traded domestic produce, textiles, hides, metals, and lumber. Most transactions were cash transactions for immediate delivery, however, these early markets greatly enhanced the ease and scope of trading all types of goods.

Chicago Board of Trade members pictured on their trading floor during the early 1900s.

Chicago Markets: History of the City

The history of modern futures trading began on the Midwestern frontier in the early 1800s. It was tied closely to the development of commerce in Chicago and the grain trade in the Midwest. Incorporated as a village in 1833, Chicago became a city in 1837 with a population of 4,107. Chicago's strategic location at the base of the Great Lakes, close to the fertile farmlands of the Midwest, contributed to the city's rapid growth and development as a grain terminal. Problems of supply and demand, transportation, and storage, however, led to a chaotic marketing situation and the logical development of futures markets.

For producers and processors in the early 1800s, supply and demand chaos was quite common. Farmers, who brought grain and livestock to regional markets at a certain time each year, often found that the supply of meat and grain far exceeded the immediate needs of packers and millers. These processors, seeing more than adequate supplies, would bid the lowest price. Often, the short-term demand could not absorb the glut of commodities at any price, however low, and grains were dumped in the street for lack of buyers.

The glut of commodities at harvesttime was only part of the problem. Inevitably, there were years of crop failure and extreme shortages. Even in years of abundant yield, supplies became exhausted, prices soared, and people went hungry. Businesses were faced with bankruptcy because they lacked raw materials to keep their operations going. In this situation, the rural people, although having sufficient food for themselves, had crops they couldn't sell and, therefore, did not have the income to pay for needed manufactured products—tools, building materials, and textiles.

Transportation difficulties and a lack of adequate storage facilities aggravated the problems of supply and demand. Throughout most of the year, snow and rain made the dirt roads from the farmlands to Chicago impassable. Although roads of wooden boards, called *plank roads*, enabled farmers to bring wagonloads of grain to the city, transportation was very expensive. In the 1840s, if a farmer had to haul a load of wheat 60 miles, he would barely break even, because it cost as much to bring the wheat to market as it did to produce it. Once commodities reached the city, buyers were faced with the problem of inadequate storage space. Underdeveloped harbor facilities impeded the shipment of grain to eastern markets and the return of needed manufactured goods to the West.

Reliable transportation was a high priority because it was vital for the further growth of Chicago and the Midwest. When commodity exchanges were organized, they became a major force behind legislative efforts to improve rural roads, build inland waterways, and expand storage and harbor facilities.

In response to the intolerable marketing conditions, farmers and merchants began to contract for forward delivery. Forward contracts in corn were first used by river merchants who received corn from farmers in late fall and early winter but had to store it until the corn reached a low enough moisture to ship and the river and canal were free of ice. Seeking to reduce the price risk of storing corn through the winter, these river merchants would travel to Chicago, where they would contract with processors for delivery of grain in the spring. In this way, they assured themselves of a buyer as well as a price for the grain. The earliest recorded forward contract in corn was made on March 13, 1851. The contract was for 3,000 bushels of corn to be delivered in June at a price of one cent per bushel below the price of corn on March 13.

Forward contracts in wheat developed later than those in corn. For wheat, however, it was the Chicago merchants and processors who faced the price risk of storing grain and, thus, sold wheat through forward contracts to eastern millers and exporters.

As grain trade expanded, a centralized marketplace—the Chicago Board of Trade (CBOT)—was formed in 1848 by 82 merchants. Their purpose was to promote the commerce of the city and to provide a place where buyers and sellers could meet to exchange commodities. During the exchange's early years, forward contracts were used.

But forward contracts had their drawbacks. They were not standardized according to quality or delivery time, and merchants and traders often did not fulfill these forward commitments. Then, in 1865, the Chicago Board of Trade took a step to formalize grain trading by developing standardized agreements called *futures contracts*. Futures contracts, in contrast to forward contracts, are standardized as to quality, quantity, and time and place of delivery for the commodity being traded.

A margining system was initiated that same year to eliminate the problem of buyers and sellers not fulfilling their contracts. (A margining system requires traders to deposit funds with the exchange or an exchange representative to guarantee contract performance.) Following these monumental steps, most of the basic principles of futures trading as we know them today were in place. But no one could have guessed how this infant industry would change and develop in the next century and beyond.

Emergence of Futures Contracts

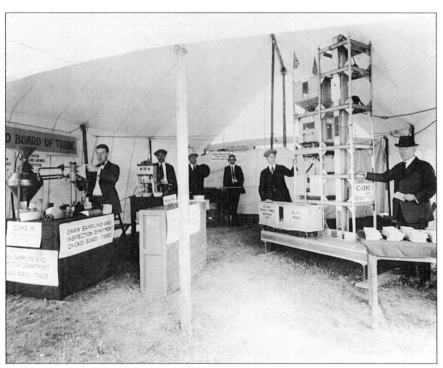

During the early years of the Chicago Board of Trade, grain was inspected to determine its quality.

Growth of the Futures Industry Since 1870

The late 1800s were critical to the scope and efficiency of futures trading. Trading practices were formalized, contracts were standardized, and rules of conduct and clearing and settlement procedures were established.

Trading became more efficient as speculators entered the picture. Lawyers, physicians, and others not connected with the grain trade began to speculate on price and buy and sell futures contracts, hoping to make an honest profit. By purchasing and selling grain that would not otherwise have been traded, speculators made the markets more liquid and helped minimize price fluctuations.

One feature of futures contracts that became standardized was the delivery month. Months were chosen, or gradually agreed upon, by grain merchants based on harvesting and transportation conditions. March was a logical choice because the end of winter made transportation possible once again. May also became an established delivery month because of the cleanup of old-crop oats and wheat (those crops harvested the previous summer). December was selected for the marketing of new-crop corn (harvested in the fall) and was the last month that farmers could move corn to market before winter weather made travel impossible. Quality and quantity standards developed as a more accurate system of weighing bushels of grain replaced measurement, and an inspection process was initiated.

Growth in futures trading increased in the late 19th and early 20th centuries as new exchanges were formed. Many types of commodities were traded on these exchanges, including cotton, butter, eggs, coffee, and cocoa. And, as the United States moved away from an agrarian-based economy, the number and variety of futures contracts grew. In addition to the traditional agricultural futures, trading developed in precious metals, manufactured or processed products, and nonstorable commodities. But the most dramatic growth and successful contracts in the futures industry were yet to come—financial instruments futures contracts.

Financial Instruments

As the world's financial structure changed because of new monetary policies and other reasons, the futures industry expanded its contract offerings so businesses and financial institutions could continue to manage price risks.

Beginning in the 1970s, the first futures contracts in financial instruments were launched with Government National Mortgage Association (GNMA) mortgage-backed certificates and foreign currency futures. GNMAs were a joint effort between the Chicago Board of Trade and members of the mortgage lending industry. Several years of extensive research went into developing the contract, which began trading in October 1975. Futures trading in foreign currencies—British pound, Canadian dollar, Deutsche mark, French franc, Japanese yen, and Swiss franc—was initiated by the Chicago Mercantile Exchange in May 1972.

Since the introduction of these first financial contracts, financial futures trading has been initiated in an increasing number of financial

Chicago Board of Trade price-reporting systems (ABEF). Exchange floor (C). Grain inspecting and weighing (D). circa 1930.

instruments, including U.S. Treasury bond futures, stock index futures, and municipal bond index futures.

By 1982, another market innovation—options on futures—was instituted. In contrast to futures, options on futures allow investors and risk managers to define and limit risk in the form of a premium paid for the right to buy or sell a futures contract. At the same time, options can provide the buyer with unlimited profit potential. Options on Treasury bond futures began trading in October 1982 at the Chicago Board of Trade as part of a government pilot program. The success of this contract opened the way for options on agricultural and other financial futures, beginning with options on soybean and corn futures contracts in 1984 and 1985, respectively.

Even before options on futures were introduced, the Chicago Board of Trade formed The Chicago Board Options Exchange, which trades stock options. One of the unique trading aspects adopted from the futures exchanges by The Chicago Board Options Exchange was the Chicago style of trading, where bids and offers are made in the pits by open outcry.

Perhaps the most remarkable thing about financial instruments futures and options is their phenomenal growth. While it took centuries for agricultural markets to develop, the financial markets sprang up in less than 15 years and surpassed the agricultural markets in many ways. Since financial instruments were first introduced at the Chicago Board of Trade in 1975, the number of financial contracts traded annually at the exchange soared from a mere 20,125 to more than 78 million in 1986. Share of total volume also increased tremendously. In 1976, for example, the majority of contracts traded were agricultural and metals futures; less than 1 percent of all contracts traded were financial instruments. Just four years later, financial instruments volume increased to 33 percent and, during 1987, reached an amazing 77 percent.

The growth in financial instruments resulted from a substantially different economic environment—an environment characterized by frequent changes in interest rates, sharp increases in the amount of government debt, and greater financial interdependence among nations.

Worldwide Market Coverage and Expanded Trading Hours

Within the last few years, the interdependence of the world's economies has become clearly evident. The U.S. futures industry, because of its sensitivity to the marketplace and its function as a risk-management mechanism, has already reacted to the need for internationalization. By linking up with foreign exchanges, expanding trading hours, opening offices overseas, and developing contracts with international impact, U.S. futures exchanges are making their markets more accessible and attractive to investors and businesses worldwide.

The first link with a foreign futures exchange was established between the Chicago Mercantile Exchange (CME) and the Singapore International Monetary Exchange (SIMEX) in 1984. The CME/SIMEX link allows traders to buy (sell) contracts on one exchange and later sell (buy) them back on the other. Such linkages provide comprehensive market coverage and are being considered by other exchanges as well.

In another move toward globalization of futures markets, some U.S. futures exchanges are adding evening trading sessions to span time zones and attract foreign investors. In April 1987, the first evening-hours session in the history of futures trading opened at the Chicago Board of Trade. The expanded trading hours provide increased liquidity, efficiency, and greater access to markets worldwide. By capturing the morning trading hours in Hong Kong, Sydney, Tokyo, and Singapore, U.S. futures exchanges can compete directly with Japanese and Far Eastern markets.

As the world business environment continues to change, new products and instruments will, undoubtedly, continue to be introduced by futures exchanges. Even now, innovations, such as early morning trading sessions, are being studied in an effort to better meet the needs of the market.

Futures markets make it possible for those who want to manage price risk, hedgers, to transfer that risk to those who are willing to accept it, speculators. Futures markets also provide price information that the world looks to as a benchmark in determining the value of a particular commodity or financial instrument on a given day and time. These important benefits—risk transfer and price discovery—reach every sector of the world where changing market conditions create economic risk, including such diverse areas as agricultural products, foreign exchange, imports and exports, financing, and investments.

Futures markets evolved gradually. In their earlier years, exchanges were essentially cash markets where physical commodities were bought and sold. As the volume of trading increased, buyers and sellers began trading futures contracts—standardized, legal agreements to make or take delivery of a specific commodity at a designated place sometime in the future.

While cash and futures contracts have common elements, they serve different market functions. This chapter briefly explains some of the differences, gives an overview of futures trading, and describes its economic importance to the world.

OVERVIEW
OF
FUTURES
TRADING

*Hedging,
Speculating,
Clearing,
Price Theory*

2

Cash Transactions

Cash contracts in the agricultural markets are sales agreements for either the immediate or future delivery of a commodity. The quality and quantity of the commodity as well as the delivery terms are agreed upon by both the buyer and seller.

Each of these factors affects the sales price. For instance, if a lower or higher quality of grain than the seller agreed to purchase is delivered, a price discount or premium is calculated in the final price. Quantity also affects the price. If a greater quantity is delivered than initially agreed upon, a price discount is sometimes negotiated.

A typical cash transaction can involve a farmer who wants to sell his grain and a grain elevator operator who wants to purchase it. Typically, the grain elevator operator acts as a middleman between farmers and grain buyers, such as flour millers, who eventually purchase the grain to process.

There are a variety of cash sales agreements used by farmers, grain elevator operators, and other marketers. One type of cash transaction involves the immediate delivery of the commodity. Many farmers use this marketing alternative in the fall. After harvest, they haul the grain to the local elevator where it is priced on the spot based on the quantity and quality of the crop.

Another alternative is a cash forward contract—an agreement in which a seller agrees to deliver a specific cash commodity to a buyer sometime in the future. For example, a farmer could enter a cash forward contract with a grain elevator operator in the winter to deliver 10,000 bushels of wheat the following July. At the time the contract is initiated, the farmer and grain elevator operator agree on the quality and quantity of grain, the delivery time and location, as well as the price. When delivery occurs, the wheat is carefully inspected and price adjustments are made according to the quality and quantity.

In many instances, a cash forward contract might be more appropriate than an immediate cash sales transaction because it allows both buyers and sellers to plan ahead. Not only do they know, in advance, the price they will have to pay or the price they will receive for a specific commodity, they can hold off delivery until they have possession of the grain or are ready to process it. This saves the expense of tying up storage facilities.

Similar cash forward transactions are prevalent in all sections of the economy, such as real estate leases, fixed-rate loans, charge cards, rents, mortgages, even magazine and newspaper subscriptions. In all cases, a product or service is agreed to be delivered sometime in the future at a specific price. Without forward contracts, it is impossible for buyers and sellers to agree on anything and price must be constantly renegotiated.

In contrast to futures contracts, forward contracts are not actively traded on exchanges nor standardized. They are privately negotiated. They also carry some risk to both parties in the agreement—the risk that one side is negotiating in bad faith or without sufficient funds. There also is the risk that future events could prevent one or both sides from fulfilling the contract.

Futures contracts are standardized and meet specific requirements of buyers and sellers for a variety of commodities and financial instruments. Quantity, quality, delivery locations—are all established. The only variable is price, which is discovered through an auctionlike process on the trading floor of an organized futures exchange.

Because futures contracts are standardized, sellers and buyers are able to exchange one contract for another and actually offset their obligation to deliver or take delivery of the cash commodity underlying the futures contract. *Offset* in the futures market means taking another futures position opposite and equal to one's initial futures transaction.

As an example, suppose an investor bought two March U.S. Treasury bond futures contracts. To offset this position, he would have to sell two March U.S. T-bond futures contracts before the contracts called for delivery. On the other hand, if the investor first sold two March U.S. T-bond futures contracts, to offset the position, he would have to buy two March U.S. T-bond futures contracts before the contracts called for delivery.

Standardization of contract terms and the ability to offset contracts led to the rapidly increasing use of the futures markets by commercial firms and speculators. Commercial firms began to realize that futures markets could provide financial protection against price volatility without the need to make or take delivery of the cash commodity underlying the futures contract. Speculators found that standardization added trading appeal because contracts could be bought and later sold, or sold and later bought, at a profit if they were correct in their forecasts of price movement.

Futures Contracts

Hedging, a major economic purpose of futures markets, is buying or selling futures contracts to offset the risks of changing prices in the cash markets. This risk-transfer mechanism has made futures contracts virtually indispensable in efforts to control costs and protect profit margins.

Hedging

Agricultural Scenario

Commercial firms, producers, merchandisers, and processors of commodities use the futures market to protect themselves against changing cash prices. They are able to do so because cash and futures prices usually respond to the same economic factors and tend to move together in the same direction. News of bad weather that would likely result in crop losses and tighter supplies is reflected immediately in higher cash prices as buyers seek to buy and store the commodity in anticipation of later shortages. Futures prices also are bid higher when buyers anticipate a commodity shortage, not only at harvest but throughout the marketing year.

Economic news, on the other hand, that signals higher-than-expected supplies is immediately registered in weakening cash prices as buyers lower bids in anticipation of easily available supplies. At the same time, buyers in the futures markets scale down bids with the prospect of increased supplies.

Commercial firms note the strong tendency for cash and futures prices to move in the same direction by roughly equal amounts, reacting to the same economic factors. These firms realize that, although a single set of economic factors might result in a loss on a cash transaction, it could be offset and sometimes turned into a profit in the futures market. This is possible if they initiate a futures position equal and opposite to their cash market position.

As an example, suppose a Midwest wheat miller agrees to ship 500,000 pounds of flour in six months to a cookie manufacturer in Minnesota. Both agree on a price today even though the flour will not be delivered for another six months. However, the miller does not own the wheat he will eventually process and is concerned that prices will rise during the six-month period.

To hedge against the risk of rising cash prices, the miller buys two wheat futures contracts for delivery in six months. When the miller goes to purchase the cash wheat, prices have risen. The miller then sells two futures contracts and makes a profit in the futures market because futures prices also have increased.

Even though the miller has to pay more for the cash wheat than he originally planned, he was able to offset his loss by making a gain in the futures market.

Financial Scenario

The economic principles that apply to traditional commodity futures contracts, such as wheat futures, also apply to nontraditional contracts like currencies, stock indexes, government bonds, and other financial instruments. These futures contracts are invaluable hedging vehicles for all types of investors.

A portfolio manager can hedge against an increase in the purchase price of bonds using Treasury bond futures. A corporate treasurer planning a bond issue can hedge against higher interest rates and lower bond prices with interest rate futures. An institution can hedge to protect the market value of stocks from a possible decline in value with stock index futures.

For instance, a major financial institution wants to sell a portion of its bond portfolio in four months. However, the company expects interest rates to rise over the next four months, which would result in lower bond prices.

To take advantage of the current bond market, the company sells U.S. Treasury bond futures contracts. In four months, the bond market falls. The company then sells its Treasury bonds in the cash market and offsets its futures position by buying Treasury bond futures contracts. Even though the institution receives less than it would have four months ago for the same portfolio of bonds, it has gained in the futures market, minimizing the potential loss.

Other users of financial futures contracts include bankers, corporate treasurers, state and local governments, insurance companies, investment bankers, money managers, mortgage bankers, pension fund managers, portfolio managers, thrifts, trust fund managers, and underwriters. (For a more complete discussion of hedging, see Chapter 8.)

In all hedging strategies, the common denominator is the desire to establish, in advance, an acceptable price or rate of interest. Every business, regardless of whether it performs a service or manufactures a product, faces some type of financial risk. For each individual or institution attempting to minimize risk, there must be another willing to assume it. Futures exchanges act as a magnet, attracting risk-avoiders (hedgers) and risk-takers (speculators).

Speculators

Speculators assume the risk hedgers try to avoid. While profit is the motive of speculators, they provide the marketplace with an essential element, liquidity, which enables hedgers to buy or sell large numbers of contracts without adversely disrupting the price in the marketplace. This is crucial to institutional investors, processors of commodities, and other commercial and financial firms who buy or sell hundreds or thousands of contracts to hedge a cash market position.

Although speculators usually have no commercial interest in commodities, the potential for profit motivates them to gather market information regarding supply and demand and to anticipate its effect on prices. By buying and selling futures contracts, speculators also help provide information about the impact of current events on expected future demands. In essence, speculators make the market more fluid, bridging the gap between the prices bid and offered by other commodity traders. (For more information on speculating, see Chapter 9.)

Clearinghouses

Essential to the marketplace is an exchange's clearing mechanism. Without it, hedgers and speculators run the risk that some market participants would not fulfill their contract commitments. This would hamper the risk-transfer mechanism of futures markets, making it difficult for traders to offset open positions.

Clearinghouses are responsible for settling trading accounts, clearing trades, collecting and maintaining margin monies, regulating delivery, and reporting trading data.

Clearinghouses act as third parties to all futures and options contracts—acting as a buyer to every clearing member seller and a seller to every clearing member buyer. Buyers and sellers of futures and options contracts do not create financial obligations to one another, but, rather, to the clearinghouses through their clearing member firms.

A clearinghouse severs the direct relationship between buyer and seller, so that each is free to buy and sell independently of the other. As a party to every trade, the clearinghouse assumes the responsibility of guarantor of every trade.

Performance Bond Margins

Exchange clearinghouses are able to guarantee all trades because they require their members to deposit performance bond margins.

Performance bond margins are financial guarantees required of both buyers and sellers of futures contracts to ensure fulfillment of the contract obligations. That is, buyers and sellers are required to take or make delivery of the commodity or financial instrument represented by the contract unless the position is offset before contract expiration.

Margins are determined on the basis of market risk. Because margins are adjusted to risk, they help assure the financial soundness of futures exchanges and provide valuable price protection for hedgers with a minimum tie-up of capital. Margins are normally set at 5 to 18 percent of the value of the commodity represented by the contract.

Price Theory and the Futures Markets

Futures markets are successful because they rely on the economics of price theory.

Supply

The price of a product is discovered by changes in its supply and demand. Supply is the quantity of a product that sellers are willing to provide to the market at a given price. Supply can be graphed as a curve with quantity shown on the horizontal axis and price shown on the vertical axis. It slants upward from left to right, as shown on the next page, and indicates the quantity supplied at a given price. When prices are high, sellers are willing to provide larger quantities of their products to the market; at lower prices, sellers are willing to furnish smaller quantities to the market. This relationship between product supply and its price is known as the *law of supply*.

There are a variety of economic factors that can cause supply to increase or decrease, thus shifting the supply curve. These include changes in production costs, prices of related goods, and number of sellers in the market.

Demand

Demand, on the other hand, is the quantity of a product buyers are willing to purchase from the market at a given price. Demand can be graphed as a curve with quantity shown on the horizontal axis and price shown on the vertical axis. It slants downward from left to right, as shown on the next page, and indicates the quantity demanded at a given price. When prices are low, buyers are willing to purchase greater quantities of a product; at higher prices, buyers are willing to purchase lesser quantities of a product. This relationship between product demand and its price is known as the *law of demand*.

Supply Curve

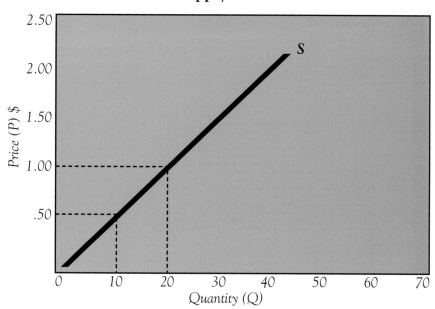

Demand Curve

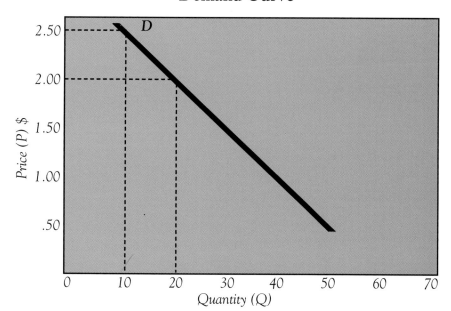

There are a variety of economic factors that can cause demand to increase or decrease, thus shifting the demand curve. These include changes in personal income, prices of related goods, and the number of buyers in the marketplace.

The price of a product or commodity depends on the relationship between supply and demand. If the supply and demand curves of a product are placed on the same graph, the point where they intersect is a product's market price, also known as the *equilibrium price*. At the market price, the quantity supplied equals the quantity demanded.

Equilibrium Price

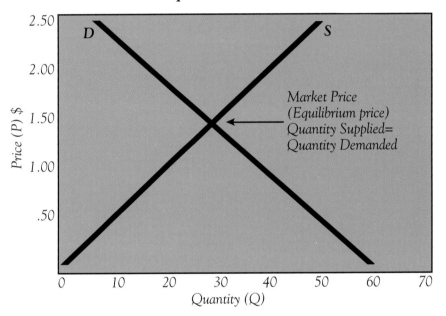

A change in the supply and/or demand for a commodity will cause a shift in the respective supply and/or demand curves. As a curve shifts, the market price may increase, decrease, or remain the same.

Price Information

Hedgers and speculators continually evaluate supply and demand factors as well as other market indicators. Based on their analysis and expectations of future price movements, trades are made and prices are discovered.

Traders constantly adjust their bids and offers to buy and sell futures contracts in relation to a continuous flow of worldwide market information.

News of Brazilian soybean crop conditions is sought, analyzed, and then reflected almost instantaneously in the prices of soybean, soybean meal, and soybean oil futures. The impact of nationalization of foreign-owned copper mines is registered in the price of copper, silver, and other related futures in New York, London, and Chicago. The release of a government report announcing that the Federal Reserve Board is putting more money into the economy is absorbed by the market and noted in the price of U.S. Treasury bond futures.

Futures prices are the most widely used pricing reference in domestic and international financial, metals, and agricultural markets. Once prices are discovered, the futures exchanges are responsible for disseminating these prices to the public on a daily basis through market report systems and newspapers.

While all U.S. futures exchanges share some general characteristics, no two are exactly alike. Many of the differences have to do with their historical development. This chapter not only discusses their similarities, but gives a brief history of each U.S. futures exchange and describes its organizational structure.

Most exchanges are not-for-profit membership associations, incorporated in the states in which they are located. Membership in each exchange is limited to a specific number of individuals, although some exchanges permit the holding of multiple memberships by members. Every membership is owned by an individual; however, companies, corporations, partnerships, and cooperatives may be registered for certain membership privileges.

The exchange conducts a thorough investigation of each member applicant. It focuses on the applicant's credit standing, financial responsibility, character, and integrity.

In recent years, special memberships or trading privileges have been offered by some exchanges. For example, an associate membership at the Chicago Board of Trade allows an individual to trade the financial instrument futures and other designated markets.

Other special memberships at the Chicago Board of Trade include a variety of membership interest holders. Of these, GIM membership interest holders may trade all futures contracts listed in the government

U.S. FUTURES EXCHANGES

Their History & Organization

3

instruments market category (financial instrument futures); IDEMs may trade all futures contracts in the index, debt, and metals markets category (gold, silver, and stock index futures); and COMs may trade all options contracts listed in the commodity options market category (all options listed for trading by the exchange).

The government of each exchange is vested in a board (called the *board of directors, board of governors,* or *board of managers*) and its officers. The board is elected by the exchange membership.

Committees

Committees are composed of exchange members either appointed by the board or elected by the exchange membership; they advise and assist the board and perform specific duties related to exchange operations.

Most exchanges have committees for the following purposes: nominations of board candidates, officers, and those committees elected by the exchange membership; management of the exchange; supervision of finances; supervision and investigation of the business conduct of members; arbitration of disputes; appeal of decisions of the committee on arbitration; examination of member applicants; supervision of trading floor activity; supervision of market price reporting; management of the physical facilities of the exchange; amendments to rules and regulations; public relations; marketing and education; supervision of trading and changes in the contracts for commodities traded; and supervision of weighing, warehousing, and inspection of commodities for delivery against the futures contract.

Staff

The administrative staff of an exchange carries out the policies and decisions of the board and the committees. Departmental organization of the staff frequently parallels the functions of the various committees, and each department is responsible to an executive officer of the exchange. The titles, responsibilities, and numbers of these executive officers and staff vary among the exchanges. Following are the histories, committees, and staffs of today's U.S. futures exchanges.

Chicago Board of Trade

The Chicago Board of Trade, founded in 1848, is the world's oldest and largest futures exchange. In addition to futures trading in grains, soybeans, and soybean products, the exchange offers futures markets in long-term U.S. Treasury bonds and notes, stock and municipal bond indexes, gold, and silver. Options on financial, agricultural, and metals futures also are traded.

Change and growth are a tradition of the Chicago Board of Trade. Most recently, the exchange has taken several steps to make its markets more appealing to an international audience. In addition to expanding trading hours to coincide with business hours in Far Eastern markets during 1987, the Chicago Board of Trade opened a London office in 1986 and a Tokyo office in 1988.

Membership	3,490 (1,402 full members, 716 associate members, 257 GIM interests, 547 IDEM interests, 568 COM interests)
Governing Body	board of directors—24 (chairman, vice chairman, 15 full member directors, 3 associate member directors, 3 nonmember public directors, and president)
Officers	chairman, vice chairman, president and chief executive officer*
Committees	Agricultural Advisory; Arbitration; Associate Members; Business Conduct; Cash Grain; Commodity Options; Computer and Telecommunications; Education and Marketing Services; Executive; Feed Grain Contract; Finance; Financial Instruments; Floor; Floor Broker; Floor Conduct; Floor Governors; Margin; Market Efficiency; Market Report and Quotations; Member Services; Membership; Membership Interest Holders; Metals; Nominating; Public Relations; Real Estate; Rules; Soybean; Soybean Meal; Soybean Oil; Statistics; Stock Index; Transportation; Warehouse, Weighing and Custodian; Wheat
Staff*	600
Executive Officers	president and chief executive officer, executive vice president, vice president/secretary, vice president/treasurer, vice presidents— (administration and planning, administration/ Office of Investigations and Audits, director/economic analysis, director/international operations, education and marketing services, floor operations, government relations,

*Not exchange members

information systems, managing director/Asia–Pacific, representative office, personnel, public relations, real estate, special counsel, technology application), general counsel, associate general counsel

Chicago Mercantile Exchange

The Chicago Mercantile Exchange (CME) traces its origins to a group of agricultural dealers who formed the Chicago Produce Exchange in 1874. This exchange was a market for butter, eggs, poultry, and other perishable agricultural products. In 1898, the butter and egg dealers withdrew from this group to form their own market, the Chicago Butter and Egg Board.

The Chicago Butter and Egg Board was reorganized for futures trading in additional commodities and was renamed the Chicago Mercantile Exchange in 1919. Since that time, the exchange has provided a futures market for many commodities, including pork bellies, live cattle, live hogs, and feeder cattle.

The International Monetary Market (IMM), a division of the exchange, was established in 1972 for foreign currency futures trading. Since then, other financial futures have been added, including futures contracts based on 90-day U.S. Treasury bills and three-month Eurodollar time deposits.

Another division of the exchange, the Index and Option Market (IOM), was opened for trading stock index futures and options on futures in 1982. Among the contracts traded on the Index and Option Market at the Chicago Mercantile Exchange are S&P 500 Stock Index futures and various options contracts.

In 1984, the Chicago Mercantile Exchange and the Singapore International Monetary Exchange initiated the world's first interexchange futures trading link. The two exchanges trade Eurodollar, Japanese yen, British pound, and Deutsche mark futures, making trading in Singapore equivalent to that in Chicago.

Membership	2,724 (625 CME, 812 IMM, and 1,287 IOM)
Governing Body	board of governors—25
Officers	chairman, 1st vice chairman, 2nd vice chairman, secretary, treasurer, special counsel and chairman of executive committee
Public and Industry Governors	6

Committees

Standing: Agricultural Advisory; American Coalition for Flexible Exchange Rates; Approved Delivery Facility; Arbitration—Agricultural Division; Arbitration—Financial Division; Building Improvement and Real Estate; Business Conduct; Butter; Cattle—Feeder; Cattle—Live; Clearing House; Commodity Representative/Customer Complaint; Computerized Trade Reconstruction; Contributions; Education; Equity Indices—Specifications; Executive; Finance; Financial Instrument Steering Committee Advisory; Floor Broker Qualification; Floor Communications; Floor Orientation; Floor Practices—Agricultural; Floor Practices—Broker Negligence; Floor Practices—Financial; Floor Services; Foreign Currency; Forest Products; Gold; Interest Rate Futures; Leasing; Live Hog; Member Services; Membership; Member Space Allocation; New Market Floor Promotion; Options; Permit Administration; Pit Supervision; Pork Products; Probable Cause; Public Affairs; Restaurant and Club; S&P Oversight; S&P Price Limit

Coordination: Agricultural Steering; Facility Coordination; Financial Instruments Steering; International Steering; Member Coordination

Staff*

867

Officers

president and chief executive officer; executive vice president and chief operating officer; executive vice president and chief economist, research; senior vice presidents—(administration and finance, government relations, legal and regulatory affairs, marketing, operations), vice presidents—(audits, clearing, commodity research and marketing, compliance, currency products, finance and administration, financial research, general counsel—legal, government relations, international financial marketing, London office, Management Information Systems, market surveillance, New York office, Post Market Trade, public affairs, special projects, strategic planning)

*Not exchange members

Chicago Rice & Cotton Exchange

The Chicago Rice & Cotton Exchange, formerly the New Orleans Commodity Exchange, moved to Chicago in September 1983 as an affiliate of the MidAmerica Commodity Exchange. In 1986, MidAm became an affiliate of the Chicago Board of Trade, and all MidAm and CRCE contracts are now traded in the Chicago Board of Trade building.

Membership	173
Governing Body	board of directors—(chairman, vice chairman, three directors, including one public director)
Committees	Cotton; Executive; Rough Rice
Staff Officers*	president, vice president, secretary, treasurer

*Not exchange members

Coffee, Sugar & Cocoa Exchange, Inc.

The Coffee, Sugar & Cocoa Exchange, Inc., known initially as the Coffee Exchange of the City of New York, was founded in 1882. The exchange was formed by a group of coffee merchants who wished to avoid the risk of a cash market collapse by organizing a market for trading in coffee futures. In 1914, the Coffee Exchange expanded to include futures in sugar, and, in 1916, it became the New York Coffee and Sugar Exchange, Inc. On September 28, 1979, the New York Cocoa Exchange, Inc., which had been in existence since 1925, was officially merged into the Coffee and Sugar Exchange, and the name Coffee, Sugar & Cocoa Exchange, Inc. was adopted.

Membership	777 (527 full, 250 associate)
Governing Body	board of managers—22
Officers	chairman, two vice chairmen, treasurer
Committees	Adjudication; Appeals; Arbitration; Board of Cocoa Graders; Board of Coffee Graders; Business Conduct; Cocoa; Coffee; Compensation; Control; Deliveries and Warehouse Procedures; Executive; Executive Floor; Finance; Floor; Margin; Membership; New Product Development; Nominating; Option Quotation; Options; Pension; Planning; Sugar; Sugar Delivery; Sugar Spot Price Roster; Warehouse and License; Warehouse Inspectors

Staff*	101
Officers	president, three senior vice presidents, secretary, three assistant vice presidents, assistant treasurer, assistant secretary, chief economist

*Not exchange members

The Commodity Exchange, Inc., (COMEX) of New York was formed in 1933 by the merger of four exchanges that had been trading in hides, raw silk, rubber, and metals. Today, COMEX trades a variety of metals contracts, including silver, gold, copper, and aluminum futures, and options on gold, silver, and copper futures.

Commodity Exchange, Inc. (COMEX)

Membership	772**
Governing Body	board of governors—25
Officers	chairman, treasurer, vice chairmen—(general, commission house, trade, floor)
Committees	Admissions; Arbitration; Audit; Business Conduct; Clearing Liaison; Control; Executive; Finance; Floor; Floor Facilities; Margin; Marketing, Public Relations, and Education; Metal Trade Committees (3); New Products; Nominating; Operations; Options; Quotations; Supervisory
Staff*	165
Officers	president, three senior vice presidents, six vice presidents, secretary, assistant secretary, controller

*Not exchange members
**Multiple memberships available

For more than 100 years, the Kansas City Board of Trade has been the world's predominant marketplace for Hard Red Winter wheat, the major ingredient in bread. In 1982, the Kansas City Board of Trade broadened its product base into the financial arena by introducing the first U.S. stock index futures contract, based on the Value Line Index. In 1984, the exchange began trading options on Hard Red Winter wheat futures, providing still another risk-management tool.

Kansas City Board of Trade

Membership	264 (Class A—196; Class B—68)
Governing Body	board of directors—14 directors and 3 officers
Officers	chairman, first vice chairman, second vice chairman, president and secretary, senior vice president, vice presidents—(compliance, marketing, operations, public affairs), treasurer, assistant treasurer, assistant secretary, assistant vice presidents—(floor operations, Grain Market Review, transportation)
Committees	Ag Options; Ag Options Pit; Appeals Arbitration (Cash); Arbitration (Cash and Futures); Budget; Business Conduct; Compliance Advisory; Country Elevators; Elevator Weighing Inspection; Employee Pension Trustees; Finance; Floor Operations; Legislation; Long Range Planning; Marketing; Market Reports Coarse Grain; Market Reports Wheat; Membership; Nominating; Rules; Transportation; Value Line Contract; Value Line Pit; Value Line Pit Complaint Sub-Committee; Wheat Contract; Wheat Pit; Wheat Pit Complaint Sub-Committee
Staff*	30
Officers	president

*Not exchange members

MidAmerica Commodity Exchange

The MidAmerica Commodity Exchange was founded in 1868 and incorporated as the Chicago Open Board of Trade in 1880. The exchange acquired its present name in late 1972. In 1986, the MidAm became an affiliate of the Chicago Board of Trade, and the MidAm trading floor is located in the Chicago Board of Trade building. MidAm is known for a wide variety of agricultural, financial, metals, and foreign currencies contracts that trade in smaller units.

Membership	1,205
Governing Body	board of directors—29
Officers	chairman, vice chairman, president and chief executive officer*

*Not an exchange member

Committees	Arbitration; Business Conduct; Executive; Floor Conduct; Floor Governors; Market Report and Quotations; Members Advisory; Membership; Pit

The Minneapolis Grain Exchange, founded in 1881, is the largest cash grain market in the world. In addition, the Minneapolis Grain Exchange trades a variety of wheat futures contracts and high fructose corn syrup futures.

Minneapolis Grain Exchange

Membership	402**
Governing Body	board of directors—15
Officers	chairman, two vice chairmen
Public Members*	1–4
Committees	Arbitration Pool; Building; Business Conduct; Changes in Rules; Clearing House; Exchange Room; Finance; Fructose; Futures Contracts; Futures Trading Conduct; Membership; New Member Orientation; Nominations; Options; Options Quotations; Personnel and Compensation; Public Affairs; Public Relations; Sampling; Spring Wheat Quotations; Transportation; Weighing; Wheat Classification; White Wheat Quotations; Sweetener
Staff*	100
Officers	president, vice president of operations and secretary, vice president of finance and treasurer, vice presidents—(marketing, public relations, real estate), assistant secretary

*Not exchange members (nonmember directors are elected by the board of directors)
**Multiple memberships available

The New York Cotton Exchange was formed by 106 cotton merchants and brokers in 1870. By 1923, the membership had expanded to 450, and the volume of trade had increased so much that the exchange was forced to seek larger quarters five times during its first 50 years. Major innovations in trading during the exchange's first half century included the adoption of

New York Cotton Exchange

the Certification System, which provided for delivery through a certificate, and the creation of the exchange clearinghouse.

Because the exchange's state charter had at one time specified trading in cotton only, expansion to include trading in other commodities had to be accomplished through the establishment of separate corporations. The Citrus Associates of the New York Cotton Exchange was founded in 1966 and trades frozen concentrated orange juice futures.

The Financial Instrument Exchange (FINEX®) was formed in June 1985 to oversee the development and introduction of financial futures and options. U.S. Dollar Index^{SM} futures and options, European Currency Unit futures, and Five-Year U.S. Treasury Note (FYTR®) futures and options are currently traded on FINEX®.

The 450 members of the New York Cotton Exchange have a "Class A" membership in each of the associate exchanges; other members of the associate exchanges hold "Class B" memberships on those exchanges. In addition, the New York Futures Exchange (NYFE) is affiliated with the New York Cotton Exchange.

Membership	450
Governing Body	board of managers—21–27
Officers	chairman, vice chairman, treasurer
Committees	Adjudication; Arbitration; Business Conduct; Bylaws and Rules; Committee Supervising Simultaneous Purchases and Sales of Cotton and Options Contracts; Control—Cotton and Options; Cotton Futures and Options Contracts; Distribution of Quotations; Executive; Finance; Floor—Cotton and Options; Futures and Options—Financial Contracts; Information and Statistics; Margin—Cotton and Options; Membership; National Advisory; Nominating; Real Estate; Reception; Supervisory; Trade Warehouse and Delivery Committee—Cotton; special committees appointed from time to time
Staff*	77
Officers	president, executive director, vice president and counsel, secretary, assistant officers

*Not exchange members

Membership	200 authorized, 157 outstanding	**Citrus Associates** Division of the NYCE®
Governing Body	board of directors—15	
Officers	president, two vice presidents, treasurer	
Committees	Arbitration; Business Conduct; Bylaws and Rules; Control; Executive; Floor; Finance; Frozen Concentrated Orange Juice; Information and Statistics; Margins; Membership; Nominating; Quotations for Spot and Futures Delivery of Frozen Concentrated Orange Juice; Supervisory; Warehouse; special committees appointed from time to time	
Staff*	served by the New York Cotton Exchange staff	
Officers	executive director, secretary, assistant secretary	

*Not exchange members

Membership	New York Cotton Exchange membership	**Financial Instrument Exchange (FINEX®)** Division of the NYCE®
Governing Body	subject generally to board of managers of the New York Cotton Exchange	
Officers	chairman, two vice chairmen, treasurer of the division	
Committees	Delivery; Executive; Finance; Floor; Futures and Options; Margins; Nominating; Offset; Oversight; special committees appointed from time to time	
Staff*	served by the New York Cotton Exchange staff	

*Not exchange members

On April 15, 1979, the New York Stock Exchange entered the financial futures industry by incorporating the New York Futures Exchange as its wholly owned subsidiary. This marked the culmination of an intensive two-year study of the opportunities and potential for financial futures markets, and the service and facilities requirements of the international financial community. The Intermarket Clearing Corporation, a wholly owned subsidiary of the Options Clearing Corporation, is the clearing agent for the exchange.

Membership	1,440
Governing Body	board of directors—23
Officers	chairman, vice chairman, president, senior vice president—(regulation, operations, and administration), vice president—(regulation and surveillance), general counsel, secretary
Committees	Appeals; Arbitration Board; Audit; Compliance and Surveillance Oversight; Finance; Floor; Hearing Board; Margin; Market Emergency; New Products; Personnel; Quality of Markets

New York Mercantile Exchange

The New York Mercantile Exchange was founded in 1872 as a market for cheese, butter, and eggs. In 1882, it acquired its present name and, in 1884, it took up occupancy in its own building in the former New York produce market area. In 1977, the exchange moved into joint facilities with other New York exchanges in the World Trade Center.

Membership	816
Governing Body	board of governors—15
Officers	at large
Public Members*	(up to) 3
Committees	Adjudication; Administrative; Arbitration; Business Conduct; Bylaws; Clearing House; Control; Crude Oil; Finance; Floor; Marketing; Membership; Metals; Natural Gas; New Commodities; Options; Petroleum Products; Storage and Delivery; Trader Qualification
Staff*	300
Officers	president, senior executive vice president, vice president and general counsel, vice presidents—(clearing, compliance, financial surveillance, floor operations, marketing, membership, operations)

*Not exchange members

The Philadelphia Board of Trade, Inc., a wholly owned subsidiary of the Philadelphia Stock Exchange, Inc., was approved as a designated contract market by the Commodity Futures Trading Commission on May 10, 1985. Futures contracts traded on the Philadelphia Board of Trade include XOC Index, British pound, French franc, Swiss franc, Deutsche mark, Australian dollar, Japanese yen, and Canadian dollar.

Philadelphia Board of Trade, Inc.

Membership	320
Governing Body	board of directors—18
Committees	Admissions; Business Conduct; Finance; Floor Procedure; Margin Allocation; Marketing; Nominating
Officers*	president, executive vice president, secretary, treasurer, vice presidents—(general counsel, operations)

*Not exchange members

In addition to the U.S. exchanges, there are approximately 50 other commodity exchanges around the world that trade a variety of futures contracts. These exchanges include the Australian Financial Futures Market, London International Financial Futures Exchange (LIFFE), London Metals Exchange (LME), Singapore International Monetary Exchange (SIMEX), Sydney Futures Exchange, Tokyo Stock Exchange, and Winnipeg Commodity Exchange.

Foreign Exchanges

Futures exchanges provide a location for buyers and sellers to meet and, through an open outcry auction process, discover a price for specific futures and options contracts. Exchanges also are responsible for disseminating these prices and guaranteeing fulfillment of traded contracts.

This activity is centralized on the trading floor of each futures exchange. While all market participants have indirect access to the floor through their brokers, only exchange members have the privilege of actually trading on the floor.

The size, arrangement, and facilities of the trading floor vary among the exchanges, but many features are common to all. Futures trading is conducted in octagonal and polygonal pits or rings, with steps descending to the center of each pit. Traders stand in groups on the steps, in the center of the pit, or around the waist-high ring according to the contract month of the commodity that they are trading. Buyers and sellers stand throughout the pit, as any trader can buy or sell at any given moment. Generally, one pit or ring is devoted to each futures or options contract traded on the exchange.

Adjacent to the pit or ring (or sometimes in its center) are market reporters, employed by the exchange to record price changes as they occur. The recorded prices are then displayed on computer-operated electronic display boards. Futures prices of commodities traded on other exchanges

EXCHANGE FLOOR OPERATIONS

Floor Trading, Price Discovery, Market Information

4

also are displayed so traders are aware of the most current price movements.

The financial trading floor at the Chicago Board of Trade

Electronic displays and video monitors on the exchange floor provide a constant stream of the latest financial, business, and commodity news from major wire services, and futures and securities exchanges. Large maps show weather development in relevant agricultural areas. Cash prices, receipts, and shipments of various commodities also are available.

To handle the thousands of calls coming from commercial traders and brokerage firms, batteries of telephone stations and sophisticated electronic equipment are strategically located near the pits. At the Chicago Board of Trade, orders received by phone clerks from various member firms are time-stamped, then rushed by messengers (called *runners*) or flashed (signaled by hand) to brokers in the pit for execution.

The price at which a trade is made and other pertinent information are jotted down by the broker on an order blank and returned by a runner to the firm's phone desk. The order is time-stamped again. Information that the trade is completed is then relayed to the office where the order originated so that the customer may be informed. (For more information on order routing, see Chapter 5.)

The result of this trade, along with the results of hundreds of thousands of other trades, is immediately displayed on quotation boards around the trading floor. At the same time, the price quotes are sent outside the exchange to more than 50 vendors of financial information who, in turn, retransmit the information in a variety of formats to hundreds of thousands of subscribers.

Price boards at the Chicago Board of Trade

Types of Floor Traders

The men and women who trade on the floor of futures exchanges perform a variety of different functions. Some traders known as *floor brokers* fill outside orders for different firms such as commission houses, commercial interests, financial institutions, portfolio managers, processors, and exporters, and the general public interested in speculating. Others trade hedging or speculative accounts for the company they work for.

Another group, known as *locals,* trade for their own account and speculate on future price movements. These speculators can fall into one of three categories: *day traders,* who initiate and offset their positions in the course of one day's trading session; *position traders,* who hold long or short positions over a period of days or weeks; or *scalpers,* who trade for small, short-term profits during the course of each trading session, rarely carrying a position overnight.

All the floor traders compete in the auction for sales and purchases of futures and options contracts. The day traders and scalpers, especially, help make the market more fluid by placing incremental prices between the wide bid and offer spreads made by other traders. This creates market liquidity and minimizes price fluctuations.

The Auction

Offers to buy or sell are made by shouting out prices in an auction style so that each trader in the pit has an opportunity to take the opposite side of a trade. This method of vocal trading is so important that it is specifically detailed in the Chicago Board of Trade Rules and Regulations.

In addition to making verbal bids and offers, pit traders also use a simple but highly efficient set of hand and finger signals. In active markets, these signals are indispensable in clarifying bids and offers.

Hand signals vary from exchange to exchange. At the Chicago Board of Trade, the position of the hands tells whether a trader is buying or selling. If a trader has the palm of his hand facing himself, he is buying; if his palm faces outward, he is selling. By holding his arm and the fingers of his hand in a horizontal position, a trader shows with finger signals the fraction above or below the most recent price at which he is making his bid or offer. Vertical finger signals are used to indicate the number of contracts the trader wishes to buy or sell at the price indicated. Traders and brokers use combinations of the signals for price and quantity to indicate a bid or offer.

An important verbal distinction also shows if a trader wants to buy or sell. Buyers call out price first and then quantity; sellers call out quantity first, then price.

When a trade is made, each trader writes the completed transaction on a trading card or multipart order form. For instance, any trade that has been carded for T-bond futures includes the contract month, the price, the trader's initials, the identity of the other trader, the name of the clearing firm on the opposite side of the transaction, and a code indicating the time.

These trading cards constitute original records, and from them the essential data are transferred to the buyer's and seller's clearing firms. Each trader is financially responsible to his clearing firm, which is a member of an exchange clearinghouse. Each clearinghouse guarantees contract performance of all contracts traded and cleared at that futures exchange. (For details on clearing, see Chapter 6.)

Price Discovery

Futures exchanges are free markets where the many factors that influence supply and demand converge on the trading floor and through open outcry auction are translated into a single figure—a price. Exchanges, such as the Chicago Board of Trade, act as barometers for price, registering the impact of the many worldwide forces on specific commodities and financial instruments being traded.

CBOT Hand Signals Indicating Quantities and Prices

Quantity

Buy four contracts

Sell two contracts

Price

Grain futures: ¼ cent
Grain options: ⅔ or ¼ cent
Treasury bond & note futures:
7, 17, & $^{27}/_{32}$ of a point
Stock index futures: .70

Grain futures: ½ cent
Grain options: ⅘ or ½ cent
Treasury bond & note futures:
9, 19, & $^{29}/_{32}$ of a point
Stock index futures: .90

Hand signals adjust to the tick size which varies for each contract. See specific contract specifications in the Appendix for more information on pricing.

Because these economic forces influence cash and futures markets similarly, futures prices parallel the actual cash values of commodities and financial instruments. This characteristic of futures prices allows hedgers and speculators to gauge the value of the underlying instrument in the near or distant future.

Millions of people all over the world use the price information generated by futures exchanges to make marketing decisions—whether or not they actually trade futures contracts. The development of new futures exchanges and special futures divisions in older commodity and financial markets in Europe and the Far East underscores the importance of this exchange function.

The rapid developments in telecommunications have created a global marketplace. Recognizing the importance of providing timely, reliable price information to the public, exchanges, like the Chicago Board of Trade, have made a commitment to use only state-of-the-art technology to transmit this vital price information. Space-age electronics and the time-honored use of the open outcry auction have combined to produce one of the most efficient methods of price discovery in the world.

Price Reporting

Transactions made on the trading floor must be reported to the membership and the general public. This is accomplished by futures exchanges through a variety of communications systems. The Chicago Board of Trade's advanced computer system, considered the most sophisticated available, is called the *Market Price Reporting and Information System* (MPRIS). Several other exchanges also have computerized price-reporting systems. Although the Chicago Board of Trade system differs in some ways from those used by other exchanges, it will be used here to illustrate modern futures price reporting.

The MPRIS, in a typical market situation, accepts four or five price transactions per second and reformats the information in less than a second. The reformatted price information is sent to the trading floor's electronic wallboards, to the exchange's price-reporting network, and to a private closed-circuit television network inside the exchange building. Additionally, this price information is available at specific computer terminals within the Chicago Board of Trade building.

At each trading pit, exchange-employed market reporters enter prices into the MPRIS through a cathode-ray (visual display) computer terminal. The terminal on the floor transmits the coded transaction to a large computer system that performs editing functions to ensure that the trade adheres to exchange regulations, such as those governing minimum price fluctuations and trading limits. If the quote is valid, the computer sends a message back to the terminal operator in the pulpit (usually a raised desk area located in each pit) indicating the time the quote entered the system. Simultaneously, the information is displayed throughout the MPRIS network. Master terminal operators communicate with the system to revise, insert, or cancel quotations if an error occurs during trading.

The MPRIS system involves multiple computers; if one fails, another automatically takes over. Also, multiple controllers for the electronic board and television systems provide ready backup to keep the board running normally in emergencies.

Electronic wallboards on the trading floor display the most current MPRIS price information and are designed to be visible from any position on the trading floor. Virtually all needed price information also is provided on each of the most actively traded commodities, including those from other exchanges.

Electronic Price Wallboards

The closed-circuit television system disseminates MPRIS price information to monitors within the Chicago Board of Trade building. Televised price information appears on at least 720 channels in several formats and carries the following information:

Closed-Circuit Television

♦ The three most recent trades for all contracts of each commodity; opening, high, low, and settlement prices; opening and closing ranges, if applicable; suspension and resumption ranges for the extended trading session, if applicable; net price change from the previous trading day.

♦ Current high and low trading limits.

♦ The most recent quotations in all commodities combined with simulated ticker tape output.

♦ Specialized display of cash grain information, spread data, and Liquidity Data Bank® (LDB)® information. LDB® is copyrighted and exclusive to the Chicago Board of Trade and offers daily volume data and time distribution of prices for every commodity traded on the exchange. (For further information on LDB®, see Chapter 10.)

As part of the MPRIS system, commodity quotations are released by the Chicago Board of Trade to the press and to its own price-reporting networks. Most subscribers to the exchange quotations service receive their information over computer terminals, although many of the larger offices of some commission houses have electronic wall displays.

Commodity Quotations

In addition to futures and options on futures prices, price-reporting networks from most futures exchanges carry other information relevant to trading. Following is a review of the kinds of information provided by the Chicago Board of Trade system.

Line transmission begins each day at approximately 6:45 a.m. with a test series. Interspersed during the test and at one-minute intervals throughout the trading session, the correct Chicago time is given as a permanent record of when specific bids, offers, and trades were made. In

Presession Data

addition, each quote transmitted contains the official Chicago Board of Trade time stamp.

Notices

Before trading begins each day, important notices are flashed across the MPRIS system. These include announcements of the last trading day for expiring futures and options contracts, new contract introductions, changes in contract specifications, and new strike prices when applicable. These notices are repeated following the close of the day trading session.

Deliveries

Each day at approximately 6:50 a.m. during a contract's delivery period, the system lists the deliveries that will be made that day. Delivery notices made the previous day are given, and the first notices of delivery that will be made the following day also are listed.

Receipts and Shipments

The next report is the Chicago Daily Receipts and Shipments of grain. The first section of the report gives the estimated number of railcars of grain in Chicago for that day. This is followed by the estimated number of Commodity Credit Corporation (CCC) railcars of grain in Chicago for that day.

Following the estimates are the previous day's receipts and shipments records, including the number of grain railcars loaded out, and the receipts and shipments of grain made by truck and barge.

Options Volume and Open Interest

About 6:55 a.m. each day, the previous day's volume and open interest figures for put and call options are listed.

Previous Day's Volume

At approximately 7 a.m. daily, the previous day's estimated volume figures for all futures contracts are transmitted, based on the clearinghouse's latest run. (During the last run, the clearinghouse makes a final check to match all trades from the previous day.) This report is released before the first trade-checking session during which exchange members reconcile unmatched trades from the previous day.

Data During the Day Session

The current day's trading session rarely opens precisely on the previous session's closing prices. Opening prices are usually a little higher or lower, reflecting changes in available supplies, news events, and a host of other factors that affect buying and selling decisions.

Open

Trading in all futures contracts does not always begin immediately after the opening bell. This is particularly true in distant contract months where trading is generally less active. However, the first trade made during the day, regardless of when it occurs, will carry the opening symbol OPG on MPRIS. This alerts the reader that a particular price is the first trade made that day.

Bids and Offers

Prices that appear on the price-reporting system may be the result of a trade, but they also could be indications of bids or offers in which no trades were made. When a price appears on the system, it means that a trade, a bid, or an offer was made at that level.

Errors

Errors in transmission usually are corrected quickly by a notation on the system. A quote might be revised or canceled; a missed quote is inserted.

Spreads

A spread refers to the simultaneous purchase and sale of at least two futures contracts. It also can refer to a sale and purchase of different options or a combination of options and futures contracts.

The Rules and Regulations of the Chicago Board of Trade and most other futures exchanges require that spreads be reported as such on the price-reporting system. It is the responsibility of the floor broker or trader who places a spread to inform the market reporters of the prices at which the spread was executed.

Price Ranges

Trading ranges usually are reported twice during the session, reflecting the highest and lowest prices on all transactions. The commodity and contract-month symbols for the nearby contract are the first to appear, followed by the highest and lowest prices. More distant contract months of the same commodity follow in sequence with the highest and lowest prices.

Close

Five minutes before trading closes, a warning bell is sounded on the trading floor. The tempo of trading increases as day traders close out positions they took earlier in the day and outside customers place orders for execution at or near the close.

Another warning bell is sounded one minute before the end of trading. The last 60 seconds is likely to be one of the most active periods in the session. Messengers race back and forth between phones and pit brokers. As soon as the traders confirm execution of their closing orders, the closing, high, and low prices for the day are transmitted through the system. Inactive contracts are shown as having a nominal price, a bid price, or an asked price. (A nominal price is used when no trade has taken place.)

Postsession Data

The settlement prices are released by the clearinghouse and reported on MPRIS 15 to 30 minutes after trading ends. The price fluctuation limits for the following day's trading are transmitted after the settlement prices are sent through the system.

Settlement

The first settlement prices to appear are for the agricultural contracts. They are followed by the price limits for each agricultural contract for the next day. Settlement prices for the nonagricultural commodities traded on the Chicago Board of Trade follow, along with the price limits for the next day's trading in these commodities. Any errors in previous transmission, especially in closing prices and high and low prices, are then corrected and reported.

Volume and Open Interest

The final volume of trading and the open interest for the previous day's trading are carried on the system at about 2:15 p.m. Volume figures for each futures and options contract month are reported, as well as total trading volume and open interest for each commodity.

Evening Session

The trading day has been adjusted to accommodate futures contracts that trade during the evening session at the Chicago Board of Trade. The board of directors determined that each extended trading day has a single official "opening," i.e., 5 p.m., and a single official "close," i.e., 2 p.m. the following day.* The end of the evening session is not referred to as a *close* but as a *suspension,* and the reopening of trading at 7:20 a.m. is officially known as *resumption.*

Wallboards and the closed-circuit television system show a suspension price or range following the conclusion of trading each evening, and show a resumption price or range each morning following the continuation of trading.

Master Reports

Master Reports are compiled by the Chicago Board of Trade's Market Information Department based on information received from various sources, including the U.S. Department of Agriculture, private and terminal markets, and storage facilities.

Visible Supply

On Monday of each week, figures on the U.S. visible supply of agricultural commodities compiled by the Chicago Board of Trade are released. The visible supply is the total stock of agricultural commodities in

---

*During the summer months, the times of the extended trading day are adjusted to allow for daylight saving time.

storage in public elevators and some private elevators in the terminal markets plus certain stocks afloat. This information is carried on the system at approximately 2:30 p.m. The figures are reported in thousands of bushels with the last three digits omitted. The first information reported is the total U.S. visible supplies of each agricultural commodity. Increases or decreases in visible supplies from the previous week also are given. Figures representing stocks on hand at the various principal markets are given with corresponding figures for one week ago and one year ago.

Crop Reports

The U.S. Department of Agriculture Crop Reports also are disseminated over MPRIS. Crop reports are compiled by the Crop Reporting Board and are released at 3 p.m. eastern standard time, and reported over the Chicago Board of Trade system at approximately 2:30 p.m. Chicago time on specific days selected by the USDA.

Planting intention reports for the various ag commodities are released from December through March. Following the planting season, production reports are released. Current figures represent estimates in planted acreage, yield per acre, and expected production as of the first of the month in which the report appears. Each crop report also includes a production comparison with the previous month and the previous year. Significant increases or decreases in the anticipated crop size can have a profound influence on grain prices as well as the prices of related commodities. As a consequence, producers, commercial firms, and speculators eagerly await the release of monthly government crop reports.

Newspaper Quotations

Newspapers vary in how they publish futures and options prices. As an example, the pages at the end of the chapter list how *The Wall Street Journal* reports futures and options on futures prices. The paper includes open, high, low, and closing prices, as well as the net change from the previous day's close and the high-low price range. These prices are quoted in units specific to each futures and options contract and are listed with the quotes. For instance, grains are quoted in cents per bushel, silver in cents per troy ounce, and cattle in cents per pound.

MIDIS-Touch Phone System

Daily price, volume, and open interest data also are available through a unique Chicago Board of Trade telephone system called MIDIS-Touch (Market Information Data Inquiry System). This voice-response system is accessed through any touch-tone telephone. It has the capability to store and update all currently active contract prices periodically during both the Chicago Board of Trade's daytime and evening trading. Prices are updated every 30 minutes during the day and every 15 minutes during the evening. The price updates are entirely computer automated and require no human intervention. Other exchanges also report price data over the telephone, but with a lag time of about a day, because the price information must be compiled, a script made, and a tape recorded.

The price discovery function of futures markets is vitally important to the economy. Futures exchanges, recognizing this role, work to disseminate timely and accurate price information and are constantly improving their price-reporting systems.

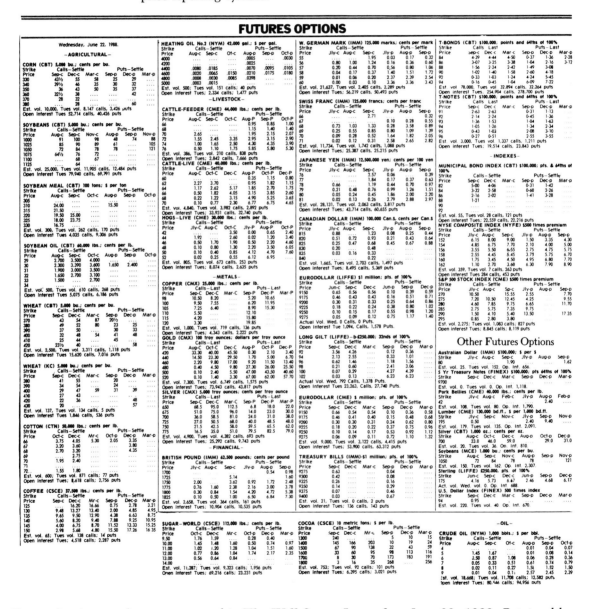

Prices of options on futures as reported in **The Wall Street Journal** *on June 23, 1988. Reprinted by permission of* **The Wall Street Journal**, *Dow Jones and Company, Inc. 1988. All rights reserved.*

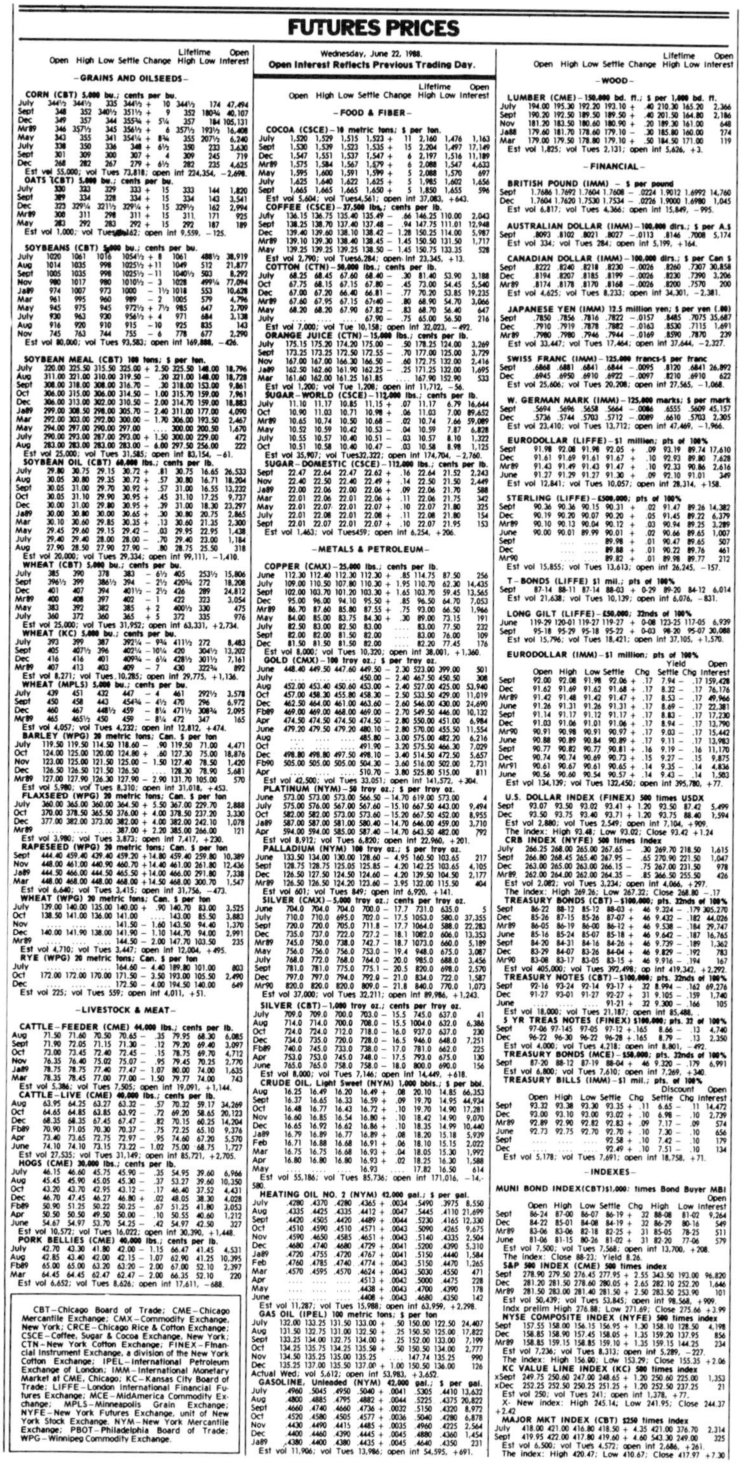

FUTURES PRICES

Wednesday, June 22, 1988.
Open Interest Reflects Previous Trading Day.

Open High Low Settle Change Lifetime High Low Open Interest

CBT–Chicago Board of Trade; CME–Chicago Mercantile Exchange; CMX–Commodity Exchange, New York; CRCE–Chicago Rice & Cotton Exchange; CSCE–Coffee, Sugar & Cocoa Exchange, New York; CTN–New York Cotton Exchange; FINEX–Financial Instrument Exchange, a division of the New York Cotton Exchange; IPEL–International Petroleum Exchange of London; IMM–International Monetary Market at CME, Chicago; KC–Kansas City Board of Trade; LIFFE–London International Financial Futures Exchange; MCE–MidAmerica Commodity Exchange; MPLS–Minneapolis Grain Exchange; NYFE–New York Futures Exchange, unit of New York Stock Exchange. NYM–New York Mercantile Exchange; PBOT–Philadelphia Board of Trade; WPG–Winnipeg Commodity Exchange.

Futures prices as reported in ***The Wall Street Journal*** *on June 23, 1988. Reprinted by permission of* ***The Wall Street Journal****, Dow Jones and Company, Inc. 1988.* *All rights reserved.*

A Futures Commission Merchant (FCM)* is a firm that transacts futures and options on futures business on behalf of financial and commercial institutions as well as the general public. A number of terms are used to describe FCMs, including *wire houses*, *brokerage houses*, and *commission houses*. FCMs are a highly diversified segment of the financial world. Some conduct business in all types of financial investments; others confine their operations to futures and options markets. There are firms that specialize in financial and commercial hedging accounts, while other firms concentrate on public speculative trading.

FCMs become registered member firms of futures exchanges in order to trade or handle accounts in the markets conducted by those exchanges. Under the rules of most exchanges, however, memberships can be held only by individuals. Usually, officers of partnerships and corporations holding exchange memberships register their memberships for the benefit of the partnership or corporation. The individual member retains full control over the membership and full responsibility for the acts of the firm and its employees under the rules and regulations of the exchange.

The basic function of the FCM—regardless of the name, size, and scope of the firm—is to represent the interests of those in the market who

*According to the National Futures Association, an FCM can be an individual or an organization.

THE CUSTOMER AND THE FUTURES COMMISSION MERCHANT

Registration, Accounts, Orders

5

49

do not hold seats on futures exchanges. Some of the many services provided by FCMs include: placing orders, collecting and segregating margin monies, providing basic accounting records, disseminating market information and research, and counseling and training customers in futures and options trading practices and strategies.

Customer Operations

Most customer operations are handled by Associated Persons (APs),** who are employed or associated with a Futures Commission Merchant, an Introducing Broker (IB), Commodity Trading Advisor (CTA), or Commodity Pool Operator (CPO). (IBs, CTAs, and CPOs perform different market services from the FCM. For a description of each, see the National Futures Association reprint on the next page.)

Because these individuals or organizations are responsible for a variety of services—determining the financial stability of prospective customers, opening new accounts, placing orders, and accepting money—they must be registered with the Commodity Futures Trading Commission (CFTC) and become members of the National Futures Association (NFA).

The CFTC, the NFA, and the exchanges have strict rules regarding registration as an Associated Person. For example, as early as the mid-1960s, the Chicago Board of Trade required any individual who was not an exchange member but traded for customer accounts to pass a futures examination. Later, the Chicago Mercantile Exchange, Coffee, Sugar & Cocoa Exchange, New York Cotton Exchange, and Commodity Exchange, Inc. adopted similar measures and required that APs pass the National Commodity Futures Examination before handling customer business.

By the mid-1980s, the Commodity Futures Trading Commission required that everyone who handles customer accounts pass the "Series 3" examination administered by the National Association of Securities Dealers and register with the CFTC. A complete listing of CFTC registration requirements and/or exemptions for registration is on the next page.

Typically, a prospective customer will discuss his financial goals with an Associated Person, who explains the risks associated with trading futures and options on futures. Customer financial requirements may vary from one FCM to another, but are usually strictly enforced to protect the customer, the integrity of the firm, the exchanges, and the CFTC.

Once it has been established that trading in futures contracts is appropriate to the financial goals of a prospective customer and that he meets the financial requirements, opening a futures account is quite simple. To open an account, the customer must supply his name, address, phone

---

**Floor brokers, individuals who execute orders for the purchase and sale of futures or options contracts for another person, also are responsible for handling customer accounts. The NFA and CFTC have specific rules regarding registration of floor brokers. For more information, see the NFA reprint published in this chapter or contact the association.

	Who Is Required to Register	The information which follows should help you determine whether, by law, you are required to seek CFTC registration. If you have any question as to whether you qualify for a particular exemption from registration, you should seek guidance by referring to the appropriate section of the Act or by consulting NFA or CFTC registration personnel.*

Category	Description of Business Activity Requiring Registration	Exemptions
Futures Commission Merchant (FCM)	Generally, an FCM is an individual or organization which does both of the following: (1) solicits or accepts orders to buy or sell futures contracts or commodity options, and (2) accepts money or other assets from customers to support such orders.	Registration is required. There are no exemptions.
Introducing Broker (IB)	An IB is a person or organization that solicits or accepts orders to buy or sell futures contracts or commodity options but does not accept money or other assets from customers to support such orders.	Registration is required unless: (a) You are registered as and acting in the capacity of an AP. *or* (b) You are registered as an FCM. *or* (c) You are registered as a CPO and only operate pools. *or* (d) You are registered as a CTA and either solely manage accounts under powers of attorney or don't receive per trade compensation.
Commodity Pool Operator (CPO)	A CPO is an individual or organization which operates or solicits funds for a commodity pool, that is, an enterprise in which funds contributed by a number of persons are combined for the purpose of trading futures contracts or commodity options.	In general, registration is required unless: (a) The total gross capital contributions to all pools are less than $200,000. *and* (b) There are no more than 15 participants in any one pool. (Cont'd on next page)

*Requests for exemption or for "no action" opinions with respect to the applicable registration requirements and requests for withdrawal from registration should be submitted to the CFTC and a copy of any such request should be provided to NFA.

Category	Description of Business Activity Requiring Registration	Exemptions
Commodity Trading Advisor (CTA)	A CTA is a person who, for compensation or profit, directly or indirectly advises others as to the value of or the advisability of buying or selling futures contracts or commodity options. Providing advice indirectly includes exercising trading authority over a customer's account as well as giving advice through written publications or other media.	Registration is required unless: (a) You have provided advice to 15 or fewer persons during the past 12 months and do not hold yourself out generally to the public as a CTA. *or* (b) You are in one of a number of businesses or professions listed in the Act or are registered in another capacity and your advice is solely incidental to your principal business or profession. *or* (c) Your advice is given through written publication or other mass media and is limited to futures contracts and commodity options traded on foreign exchanges.
Associated Person (AP)	An AP is an individual who solicits orders, customers, or customer funds (or who supervises persons so engaged) on behalf of an FCM, IB, CTA, or CPO. An AP is, in effect, anyone who is a salesperson or who supervises salespersons for any of these categories of individuals or firms. Certain multiple associations are prohibited (e.g. simultaneous association with two FCMs, two IBs or with an FCM and an IB). The registration requirement applies to any person in the supervisory chain of command and not only to persons who directly supervise the solicitation of orders, customers, or funds.	Registration is generally required unless: (a) You are already registered as an FCM, IB, or Floor Broker. *or* (b) You are already registered as a CPO if you are to be associated with a CPO. *or* (c) You are already registered as a CTA if you are to be associated with a CTA. *or* (d) You are already registered with the National Association of Securities Dealers and only act in the capacity of an AP associated with a CPO.
Floor Broker (FB)	An FB is an individual who executes any orders for the purchase or sale of any commodity futures or options contract on any contract market for any other person.	Registration is not required of an exchange member who trades solely for his own account.

Reprinted with permission from NFA. An *Application Guide: NFA Membership and CFTC Registration.*

number, social security or tax I.D. number, and business, personal, and banking references.

CFTC regulations require that the Associated Person provide the prospective customer with a risk disclosure statement. Before an account can be opened, the customer must read the statement and sign a document stating that he has read and fully understands it. A separate risk disclosure statement is required for those who wish to trade options.

An example of a futures risk disclosure statement and two other basic commodity account documents—commodity account agreement form and hedge account certificate—are included in the chapter. The commodity account agreement form outlines how the account will be handled by the FCM and the obligations of the account holder. The hedge account certificate lists the cash commodities owned or expected to be owned, or sold or expected to be sold, by the customer.

Other documents not shown include a new account fact sheet, an options risk disclosure statement, a disclosure statement for noncash margin deposits, and a bankruptcy disclosure statement for hedge accounts. These documents can be obtained from an FCM.

While the amount of paperwork may seem excessive at first, it is designed to ensure that customers understand their financial commitment and the risks associated with a futures and options account.

Types of Accounts

Futures and options accounts may be opened on an individual or joint basis. In individual accounts, trading decisions are made by the individual. In joint accounts, all parties have input on trading decisions. Either type of account may be opened for hedging or speculating purposes.

A third type of account—a discretionary account (also known as a controlled or managed account)—can be set up, in which the customer authorizes another person to make all trading decisions. Each exchange and FCM, especially if an Associated Person will be exercising discretion, has specific rules for handling discretionary accounts. One of the most essential is the customer's written power of attorney to exercise discretion.

Exchange regulations also govern those individuals who handle discretionary accounts. On the Chicago Board of Trade, for example, only those APs who have been registered for at least two continuous years may handle such accounts. All discretionary accounts must be supervised by an officer or partner of the FCM. The AP must record, in writing, every transaction for the account, with subsequent confirmation sent to the customer. The customer receives a detailed monthly statement showing the number, size, and terms of the transactions with net and open positions.

The only way to terminate the trading authority established in a discretionary account is by written revocation of the power of attorney either on the part of the customer or the person controlling the account.

Margins

Futures market participants are required to post performance bond margins. Performance bond margins are financial guarantees required of both buyers and sellers to ensure they fulfill the obligation of the futures contract. That is, they are required to make or take delivery of the commodity represented unless the position is offset before expiration of the contract.

The main purpose of a performance bond margin is to provide contract integrity. It is not at all like margin in the securities industry, which involves a down payment and a loan by the broker/dealer for the purchase of equities.

Margin requirements for futures contracts usually range between 5 and 18 percent of a contract's face value and are set by the exchanges where the contracts are traded. However, brokerage firms can, and often do, require a larger margin than the exchange minimum; they cannot require less.

Futures margins are determined on the basis of risk. In a volatile (or risky) market, a higher margin is usually required; and in a less volatile (or less risky) market, a lower margin is usually required. Margin levels also vary for hedging and speculating accounts. For example, exchanges and brokerage firms generally require lower margins for hedging accounts because they carry less risk than speculating accounts.

Initial margin is the amount a market participant must deposit into his margin account at the time he places an order to buy or sell a futures contract. Then, on a daily basis, the margin account is debited or credited based on the close of that day's trading session. This debiting and crediting is referred to as *marking-to-the-market*. In this way, buyers and sellers are protected against the possibility of contract default.

A customer must maintain a set minimum margin known as *maintenance margin* (per outstanding futures contract) in his account. On any day that debits resulting from a market loss reduce the funds in the account below the maintenance margin, the broker calls on his customer for an additional deposit to restore the account to the initial margin level. Requests for additional money are known as *margin calls*.

FCMs are responsible to see that their customers deposit the required margin promptly. The CFTC requires customer margin monies to be held in segregated accounts from commission house assets, margins on house accounts, and other customer margin funds for commodities not subject to U.S. federal regulations such as London cocoa or sugar.

To ensure the margin system performs efficiently, each exchange has a clearing organization, which not only reconciles the day's trading activity but makes sure brokerage firms have sufficient margin in their accounts to cover their customers' open positions. Just as every buyer or seller of a futures contract must maintain adequate funds in his margin account with the brokerage firm, so must each brokerage firm maintain adequate funds in its margin account with the exchange clearinghouse. (Smaller brokerage houses that are not members of the clearinghouse accomplish this through a firm that is a member.)

(For more detailed information on clearing margins and practices, see Chapter 6.)

Handling margins is an important function of the FCM. Responsibility for placing orders, collecting margin deposits, overseeing the account, making margin calls, and notifying the customer when he has surplus margin usually falls on the shoulders of the AP.

Orders

Understanding the customer's objectives and properly relaying orders are vital functions of the AP. He must write and enter orders without vagueness or ambiguity to ensure that they are properly handled on the trading floor. A mistake in this process can be very costly, therefore, both the customer and the AP must accurately communicate the order.

Some of the more common orders follow:

Market

Perhaps the most common type of order is the market order. In a market order, the customer states the number of contracts of a given delivery month he wishes to buy or sell. He does not specify the price at which he wants to initiate the transaction, but simply wants it placed as soon as possible at the best possible price.

Price Limit

The price limit order specifies a price limit at which the customer's order must be executed. It can be executed only at that price or better.

Fill-or-Kill

A fill-or-kill order is a price limit order that must be filled immediately or canceled.

Stop

A stop order is not executed until the market reaches a given price level. For instance, a stop order to buy becomes a market order when the futures contract trades (or is bid) at or above the stop price. A stop order to sell becomes a market order when the futures contract trades (or is offered) at or below the stop price.

Stop orders normally are used to liquidate earlier transactions, to cut losses, or to protect profits. Let's assume a customer bought a U.S. Treasury bond futures contract for $100,000. To prevent a large loss in the event bond prices fall, the customer could place a stop order (also known as a *stop-loss* or *sell-stop order*) at $96,000. His position is liquidated if and when the market price declines to $96,000. Once the market reaches $96,000, the stop-loss order becomes a market order and could be filled at a lower price, say $95,500, rather than the price designated in the order.

Stop orders also can be used to enter the market. Suppose a trader expected a bull market only if it passed a specific price level. In this case, he could use a stop-buy order when and if the market reached this point.

Stop-Limit Order

One variation of a stop order is a stop-limit order. With a stop-limit order, the trade must be executed at the exact price or held until the stated price is reached again. If the market fails to return to the stop-limit level, the order is not executed.

Market-if-Touched

A board or market-if-touched (MIT) order may be executed only if the market reaches a particular price. An MIT to buy becomes a market order if and when a futures contract trades at or below the order price. An MIT order to sell becomes a market order if and when a futures contract trades at or above the order price.

Time Limit

Several types of orders specify the time an order must be executed. For instance, a day order must be placed at a given price sometime during that day's trading session. At the Chicago Board of Trade, all orders are assumed to be day orders unless otherwise specified.

A time limit order is good until a designated time during the trading session. If the order has not been filled by that time, it is automatically canceled. An open or good-till-canceled (GTC) order can be executed any time up until the customer cancels the order or the contract expires.

Orders also may be limited to purchases or sales at the open or close of a trading session. These transactions do not have to be the first or last of the session, but must be executed within the opening or closing ranges of a trading session as defined by the rules of the exchange. It is also possible to specify a certain portion of the day or time that an order must be executed.

Opening and Closing Orders, Cancellations

On the Chicago Board of Trade, all orders that reach the trading floor 15 minutes or less before the open or close of trading are accepted solely at the risk of the customer on a "not held" basis. This is because they could involve extraordinary problems if floor brokers don't have enough time to prioritize and organize their orders for execution in the pit.

Canceling

A straight cancel order deletes a customer's previous order.

A cancel-former-order (CFO) eliminates a previous order but replaces it with new instructions. It is most often used to change the price level in a price limit order.

Combination

Combination orders are used to enter two orders at the same time. One example of a combination order is a one-cancels-other (OCO) order. It is a two-sided order in which the execution of one side cancels the other. For instance, a trader, who is long January U.S. Treasury bonds at $98,000 with a price objective of $103,000 and a desired stop point at $96,000, might enter the following OCO order: Sell one January U.S. Treasury bond contract $103,000 limit/$96,000 stop. (**Note:** This type of order may not be accepted on all exchanges.)

Spread orders also are considered combination orders and refer to the simultaneous purchase and sale of at least two different futures contracts. There are a variety of spread orders that can involve the sale and purchase of futures contracts of different delivery months (intramarket or interdelivery spread), the same commodity on different exchanges (intermarket spread), or different but related futures contracts (intercommodity spread).

With respect to options on futures, spread trading takes many forms. Among the most commonly used are vertical spreads (buying and selling options of the same expiration month at different strike prices), conversions (buying a put option, selling a call option, and buying a futures contract), and reversals (buying a call option, selling a put option, and selling a futures contract).

Order Routing

Orders received from customers are sent immediately by an AP by direct transmission to the exchange on which the order is to be executed. A sufficient number of telephone stations are located on the periphery of the trading floor to handle the many orders coming to the exchange from companies and individuals. At the Chicago Board of Trade, for example, there are several steps taken once an order is received on the exchange floor that are described on the next page.

Accounting Services

Written confirmation of all commodity futures and options on futures orders on a same-day basis is the objective of most FCMs even though the confirmation may have been made by telephone.

Confirmation is just the first step in a series of important accounting services that FCMs provide their customers. In addition, firms provide purchase and sales (P&S) statements that show the number of contracts purchased and/or sold in specific futures markets at specific prices and current cash balances.

A customer may obtain full information on the net status of his account by asking his AP. The customer normally receives a regular monthly statement that shows all trading activity, net position, and margin balance less commission and fees.

Route of an Order

The order is time-stamped.

A member firm employee, known as a runner, rushes the order to a broker in the trading pit. (Some orders are flashed by hand signals to brokers in the trading pit and fills are flashed back to the order station. This is generally the practice in many of the financial futures markets.)

The broker fills the order using open outcry and hand signals to communicate price and quantity.

Once the order is filled, the broker reports the price to exchange price reporters in raised pulpits looking down onto each pit. The pit reporters relay price changes as they occur to central quotation computers.

The computer then transmits the price information to electronic price boards facing the trading floor and around the world via information services.

The completed order is picked up by a runner and returned to the telephone desk. The order is time-stamped again. The customer is notified that his order has been filled.

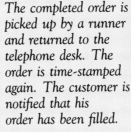

One of the most important FCM services is disseminating market information to its customers. This service can take the form of daily or weekly market letters, prepared by futures specialists, that outline the fundamental supply/demand factors and price outlook.

Some FCMs also provide technical advisory and price-charting services that track historical patterns of price movement, volume, and open interest data as indicators of future price movement.

Market Information and Research

Several exchanges have strict standards for advertising and promotional materials distributed by their member firms and aimed at prospective customers. In general, ads have to be truthful and in good taste. Advertising and sales promotion appeals should avoid misrepresentations about profit potential. Periodically, exchanges will review advertising done by their member firms to make certain it meets generally high standards. In the case of options on futures, all promotional material must be submitted to the exchanges for review. The exchanges' rules on advertising are meant to protect the customer, member firms and their employees, and the exchanges themselves.

Advertising and Promotion

FCMs, futures exchanges, the NFA, and the CFTC share important responsibilities for protecting public customers in futures and options on futures markets. The FCMs, together with the exchanges, are responsible for informing the public not only of the investment potential, but also of the possibility of losses in futures and options on futures trading. They must communicate that gains in futures trading are the product of attentive observation of price movement and a thorough understanding of the economic factors underlying the market, and that there is no guarantee of profit.

By their regulations, auditing procedures, and financial requirements, FCMs and exchanges make certain that customers are prepared to fulfill their financial commitments in futures and options on futures trading. Regulation of the business conduct and financial soundness of member firms, margin requirements, standards of performance for APs, and the segregation of customer margins are not guarantees against customer losses due to adverse price movements, but they do ensure against customer losses due to financial failure or improper handling of customer funds.

Customer Protection

NAME OF FIRM

RISK DISCLOSURE STATEMENT

This statement is furnished to you because rule 1.55 of the Commodity Futures Trading Commission requires it.

The risk of loss in trading commodity futures contracts can be substantial. You should therefore carefully consider whether such trading is suitable for you in light of your financial condition. In considering whether to trade, you should be aware of the following:

1) You may sustain a total loss of the initial margin funds and any additional funds that you deposit with your broker to establish or maintain a position in the commodity futures market. If the market moves against your position, you may be called upon by your broker to deposit a substantial amount of additional margin funds, on short notice, in order to maintain your position. If you do not provide the required funds within the prescribed time, your position may be liquidated at a loss, and you will be liable for any resulting deficit in your account.

2) Under certain market conditions, you may find it difficult or impossible to liquidate a position. This can occur, for example, when the market makes a "limit move."

3) Placing contingent orders, such as a "stop-loss" or "stop-limit" order, will not necessarily limit your losses to the intended amounts, since market conditions may make it impossible to execute such orders.

4) A "spread" position may not be less risky than a simple "long" or "short" position.

5) The high degree of leverage that is often obtainable in futures trading because of the small margin requirements can work against you as well as for you. The use of leverage can lead to large losses as well as gains.

This brief statement cannot, of course, disclose all the risks and other significant aspects of the commodity markets. You should therefore carefully study futures trading before you trade.

I have read and understand the above risk disclosure statement furnished to me by Name of Firm.

_____	_____	_____
Date	Signature	Print Name
_____	_____	_____
Date	Signature	Print Name
_____	_____	_____
Date	Signature	Print Name

HEDGE ACCOUNT CERTIFICATION

The undersigned certifies that trades in futures and/or options on futures contracts in his/her account with Name of Firm are bona fide hedging transactions and that the positions maintained are bona fide hedge positions.

The undersigned further certifies that provided below is a true and accurate list of the cash commodities owned or expected to be owned, or sold or expected to be sold by the customer; and that checked below are futures therefore eligible as bona fide hedge positions.

		COMMODITY FUTURES	CASH COMMODITY
_____	A.	Grains-wheat, corn, oats, soybeans-meal, oil, etc.	_____
_____	B.	Meats-cattle, hogs, broilers and products, etc.	_____
_____	C.	Metals-gold, silver, copper	_____
_____	D.	Financials-T-bills, T-bonds, GNMA, Eurodollars, CDs, etc.	_____
_____	E.	Currencies-Brit. Pounds, Mex. Pesos, Swiss Francs, Jap. Yen, etc.	_____
_____	F.	Sugar, Coffee, Cocoa	_____
_____	G.	Cotton, Frozen O.J.	_____
_____	H.	Petroleum Products-unleaded gas, heating oil, etc.	_____
_____	I.	Forest Products-lumber	_____
_____	J.	Indexes-NYSE Index, S&P, Value Line, MMI, etc.	_____

CFTC regulations require that all commodity brokers notify their hedge customers of the following: You have the opportunity to state at this time whether in the unlikely event of this company's bankruptcy you prefer that open contracts held in your hedging account be liquidated by the trustee without seeking your instructions.

_____   I would not prefer such liquidation.   _____

Customer's Signature

_____   I would prefer such liquidation.   _____

Customer's Signature

COMMODITY ACCOUNT AGREEMENT

_____   _____
Name   Account No.

1) In consideration of the agreement of Name of Firm to act as broker for the undersigned in the purchase or sale of commodities (which term shall include contracts relating to immediate or future delivery of commodities and options thereon) the undersigned agrees, in respect to all commodity accounts which the undersigned now has or may at any future time have with the firm, or its successors including accounts from time to time closed and then reopened, as follows:

2) Orders for the purchase or sale of commodities shall be received and executed with the express intent that actual delivery is contemplated. All transactions shall be subject to the constitution, by-laws, rules, regulations, customs and usages of the exchange or market where executed (and of its clearing house if any) and to any law, rule and regulation applicable thereto, including but not limited to, the provisions of the Commodity Exchange Act, as amended, and the rules and regulations thereunder. The firm reserves the right to refuse to accept any order.

3) If the undersigned should die or become incompetent, any pending order shall be validly executed by the firm, up to the time it receives written notice of the death or incompetence of the undersigned, and the firm is hereby indemnified against loss arising therefrom.

4) To secure any indebtedness or other obligation owed by the undersigned to the firm, the firm is hereby granted a lien on all of the undersigned's property at any time held by the firm. The firm may without notice transfer any money or other property interchangeably between any accounts of the undersigned except that any transfer from a commodity account which is subject to regulations under the Commodity Exchange Act to a nonregulated account shall have such other authorization by the undersigned as is required by such regulations.

5) The undersigned recognizes that margin deposits are due and must be paid immediately upon entering into positions on commodity exchanges and from time to time as market conditions dictate and agrees to make such deposits immediately on demand. The firm shall have absolute discretion to set and revise margin requirements. Customer acknowledges the firm's right to limit, without notice to customer, the number of open positions which customer may maintain or acquire through the firm.

6) The undersigned agrees to pay promptly on demand any and all sums due to the firm for monies advanced, with interest thereon at 1% over the prime rate. The undersigned agrees to pay when due the firm's charges for commissions at rates established between us and to pay interest at 1% over the prime rate on past due commission charges.

7) The firm shall have the right, whenever in its discretion it considers it necessary for its protection, or in the event that a petition in bankruptcy or for the appointment of a receiver is filed by or against the undersigned, or in the event of the death of the undersigned, or in the event the undersigned is adjudged incompetent, to sell any or all commodities, or other property in any account of the undersigned and to buy any or all commodities which may be short in any account of the undersigned, and to close out

and liquidate any and all outstanding contracts of the undersigned, all without demand for margin or additional margin, notice of sale or purchase, notice of advertisement of any kind whatsoever, and any such sales or purchases may be made at the firm's discretion on any exchange or other market where such business is then usually transacted, and on any such sale the firm may be the purchaser for its own account; it being understood that a prior demand, or call, or prior notice of the time and place of such sale or purchase, if any be given, shall not be considered a waiver of the firm's right to sell or to buy without demand or notice as herein provided; and the undersigned shall at all times be liable to the firm for the payment of any debit balance owing in the accounts of the undersigned with the firm, and shall be liable for any deficiency remaining in any such account in the event of the liquidation thereof in whole or in part, and shall be liable for any reasonable costs of collection including attorneys' fees.

8)   Any notices and other communications may be transmitted to the undersigned at the address, or telephone number given herein, or at such other address or telephone number as the undersigned hereafter shall notify the firm in writing, and all notices or communications shall be deemed transmitted when telephoned or deposited in the mail or telexed or telegraphed by the firm or the firm's representative, whether actually received by the undersigned or not. Confirmations, purchase and sale statements and account statements shall be deemed accurate unless objected to in writing within 5 business days from the date of such notice and delivered to the firm.

9)   The firm will not be responsible for delays or failure in the transmission of orders caused by a breakdown of communication facilities or by any other cause beyond the firm's reasonable control.

10)   The undersigned represents that he or she is 18 years of age or over and that he or she is not an employee of any exchange nor of any corporation of which any exchange owns a majority of the capital stock. The undersigned further represents that he or she is not an employee of a member of any exchange nor of a firm registered on any exchange or if he or she is so employed then a written consent of his or her employer is attached herewith.

11)   This agreement is made under and shall be governed by the laws of the State of Illinois in all respects, including construction and performance.

12)   The undersigned acknowledges that the firm is a wholly owned subsidiary of Company A and that the market recommendations of the firm may or may not be consistent with the market position or intentions of Company A, its subsidiaries and affiliates. The market recommendations of the firm are based upon information believed to be reliable, but the firm cannot and does not guarantee the accuracy or completeness thereof or represent that following such recommendations will eliminate or reduce the risks inherent in trading commodities futures.

13)   The firm is hereby granted permission to record telephone conversations between its employees and the undersigned.

14)   This agreement shall be irrevocable as long as the undersigned shall have any account with the firm; it shall be binding upon the undersigned and upon the undersigned's executors, administrators, heirs and assigns; it can be amended only in writing duly signed by the undersigned and an officer of the firm.

Clearinghouses of U.S. commodity exchanges are an integral part of futures trading. Their responsibilities include settling accounts, clearing trades, collecting and maintaining margin monies, regulating delivery, and reporting trading data. In addition to guaranteeing that all trades and accounts are checked and balanced before the next trading session opens, clearinghouses ensure the financial integrity of the marketplace. Their operations have greatly contributed to the rapid growth and efficiency of futures trading.

In the mid to late 1800s, commodity exchanges were essentially cash markets. Buyers and sellers met, agreed on a price, and arranged for delivery of their commodities. But, as the volume of trading grew, direct transactions between buyers and sellers became impractical. A contract might be bought and resold several times before it was actually offset or delivery was taken.

To handle this complex chain of transactions, brokers became the mediators between buyers and sellers, making contractual agreements, arranging for delivery, and transferring funds. Settlement clerks of brokerage houses maintained daily accounting records of customer transactions in ring notebooks. This method of record keeping became known as the *ring method*.

For example, suppose a broker received an order from his customer, Jones, to buy wheat futures contracts. The broker executed the order with

CLEARING OPERATIONS

Preserving the Integrity of the Markets

6

Stanley; his settlement clerk's records showed that Jones bought from Stanley. Later, Jones, seeing a profit due to a price increase, decided to offset or liquidate his position by selling back the same number of wheat futures contracts. Jones gave an order to that effect to his broker and the contracts were offered on the market. They were bought by a man named Larson, who, two days later, because of a price decline, decided to offset his position to cut his losses. The contracts were offered in the market and were purchased by Smith, a flour miller, who wanted to take delivery of the wheat when the contracts reached maturity. Smith's broker arranged for delivery and payment between Smith and the original seller of the contracts, Stanley. Any obligation undertaken by Jones or Larson had been offset by equal and opposite futures transactions. Often, this kind of chain of buyers and sellers involved as many as 50 or more persons.

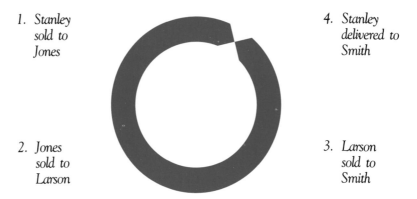

1. *Stanley sold to Jones*

2. *Jones sold to Larson*

3. *Larson sold to Smith*

4. *Stanley delivered to Smith*

Formal Clearing Organizations

The ring method of settlement served futures markets well from the early 1900s until the 1920s when the first formalized clearing operations were developed, either as part of an exchange, or as a related but separate entity. Today, clearing of U.S. futures contracts is conducted by clearinghouses of the exchanges or by separate clearing corporations.

Unlike memberships on commodity exchanges, which are held by individuals only, memberships in clearing organizations are usually held by companies. Membership rosters of clearing organizations include international commission houses, commercial processors, independent trading companies, and financial institutions. On some exchanges, an individual may apply for clearing privileges but is only permitted to clear trades for his own account and not for customers or third parties.

The level of capitalization required for clearing member firms varies depending upon the type and size of their business. Financial requirements also vary among exchanges but are uniformly rigid to help ensure the financial soundness of the clearinghouses. Some clearing firms even require members to purchase and hold shares in the clearing organization.

Clearinghouses act as third parties to all futures and options contracts—acting as a buyer to every clearing member seller and a seller to every clearing member buyer. Buyers and sellers of futures and options contracts do not create financial obligations to one another, but, rather, to the clearinghouse through their clearing member firms.

A transaction in which Smith sells futures to Adams means that Smith's clearing firm would be obligated to the clearinghouse to make delivery or offset before the contract expires. Adams's clearing firm also would be obligated to the clearinghouse to take delivery or offset. The clearinghouse would act as the buyer to Smith's clearing firm and the seller to Adams's clearing firm.

Because the direct relationship between buyer and seller is severed, each is free to buy and sell independently of the other. As a party to every trade, the clearinghouse assumes the responsibility of guarantor of every trade.

A Typical Order Process

1. Customer places order through a brokerage firm.

2. Brokerage firm fills order.

3. Order is cleared through a clearing member firm. (If the brokerage firm is not a member of a clearinghouse, it clears through another firm that is a clearinghouse member.)

4. Clearing member firm transmits order to clearinghouse.

5. Clearinghouse confirms order, guarantees trade, and adjusts clearing firm's account based on the gain or loss from the transaction.

Third-Party Guarantors

Clearinghouses are able to guarantee all trades made on the floor of exchanges because they require members to deposit margin monies based upon their customers' positions. Clearing margins act as financial safeguards to ensure that clearing member firms perform on their customers' open futures and options contracts. These margins are recommended by the clearinghouse margin committee and set by the board of directors. Clearing margins are distinct from the brokerage margins that individual buyers and sellers of futures and options contracts are required to deposit with their brokers. (Refer to Chapter 5 for more information on these margins.)

The initial clearing margin is the amount a clearing member firm must have on account at the time an order is placed to buy or sell a futures contract. On the Chicago Board of Trade and most other exchanges, a clearing member's initial clearing margin deposits are based on the net long (buy) or net short (sell) futures position. As an example, a clearing member firm with a short position of 10 corn futures contracts and a long

Clearing Margins

position of 5 corn futures contracts would be required to deposit margin money on the net short position of 5 corn contracts.

The clearinghouses of the Chicago Mercantile Exchange and the New York Mercantile Exchange require margin deposits on both the long and short futures positions in each commodity rather than on the net position.

(For options contracts, however, margin is required only from the short position. Options on futures are explained more fully in Chapter 12.)

Margin levels are set consistent with market risks. Typically, margin requirements range between 5 and 18 percent of a contract's face value. Naturally, market participants assuming greater price risks are required to post more margin.

Clearing margins may be posted in three forms or in combinations of the following: cash, interest-bearing obligations of the federal government, and letters of credit issued by approved banks. The member firm does not have access to this money until it is released by the clearinghouse.

As a member's position changes from day to day, so does the required margin. After each trading session, the clearinghouse recomputes the margin requirement for each clearing member. Every evening, the clearinghouse provides a margin statement to the clearing firm. If a net position increases, additional margin must be deposited before the market opens the next day. If a net position declines, excess margin money may be returned to the clearing member firm. Some firms prefer to keep their surplus margin in reserve rather than to draw it back on a daily basis.

In most cases, initial margins are sufficient to cover daily maximum price fluctuations. At the Chicago Board of Trade, initial margin deposits are collected within 24 hours of the time a trade is executed (in some instances, within 10 hours).

Clearinghouses monitor the markets as well as the members' positions. For example, the Board of Trade Clearing Corporation uses a sophisticated computer risk-analysis program known as *Simulation Analysis of Financial Exposure* (SAFE). SAFE monitors the risk of clearing members and large-volume traders. It evaluates the risk of open positions by calculating the risk a firm is carrying if there is a change in market prices or volatility.

In periods of great market volatility or in the case of high-risk accounts, the clearinghouse can call on a member firm to deposit additional margin money at anytime during a trading session to cover adverse price changes. This call for additional money is known as a *variation margin call*, and, within one hour, the member firm must pay the amount called for by wire transfer of funds. This amount is applied to the settlement for the day and does not go into the standing or initial margin account.

In this way, the clearinghouse maintains very tight control over margins as prices fluctuate. It ensures that sufficient margin money is on deposit at all times—another means of ensuring the financial integrity of futures contracts.

Every day, the clearinghouse settles each account on its books. All futures accounts, long or short, whether traded during the most recent session or not, are adjusted daily as to gain or loss. This debiting and crediting on the basis of price changes takes place following the close of each trading day. It is called *marking-to-the-market*. Accounts are adjusted by calculating the difference between the day's settlement price and the price at which the position was initiated. In the case of options on futures, the full premium is received from the buyer and passed on to the seller.

Although the method of determining the settlement price varies among exchanges, the following methods are the most common. When there is a single price at the close of trading, that price becomes the settlement price. However, in the flurry of last-minute trading, it is common for several separate transactions to be made at different but closely related prices. In this circumstance, averaging the closing range is the most common way to determine the settlement price.

Daily Settlement of Accounts

All futures positions are either offset or delivered against the contract. The vast majority are settled by offsetting trades, and only 1 to 3 percent result in delivery of the actual commodity.* Yet, the fact that buyers and sellers can take or make delivery helps assure that futures prices reflect the actual cash value of the commodity.

Clearinghouses generally do not make or take delivery of the actual commodity.** Rather, they provide the mechanism that enables sellers to make delivery to qualified buyers. The delivery process varies somewhat from exchange to exchange but, in all cases, delivery is possible by completing a series of steps. As an example, the following three-day delivery process is required by the rules of the Chicago Board of Trade.

Delivery

Day 1 (Position Day)

The clearing firm representing the seller notifies the Board of Trade Clearing Corporation that its customer wants to deliver on a futures contract.

Day 2 (Notice Day)

Prior to the market opening on Day 2, the clearing corporation matches the buyer with the oldest reported long position to the delivering

---

*The advent of index-based futures contracts, such as stock index and municipal bond index futures, has seen the development of cash-settled contracts. Rather than specifying delivery of a commodity or financial instrument, transactions are settled in cash based on the actual value of the index on the last trading day.

**For some contracts, the clearinghouse does make or take delivery. For example, the Chicago Mercantile Exchange and MidAmerica Commodity Exchange will make or take delivery on currencies and cattle futures.

seller. The clearing corporation then notifies both parties.

The clearing firm representing the seller prepares and sends an invoice to the Board of Trade Clearing Corporation for distribution to the clearing firm representing the buyer. The seller's clearing firm also must prepare a copy of the invoice for the clearing corporation. The buyer's clearing firm receives the seller's invoice from the clearing corporation.

Day 3 (Delivery Day)

Upon receiving a check from the buyer's clearing firm, the seller's clearing firm gives the warehouse receipt[†] to the buyer's clearing firm. The buyer's clearing firm presents the delivery notice with a certified check for the amount due at the office of the seller's clearing firm.

Market Information

Daily recording of trading volume and open interest is a service provided by all clearing organizations. (Trading volume is the number of contracts traded each delivery month of every futures and options contract, and open interest is the number of open futures and options positions.)

Exchanges are required to make this information available to the general public, on a daily basis, according to the Commodity Exchange Act, as amended in 1974. Open interest and trading volume are used by the Commodity Futures Trading Commission to compile monthly reports that analyze traders' positions based upon the size of accounts and whether trades are used for speculative or hedging purposes. Both daily and monthly open interest and volume information are reported in the newspaper.

[†]Only certain commodities require a transfer of a warehouse receipt.

U.S. futures markets have a long history of self-regulation that dates from the mid-1800s, predating both state and federal regulation.

The rules and regulations of the exchanges are extensive and are designed to support competitive, efficient, liquid markets. Most state and federal regulation, which began shortly after futures trading developed in the United States, has been designed to enforce self-regulation by the exchanges.

This chapter reviews some of the principal rules and trading practices followed on most U.S. exchanges, as well as federal and industry regulation of futures trading. Keep in mind that rules may vary among exchanges due in part to their highly diverse histories and patterns of development, but those described here are based on the Rules and Regulations of the Chicago Board of Trade.

Note that the rules and regulations are scrutinized continuously by the exchanges, and are periodically amended to reflect the needs of market users. The adoption of many new rules and regulations, as well as the amendment of existing ones, requires the approval of the Commodity Futures Trading Commission (CFTC), the U.S. federal regulatory agency for futures and options on futures trading.

REGULATION OF FUTURES TRADING

Exchange, Industry, Federal Regulation

7

EXCHANGE REGULATION

Exchange rules and regulations cover many areas of futures trading—from contract specifications to trading practices to arbitration procedures. Following are some of the more important rules, which should serve as a useful guide to exchange self-regulation.

Open Market

All transactions must be made in the open market. This means that all bids and offers are shouted in the trading pit, i.e., made in open outcry, and are available to all members present.

Nonclearing and Clearing Members

Nonclearing members must follow certain clearing procedures when trading futures and options on futures contracts. Most importantly, nonclearing members are required to clear all trades through a clearing member firm; the clearing member is liable for those trades until the clearing arrangement is officially terminated through procedures specified by the exchange. Immediately following a trade, a nonclearing trader or broker must report the name of his clearing firm to the trader on the other side of the transaction. (Clearing operations are described in Chapter 6.)

At the Chicago Board of Trade, buyers and sellers must verbally check a trade not longer than 15 minutes after the time it is executed and provide the name of their clearing member within 30 minutes. The Chicago Mercantile Exchange and most others also require that this information be exchanged within a reasonable amount of time following a trade.

Nonmembers: Floor Personnel

Nonmember employees on the trading floor have very specific job descriptions as defined in the rules and regulations of most futures exchanges. For example, floor messengers and clerks are authorized to deliver and receive messages, write broker cards from endorsed orders, operate teletype machines, and perform other routine clerical and telephone functions. Trade checkers may only check trades.

Position Limits

Position and daily trading limits are designed to ensure the market's financial integrity and reduce price volatility. A position limit is the maximum number of futures and/or options on futures contracts that may be held by a market participant and is determined by the CFTC and/or the exchange where the contract is traded. The daily trading limit refers to the maximum price range allowed each day for a contract and is set by the exchange.

Limits on the long or short positions of a given commodity are usually listed in the contract specifications. Positions at or above specific levels must be reported daily to the CFTC and/or the exchange where the contract is traded.

Position limits apply to speculative as well as hedging accounts, however, there are certain procedures a hedger can take to expand his position limits.

Daily trading limits are listed in the contract specifications. Trading is prohibited outside of an established price range, which is based on the settlement price of the previous business day plus or minus an amount set for each futures contract.* For example, if soybeans close at $6.64 per bushel and the normal daily trading limit is 30 cents per bushel, beans may be traded within a range of $6.34 and $6.94 on the following business day.

During periods of extreme price volatility, the Chicago Board of Trade has a variable limits provision under which the price limit of a futures contract is automatically expanded by 50 percent of the daily price limit. The provision applies when three or more delivery months of a given commodity in a particular contract year experience limit bid or limit sellers moves** on a single day. For instance, the daily trading limit for soybeans is 30 cents per bushel. Under the variable limits provision, the daily trading limit in soybeans for the following business day would be increased by 50 percent of the normal daily limit, or 15 cents. The variable price limit would then be 45 cents.

Variable limits stay in effect for a minimum of three days. If the markets move limit bid or limit sellers on the third day, the expanded position limits continue for another three days. If the markets do not move limit bid or limit sellers on the third day, price limits drop back to their original level.

Other exchanges, including the Chicago Mercantile Exchange, also have provisions for expanded daily trading limits in periods of unusual price volatility. These regulations are complex, and the rule books of the individual exchanges should be consulted.

Types of orders that are permitted vary among the exchanges. The following are acceptable for execution on the Chicago Board of Trade:

Types of Orders

♦ Market orders to buy or sell
♦ Closing orders to buy or sell
♦ Limit orders to buy or sell
♦ Stop orders to buy or sell

---

*For some futures contracts, the price limit does not apply on or after two business days preceding the first business day of the current month.
**Limit bid: The market closes at an upward price limit on an unfilled bid.
Limit sellers: The market closes at a downward price limit on an unfilled offer.

- Stop-limit orders to buy or sell
- Limit or market spread orders

On several exchanges, various time and contingent orders are generally prohibited on the last day of trading, but are otherwise accepted. (Various orders and their purposes are discussed in more detail in Chapter 5. Consult the rule books of the individual exchanges to determine the kinds of orders that each exchange accepts.)

Price Reporting

Both traders in a transaction are generally responsible for ensuring that the market reporter has accurately recorded the price of the trade. In those market situations when a price is not recorded by a market reporter, exchange pit committees are authorized to insert prices. However, each exchange has specific rules governing price insertion.

On the Chicago Board of Trade, pit committees are authorized to change an opening range only within 30 minutes after an opening and to change a closing range only within 15 minutes of the close of that day's market. Only the board of directors has the authority to insert prices that affect an open, high, low, or closing price after that time, though it is not a common practice. The Chicago Mercantile Exchange has a 15-minute limit on inserting prices after the opening and a 5-minute limit on the close. Most other exchanges follow similar practices.

Offenses

The following acts are considered offenses on most exchanges, and will likely result in suspension, expulsion, or fines for the members or member firms:

- Violating any rule or regulation of the exchange regarding the conduct or business of members, or violating any agreement made with the exchange
- Fraud, dishonorable conduct, behavior inconsistent with equitable principles of trade, and default
- Making a fictitious transaction or giving an order for the purchase or sale of a futures contract that, when executed, would involve no change in ownership
- Purchases or sales, or offers to buy or sell, that are made to upset market equilibrium and result in prices that do not reflect fair market values
- A false statement made to the board of directors, a standing or special committee, or on a membership application

♦ Any act detrimental to the interest or welfare of the exchange such as reckless and unbusinesslike conduct

♦ Circulating rumors to manipulate the market and affect prices

♦ Failing or refusing to submit books or papers to the board of directors or to a standing or special committee when requested

♦ Attempted extortion; trading against orders or positions of customers; manipulation of prices or attempts to corner the market; giving out false market information; trading or accepting margins after insolvency; trading for the account of a clearing member, or giving up the name of any clearing member without authority; failing to comply with an order of the Arbitration Committee

Most exchanges also have rules dealing with trading behavior. The following practices are prohibited:

Trading Behavior Rules

♦ Disclosing an order at any time, or divulging, trading against, or taking the other side of any order revealed to a member through his relationship with a customer

♦ Trading with yourself

♦ For a member to withhold from the open market any order or part of any order for the convenience of another member

♦ Buying or selling as an accommodation to another trader (such as prearranged trading) at any time; using one order to fill another order or part of an order; buying or selling simultaneously at a prearranged price

♦ For a broker to trade for his own account (at the market price or customer's requested price) before filling customer orders

♦ For traders to fail to make sure that the market reporter has accurately recorded the price of a trade

FCM Responsibility

Grievances

Futures Commission Merchants (FCMs) and floor brokers are liable for losses that occur due to error or mishandling of a customer order.

Responsibility for the customer account is assumed immediately after accepting an order. If an error occurs, the floor broker, FCM, or both are held responsible for the loss, depending on who made the error.

Defaulting on Contracts

Chicago Board of Trade members who default on exchange contracts may be suspended until the contract is performed or the debt is satisfied. If the default is denied, then the member is entitled to arbitration of the claim.

Arbitration

The rules and regulations of most exchanges have long defined procedures for arbitration of disputes between members, and between members and customers. As early as 1859, the Chicago Board of Trade had arbitration committees to settle disputes that were voluntarily submitted.

Information regarding arbitration procedures can be obtained from the current rule books of the individual exchanges and current CFTC regulations.

Committees

Floor Governors

On most exchanges, floor trading practices are governed by one or more committees called the Floor Governors Committee, the Floor Practices Committee, or the Exchange Room Committee. This committee oversees the practices and conduct of members on the trading floor to ensure compliance with exchange rules and regulations. It also determines activities that nonmember employees are allowed to perform on the trading floor, and controls nonmember access to the floor.

When charged with a violation, a member is entitled to a hearing before the committee and faces possible disciplinary action. The committee may reprimand, fine, and/or suspend a member from the trading floor. For serious violations, the committee may file charges against a member and bring the matter before the board of directors for a hearing. In addition to a reprimand and fine, the board may suspend or expel the member from the exchange.

Business Conduct

Each of the exchanges has a committee governing the business conduct of its members and member firms. On the Chicago Board of Trade, the Business Conduct Committee is responsible for preventing manipulation of prices, the cornering of any futures contract, and overseeing the "back office" activity of member firms.

The committee reviews staff investigations of transactions and financial conditions of members. The committee may examine members' books and papers and prescribe appropriate capital requirements. Members are required to stop any activity or business conduct that the committee finds unfair, in violation of exchange rules, or damaging to the exchange's reputation. Any member or member firm may appeal a disciplinary decision of the Business Conduct Committee by filing a written notice of appeal to the board of directors within 10 business days.

Members can be charged with an offense against the exchange for failing to appear before the committee when requested, failing to submit books and papers for examination, or violating any order of the committee. If found guilty, members may be expelled, suspended, or fined.

Exchanges have various methods to enforce rules and monitor their markets. At the Chicago Board of Trade, for example, the Office of Investigations and Audits conducts surveillance programs, such as the Computerized Trade Reconstruction (CTR) system. Developed by the Chicago Board of Trade in 1986, CTR is able to pinpoint in any trade, the traders, the contract, the quantity, the price, and time of execution to the nearest minute. A program within the system—CTR PLUS®—is able to reconstruct the trading activities of members and member firms to detect patterns of conduct that might indicate rule violations.

In addition, as of the 1980s, futures, stock, and options exchanges are pursuing different ways to enhance market efficiency and regulatory compliance through cooperative efforts. This includes sharing financial information of common member firms as to their overall risk exposure in related markets. Also, registered firms of several different futures, stock, and options exchanges generally have been able to undergo a single financial audit by one exchange, which is then shared with the other exchanges.

Ensuring Compliance

FEDERAL AND INDUSTRY REGULATION

U.S. futures exchanges are required by state and federal laws to regulate the conduct of exchange members, member firms, and their employees. The obligations of the exchanges to enforce their own rules and regulations were enhanced in the 1900s with the passing of several federal acts, including the Grain Futures Act of 1922, the Commodity Exchange Act of 1936, the Commodity Futures Trading Commission Act of 1974, and the Futures Trading Acts of 1978, 1982, and 1986.

The farm depression following World War I generated intense speculation in grain futures. The Futures Trading Act, the first federal law regulating futures trading, was passed in 1921. Shortly thereafter, it was declared unconstitutional by the Supreme Court. In 1922, Congress passed the Grain Futures Act, based on the interstate commerce clause of the Constitution.

Under the Grain Futures Act, futures trading in specific commodities could take place only on federally licensed exchanges. This legislation focused on exchange responsibility for preventing market manipulation by their members, member firms, and employees. If an exchange failed to adequately supervise market activity, its license could be revoked.

Grain Futures Act of 1922 and Amendments

Commodity Exchange Act of 1936

U.S. Department of Agriculture (USDA) studies over a period of several years led to the introduction of a number of amendments designed to strengthen the government's regulatory powers. In 1936, these revisions and additions to the law were consolidated in new legislation, the Commodity Exchange Act, which extended regulation from the grains and flaxseed to cotton and other agricultural commodities.

The new act created the Commodity Exchange Commission, which was comprised of the Secretary of Agriculture, the Secretary of Commerce, and the Attorney General, or their designated representatives. The commission was responsible for: (1) licensing futures exchanges, (2) determining procedures for registering Futures Commission Merchants and floor brokers, (3) protecting customer funds, (4) setting position and trading limits for speculative trading, (5) prohibiting price manipulations, false market information, and illegal trading, and (6) enforcing the Commodity Exchange Act and dealing with violations.

The Commodity Exchange Act was administered by the Commodity Exchange Commission until 1947 when the Commodity Exchange Authority was established. In addition to administering the act, the Commodity Exchange Authority provided information on futures trading to the general public.

Changing Needs for Regulation

During the early 1970s, rising affluence in many of the world's industrially developed countries was coupled with declines in crop production in several major producing nations. During the same period, two devaluations of the U.S. dollar made imports of U.S. agricultural goods less expensive and stimulated foreign sales. The result was heavy new demand on reduced supplies of feed grains and vegetable protein. In less than three years, previously ample USDA Commodity Credit Corporation holdings of surplus grain shrunk significantly. By late 1974, it was widely estimated that world feed-grain supplies had dwindled to the level of a month's supply.

As supplies continued to shrink and demand and grain prices rose, the public and members of Congress began to question the existing regulation of the futures markets. There also were new pressures to extend regulation to other futures markets not covered by the Commodity Exchange Act, such as metals, lumber, and currencies.

In response, the government began a series of hearings in September 1973 on proposed regulatory changes. The result was the Commodity Futures Trading Commission Act of 1974.

CFTC Act of 1974

The new act amended the Commodity Exchange Act and created an independent Commodity Futures Trading Commission (CFTC) to replace the Commodity Exchange Authority of the USDA. Existing Commodity Exchange Authority and Commodity Exchange Commission personnel, records, and appropriations were transferred to the new commission. And, on April 21, 1975, the CFTC assumed federal regulatory authority over all commodity futures markets.

The agency's five full-time commissioners are appointed by the President with Senate confirmation. They serve staggered, five-year terms with one designated to serve as chairman. There are three staff divisions—Economic and Analysis, Trading and Markets, and Enforcement. Each division director reports to the commission chairman, who performs the daily administrative duties.

The legislation creating the CFTC contained a sunset provision under which the commission would have ceased to exist on September 30, 1978, unless it was reauthorized. Extensive hearings were conducted early in 1978, resulting in the Futures Trading Act of 1978, which extended the life of the agency for another four years. CFTC reauthorization continues on a regular basis. The most recent reauthorization occurred in 1986, and is subject to renewal in 1989.

The Futures Trading Act of 1978 also expanded the jurisdiction of the CFTC, clarifying some earlier provisions of the Commodity Exchange Act.

Futures Trading Act of 1978

The amended Commodity Exchange Act gave the CFTC the authority to regulate trading in all futures contracts—those currently trading as well as those that will be traded in the future. Prior to 1974, several futures contracts—such as currencies, financial instruments, and metals—were not regulated by the federal government.

CFTC regulation of options on financial futures began in 1981 with the initiation of a pilot program. The success of this program led to the approval of nonagricultural options in 1982. Then, in 1984, the CFTC extended trading in options to agricultural futures.

Requirements of the CFTC Act

During the 1982 reauthorization of the CFTC, Congress adopted the Shad/Johnson Accord Index Act, developed by CFTC Chairman Johnson and SEC Chairman Shad, to define the jurisdiction of the CFTC and the Securities and Exchange Commission (SEC) over stock indexes.

The amendments gave the CFTC exclusive jurisdiction over stock index futures and options on stock index futures contracts. The SEC, on the other hand, is responsible for the trading of options on any security or index of securities or options on foreign currencies traded on a U.S. securities exchange.

Shad/Johnson Accord

The CFTC's regulatory powers extend to exchange actions and to the review and approval of futures contracts proposed by an exchange. Before a new contract is approved for trading, the CFTC must determine that a futures contract is in the public interest. In making that assessment, the commission examines how contracts are used commercially for pricing and

CFTC Regulation of Exchange Actions

hedging to ensure that they serve an economic purpose.

One of the first actions taken by the commission in 1975 was to redefine the term *hedge*. The definition was broadened to permit anticipatory hedging and cross-hedging within certain limits. Anticipatory hedging allows market users to buy or sell a futures contract before they actually own the cash commodity. Cross-hedging enables market users to hedge a cash commodity using a different but related futures contract when there is no futures contract for the cash commodity being hedged and the two markets follow similar price trends. For example, a hedger could use corn futures to hedge barley, or soybean meal futures to hedge fish meal.

Exchanges must submit all proposed trading rules and contract terms to the CFTC for approval. When reviewing trading rules, the commission tries to assure that the rule will not restrict competition, and may require the exchange to amend its proposal. Exchange regulations of major economic significance must be made available to the public, and are published in the Federal Register.

Delivery points for commodities that underlie futures contracts also are governed by the CFTC. The commission has the right to require an exchange to add or change delivery locations when necessary.

Review of Exchange Actions

Review of exchange actions—denying membership, access privileges, or disciplining members—is another responsibility of the CFTC. In reviewing actions, the commission may affirm, modify, or set aside an exchange's decision. The commission also is authorized to take emergency steps in the markets under certain conditions, such as actual or threatened market manipulation, or some other event that prevents the market from reflecting true supply/demand factors.

Regulation of Market Participants

The CFTC has broad regulatory powers over floor brokers, Futures Commission Merchants (FCMs), Associated Persons (APs), Commodity Pool Operators (CPOs), Commodity Trading Advisors (CTAs), Introducing Brokers (IBs), and other market participants. For example, the commission is authorized to register Associated Persons and office managers, and to establish eligibility requirements which may include proficiency tests.

Federal authority to establish minimum financial requirements for Futures Commission Merchants was established in the Commodity Exchange Act of 1936. This same legislation required Futures Commission Merchants to segregate customers' margin deposits from company funds, and prohibited the use of one customer's funds to meet the margin requirements of another customer's account. These requirements are enforced today by the CFTC.

Arbitration

Exchanges are required to have arbitration or claims settlement procedures to handle customer claims against members or their employees. The act stipulates that the CFTC establish procedures that can be used as an alternative to exchange arbitration or civil court actions.

Reparations

The CFTC provides a reparation procedure for investors to assert claims based on violations of federal commodities law. Claims are heard by an administrative law judge whose decision can be reviewed by the CFTC. The procedure is flexible depending on the amount of money involved and the consent of the parties.

Powers of Injunction

The former Commodity Exchange Authority did not have the power to prohibit an exchange or exchange member from violating the Commodity Exchange Act. However, the Commodity Futures Trading Commission has that power and, in addition, may require an exchange or exchange member to perform a specific act. In the case of a violation that is also a criminal offense, criminal penalties may be imposed.

Daily Trading Record Requirements

Exchanges and their clearinghouses are required by the CFTC to maintain daily trading records. Also, exchanges must publish daily trading volume before the next day's opening, if practical.

Under the CFTC Act of 1974, the futures industry was authorized to create registered futures associations. One such organization is the National Futures Association (NFA)—an industrywide, industry-supported, self-regulatory organization for the futures industry.

National Futures Association

NFA was formally designated a registered futures association by the CFTC on September 22, 1981, and became operational on October 1, 1982. The primary responsibilities of NFA are to: (1) enforce ethical standards and customer protection rules, (2) screen futures professionals for membership, (3) audit and monitor futures professionals for financial and general compliance rules, (4) provide for arbitration of futures-related disputes, and (5) promote consumer and member education concerning NFA's role in the futures industry.

Customer Protection

To protect customers, NFA's ethical standards prohibit fraud, manipulative and deceptive acts and practices, and unfair business dealings. In addition, employees who handle discretionary accounts must follow procedures similar to CFTC requirements.

Membership Screening

Membership in NFA and CFTC registration are mandatory for Futures

Commission Merchants, Commodity Trading Advisors, Commodity Pool Operators, and Introducing Brokers working with customer accounts.

The CFTC requires associate membership in NFA and CFTC registration for most Associated Persons. Associated Persons solicit orders, customers, or customer funds for FCMs, IBs, CTAs, or CPOs. Membership is voluntary for futures exchanges, commercial banks, and commodity-related commercial firms.

Regulation of futures professionals begins with applicant screening. In addition to approving applicants for NFA membership, NFA is authorized by the CFTC to screen and approve applications for federal registration. Eligibility requirements are strict and specific, and are designed to ensure high standards of professional conduct and financial responsibility.

NFA staff handle the initial screening process. If an applicant is denied membership or registration, then the final decision is made by the NFA membership committee.

Proficiency testing is another NFA activity and is now required for CFTC registration. FCMs, IBs, CTAs, CPOs, and APs applying for registration must pass the National Commodity Futures Exam (Series 3) which tests their knowledge of trading futures and options on futures and understanding of exchange, industry, and federal regulations.

Financial and General Compliance

One of NFA's major functions is to establish, audit, and enforce minimum financial requirements for its FCM and IB members. No such requirements are currently established under NFA rules for other NFA members, such as Commodity Pool Operators and Commodity Trading Advisors.

NFA conducts unannounced audits of all its members except those that are members of an exchange. In those cases, the audits are conducted by the exchange.

NFA audits are all-inclusive and cover every facet of the firm's futures-related business activities. Rule violations may be referred to Regional Business Conduct committees for appropriate disciplinary action.

General compliance rules require members to maintain complete and timely records, and segregate customer funds and accounts. Advertising and sales practices must be clear and honest, and customer orders equitably handled.

NFA financial requirements are patterned after existing financial standards of futures exchanges, as approved by the CFTC. NFA's computerized Financial Analysis Auditing Compliance Tracking System (FACTS) maintains financial records of NFA member firms and assists in monitoring their financial conditions.

Certain financial matters, such as the setting of margin levels, remain exclusively with the exchanges.

NFA has an Office of Compliance responsible for financial auditing and ethical surveillance. If an audit or investigation reveals a possible NFA rule violation, the infraction is reported to one of three regional Business Conduct committees. Each committee is made up of individuals associated with NFA members in the region where the member under investigation lives. The committee either closes the matter or serves a formal complaint against the member accused of violating a rule. In the latter case, the member must answer the complaint and is entitled to a hearing before the committee. If the committee decides against the member, he may appeal the decision to the Appeals Committee (a subcommittee of the NFA Board of Directors). The decision of the Appeals Committee is final, following a review by the CFTC.

NFA has authority to discipline any member (other than floor brokers or traders). NFA may expel, suspend, prohibit contact with members, censure, reprimand, or impose fines of up to $100,000. In emergency cases, when there is imminent danger to the markets, customers, or other members, NFA's president with the agreement of the Executive Committee or board can require the firm to stop doing business immediately. This action may be issued with or without a hearing. If a hearing is not held before the action is taken, a hearing will be scheduled as soon as possible before the appropriate Business Conduct Committee.

Arbitration

Another important function of NFA is to provide a centralized, uniform arbitration system. In most cases, when requested by a customer, arbitration is mandatory for all NFA member firms and their employees including FCMs, IBs, CPOs, CTAs, and APs. Counterclaims made by members and disputes between NFA members also may be heard by NFA arbitrators. Decisions of the arbitrators are generally final and may not be appealed to NFA. Alternatives to NFA arbitration include the CFTC's reparation procedure, exchange arbitration, or any other arbitration system mutually agreed to by the member and customer. After a particular method is chosen, no other may be used unless both parties agree.

Under NFA compliance rules, any NFA member or employee of a member is subject to disciplinary action for failure to comply with an arbitration decision.

Education

NFA educational efforts are directed to both members and the investing public. Members are assisted in complying with NFA rules and CFTC registration. For the investing public, NFA produces materials concerning such topics as the fundamentals of futures trading and identifying fraud.

NFA is governed by a 42-member board of directors. This board makes decisions concerning priorities, policies, plans, funding, budget, and bylaws. It represents all sectors of NFA membership as follows: 14 directors

Structure

represent Futures Commission Merchants; 3 directors represent Commodity Trading Advisors; 2 represent Commodity Pool Operators; 2 directors represent Introducing Brokers; 3 represent commodity-related commercial firms; 2 represent commercial banks; and 13 represent futures exchanges. The remaining 3 are public directors, that is, individuals with no present direct affiliation with the futures industry. All, except for the public directors, are selected by NFA members during the annual election held in January. Public directors are chosen by the board; all directors serve three-year terms.

Executive Committee

Although the full NFA board makes all major decisions, the direction and supervision of day-to-day operations are provided by an Executive Committee. The Executive Committee is comprised of 10 members including the NFA president, the chairman of the board of directors, plus 8 other members of the board. Of the 8 directors, 3 represent FCMs or IBs, 2 represent exchanges, 2 represent industry participants (CTAs, CPOs, commercial firms and banks), and there is 1 public director.

Both the board and Executive Committee are designed to provide balanced representation by membership category and geographic location. Thus, the number of directors allowed from the same NFA geographic region (Eastern, Central, or Western) is limited for each category.

A primary economic function of futures markets is price-risk management, the most common method of which is hedging. Hedging, in its simplest form, is the practice of offsetting the price risk inherent in any cash market position by taking an equal but opposite position in the futures market. Hedgers use the futures markets to protect their businesses from adverse price changes.

Price risk exists throughout all business, commerce, and finance. In agriculture, for instance, a prolonged drought affects a farmer's crop supply as well as the income he receives. But the drought also affects the price paid by grain companies for corn, wheat, soybeans, and oats. Those prices, in turn, directly impact consumer prices for cereals, cooking oils, salad dressings, bread, meat, poultry, and countless other items purchased at the local supermarket.

For manufacturers, an extended labor strike or the embargo of a raw material could result in a diminished supply and eventually a sharp price increase of a specific manufactured product. These economic factors directly affect the price manufacturers and consumers pay for an array of commodities ranging from gasoline and home heating oil to jewelry. For a bank, savings and loan, or other financial institution, an increase in interest rates affects the rate the institution pays on certificates of deposit as well as the cost of an automobile or home loan.

There's no escaping the varying degrees of price fluctuation, i.e., risk,

Hedging in the Futures Markets

Economic Justification for the Futures Markets

8

89

in every sector of today's economy: agriculture, manufacturing, business, and finance. Hedging in the futures markets minimizes the impact of these unwanted price changes.

PROTECTION AGAINST PRICE CHANGES

Although we may not give it much thought, hedging is a dominant feature of our daily lives. The buyer of an automobile acquires insurance to protect against collision damage and the possibility of total loss of that vehicle. A homeowner takes out an insurance policy to protect against possible fire or storm damage. Because the insurance can be purchased for a fraction of the home's value, the local bank or savings and loan is more willing to lend funds for the purchase of the home. Likewise, to guard against the cost of replacing an appliance, one may choose to purchase, for a minimal cost, an extended warranty covering part replacement and labor charges. Or, a family—contemplating the cost of college for a newborn son or daughter—may begin a savings program to help meet the rising cost of a higher education.

These everyday examples illustrate hedging by consumers—a defensive strategy to protect against unwanted price change and the possibility of total loss. Hedging functions the same in the futures markets. It is a conscious effort to reduce the price risk inherent in buying, selling, or even holding a cash market commodity.

Who Hedges with Futures

Hedgers are individuals or companies that own or are planning to own a cash commodity—corn, soybeans, wheat, U.S. Treasury bonds, notes, bills, etc.—and are concerned that the cost of the commodity may change before they either buy or sell it. Virtually anyone who seeks to protect cash market commodities from unwanted price changes can use the futures markets for hedging—farmers, grain elevator operators, merchandisers, producers, exporters, bankers, bond dealers, insurance companies, money managers, pension funds, portfolio managers, thrifts, manufacturers, and others.

For example, suppose a soybean processor agrees to sell soybean oil to a food manufacturer six months from now. Both agree on a price today even though the oil will not be delivered for six months. The soybean processor does not yet own the soybeans he will eventually process into oil, but he is concerned that soybean prices may rise during the next six months, causing him to lose money.

To hedge against the risk of rising prices, the soybean processor buys soybean futures contracts calling for the delivery of the soybeans in six months. When five and a half months have passed, the soybean processor purchases the soybeans in the cash market and, as feared, prices have risen. However, because he hedged in the futures market, the soybean processor can now sell his futures contracts at a profit, since futures prices also have increased. He uses the gain on the futures contracts to offset the higher cost of soybeans, protecting his profit on the sale of the soybean oil.

Hedging works the same way in the financial markets. Suppose a major financial institution holds a significant amount of long-term U.S. Treasury bonds. The firm's financial officers are concerned that interest rates may rise in the near term, causing a decline in the value of the bonds. Knowing there is a substantial risk in holding this unhedged cash position, they elect to sell U.S. Treasury bond futures.

A month later, as expected, interest rates rise and bond prices decline. In offsetting its futures position by purchasing U.S. T-bond futures, the firm succeeds in protecting the value of the cash bonds, because the profits from closing out the futures position offset the decline in the cash market value of the Treasury bonds.

Of course, the market does not always move as expected. But a hedger accepts that possibility even though he may forfeit the opportunity to make a gain in the market. To an experienced hedger, it is more important to establish a market objective that protects his investment rather than worry about the possibility of a missed profit opportunity.

Cash market transactions involve the purchase and sale of actual commodities at current prices. For instance, the term *cash corn* refers to the actual physical product—kernels of corn that are either fed to livestock or processed into various animal feeds, human food, or industrial products. Delivery of the commodity can be immediate or within a few days of the transaction.

Cash-Futures Relationship

In the futures market, however, buyers and sellers agree to take or make delivery of a specific commodity at a predetermined place and time in the future. The date of the purchase or sale may be weeks or months away—hence the term *futures*.

What Is Basis?

The difference between the cash price of a commodity at a specific location and the price of a specific futures contract for the same commodity is defined as the *basis*. To calculate the basis, subtract the futures price from the cash price: cash price − futures price = basis. It is assumed, when speaking of basis, that one is referring to the nearby futures month (the contract month closest to delivery), unless otherwise specified.

For instance, if a country elevator operator in central Illinois buys soybeans from a farmer at $7.80 a bushel on October 3, and the November soybean futures contract is $7.90 on the same day, the basis at the local grain elevator would be 10 cents under (−10 cents) the November contract. If a Nebraska farmer is selling wheat, and the local cash price on June 10 is $4.10 a bushel and the July wheat futures contract is $3.60, the basis at the Nebraska location is 50 cents over (+50 cents) the July futures contract.

Calculating the basis for financial instruments is essentially the same. If the cash market price of a U.S. Treasury bond is 88-16,* and the June adjusted futures price is 90-22, the basis is 2-06 under the June contract.

Given the variety of U.S. Treasury bonds and notes that are eligible for delivery against the Chicago Board of Trade's U.S. Treasury bond and note futures contracts, a modification in calculating the basis occurs. This is done by adjusting the bond or note futures price to a futures-cash equivalent. The change to a cash equivalent is made using a conversion factor to compare the cash market Treasury bond or note with the 8 percent coupon standard of the T-bond or note futures contract. The conversion factor is multiplied by the futures price to obtain the cash equivalent.

Suppose in late February the March T-bond futures contract, which calls for a nominal 8 percent coupon, is priced at 67-02. The cash market notes and price of a U.S. Treasury bond carrying a 12 percent coupon and maturing August 15, 2013, is 97-00.

Although there is a specific equation to calculate the conversion factors for T-bonds and T-notes, a booklet is available from the Chicago Board of Trade that lists the different conversion factors for cash market notes and bonds of varying maturities and coupon rates. In this case, assume the conversion factor of the 12 percent T-bond is 1.4251. Because cash and futures prices are quoted in 32nds, the first step in calculating the cash equivalent is converting the quoted futures price to a decimal ($67\frac{2}{32}$ = 67.0625). The futures-cash equivalent is obtained then by multiplying the conversion factor by the futures price:

Futures-cash equivalent = 67.0625 × 1.4251

= 95.57 or $95\frac{18}{32}$

Once the futures-cash equivalent is calculated, the basis is the difference between the cash price and the futures-cash equivalent:

Basis = (bond cash price) − (futures price × bond conversion factor)
Basis = 97-00 − 95-18 = $1\frac{14}{32}$

As these examples illustrate, the basis can be either positive or negative, depending upon whether the cash price is higher or lower than the futures price. If the basis moves from 10 to 1, it has become more negative (less positive). On the other hand, if the basis moves from −5 to 2, the basis has become more positive (less negative). If the cash and futures prices are the same, the basis is expressed as zero.

*T-bond futures contracts are quoted in 32nds but the prices generally are written as follows: $88\frac{16}{32}$ = 88-16.

Factors Affecting Basis

There are a variety of factors that can cause the basis to change. If the demand for cash grain is strong and/or the available supply is small, cash market prices could rise relative to futures prices. However, if there is a large supply of grain and little demand, cash prices could fall relative to futures prices.

Other factors that affect the basis of ag commodities include:

♦ Carryover stocks from the previous year
♦ Expectations of the current year's production
♦ Supply and demand of comparable substitutes
♦ Foreign production
♦ Foreign demand
♦ Storage costs
♦ Availability of sufficient storage facilities
♦ Transportation costs
♦ Transportation problems
♦ Insurance costs
♦ Federal policies
♦ Seasonal price fluctuations

Similarly, several factors affect the basis for financial instruments. These factors include:

♦ The cost of money, i.e., the interest rates
♦ Federal Reserve Board monetary policies
♦ Congressional and Presidential fiscal policies
♦ Time until expiration of the futures contract
♦ Cost of funding margin requirements
♦ Coupon of the cash market instrument being hedged against the 8 percent futures contract coupon standard
♦ Supply of deliverable cash market instruments
♦ Domestic and foreign demand for cash market instruments
♦ Inflationary expectations
♦ General level of business activity
♦ Seasonal factors (such as estimated quarterly tax payments by corporations and self-employed individuals)
♦ Liquidity of nearby versus distant month contracts

The basis cannot be predicted precisely, but it is generally less volatile than either the futures or cash price. By knowing the basis, the hedger replaces the risk of price fluctuation with the lesser risk of a change in the relationship between the cash and the futures price of the commodity. Even so, a change in the basis during the time of the hedge can influence the results of a transaction. Hedgers must pay close attention to this relationship. Without a knowledge of the usual basis and basis patterns for a given commodity, it is impossible for a hedger to make a fully informed decision about whether to accept or reject a given price (cash or futures); whether, when, and in what delivery month to hedge; when to close a hedge; or when and how to turn an unusual basis situation into a possible profit opportunity.

Price Relationships: Grains

Grain generally is harvested within a span of a few months each year, but only a small portion is actually used at harvest. The rest is stored until needed for feeding, processing, exporting, and so forth. The expenses of storage—known as *carrying charges*—normally are reflected in futures prices for different delivery months. They include not only the cost of using storage facilities for the grain, but also such costs as insurance on the grain and interest on the invested capital.

Buyers usually are willing to pay a higher price for grain as the marketing year progresses to cover the carrying charges. Consequently, these carrying charges tend to be reflected in the price of futures contracts. More distant or deferred futures contracts tend to trade at higher prices than do nearby futures contracts. For example, futures prices for delivery within the same marketing year** are normally stair-stepped upward from one delivery month to the next. If the total cost of storing corn were, say, 4 cents per bushel a month, and if futures prices reflected the full carrying charge, the prices for the different delivery months might look something like this:

Dec	Mar	May	Jul	Sep
$2.00	$2.12	$2.20	$2.28	$2.36

This example illustrates normal market conditions. In reality, the market may reflect less than full carrying charges or even negative carrying charges, which is referred to as an *inverted market*. An inverted market can occur for a variety of reasons, including a strong immediate

**The crop marketing year varies slightly with each ag commodity, but it tends to begin following harvest and end before the next year's harvest, e.g., the marketing year for soybeans begins September 1 and ends August 31. The futures contract month of November represents the first major new-crop marketing month and the contract month of July represents the last major old-crop marketing month for soybeans. At the beginning of the soybean marketing year, November is considered the nearby month, and subsequent contract months are referred to as *deferred months*.

demand for cash grain or the willingness of elevator owners to store grain for their own accounts at less than the full storage rate.

The basis for debt instruments is almost totally dependent upon interest rates, so the historical basis behavior does not carry the same emphasis as it does for the grains. There are repetitive tendencies, however, within the financial markets. For example, those individuals and companies in the financial cash and futures markets know estimated quarterly tax payments due from corporations and self-employed individuals may have a tendency to unduly affect short-term (usually overnight) interest rates on the 15th of April, June, September, and December. These abrupt changes in short-term rates may impact long-term prices in both the cash and futures markets a day or two before and after the 15th.

In another case, the equity markets during the 7- to 10-day period marking the end of each calendar quarter (March, June, September, and December) are closely watched for changes in equity cash and futures prices. Because a portfolio manager's performance is sometimes measured against the Standard & Poor's 500 Index, managers often adjust their market positions (that is, sell losing positions and/or buy winning positions) before the end of the quarter and the subsequent release of reports to clients.

In the case of interest rate futures, deferred futures months (those that expire later in the year) are generally priced lower than the nearby futures month (the next contract month that will stop trading) in a normal market. On September 13, 1988, for example, U.S. Treasury bond futures prices closed at 88-22 (Dec '88); 88-03 (Mar '89); 87-16 (Jun '89); 86-30 (Sep '89); 86-13 (Dec '89); 85-29 (Mar '90); and 85-14 (Jun '90).

Furthermore, interest rate futures prices are normally lower than cash prices, reflecting what is referred to as the *positive cost of carry*. The cost of carry reflects the actual costs of financing an investment. It includes any interest payments received, less any short-term borrowing costs, initial margin deposit, variation margin requirements, if any, and transaction costs.

The cost of carry can be either positive or negative. If it is positive, as illustrated in the example below, it can be profitable to hold the instrument until delivery. Suppose the cost to finance a 12 percent $100,000 U.S. Treasury bond selling at par for one month is 10 percent. Under these circumstances, the investor earns $167 a month by holding the T-bond.

Annual coupon payment	$100,000 × 12%	= $12,000
Annual finance cost	$100,000 × 10%	= $10,000
Annual cost of carry	$ 12,000 − $10,000	= $ 2,000
Monthly cost of carry	$ 2,000 / 12	= $ 167

Price Relationships: Financial Instruments

Under this "normal" market environment, the cash instrument is priced at a premium to the futures contract. Since these gains increase as the holding period increases, the nearby futures contract trades at a premium to the deferred futures month, as noted in the September 13, 1988, example of T-bond futures prices. On the other hand, if the cost of carry is negative, the investor loses money holding the investment until delivery. Suppose the cost of financing the same security rises to 14 percent. In this instance, the cost of carry is negative and the investor loses $167 a month carrying the bond until delivery.

Annual coupon payment	$100,000 × 12%	= $12,000
Annual finance cost	$100,000 × 14%	= $14,000
Annual cost of carry	$ 12,000 − $14,000	= ($ 2,000)
Monthly cost of carry	($ 2,000) / 12	= ($ 167)

To compensate for his negative carry, the investor trades the cash instrument at a discount to the futures contract. Since carrying costs rise as the holding period increases, the futures price of the nearby contract month trades at a discount to the deferred contract month.

Yield Curve

The cost of carry—the relationship between long-term and short-term interest rates—is reflected in the yield curve. The yield curve is a chart or graph visually depicting the current yield for all debt instruments with the same rating over an extended time period. U.S. government debt instruments (short-term Treasury bills, intermediate-term Treasury notes, and long-term Treasury bonds) are most often used because all government debt carries the same credit rating and offers investors maturities ranging from days up to 30 years.

Positive Yield Curve

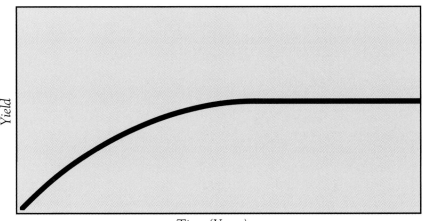

Time (Years)

The yield curve is positive when long-term rates are higher than short-term rates. In such an environment, investors are willing to accept a lower yield on short-term investments and are compensated for lending their money for an extended time period.

However, when short-term rates are higher than rates on long-term investments, the yield curve is negative or inverted. A negative yield curve typically occurs during inflationary periods, when heavy credit demand pushes short-term rates higher than long-term rates.

Negative Yield Curve

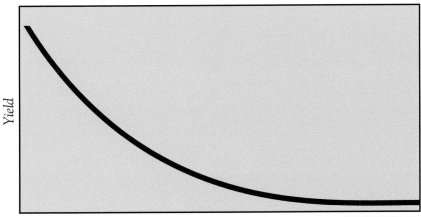

Time (Years)

A crucial relationship exists between interest rates and prices in both the cash and the futures markets: when interest rates rise, the prices of interest rate futures and cash market instruments decline; when interest rates decline, prices of interest rate futures and cash market instruments rise.

ECONOMIC LOGIC OF HEDGING

The fundamental reason why hedging works is that futures and cash prices of a related commodity tend to respond to the same economic factors. And, as a futures contract nears expiration, cash and futures prices tend to converge; that is, the basis approaches zero. There are several market factors that allow this to occur.

For one, futures contracts for traditional commodities, such as grains, require all market participants holding contracts at expiration to either take or make delivery of the underlying commodity. This responsibility to make

Delivery

or take delivery of the actual commodity assumes that futures prices will reflect the actual cash value of the commodity.

Like other contractual obligations, predetermined delivery steps must be completed within a specific time period to comply with the terms of the agreement. For example, the Chicago Board of Trade specifies that in the case of corn, the deliverable grade is No. 2 Yellow or permitted substitutions at differentials established by the exchange. Delivery of financial instruments also must satisfy established criteria. A particular U.S. Treasury bond is eligible for delivery against the T-bond futures contract if it has a remaining time to maturity, or time to call if callable, of at least 15 years as of the first day of the delivery month.

Cheapest Deliverable Bond or Note

The pricing of futures contracts on government debt instruments (e.g., 5-year notes, 10-year notes, and bonds) remains highly correlated to the value of the deliverable instrument at expiration. Both bond and note contracts are designed to accept a range of issues for delivery, and, at any given time, one of these issues will be more economical than the others to acquire in the cash market and deliver against the futures contract. Because anyone trading bond futures can assume that a seller will deliver the most economical instrument, these contracts tend to trade to the price of that issue. Therefore, in addition to following the credit markets in general, it is important to track the price of whichever bond or note is least expensive to deliver at any point in time.

One technique for identifying the cheapest bond or note to deliver against a particular contract is to identify which bond has the smallest basis. But it is important to remember that price relationships between cash market instruments change daily. Therefore, reconfirming the cheapest deliverable bond or note at the close of each trading session is essential. This method, however, is only a quick rule-of-thumb procedure.

Cash Settlement

Futures contracts that track indexes (e.g., stock or bond index futures contracts) are cash settled. Cash-settled futures contracts are specifically designed to converge with the value of the underlying index at expiration, ensuring that delivery month pricing remains correlated to the underlying index.

While delivery acts as a link between cash and futures prices, only about 3 percent of all futures contracts are actually delivered. Instead, most are offset before they expire. To offset a futures position, a hedger takes a second futures position opposite his initial transaction. For instance, if an open position is established with the sale of five July wheat contracts, that position can be closed with an offsetting transaction—the purchase of five July wheat contracts. In other words, most futures traders use the futures market as a pricing mechanism; few actually deliver or take delivery of the cash commodity.

Second, if cash prices are higher than the futures prices, or vice versa, traders generally buy the lower-priced, or "cheaper," instrument and sell in the higher-priced, or "dearer," instrument, thereby quickly minimizing any price disparities. If cash prices are well below futures prices (after carrying costs are netted out), then a trader can sell the futures contract, buy the cash instrument, and make a profit. Because many traders attempt to capitalize on these price distortions, their actions have the net effect of forcing prices back into line.

This trading practice is known as *arbitrage*. Arbitrage is crucial to preserving the relationship between the cash and futures markets and helps ensure that the basis approaches zero by the time the contract expires. Without this equilibrium, it would be impossible for hedgers to transfer their unwanted risk because the futures contract might have little, if any, price correlation to the cash market.

In addition to making or taking delivery of a commodity, hedgers can enter into an exchange for physicals (EFP) transaction. Also known as *against actuals* or *versus cash*, EFPs generally are used by two hedgers who want to "exchange" futures for cash positions. EFPs are the only type of futures transaction allowed to take place outside the trading pit and are permitted according to specific exchange and Commodity Futures Trading Commission rules.

For instance, assume a grain exporter commits to a forward sale of grain and simultaneously hedges with a futures purchase. On the day he must acquire the grain for shipment, he makes a cash bid to an elevator operator expressed in basis. The elevator operator also has hedged, but with a short futures position to protect against a possible decline in value of the stored grain. Both the exporter and elevator operator agree to the basis price.

The elevator operator (short hedger) delivers the actual cash grain to the exporter (long hedger) in exchange for a long futures position. That long position offsets the elevator's initial short futures position, thus ending the hedge. The grain exporter, in turn, acquires the actual grain needed for shipment and assumes a short position, which automatically offsets his initial long futures position. Payment for the cash contract between the elevator operator and grain exporter is made on the agreed-upon basis.

EFPs involving financial instruments, usually fixed-income instruments, frequently occur. Institutions with opposite cash-futures positions find it profitable and convenient to use U.S. Treasury bonds, notes, or bills in EFP transactions. Related to this, EFPs have occurred with the Major Market Index futures contract, which trades at the Chicago Board of Trade. That is because the small composition of the index, 20 stocks in total (16 of which are in the Dow Jones Industrial Average), makes it feasible to engage in EFPs.

Exchange for physicals are important to commercial users because if

Arbitrage

Exchange for Physicals

both the long and short hedger were required to liquidate their futures positions by open outcry auction in the pit, they might have to do so at different prices. This would mean that the effectiveness of the agreed-upon basis for both buyer and seller would be lost. Consequently, many cash commodity dealers who trade the basis often specify when trading the cash market commodity that they will do so only against an exchange of futures.

THE BASICS OF HEDGING

Hedging in the futures market is a two-step process. Depending upon the hedger's cash market situation, he will either buy or sell futures as his first position. The hedger's next step will be to offset his opening position before the futures contract expires by taking a second position opposite the opening transaction. The contract in both the opening and closing positions must be the same commodity, number of contracts, and delivery month.

If a hedger's first position involves the sale of futures contracts, it is referred to as a *selling*, or *short*, *hedge*. On the other hand, if the hedger's first position involves the purchase of futures contracts, it is referred to as a *long*, or *buying*, *hedge*.

Institutions and individuals use selling, or short, hedges as a temporary substitute for a later cash market sale of the underlying commodity, and the purpose of the short hedge is to lock in a selling price. With financial instruments, primarily fixed-income assets such as U.S. Treasury bonds, the selling hedge not only locks in a sale price, it also locks in a yield because of the price/yield correlation between interest rates and price.

The purchasing hedge, or long hedge, is used by institutions and individuals planning to buy the actual cash commodity at a later date. The purpose of the long hedge is to establish a fixed purchase price. With financial instruments, the long hedge not only establishes a purchase price, it locks in a yield.

> The following examples illustrate basic short and long hedging applications. For purposes of explanation, assume the basis is the same when each hedge was established and closed. The only exception is the example on short hedging for protection against falling soybean prices in which the basis changed. (When the basis remains unchanged, it is defined as a perfect hedge, i.e., a gain in one market perfectly offsets a loss in the other market.)

Consider a pension fund manager who holds $1 million face value 10¾ percent U.S. Treasury bonds maturing August 15, 2005. The bonds are priced in the cash market in September at 99-00.† However, the manager fears interest rates will rise sharply during the next few months, reducing the market value of the bonds. He wants to protect the bonds from the expected decline in resale value and decides to initiate a short hedge by selling 10 Dec T-bond futures at 83-00.

As expected, interest rates rose, causing the cash market value of the T-bonds to fall by $90,000 to 90-00. However, the fund manager offset some of the decline with a gain in his T-bond futures position. Remember, the initial futures position was a sale; to close the position, the futures contracts were bought, at a lower price of 75-00.

Cash	Futures
Sep	
Holds $1,000,000 T-bonds at 99-00, or $990,000 total	Sells 10 Dec T-bond contracts at 83-00, or $830,000 total
Nov	
Market value falls to 90-00, or $900,000	Buys back 10 Dec T-bond contracts at 75-00, or $750,000 total
Result	
($90,000)	$80,000

This and other examples in this chapter do not include commission or transaction costs.

Because the futures position produced a profit, the cash market loss was almost entirely offset. And, the results of this hedge could have been improved by "adjusting" the number of futures contracts used to hedge the cash market position.

Weighted Hedge

To compensate for the greater decline in the dollar value of a cash bond versus the decline in the futures price, a weighted hedge is used. In a weighted T-bond hedge, one way to determine the number of futures

---

†In this example, the size of the T-bond futures contract equals $100,000 worth of U.S. Treasury bonds, and prices are quoted in ¹⁄₃₂ of a percent of the contract size. A price quote of 99-00 means the contract is worth 99 percent of $100,000 or $99,000. A ¹⁄₃₂ of a percent change of $100,000 equals $31.25 ($100,000 ×.01)/32. So, a price quote of 99-16 (or 99¹⁶⁄₃₂) equals $99,500 (($31.25 × 16) + $99,000).

contracts needed to effectively hedge a cash position is by multiplying the conversion factor of the T-bond by the par value of the cash bonds divided by the par value of the futures contract. In this example, the conversion factor for T-bonds maturing August 15, 2005, is 1.2495.

$$\text{Number of futures contracts} = 1.2495 \times (\$1,000,000/\$100,000)$$
$$= 1.2495 \times 10$$
$$= 12.495$$

In this instance, the portfolio manager rounds 12.495 to the lowest whole number, 12. Given the same situation in the previous example, the results obtained using the weighted hedge are significantly different.

Cash	Futures
Sep Holds $1,000,000 T-bonds at 99-00, or $990,000 total	Sells 12 Dec T-bond contracts at 83-00, or $996,000 total
Nov Market value falls to 90-00, or $900,000 total	Buys back 12 Dec T-bond contracts at 75-00, or $900,000 total
Result ($90,000)	$96,000

The advantage of using the weighted hedge is clear. The portfolio manager not only offset the entire decline in the cash market value of the Treasury bonds, but realized a small net profit of $6,000. **Note:** Since hedging is a defensive strategy, it is unlikely to produce net profit results such as those just illustrated. Nonetheless, the example illustrates how futures are used to offset the risk of holding U.S. government securities.

Short Hedging for Protection Against Falling Soybean Prices

A farmer can use the futures markets to establish a price for his crop long before he sells it. But to do so requires calculating the basis.

Assume in June a farmer expects to harvest at least 10,000 bushels of soybeans during September. By hedging, he can lock in a price for his soybeans in June and protect himself against the possibility of falling prices.

At the time, the cash price for new-crop soybeans is $7 and the futures price of November soybean futures is $7.25. The delivery month of

November marks the beginning of the new-crop marketing year for soybeans. The current basis of 25 cents under is slightly weaker than the historical harvest level and the farmer sees the potential to gain a couple of cents per bushel if the basis becomes less negative between now and the time he sells cash beans.

With this market information, the farmer short hedges his crop by selling two November 5,000-bu. soybean futures at $7.25. (Typically, farmers do not hedge 100 percent of their expected production, as the exact number of bushels produced is unknown until harvest. In this scenario, the producer expects to produce more than 10,000 bushels of soybeans.)

By the beginning of September, cash and futures prices have fallen and the basis became less negative moving from -25 cents to -23 cents. When the farmer sells his cash beans to the local elevator for $6.72 a bushel, he lifts his hedge by purchasing November soybean futures at $6.95. The 30-cent gain in the futures market offsets the lower price he receives for his soybeans in the cash market.

Cash	Futures	Basis
Jun		
Price for new-crop soybeans at $7.00/bu	Sells 2 Nov soybean contracts at $7.25/bu	−$0.25
Sep		
Sells 10,000 bu soybeans at $6.72/bu	Buys 2 Nov soybean contracts at $6.95/bu	−$0.23
Result	Cash sale price	$6.72/bu
	Futures gain	0.30/bu
	Net selling price	$7.02/bu

Had the farmer not hedged, he only would have received $6.72 a bushel for his soybeans—30 cents lower than the price he received. Since the basis strengthened from 25 cents under the November contract to 23 cents under, the farmer's selling price was actually 2 cents higher than his initial price objective of $7 a bushel. If the basis had become more negative instead, the farmer's selling price would have been lower than his expected price objective, but he would have been protected from the drop in the cash price, since he was hedged.

Long Hedge to Establish the Price of Silver

Suppose a film manufacturer wants to establish a ceiling price for the 20,000 troy ounces of silver he plans to purchase during December and January. Anticipating a price increase, he would like to take advantage of the current cash price of $5.21 per troy ounce but does not want to buy the silver right now.

On June 15, silver futures for December delivery are trading at $5.71 per troy ounce. The manufacturer decides to purchase 20 December silver futures contracts.

Several months elapse, with silver prices continuing to rise. The manufacturer decides to purchase silver in the cash market at $9 and close his futures position by selling 20 December silver contracts at $9.45.

Cash	Futures
Jun Needs 20,000 oz of silver in Dec.; silver at $5.21/troy oz	Buys 20 Dec silver contracts at $5.71/troy oz (contract size: 1,000 troy oz)
Nov Acquires 20,000 oz of silver at $9.00/troy oz	Closes long position by selling 20 Dec silver contracts at $9.45/troy oz
Result Cash sale price	$9.00/troy oz
Futures gain	$3.74/troy oz
Net purchase price	$5.26/troy oz

In this instance, the futures gain of $3.74 per troy ounce cushioned the cash price increase, resulting in an additional cost of only 5 cents per troy ounce from what he initially expected to pay. By hedging, the manufacturer only paid $5.26 per troy ounce versus the $9 per ounce he would have had to pay if he had not hedged in the futures market.

Long Hedging Using Treasury Note Futures

Institutional investors frequently use the futures markets to reduce their exposure to the risk of fluctuating interest rates. For instance, the investment manager of a manufacturing firm wants to take advantage of the high yield offered on U.S. Treasury notes in May but won't have $10 million in cash to invest until September. At the time, long-term September Treasury note futures are trading at 84-12, while the cash notes are priced at 99-16. Desiring to purchase the 8½ percent T-notes maturing May 15, 1997, he calculates that a weighted hedge requires 103 September T-note futures and buys them at 84-12 in May.

During the next couple of months, interest rates decline, raising the cash market value of the T-notes to 101-04. The price of the T-note futures rises to 86-00.

Cash	Futures
May	
T-notes at 99-16, or $9,950,000 total for $10,000,000 par value	Buys 103 Sep T-note contracts at 84-12, or $8,690,625 total
Aug	
T-notes at 101-04, or $10,112,500	Sells 103 Sep T-note contracts at 86-00, or $8,858,000 total
Result	
($162,500)	$167,375

Had the investment manager not established a long hedge, it would have cost him an additional $162,500 to purchase the Treasury notes in the cash market. Using T-note futures to hedge the purchase price, the investment manager not only avoided that additional cost, but generated a modest profit of $4,875, which reduced the effective purchase price.

While the previous example illustrates a hedge in which an investment manager made an additional profit on his futures position, this is not always the case. If T-note futures and cash prices had fallen, to 81-00 and 96-04, respectively, instead of rising, the investment manager would have lost money on his futures position. However, his losses on his futures contracts would be offset by a lower purchase price of T-notes in the cash market. Remember, one of the primary reasons hedging works, is that cash and futures prices tend to follow parallel price trends. So if the cash price of a commodity falls, the futures price tends to follow a similar trend.

Cash	Futures
May	
T-notes at 99-16, or $9,950,000 total for $10,000,000 par value	Buys 103 Sep T-note contracts at 84-12, or $8,690,625 total
Aug	
T-notes at 96-04, or $9,612,500	Sells 103 Sep T-note contracts at 81-00, or $8,343,000 total
Result	
$337,500	($347,625)

Even though the investment manager may have lost $347,625 on his futures position, the purchase price of the T-notes in the cash market is $337,500 lower than he anticipated. He reminds himself that a few weeks ago when he initiated the hedge, he was satisfied with a purchase price of 99-16 on his cash bonds. In fact, the price hedgers pay for protection is the inability to take advantage of a price move after a hedge has been established. An experienced hedger is willing to forfeit this opportunity so he can have price protection.

Conclusion

Hedging is an indispensable risk-management tool for institutional and individual investors. The futures markets offer a forum for reducing undesired cash market price change. Because there is always some price risk in buying, selling, or holding a commodity for any length of time—grains, metals, even money itself—it is important that financial managers, farmers, grain companies, and other institutional and individual investors take advantage of the opportunities to protect their business profit margins against unwanted and unforeseen price fluctuation. The futures markets perform a critical economic function by offering hedgers an outlet to offset unwanted price risk in an increasingly volatile and globally linked marketplace.

Speculators in futures markets fulfill several vital economic functions that facilitate the marketing of basic commodities and trade in financial instruments.

Most importantly, speculators assume risk—risk that already exists for producers and users of commodities or financial instruments. Speculators are risk-takers. They provide vital risk-shifting opportunities to hedgers, which add liquidity and capital to the market.

In a market without these risk-takers, it would be difficult, if not impossible, for hedgers to agree on a price because the sellers (or short hedgers) want the highest possible price, while the buyers (or long hedgers) want the lowest possible price. Finding offsetting hedging trades would be very time-consuming, if not impossible, without speculators bridging the gap.

When speculators enter the marketplace, the number of ready buyers and sellers increases, and hedgers are no longer limited by the hedging needs of others.

In addition to assuming risk and providing liquidity and capital, speculators help to ensure the stability of the market. Active speculation in futures markets tends to dampen extreme price movement. For example, by purchasing futures when prices are low, speculators add to demand. The effect of rising demand is an increase in price. And by selling futures when prices are high, speculators decrease demand and,

SPECULATING IN THE FUTURES MARKETS

An Essential Ingredient for Liquidity

9

therefore, help to lower price. Thus, the extreme price swings that might otherwise occur are often softened by speculative activity.

Speculators trade futures markets to profit from natural price fluctuations. There are many external factors that can affect the price of a commodity or financial instrument. The price of grain, for example, changes along with supply and demand. Plentiful supplies at harvesttime usually mean a low price for grain. Higher prices may result from such things as adverse weather conditions during the growing season or an unexpected increase in export demand (both of which decrease grain supplies). Financial instruments fluctuate in price due to changes in interest rates and various economic and political factors.

Buy Low, Sell High

When speculating in futures markets, both profits and losses are possible—just as in owning the actual cash commodity. But speculators rarely have an interest in owning the cash commodity or financial instrument that underlies a futures contract. They buy contracts when expecting prices to increase, hoping to later make an offsetting sale at a higher price and, thus, a profit. They sell contracts when expecting prices to fall, hoping to later make an offsetting purchase at a lower price and, again, a profit. What is unique about futures is that a speculator can enter the market by either purchasing a futures contract or by selling a futures contract. The speculator's decision of whether he should buy or sell first depends on his market expectations.

The profit potential is proportional to the speculator's skill in forecasting price movement. Potential gains and losses are as great for the selling (short) speculator as for the buying (long) speculator. Whether long or short, speculators can offset their positions and never have to make or take delivery of the actual commodity.

Types of Speculators

There are several ways of classifying speculators. The simplest, or most direct, is to refer to speculators as *long* or *short*. If a speculator is long futures, then he has purchased one or more futures contracts; if a speculator is short futures, then he has sold one or more futures contracts.

Large or Small

In addition to long or short, speculators may be classified by the size of their positions as designated by the Commodity Futures Trading Commission (CFTC). Speculators' futures and options positions must be reported periodically to the CFTC after they reach a specific number of open contracts. These speculators are classified as large position holders and include professional traders who hold memberships on futures exchanges and public speculators who actively trade through commission houses.

Public speculators who carry smaller positions are not required to report their positions to the CFTC.

Fundamental or Technical Analysis

Another method of categorizing speculators is by the price forecasting methods they use. Fundamental analysts look at supply and demand factors; technical analysts use charts to plot price, volume, and open interest movements in current and recent years. (Price forecasting methods are discussed in Chapter 10.)

Position Traders, Day Traders, and Scalpers

Still another means of classifying speculators is by their trading methods. One type is the position trader who initiates a futures or options position and then holds it over a period of days, weeks, or months. Position trading is used by both public and professional traders.

A day trader, on the other hand, holds market positions only during the course of a trading session and rarely carries a position overnight. Most day traders are futures exchange members who execute their transactions in the trading pits.

Scalpers are professional traders who trade for themselves in the pits. The technique is to trade in minimum fluctuations, taking small profits and losses on a heavy volume of trades. Scalpers' willingness to buy at the bid price and sell at the asking or offer price creates the largest amount of total speculative liquidity. Like day traders, scalpers rarely hold positions overnight.

Spreaders

Finally, speculators also may be spreaders. Spreaders observe the market and note the shifting price relationships between different delivery months of the same commodity, between the prices of the same commodity traded on different exchanges, between the prices of different but related futures contracts, or between cash and futures prices of the same commodity. In each case, there are normal relationships that exist from month to month reflecting usual market situations. When those price relationships vary from their usual patterns, spreaders sell the overpriced market and buy the underpriced market. Their actions serve an important economic function by pulling prices back to a more normal relationship. (Spreading is discussed in Chapter 11.)

Leverage, which is inherent in futures trading, is an important part of futures markets. Leverage is an attractive feature of futures markets for speculators because it enables them to control the full value of a futures contract with relatively little capital.

As an example, if a trader buys one soybean contract (5,000 bushels) at $6.50 per bushel ($32,500 for the contract), the required margin might

Leverage

be $3,000 (approximately 9 percent of the contract value or about 60 cents per bushel). This capital requirement is not a down payment for the futures contract, it is a security deposit to ensure contract performance. If the market moves against the position, the speculator will be required to deposit additional margin. And if the market moves in favor of the position, his account is credited.

Trading Strategy

When speculating in futures markets, it is important to develop a trading strategy or plan to guide market activity. Although such a strategy must be geared to the individual speculator, a systematic approach to speculating is helpful.

Know Your Futures Contract

In order to make sound judgments about price movement, it is essential to have adequate knowledge about the contract being traded and to limit the number of contracts that are followed. This is true whether using fundamental analysis, technical analysis, or a combination of both trading techniques. Even experienced traders usually have difficulty following more than three different futures contracts at a time.

Profit Objective/Maximum Loss

Price forecasts must be combined with a realistic and potentially profitable trading strategy. And the profit potential should be large in relation to risk. When deciding whether or not to initiate a futures position, traders should specify profit objectives as well as the maximum losses they are willing to sustain. Personal preferences determine the acceptable minimum levels for profits and maximum levels for losses.

Determine Risk Capital

After the profit objective and loss limit have been set, determine the amount of money to be risked. To maximize returns, experienced speculators often recommend limiting the amount of money risked on a single trade. Also, open positions should be limited to as many as can be adequately followed, and some capital should be reserved for additional opportunities.

Successful speculators often advise that additions to an initial position should be made only after the initial position has proven correct (that is, when it shows a profit). Additional investments should be in amounts less than the initial position. Liquidation of a position should be based on the original trading plan. Market conditions may change, however, so it is essential that speculators maintain some degree of flexibility.

The desirability of a trade (based on potential profits compared to risks) depends on a speculator's experience and preferences. Determining profit objectives and loss limits, additions to the original position, and when to close a position also depend on personal preference and experience. Successful price forecasting and trading are ultimately influenced by individual temperament and objectivity, as well as the analysis and trading plan that were developed.

In addition to a systematic approach, many successful speculators follow a number of useful guidelines. Listed below are a few that they may use:

Guidelines

♦ Before initiating a futures position, they carefully analyze that market. They avoid quick actions based on rumors and tips.

♦ They do not speculate without a trading plan, or if there is doubt about the price forecast.

♦ Speculators rarely are able to buy at the lowest market price or sell at the highest. Orders are generally executed close to the best possible prices.

♦ Speculators give equal priority to forecasts of falling prices and short positions as they do to forecasts of rising prices and long positions.

♦ They speculate when the potential profit is great relative to risk.

♦ Successful speculation requires limiting losses and letting profits run. Traders should be prepared to accept numerous small losses; a limited number of highly profitable trades should offset those losses.

♦ In addition to a careful analysis of futures contracts, successful speculation requires a well-developed trading plan. This includes limiting the amount of money risked on any single trade and maintaining capital in reserve.

The 1975 corn futures market offers a good example of how a variety of fundamental and technical factors affect corn prices. The following example of a long corn position illustrates that speculators need to know the most current market conditions as well as to watch changing events and shifting market attitudes.

Long Position in Corn

On June 30, 1975, the December 75 corn futures contract marked a new seasonal low of $2.32½ per bushel. A seasonal low (or high) is the lowest (or highest) price a particular futures contract has traded at since it opened. Among the bearish fundamental factors was an excellent outlook for the new crop. This was highlighted in a subsequent U.S. Department of Agriculture (USDA) crop report indicating that farmers had planted 1.8 million more acres in corn than had been estimated in the March 1 planting intentions report. In addition, weather conditions had been ideal for fieldwork, planting, and early corn growth, and export sales had been slow.

Also, domestic demand for corn was down due to lower livestock numbers. Thus, it appeared that the fundamental situation was basically bearish as the supply prospect seemed to be increasing and the demand outlook appeared to be deteriorating. Both situations implied an increased carryover supply at the end of the crop year. However, despite this prevailing bearish sentiment, the technical indicators gradually began to indicate that a change was occurring in the value of corn and its price.

Bullish Market Trend

Within six trading sessions after the market's new seasonal low, the December contract advanced by more than 25 cents per bushel to $2.58 on July 9. In the process, prices exceeded the highs of the previous month. This price rise also occurred with increasing volume, which was a technically positive indicator.

At about the same time, the fundamental supply/demand picture began to change. On July 10, the USDA crop estimate was reported at 6.05 billion bushels, a figure below previous expectations, which had ranged as high as 6.5 billion to 7 billion bushels. Temperatures continued above normal in the second half of June and into July for the Corn Belt and the southeastern United States. These above-normal temperatures during the critical tasseling stage for corn raised concerns that U.S. corn production could be lower than normal.

Furthermore, unconfirmed reports began to filter into the marketplace suggesting that Soviet crop conditions also were deteriorating due to record high temperatures and below-normal precipitation.

Bought December Corn

After carefully reviewing and analyzing these various factors, and considering that the majority opinion was quite bearish just the week before, a speculator decided to initiate a long corn futures position. So, at the market opening on July 11, the speculator bought one December corn futures at $2.55. Although the speculator assumed that prices would continue moving up and planned to sell his position at around $2.85, he entered a protective 10-cent stop-loss order to sell at $2.45 in the event that his timing or market judgment proved to be wrong.

Later that day, corn futures prices advanced sharply, closing at $2.64¼, reflecting reports of Russian ocean-freight bookings, and further reports of hot, dry weather in the United States and abroad. After the market close, the CFTC released the June 30 report on Commitments of Traders which showed the average speculator had a large net short position. This was due to the generally bearish opinion that had prevailed just 11 days earlier.

On Monday, July 14, there was further buying and short-covering (buying futures to offset short futures positions), and the December contract reached $2.69. At that point, the speculator already had a potential profit of 14 cents per bushel. But since the uptrend was expected to continue, he held on to the position. However, the most aggressive traders that day were sellers on the probable thought that the 36½-cent advance in only two weeks was sufficient to discount the still minor concern over domestic and Russian crop supplies.

On that day, July 14, the market closed at $2.59½. During the balance of the week, prices fluctuated between a high of $2.71 and a low of $2.54¼, and finally closed Friday, July 18, at $2.55¼. This closing price was only a quarter of a cent above the speculator's purchase price. His profit opportunity appeared to have been lost.

Although discouraged at having possibly missed the chance to profit, he reviewed the fundamental situation and the technical indicators and decided to stick with his basic plan.

By the next Friday, the December contract closed at $2.70¼ after an earlier high of $2.74¾. At $2.74¾, he had potential gain of nearly 20 cents per bushel. Once again, the trader reviewed the multitude of technical and fundamental information and decided to stay with his initial trading plan.

More adverse crop news was reported over the weekend. This led to a limit-up move Monday and again Tuesday that pushed the December price to $2.90¼. Although the speculator's initial plan was to sell at around $2.85, the market action, the severity of the crop news, and the weather forecast caused him to revise his basic plan. He raised his profit objective another 30 cents per bushel to $3.15, and placed a new protective stop-loss order to sell at $2.65 to lock in at least an 8- to 10-cent profit should the market reverse itself. Subsequently, the December contract sold down to $2.75½, but still held above his stop.

Based upon news and the basic uptrend, he decided to hold the position. Later, the market advanced and closed August 8 at $3. On the following Friday, August 15, the market closed at $3.18¾ after reaching a high of $3.25. The speculator again revised his profit objective because he was more and more impressed with the market's strength and the substantial uptrend. In addition, there was very bullish news coming from Iowa, Nebraska, and the Soviet Union regarding the deteriorating condition of the crops. Also, the hog and cattle markets were making new highs, which suggested that domestic feed demand would improve as farmers increased livestock production.

Once again, he raised his profit objective by 30 cents per bushel to $3.45 and raised his stop-loss order another 20 cents to sell at $2.85. He felt this stop would probably assure him of at least his original profit objective of 30 cents per bushel.

Position Offset

The following week, prices again advanced, and the December contract reached $3.30¼ on August 21. However, somewhat surprisingly, the market reacted sharply late in the session and closed about 4 cents lower on a day with the heaviest trading volume since the uptrend had begun in early July. Though not conclusive, this negative technical signal suggested that the trader needed to make a critical review of the market's technical and fundamental factors. As a result, the speculator raised his sell stop-loss order to the previous low of that week, $3.10. A penetration of that price level, following the high volume reversal that occurred on August 21, would suggest that the uptrend might be over. The following week, prices did decline as the weather pattern changed, and the speculator's position was stopped out on that Wednesday's market opening at $3.08 per bushel.

Date	Action
Jul 11	Buys 1 Dec corn contract at $2.55/bu
Aug 27	Sell-stop order executed at $3.08/bu
Result	Gains $0.53/bu or $2,650 on 1 contract

In this example, the speculator did not buy at the bottom or sell at the top of the market. That rarely happens. However, considering his risk/reward ratio, he made the decision to buy when he recognized a clearly developing uptrend and took his profit when the market seemed to suggest that his position had reached its potential.

Long Position in Treasury Bonds

This example, based on events surrounding the stock market decline of October 19, 1987, highlights the importance of analyzing the economic factors and conditions that both directly and indirectly affect futures markets.

Before the Stock Market Decline

A speculator has been studying the bond and equities markets since the beginning of 1987. For the first three months, bond prices were relatively stable. By late March, however, bond prices began to fall as interest rates rose. Several interrelated factors appeared to be affecting the direction of bond prices:

♦ Weakness of the U.S. dollar—there was widespread fear among investors that a weak dollar would produce greater inflation and higher interest rates (lower bond prices).

♦ U.S. trade deficit seemed to be worsening—this occurred despite efforts to spur U.S. exports and decrease imports through a weaker dollar.

♦ Appearance that the Federal Reserve was tightening monetary policy—because of a weakness in the dollar and/or market worries about inflation.

During the summer, bond prices continued to drop and the market sentiment remained primarily bearish. Despite the bearish mentality and expectations of higher interest rates, several noted economists predicted a market turnaround. These economists believed the bond market was in the process of establishing a major bottom. Prices had been falling for nearly two years, and reached a two-year low on Friday, October 2, before closing up for the day. In fact, bond prices actually closed up for that week. It had been a month since bond prices had closed higher for the week (Monday through Friday) and over three months since the bond market had closed higher from one Friday to the next. These technical indicators seemed to be pointing to a bond market rally.

In addition, some economists focused on the state of the stock market—claiming that the market was overbought and stocks were overvalued—forecasting an end to the five-year bull market that had tripled stock prices.

Bought T-bonds

Taking all of these factors into consideration, the speculator believed that the bear market in bonds was about to end or at least take a breather. He was worried about the highly overvalued stock market and felt that a major break was about to occur—a break that would send investors flocking to bonds. On October 12, the speculator decided to take a long futures position in bonds and bought two December T-bond futures contracts at 79-08* or $79,250 per contract.

Events throughout the week led to a drop in bond prices. The huge trade deficit number released October 14 especially impacted bond prices, and the December T-bond contract closed down for the week at 77-30 (a loss of 1-10 or $1,312.50 × 2 on the position). The speculator continued to hold the opinion that the market was bullish, however, and stayed long bonds.

Over the weekend, investors began to lose confidence in the U.S. stock market. Comments made by then U.S. Treasury Secretary James Baker threatening to let the dollar drop made foreign investors nervous. There was worldwide uncertainty and fear regarding the status of the U.S. economy, and by Sunday night, European and Japanese investors had begun selling stocks heavily.

Events of October 19

When the markets opened Monday, October 19, panic had already set in. There was selling pressure from foreign investors and portfolio insurers as everyone tried to get out of stocks and into other investment vehicles.

---

*T-bond futures contracts are quoted in 32nds but the prices generally are written as follows: 70$\frac{8}{32}$ = 70-08. The minimum price fluctuation for one Chicago Board of Trade T-bond futures (contract value of $100,000) is $\frac{1}{32}$ of a percent. A $\frac{1}{32}$ of a percent change on a $100,000 contract equals $31.25 (100,000 × .01)/32.

The Dow Jones Industrial Average plunged a record 508 points on the 19th, and cash bond prices, in response to falling stock prices and selling pressures that had begun on the New York Stock Exchange, rallied 2 points immediately following the futures market close at 2 p.m. The speculator's decision to stay long bonds turned out to be a good one.

After the Decline

The immediate impact of the stock market crash was heightened uncertainty over the future direction of interest rates, the value of the dollar, and the health of the economy. Many economists and market analysts began predicting a recession—and possibly even a depression—for 1988.

To ensure the liquidity of the financial system and avert the collapse of securities firms, the Federal Reserve decided to suspend its tight monetary policy. By acting as the ultimate supplier of funds, the Fed flooded the banking system with dollars by purchasing government securities, thus driving down interest rates.

Bond prices rallied significantly as interest rates fell and investors began pouring money into fixed-income securities.

In what is termed a *flight-to-quality*, investors transferred their dollars from stocks to bonds as they sought a safe harbor for their funds. Within just one week's time, the December T-bond futures contract rose almost 12 percent—the closing price of 77-30 on October 16 had increased to 86-18 by the close of trading on October 23.

Profits for the speculator at this point, if he had chosen to offset his position, were $14,625. After reviewing the current market, the speculator decided to stick with his position. It was expected that the Fed would continue its easy monetary policy (lower interest rates) to ensure market liquidity, and predictions of a recession for 1988 were still being made.

Throughout the next few weeks, bond prices continued to climb, reaching a high of 90-15 the week of November 2. During the next two weeks, the December T-bond contract more or less stabilized, fluctuating between 88-00 and 89-00. The speculator kept a close watch on market conditions, especially the dollar, economic growth, and the Fed's monetary policy. By mid-November, fears of a recession for 1988 were beginning to subside. The impact of the crash on the overall economy was not clear and the economy was stronger than expected. Some experts began again to worry about the possibility of inflation and the higher interest rates that would be needed to contain it.

Toward the end of November, bond prices began to fall. On November 27, the December T-bond contract closed down for the week at 87-02; and throughout the following week, prices ranged from a high of 88-13 to a low of 86-15. Considering the mixed economic statistics following the crash, the various predictions of recession or inflation for 1988, and the recent downtrend in prices, the speculator reviewed his position and decided that it was time to close his position. Following the opening of trading on December 7, the speculator offset his position by selling two December T-bond futures contracts at 87-20. The profit on the position was $16,750, or $8,375 per contract.

Date	Action
Oct 12	Buys 2 Dec T-bond contracts at 79-08
Dec 7	Sells 2 Dec T-bond contracts at 87-20
Result	Gains 8-12 ($8,375 per contract or $16,750 on the position)

Note: The time frame and trading opportunities summarized in this example may not be representative of most market conditions due to the unusually wide price swings that occurred following the stock market decline in October 1987.

The following example is based on the price of gold in 1978. (It should be noted that gold has since moved to much higher levels, accompanied by even greater volatility. Although the Chicago Board of Trade currently trades a 100-ounce gold futures contract and a kilo gold futures contract, this example uses 100-ounce gold futures.)

Short Position in Gold

A speculator had been studying the gold market and found that most indicators pointed to a decline in cash and futures prices of gold. Among these indicators were a reported tapering off of a previously heavy demand for gold jewelry and industrial uses, and an improvement in the exchange rate of the U.S. dollar versus foreign currencies. On March 8, gold was trading at $184 per troy ounce on the spot market, and the September gold futures were trading between $197 and $200 per troy ounce.

Sold Gold Futures

The speculator decided the time was right to take a short position and told his broker to sell three September contracts at the market price. (A market order does not specify an exact price, but is to be filled as soon as possible at the best price available in the trading pit.) Later, the broker informed his customer that the order was filled at $198 per troy ounce.

In the following weeks, the speculator's expectations of falling gold prices became a reality. There was, along with improvement of the U.S. dollar exchange rate with foreign currencies, a decline in European demand for gold as an investment and a decline in U.S. and European demand for gold jewelry. By March 30, weak demand pushed the September futures price down to $188 per troy ounce, for a gain on the speculator's position of $10 per troy ounce. This amounted to $1,000 per contract, or $3,000 on his position. After reviewing his position, the speculator saw no sign of a trend reversal. He resisted the temptation to take his profit and let the position stand.

Position Closed—Bought Gold Futures

By April 21, September gold futures prices were about $175. However, when the price moved to $171.80, large buying developed, apparently due to speculative profit-taking on signs of an oversold market. The speculator believed that this was the beginning of a trend reversal. On May 4, he called his broker and told him to buy three September contracts at the market. Later, the broker confirmed that the order was filled at $177.60 per troy ounce. The result of the speculator's position was:

Date	Action
Mar 8	Sells 3 Sep gold contracts at $198/troy oz
May 4	Buys 3 Sep gold contracts at $177.60/troy oz
Result	$20.40/troy oz gain or $2,040 per contract or $6,120 on the position

This and other examples in this chapter do not include commission or transaction costs.

Note: In all three scenarios, the speculators realized a profit. However, if the speculators had been incorrect in their price forecasts or overlooked one or more changing market conditions, any of the positions could have resulted in a loss. This is why it is important to keep a close watch on the market and develop a trading plan before initiating a futures position.

Two basic techniques are used by market analysts to forecast price movement in futures markets: fundamental and technical analysis. While there are purists of both techniques, many traders use a combination of fundamental and technical analysis to forecast price. Forecasting price movement based on the fundamental approach requires the study of supply and demand factors affecting the price of a commodity or financial instrument, whereas the theory behind technical analysis states that prices can be projected based on historical price movement and current market activity. Technical and fundamental factors affect prices and some knowledge of both methods is important to understanding price movements in the futures market.

PRICE ANALYSIS

*Fundamental &
Technical
Approaches*

THE FUNDAMENTAL APPROACH

The trader who uses fundamental analysis watches the economic factors that affect supply and demand in attempting to forecast prices and develop profitable trading strategies. Fundamental analysts operate on the principle that any economic factor that decreases the supply or increases the use of a commodity tends to raise prices. Conversely, any factor that increases the supply or decreases the use of a commodity tends to increase

10

stocks and lower prices. A good example of how price is affected by changes in supply and demand occurred in 1983 when the price of corn fluctuated greatly. The United States had a huge supply of corn in storage following a bumper crop in 1982. Many market participants expected farmers to plant another large corn crop in 1983. The expectation of a potential corn glut drove prices to record lows. To curtail additional surpluses, President Reagan announced the Payment-In-Kind (PIK) acreage-reduction program in January 1983. Later that year, drought and hot weather brought corn production down, lowering potential supplies even more. These factors led farmers and traders to believe that corn prices would skyrocket.

However, potential buyers of corn, anticipating rising prices, chose to reduce the amount of corn they would need by cutting livestock numbers, using other grains as feed, or substituting or decreasing the amount of corn sweetener used in prepared foods and beverages. As demand for corn dropped, so did prices.

The scenario described involved some of the basic fundamental factors that can affect agricultural commodities—weather, yield, other feed grain usage, carryover, and politics.

The supply and demand factors a fundamentalist needs to study depend on the commodity or financial instrument he is interested in trading. (Specific supply and demand information for each commodity is discussed in Chapters 13–17.)

Agricultural Markets

Carryover stocks of agricultural commodities are among the most critically watched factors by fundamentalists. (Carryover is the amount of grain or oilseeds that remains at the end of a marketing year.) The size of the carryover affects the strength or weakness of the price of the commodity in the near or distant future.

Carryover

Carryover indicates the tightness of supply. A tight supply would be reflected in higher prices, while an ample supply would lower prices. The projection of ending stocks rises or falls based on the level of projected demand and production. With the exception of some nonstorable commodities such as livestock, fundamentalists keep a constant watch on stock levels as price indicators. And, even in the case of livestock, the inventory of breeding animals, the livestock on feed, and the number of livestock brought to slaughter help to forecast meat production.

In using carryover figures to forecast price movement, other factors also must be considered. The size of the upcoming crop, for example, may be more important in predicting prices than the current carryover.

Yield

Yield is the amount of grain harvested per acre planted, and it directly affects the attitude and action of buyers in the marketplace. This attitude determines how high or low prices will move. Production of agricultural commodities such as corn is a combination of acreage and yield, with yield per acre dictated by weather and the latest farm technology.

Monitoring the production of agricultural commodities requires the fundamental analyst to watch the regularly scheduled government and private reports on farm production in the United States and abroad.

Agricultural Reports

Numerous U.S. Department of Agriculture (USDA) reports exist for all types of agricultural products from livestock to orange juice. The information for these reports is gathered by each state and compiled in Washington, D.C. Because traders place such importance on these national figures, safeguards are taken to ensure that the statistics are released at precisely the scheduled time.

Corn and wheat reports, for example, are issued monthly. The reports early in the calendar year show the number of bushels produced the previous year. Later reports indicate the number of acres farmers are expected to plant. Information released through the summer months details the size of the crop and, at the end of the year, the harvested crops. (For more detailed information on government crop reports, see the Appendix.)

The uncertainty of weather can cause more anxiety in the marketplace than all other fundamentals combined.

Weather

Traders monitor the amount of moisture, the time of frost, and the temperature during the growing season and its impact on world growing conditions to gauge how crop production is affected around the world. Weather conditions also influence livestock production. During periods of drought, livestock producers are forced to reduce livestock numbers due to the high cost of feed. This presents a glut of meat and lower prices in the short term. But in the long term, meat prices rise due to a shortage of livestock after the drought-related slaughter. During winter months, blizzards can close roads, temporarily delaying livestock shipments to market.

Domestic and international economic conditions also affect commodity prices.

Economic Conditions

There is a direct relationship between the supply and demand of livestock and grains. For instance, the affluent consumer is more likely to eat red meat, which, in turn, influences the demand for livestock. A rise in livestock numbers increases consumption of feed, which contains large amounts of corn. This eventually decreases the supply of corn. On the other hand, the less money available to consumers, the less spent on more expensive foods like red meat.

Livestock feeders make a larger profit when grain prices are low, which encourages the number of livestock to increase. When livestock supply becomes too large, livestock prices drop. Feeders are forced to cut their herds, which leads to lower grain usage and, eventually, lower grain prices.

Another important variable monitored by the fundamentalist is the pattern of consumption for a commodity. Take, as an example, the breakdown of U.S. corn usage: 65 percent, livestock and poultry feed; 25 percent, exports; and 10 percent, industry, food, and seed uses.

Other Factors to Watch

Competition with Other Commodities

The ability to substitute one commodity for another in a product can have a great effect on price. For instance, when soybeans are scarce and priced high, livestock producers may substitute cottonseed meal as a feed additive, or vegetable oil manufacturers may use coconut or palm oil as a base rather than soybean oil. Of course, each substitute has specific qualities and one may be more appropriate to use than another.

Politics

Policies made by different governments regarding agricultural production can influence the prices of commodities both domestically and worldwide.

In the United States, for instance, the government offers special acreage-reduction programs to farmers to cut the number of acres planted in specific crops. This lowers production and, eventually, reduces supply; lower supplies can lead to higher prices.

Other U.S. programs of particular importance to the supply of various commodities include feed-grain and loan programs, as well as the management of stocks accumulated from defaulted loans.

Other countries or organizations such as the European Economic Community offer similar programs to farmers in an effort to control production and prices.

Worldwide Competition

The United States is a major producer of several agricultural commodities including soybeans, corn, and wheat. These crops and others also are grown in many other countries throughout the world. As an example, Australia and Canada produce large quantities of wheat for export. The Soviet Union also is a major wheat producer but, at times, imports large quantities of wheat. Brazil and Argentina are expanding their export markets, especially for soybeans.

Because these countries as well as several others are either large exporters or importers of agricultural commodities, the growing conditions there are closely monitored by fundamentalists. Both devastating weather conditions and optimum growing environments can greatly affect production and, thus, the supply and price of crops.

Other long-term factors influencing the supply of and demand for agricultural commodities include: seasonal usage trends; the number of potential producers of a commodity and their capacity to produce that commodity; international trade; foreign exchange rates; and general economic conditions, such as interest rates, unemployment rates, inflation, and disposable income.

Fundamental price analysis in the financial instrument area involves forecasting the supply of and demand for credit and the price of fixed-income securities. It is the simultaneous evaluation of economic information, political forces, and investor attitudes as they interact.

Financial Instruments

U.S. monetary policy is formed by the Federal Reserve Bank Board and is administered through the Federal Reserve System. Because the Federal Reserve controls the circulation of money, its policies and actions have a great impact on interest rate levels. In a slow economy, the Federal Reserve can lower the discount rate* in an effort to increase spending. And, during inflationary times, the Fed can raise the discount rate to reduce borrowing.

Federal Reserve System

The demand for money is comprised of four major areas of financing: business, consumer and personal, mortgage, and government. Each of these financial areas competes with the others for available capital. In an expanding economy, the combined money needs of these sectors tend to create upward pressure on interest rates. Theoretically, interest rates rise to a level at which the demand for money is curtailed until interest rates fall back to more attractive levels. On the other hand, in periods of sluggish economic activity, interest rates generally decline as the banking industry attempts to stimulate lending.

Private and government issuers of debt instruments compete for available capital by adjusting the interest rates they pay lenders and investors. Among the financial instruments affected by these influences are: long-term U.S. Treasury bonds, long- and intermediate-term U.S. Treasury notes, short-term U.S. Treasury bills, foreign currency, precious metals, stocks, corporate and municipal bonds, and prime commercial paper of various maturities.

The task of a fundamental analyst is to sort through the volume of financial information, pinpoint the significant factors, and accurately weigh their effect on the supply and demand for credit.

Economic reports released by the U.S. government are excellent sources of financial information. The elements that make up these reports can be grouped into three categories: leading, concurrent, and lagging indicators.

Government Reports

---

*If a bank is short on reserves relative to its loan demands, it may borrow funds from the Federal Reserve. The bank is required to pay an interest rate, set by the Fed, that is known as the *discount rate*.

Leading Indicators

Leading indicators signal the state of the economy for the coming months. They imply possible changes in the business cycle and, as a result, provide the analyst with an early indication of interest rate trends. The U.S. government has combined a number of these statistical elements into a single index called the Leading Indicator Index. Components of the index are:

◆ Average workweek of production and manufacturing workers

◆ Manufacturing layoff rate

◆ New orders for consumer goods and materials

◆ Percentage of companies reporting slower deliveries

◆ Net business formation

◆ Contracts and orders for plants and equipment

◆ New building permits for private housing units

◆ Net change in inventories on hand and on order

◆ Changes in total liquid assets

◆ Stock prices of 500 common stocks

◆ Money supply

A value change in one of the index's components is often an early signal of a production and/or investment change within the economy. An increase in demand for goods requires additional labor, which, more than likely, would be seen first in the lengthening of the manufacturing workweek. Eventually, there would be an increase in the number of manufacturing workers hired. Similarly, when demand for goods falls, a cut in hours worked precedes layoffs.

Traders usually react immediately to these indicators as they are released throughout the month, resulting in short-term volatility in prices.

Concurrent and Lagging Indicators

Concurrent and *lagging* indicators show the general direction of the economy and confirm or deny a trend implied by the leading indicators. The market adjusts quickly as investors react to these economic signals.

Some key concurrent and lagging monthly indicators are:

◆ Unemployment—released at the start of the month, reports the change in employment for the preceding month and shows current economic activity.

◆ Trade balance—reveals the difference between imports and exports of merchandise over a period of time. The balance of trade can indicate the strength of the dollar, which is followed very closely by the market as an indicator of potential foreign purchases of securities. A strong dollar increases private foreign buying but often causes foreign central banks to sell financial securities.

♦ Domestic car sales—lists the number of cars sold during the previous month. This is a good measure of consumer confidence and overall economic activity.

♦ Retail sales—summarizes the value of credit and cash retail purchases, and is a good indicator of consumer confidence and overall economic activity.

♦ Producer Price Index (PPI)—shows the cost of resources needed to produce manufactured goods during the previous month. PPI lists the rate of inflation for raw materials, and is a good indication of future consumer price increases.

♦ Business inventories—reflects the demand for short-term credit by businesses. As inventories build, they are usually financed through bank loans or commercial paper. Therefore, inventory increases or decreases usually signal changes in the demand for short-term credit. Inventory levels also generally indicate the duration and intensity of business slowdowns or speedups. If inventories are high when a slowdown begins, a longer and more severe recession is usually expected because factories then run at reduced levels until inventories are sold off. High inventories also may act as short-term support for interest rates. When inventories are high and the economy is in a business slowdown, demand for credit to finance inventories can keep interest rates higher longer than normal. Low inventories going into an upturn in the business cycle can result in a short inflation spurt and a quick acceleration of business activity. Rebuilding inventories creates jobs and ultimately causes consumer demand to increase. This demand often cannot be met by existing inventories, so prices climb, economic activity increases, and factories are opened.

♦ Housing starts—shows the demand for long-term mortgage money and short-term construction loans. They also are indicators of the number and type of mortgage-backed securities that the market will need in the near future.

♦ Industrial production—gives the level of factory output in the previous month and shows the level of intensity for economic recessions and booms.

♦ Personal income—reflects consumers' buying power and weighs potential demand for goods and services.

♦ Gross National Product (GNP)—reports the total value of final goods and services produced in the United States over a specific time period, usually one year, and confirms the direction and magnitude of economic change.

♦ Consumer Price Index—measures inflation and is a key factor in bond prices, as investors usually demand a real rate of return of at least 2 percent for government bonds over the long term. Traders watch these numbers closely, since they usually indicate future changes in long-term bond and money market rates.

These indicators and figures are reported in daily newspapers as information is released. Market experts, however, make forecasts of the data prior to the actual release, because the market often begins to react before the news is actually announced.

No one indicator permanently dominates and "the most important" indicators replace each other as factors in the market. Sometimes the market will concentrate on one or two elements and ignore others for a time. It is the job of the fundamental analyst to identify the factors currently of most concern.

For example, during most of 1982, many market analysts watched the money supply and ignored other indicators. (Money supply is the amount of money in the economy consisting primarily of currency in circulation plus deposits in banks.) The feeling was that the Federal Reserve was going to dominate the market and make policy decisions based on money growth and inflation rates. Later that year and in early 1983, money supply and inflation were downplayed as other economic indicators showed that the economy was in a general slide, and the Fed indicated it was going to pay less attention to money supply in policy-making.

Information Available from the Federal Reserve

The Federal Reserve system provides information that is helpful in analyzing the economy and predicting Federal Reserve activity. These weekly reports contain information on:

♦ The money supply growth on a one-week lagged basis
♦ Loan demand
♦ The average rates for fed funds
♦ Dealers' positions in Treasury issues
♦ The condition of the accounts at the New York Federal Reserve Bank

The Fed reports the level of reserves the banks must maintain at the central bank, which provides information about transactions that affect the federal funds rate. The fed funds rate is the interest rate charged among banks for reserves borrowed and lent to each other. It is watched as a good indicator of short-term Federal Reserve policy.

The total of commercial paper and industrial loans outstanding at financial and nonfinancial institutions is also reported weekly by the Fed. These statistics show the overall demand for credit and the sectors of the economy demanding it.

The minutes of the Federal Reserve Open Market Committee monthly meeting are another important source of fundamental information.

The information needed by fundamentalists to forecast prices of agricultural, metals, and financial markets is vast and complex. Many fundamentalists collect these figures on their own, but services are also available that gather this information.

According to price theory, the point where the quantity demanded and the quantity supplied are equal is called the *equilibrium* or *market price*. The purpose of fundamental analysis is to pinpoint and recognize the major factors in the market and to predict their effect on the equilibrium price of a commodity. Profit opportunities exist when a fundamentalist can project how these factors will affect both the short-term and long-term equilibrium price.

Using fundamental analysis involves formulating an economic model—a systematic description of the various supply-and-demand factors that interact to determine price. The sophistication of these economic models varies greatly—from complex models with thousands of variables to a simple equation that relates the price of a commodity to a few key demand and supply statistics.

Use of Computers

In the last few years, technological advances in computer hardware and software programs have been applied to fundamental analysis. This has resulted in the development of even more sophisticated and complex fundamental analysis systems. Using computer analysis and modeling techniques to describe in mathematical terms the relationship between economic factors such as interest rates, government policies, and capital is known as *econometrics*.

The use of computers by fundamentalists, however, still requires a measure of judgment since each piece of data fed into the computer must be weighted as to its particular significance. Such evaluation is an inherent part of the use of economic models as price-forecasting tools.

What is important to remember is that, while the indicators of supply and demand may vary greatly from one commodity to another, the process of fundamental analysis is similar for all.

THE TECHNICAL APPROACH

Although fundamental analysis provides some very general indicators of price, many traders believe that even if all the supply and demand information affecting a particular product were known, one still would not be able to forecast price movement. They believe that to know and understand every factor that may affect supply and demand is impossible, and that, at times, a trader may overlook something that could substantially affect the market.

Using Fundamental Analysis

Treasury Bonds
September 1988
Chicago Board of Trade

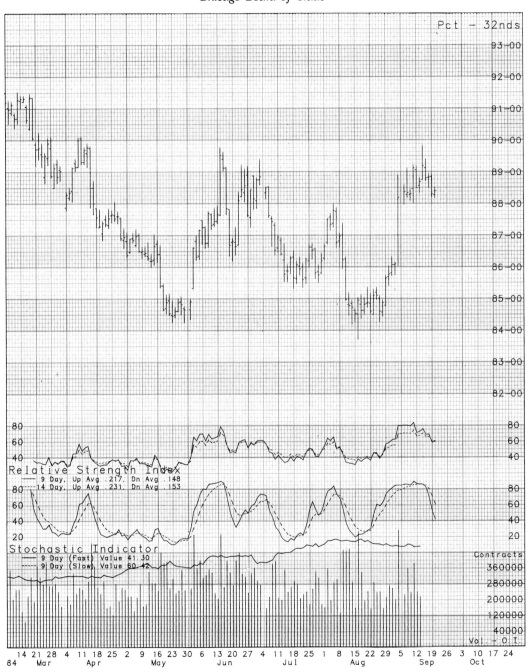

Source: Data Lab Corporation, Niles, Illinois

These traders prefer to anticipate market movement by studying price patterns in the past using historical prices, trading volume, open interest, and other trading data. They are called *technicians* and the technique they use to forecast prices is referred to as *technical analysis*.

Probably the oldest method of technical analysis is known as *charting*. There are two basic price charts—bar charts and point-and-figure charts. Both are quite simple to construct if a trader has price information, volume, open interest, graph paper, and pencil. However, if a trader doesn't want to spend the time constructing his own charts, there are a variety of companies that provide ready-made charts for a fee.

Charting

Bar Charts

Bar charts are one of the most common types of price charts. An example of a bar chart is shown to the left that also displays open interest and trading volume.

In a bar chart, the vertical axis represents price and the horizontal axis represents time. For daily bar charts, each trading day is represented by a vertical line that connects the lowest and highest price of the day. The day's closing price is indicated by a horizontal bar that crosses the vertical line.** Prices for the following days are plotted to the right of the first bar. Typically, most bar charts illustrate five vertical bars per week, representing the number of business days in a week. If there is a weekday holiday, the bar chart for that day is omitted. Not only can bar charts be graphed on a weekly basis, many traders plot this information over a month's period. Another type of bar chart tracks the daily price movement of the nearby delivery month for a specific commodity throughout the life of the contract. When the contract expires, the prices of the next delivery month are graphed on the same chart.

As price data are plotted, technicians begin to see different chart formations that tend to recur over time. Analysts use this information to predict future price movement. While it is impossible to explain every possible chart, this chapter reviews some of the most prominent bar formations.

Day Formations

Bar Chart Formations

The *inside day* is one in which the high and low prices of a trading day are within the previous day's price range. The close on such a day is not perceived as too significant. What is important to watch is the way prices move out of the narrow range in subsequent trading. The technician will either buy or

**Depending on the charting service, some bar charts indicate the opening price by a horizontal bar marked to the left and the closing price by a horizontal bar marked to the right of the vertical axis.

Live Cattle
August 1987
Chicago Mercantile Exchange

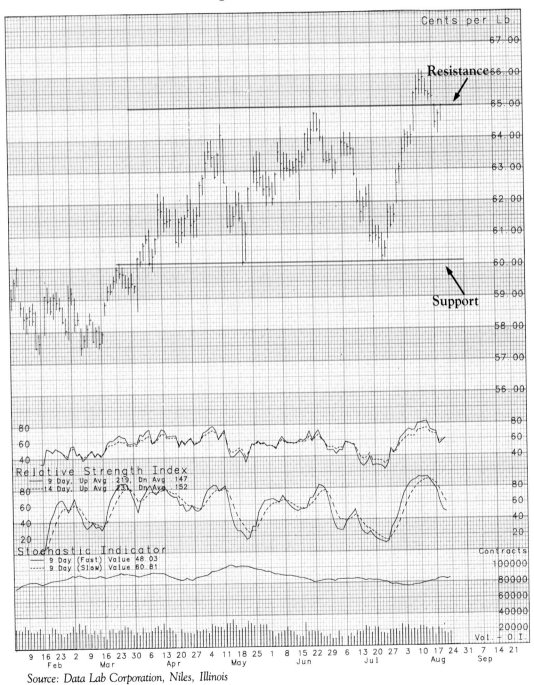

Source: Data Lab Corporation, Niles, Illinois

sell depending on which end of the range prices surpass in the days ahead.

The *outside day* formation—the opposite of the inside day—occurs when the high/low prices exceed the previous day's range. In this case, the closing price is given great weight. The chartist adjusts or adds to his position in the direction of the closing price.

The *closing price reversal* is a formation in which prices initially continue in the same direction as the previous trading day but reverse to close opposite the previous day's close. This type of price action is viewed as a strong warning signal that a price trend may have ended.

The *key reversal* combines the outside day and the closing price reversal. The essential pattern difference from the closing price reversal is that both opening and closing prices exceed the extremes of the previous day's range. The key reversal, particularly on a weekly chart, is perceived as the probable forerunner of the end of a trend. Many technicians reverse their position in the market after one occurs.

Support and Resistance

The chartist uses several terms to describe different market conditions. For example, sometimes the market rallies and then falls back to a previous price range or there may be a price decline that is stopped due to buying pressure. Traders use several different terms for these formations. One of the terms is *support*—the place on a chart where the buying of futures contracts is sufficient to halt a price decline.

The opposite of support is *resistance.* The market rallies to a particular price level then falls back to a previous price area. Resistance on a chart indicates a price range where selling pressure is expected to stop a market advance.

After a trading range is established for at least a month or two of sideways price movement, prices tend to meet support at the lower end of the range or resistance at the upper end of the range. If prices break out of a specific support or resistance area, some traders use this information to make buying or selling decisions.

Trends

A standard definition of an uptrend is a sequence of both higher highs and higher lows and is considered to be intact until a previous low point is

Weekly Nearby Corn Futures
1976-1985
Chicago Board of Trade

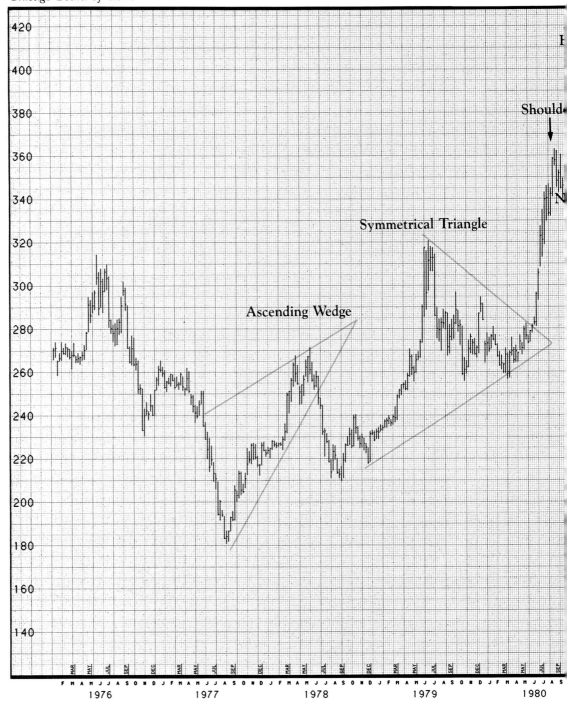

Source: Commodity Perspective, A Knight-Ridder Business Information Service, Chicago, Illinois

Shoulder

Downtrend

Uptrend

1982   1983   1984   1985   1986

Oats
March 1988
Chicago Board of Trade

Source: Commodity Trends Service, North Palm Beach, Florida

broken. Conversely, a downtrend is a sequence of lower lows and lower highs and is considered to be intact until a previous rally is surpassed. It is important to realize, however, that a break in a pattern of higher highs and higher lows (or lower highs and lower lows) should be looked at as a clue and not as an indicator of a possible long-term trend reversal.

Uptrends and downtrends also are defined in terms of trend lines. An uptrend line connects a series of higher lows and a downtrend line connects a series of lower highs. Trend lines are considered more reliable if they are at approximately a 45-degree angle to the horizontal axis representing time. However, it is not uncommon for a trend to start at a much sharper angle.

Channels

Sometimes the lines connecting highs and lows run almost parallel to a trend line. This type of price movement creates channels, and if it breaks a major trend line, it may indicate a substantial market move in the direction of the penetration.

Chart analysts rely on specific chart formations that recur over time to forecast future price movements. After trend lines and channels have been established, one of the most important decisions a trader has to make is determining a major top in a rising market or a major bottom in a declining market.

The most common chart indicators are:

- Head-and-shoulders or inverted head-and-shoulders
- Double tops and double bottoms
- Gaps
- Rounded tops and rounded bottoms

Head-and-Shoulders

The *head-and-shoulders* formation is one of the most reliable patterns indicating a major reversal in the market. This formation consists of four phases: the left shoulder, the head, the right shoulder, and a penetration of the neckline. The head-and-shoulders formation is complete only when the neckline penetration occurs. Some theorists believe that once prices break through the neckline, the distance from the top of the head to the neckline signals the extent of the movement away from the neckline. The head-and-shoulders occurs in a rising market; its opposite, the *inverted head-and-shoulders,* occurs in a declining market.

Double Tops and Double Bottoms

Double tops and *double bottoms* are exactly what their names suggest and have a tendency to indicate major market moves. These formations are

Corn
December 1988
Chicago Board of Trade

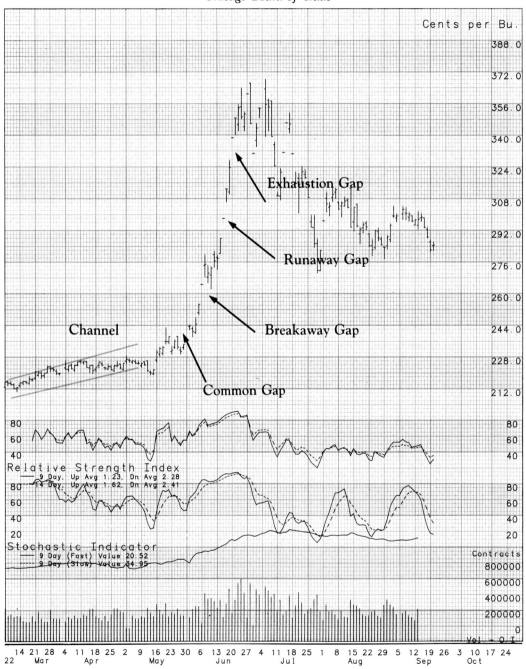

usually considered complete when prices move past the first reaction point following the first top or bottom.

Rounded Tops and Rounded Bottoms

Rounded tops or *rounded bottoms* (also called *saucers*) are usually reliable indicators of future price movement. The size of the saucer frequently signals the extent of an upcoming price advance or decline. An additional feature of this formation may be the development of the platform that is generally the forerunner of the primary price move.

Gaps

Gaps in price charts also are watched with interest by the chartist. Gaps represent a price area where the market did not trade. There are several types of gaps including the common gap, the breakaway gap, the runaway gap, and the exhaustion gap.

The *common gap* can appear at any time and has no particular significance. Frequently, this gap is filled in during later trading. The *breakaway gap* occurs when prices jump beyond a trading range leaving an area in the chart where no trading took place. A breakaway gap is useful in predicting the end of a consolidation phase of the market, and it can signal a dynamic move. A *runaway gap* appears when a trend accelerates and is quite typical of a strong bull or bear market. The *exhaustion gap* occurs after a relatively long period of steadily higher or lower prices. As the name implies, chartists theorize that the exhaustion gap signals the imminent end of a trend.

Other Patterns

Triangles, in many forms, recur in futures price charts. Their reliability as a means of predicting price behavior, however, is open to some question, and they frequently become part of other chart formations. The three triangle patterns are the ascending triangle, the symmetrical triangle, and the descending triangle.

The *ascending triangle* can point to a breakout on the upside of the triangular area. Conversely, the *descending triangle* can point to a breakout on the downside of the triangular area. The *symmetrical triangle*, also referred to as a *pennant*, is the least dependable of the three and merely forecasts that a substantial move out of price congestion may take place. The symmetrical triangle is often a continuation of a formation in which a breakout will probably favor the previous price trend.

Two more important chart patterns are the flag and the ascending wedge, formations that are the reverse of each other. The *flag* is formed when a substantial upward price move is followed by a modest downward price drift, giving the appearance of a flag on a pole in the absence of wind. After the flag is formed, the upmove is abruptly resumed. An upside

Other Bar Chart Formations

Pennant

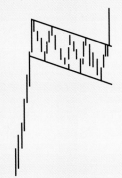

Flag

Rounded Top

Rounded Bottom

Double Bottom

objective is calculated by measuring the length of the pole and adding that amount to the low point of the flag.

The *ascending wedge* starts the same way with a significant price trend upward followed by a series of further up days that fail to accelerate as quickly as the initial uptrend. The irony of the wedge is that even though prices are rising, the upscale movement is usually not significant compared to the initial days of the formation. To the trained chartists, this is a negative pattern that will reverse to the downside.

Point-and-figure charts are unique in that they illustrate all trading as one continuous path and ignore time. As with bar charts, the vertical axis of the point-and-figure chart represents prices, however, there is no time reference along the horizontal axis.

Point-and-Figure Charts

The point-and-figure chartist uses an *x* to indicate an uptick and an *o* for a downtick. Generally, point-and-figure chartists set their price objective by counting the *x*s and *o*s of specific chart formations. The point-and-figure chartist theorizes that the amount of price movement at a given level is important in forecasting prices, which is quite similar to the logic of support and resistance used in bar charting.

Point-and-figure charts are used to track intraday price moves or long-term trends. As with bar charts, there are several formations revealed in point-and-figure charts as shown on the next page.

While the methods of charting—bar charts and point-and-figure charts—described here are used to identify trends, traders also try to recognize different price trends through statistical methods, which is known as *statistical analysis*.

Statistical Analysis

Moving-Average Charts

Probably one of the simplest and best-known statistical approaches is the moving average—an average of a series of prices. Moving-average changes are calculated for any period of time such as 3 days, 5 days, 10 days, or 30 days. One advantage of the moving average is that it tends to smooth out some of the price irregularities that can occur. However, the moving-average value always lags behind the current market by a day.

Deciding the average to use depends on several elements. The technician has to ask how sensitive he wants the average to be relative to the market. The more sensitive a trader wants the average to reflect turning points in a trend, the fewer the number of days that should be averaged. On the other hand, the more days incorporated in the average, the less the effect short-term market factors will have on the average price.

To calculate a moving average, a trader can use opening, closing, average, high, or low prices for a given day, however, most tend to use closing prices. Each price average—number of days and the price

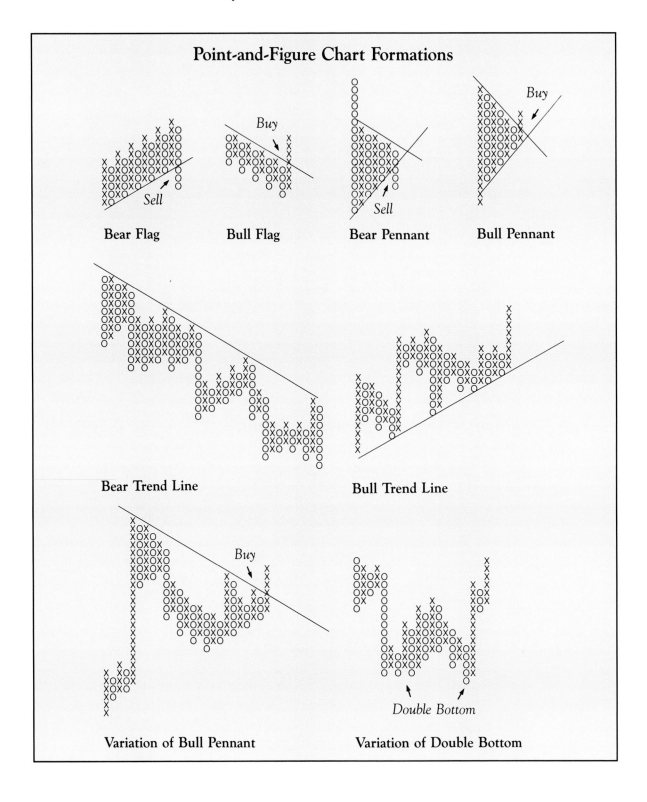

Point-and-Figure Chart Formations

Bear Flag

Bull Flag

Bear Pennant

Bull Pennant

Bear Trend Line

Bull Trend Line

Variation of Bull Pennant

Variation of Double Bottom

selection—serves a different purpose, so a trader has to look at his market objective and determine the type of moving average most appropriate to his market needs.

While it is beyond the scope of this text to explain how to calculate every type of moving average, there are a variety of books referenced in the Appendix that cover the topic of moving averages. However, one example of a three-day average is described here.

A three-day average is calculated by adding prices from three consecutive days. That total price is then divided by three to determine the first moving-average point. As an example, suppose the closing prices of silver futures for three consecutive days were $6.69, $6.62, and $6.68. Adding these three numbers equals $19.99. If $19.99 is divided by three (since this is the time frame of the moving average in this example), $6.66 is obtained. The $6.66 becomes the first moving-average point.

After the close on the fourth trading day, substitute the fourth closing price for the first and determine a new three-day average. Assume the closing price for silver on the fourth day was $6.81. Averaging the closing prices of the three previous days, $6.62, $6.68, $6.81, equals $6.70—the second point of this particular moving average.

A technician could determine the moving average for a particular contract as long as it traded if he chose to. If the closing prices for the next five trading days were $7.33, $7.36, $7.32, $7.18, $7.23, the moving average would be calculated as follows:

	Closing Prices Used	Total	Average
Day 5	$6.68 + $6.81 + $7.33 =	$20.82	$6.94
Day 6	$6.81 + $7.33 + $7.36 =	$21.50	$7.17
Day 7	$7.33 + $7.36 + $7.32 =	$22.01	$7.34
Day 8	$7.36 + $7.32 + $7.18 =	$21.86	$7.29
Day 9	$7.32 + $7.18 + $7.23 =	$21.73	$7.24

In a graph of a moving average, the horizontal axis represents the trading day or calendar day and the vertical axis represents price. The average points are plotted and a line can be drawn to connect the points. An example of a moving-average graph is illustrated on the next page.

The problem many technicians have is distinguishing false signals from the true ones. The trader might find himself buying on the high or selling on the low, with the unfortunate consequence of having to close out these positions at a loss. Therefore, the trader must learn to interpret different signals before taking action.

Some traders adjust their trading rules to accommodate the possibility of false signals by delaying entering or exiting the market a day or two.

Corn
September 1988
Chicago Board of Trade

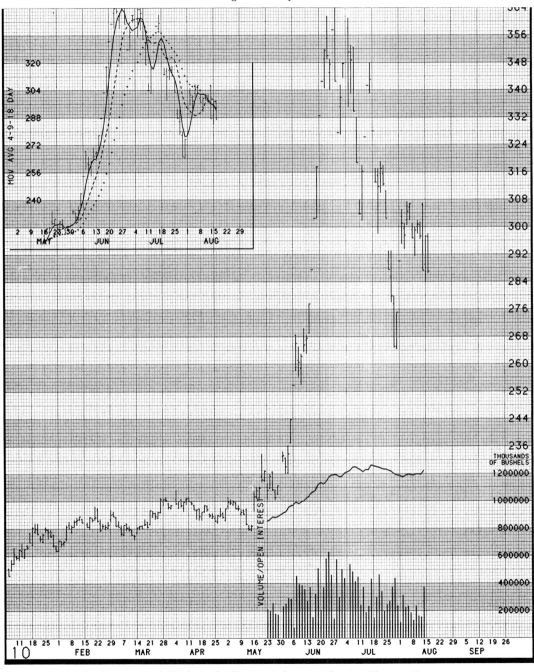

Source: Commodity Perspective, A Knight-Ridder Business Information Service, Chicago, Illinois

This allows more time for a trend to develop or for a false signal to reveal itself.

Oscillator

Many analysts use moving averages to forecast prices in trending markets. In sideways markets, technicians use oscillators. An oscillator is a technical indicator that allows a trader to measure overbought or oversold conditions in sideways markets.

The simplest example of an oscillator is the difference between the current closing price and the closing price a specific number of days earlier. As long as prices trend upward, the oscillator will be positive. However, for the oscillator to increase, prices must rise at an accelerated rate. The fact that sharp increases or decreases in the oscillator can occur only in markets that witness accelerated advances or declines suggests that this measure of price movement might be used as an overbought or oversold indicator.

Many moving-average and oscillator programs are computerized so technical analysts have this information at their fingertips. In addition, there are other price information programs for computers that analysts can either develop or purchase. In fact, several firms write their own computer programs for price analysts and have formed membership organizations. Members subscribe to these services and, thereby, have access to the most up-to-date price analysis programs.

Technical Analysis by Computer

In addition to charting and statistical analysis, a technician may use other techniques to assist him in predicting future price moves. Volume and open interest analyses are important examples.

Trading volume is the total number of contracts traded for a given period of time. Technical traders hypothesize that changes in volume are associated with price movements in the same direction. For example, a gradual increase in volume during a downtrend often indicates a continuation and acceleration of the price decline, while gradually increasing volume during an uptrend suggests a further rise in prices. Rapidly accelerating volume after a substantial price move, however, often signals the approach of a major high or low and an impending price reversal.

Open interest refers to the number of contracts that have been entered into and not yet liquidated by delivery or offset. As with volume figures, each contract represents both a long and a short position. Some technicians use open interest figures to get a handle on future price moves as the following examples illustrate.

Other Technical Tools

♦ A rise in both prices and open interest indicates that new buyers are entering the market. Since there is an increase in open interest, new contracts are being created, and the rise in prices means buyers are more aggressive than sellers.

♦ A rise in open interest and a decline in prices signal that traders are selling contracts. Once again, with open interest rising, new contracts are being established, but since prices are decreasing, sellers are more aggressive than buyers.

♦ A decline in both open interest and prices shows previous selling pressure. An increase in open interest and declining prices indicate new selling pressure.

♦ A decline in open interest accompanied by a rise in prices suggests that traders are covering their short positions.

Trading Positions

Around the 10th of each month, the Commodity Futures Trading Commission publishes a breakdown of the open interest in all futures and options on futures contracts as of the last trading day of the previous month. The report shows the total number of open positions held by large-volume traders, speculators, and hedgers, as well as those held by market participants with smaller positions.

Technicians study these reports very carefully, noting in particular any unusual changes in the various trading categories that may indicate differences of opinion between large commercial and speculative interests and smaller speculators and hedgers.

Trading positions also allow analysts to determine the resiliency of the market. Small-position traders tend to be more unstable than large-position traders who have more market "staying power." That is because large-position holders are usually higher capitalized. As an example, a market that has been experiencing a price increase is more likely to break if there is a large amount of smaller-position traders in the market who will not be able to afford a market shift.

While many veteran traders avow that knowledge of the composition of the market—who is long and who is short—is the most useful of all clues to future price moves, it should be cautioned that the data available for determining this are less than perfect. Daily volume and open interest figures do not segregate spreading activities and positions. They may obscure or give a false indication of actual new buying and selling pressure.

The monthly figures, on the other hand, segregate spreads, but the small speculator figure is calculated by subtracting the number of positions held by large traders from the number of positions held by all traders. Another disadvantage of these figures is that they are two weeks old before they are distributed.

Contrary Opinion

Similar reasoning is often applied to the opinions of market analysts who publish advisory services. The theory of contrary opinion holds that when more than 80 percent of these analysts are bullish, it can be assumed that they and their followers have taken long positions, leaving fewer potential additional buyers to absorb any selling that develops. Conversely, if 80 percent are bearish, the market is likely to become badly oversold, and a sharp price rally is likely to develop soon.

This theory often is applied after there has been a substantial move lasting an extended time period. And, it must be remembered that, after such a significant move, those who have opposed the move may be in financial difficulty. Thus, large moves tend to last longer than might reasonably be expected, and it can be very costly to take a contrary position too soon. This barometer is most useful as an early warning and is often used by prudent traders as the clue to take profits but not to reverse their positions.

CBOT Market Profile®

The Chicago Board of Trade's Market Profile® is an information service that helps technical traders analyze price trends. CBOT Market Profile® consists of a Time and Sales quotation ticker and the Liquidity Data Bank (LDB)®.

The Time and Sales ticker is an on-line graphic service that transmits price and time information throughout the day to computer subscribers. The second half of the system is the LDB®, which summarizes the entire day's trading activity including volume and a breakdown to the nearest 30 minutes of when specific trades were made. Traders use this information to recognize specific trends and forecast price movement.

Cyclical Theories

Cyclical theories are another growing area of interest for technical analysts. Cyclical theories are based on the premise that in nature certain phenomena have cycles and some analysts use this theory in forecasting price. One cyclical or wave theory, which is attracting a lot of attention, used to project price movement is the Elliot Wave Principle. (To learn more about this particular subject, check the Sources of Information in the Appendix.)

Traders frequently use a combination of fundamental and technical methods to forecast price. For example, many traders obtain a forecast of price movement using fundamental analysis and then choose the time for initiating or liquidating a position on the basis of technical factors.

But no matter what method or combination of methods for price analysis are used, none can be taken as foolproof. The process through which price is discovered in the futures markets represents the collective wisdom of all market participants trying to estimate future prices.

Combining Approaches

Futures markets provide a variety of trading opportunities. In addition to profiting from rising prices by purchasing futures contracts or from falling prices by selling futures contracts, there is the opportunity to profit from spreads. A spread refers to the simultaneous purchase and sale of two different futures contracts. When establishing or putting on a spread, a trader looks at the price relationship between contracts rather than the absolute price levels. The contract that is viewed as "cheap" is purchased, while the contract that is viewed as "expensive" is sold. If market prices move as expected, the trader profits from the change in the relationship between the prices of the contracts.

The economic contributions of spreading to the market are twofold: spreading provides market liquidity and restores prices to more normal relationships following a distortion in those relationships. An understanding of spread trading is important, therefore, to all market participants.

This chapter examines some of the underlying economic factors that account for the normal price relationships between different futures contracts. Also included are a few examples of spreading and explanations of some of the more common agricultural and financial spreads.

A trader initiates a spread when expecting the price difference between two futures contracts to change. To put on a spread, a trader

USING SPREADS IN FUTURES MARKETS

*Bulls,
Bears,
Butterflies*

11

Jul/Nov Soybean Spread
1984
Chicago Board of Trade

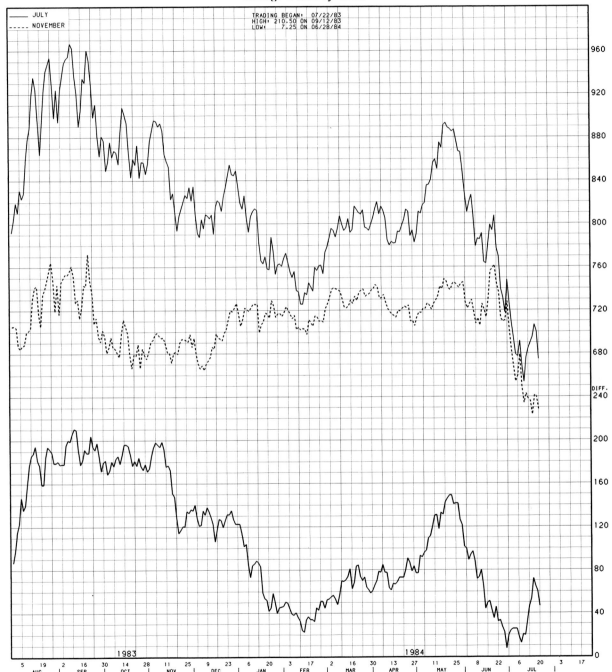

Source: Commodity Perspective, A Knight-Ridder Business Information Service, Chicago, Illinois

simultaneously buys one futures contract and sells the other. He later liquidates his spread position following a change in the price relationship. Spread orders may specify prices at which the long or short positions should be put on, or the price difference at which the spread should be established.

Spreads are quoted as the price difference between two related contracts. As an example, to calculate a particular agricultural spread such as the July/November soybean spread, one would subtract the price of the November contract from the July contract. This difference would generally result in a positive number because ag commodity prices are typically lowest at harvest and trend higher during the marketing year* as storage, interest, and insurance costs accumulate. As a result, July soybeans (old-crop beans) are usually priced higher than November soybeans (new-crop beans).

The July/November soybean 1984 spread graphed to the left illustrates the price difference between July 1984 soybeans and November 1984 soybeans.

The vertical axis of the chart represents the July/November bean spread value in cents per bushel; the horizontal axis is the trading day. The top line indicates the price of July futures, which fell nearly $1.75 between November and February, then rebounded to its original level by May, but tumbled $2.40 by July. During the same period, the middle line, which indicates November futures, depicts a gain of about 40 cents in a choppy pattern between November and May and a subsequent $1 plunge by July. The actual spread between July and November beans is illustrated on the bottom of the graph.

For the spread between two contracts to change, such as July soybeans to gain on November soybeans, there are four possible market scenarios:

♦ In a bull market, July soybeans rise faster than November soybeans;
♦ In a bear market, July soybeans fall slower than November soybeans;
♦ July soybeans remain unchanged while November soybeans fall;
♦ July soybeans rise while November soybeans remain unchanged.

Those who trade spreads do so for two important reasons—lower risk and attractive margin rates.

*The futures contract month of November represents the first major new-crop marketing month and the contract month of July represents the last major old-crop marketing month for soybeans. This is because the crop year tends to begin following harvest in the fall and end before the next year's harvest, e.g., the marketing year for soybeans begins September 1 and ends August 31.

Lower Risk

Because of their hedged nature, spreads generally are less risky than outright positions. Since the prices of two different futures contracts for the same commodity exhibit a strong tendency to move up or down together, spread trading offers protection against losses that arise from unexpected or extreme price volatility.**

This "protection" occurs because losses from one side of the spread are more or less offset by gains from the other side of the spread. For example, if the short (sold) futures side of a spread results in a loss due to a price increase, the long (bought) side should produce a profit offsetting much of the loss.

Attractive Margin Rates

Because spreads usually are less risky than outright positions, spread margin rates are generally lower than those for outright positions. Lower margin rates allow traders to diversify their portfolios with a smaller amount of capital.

SPREADING IN AG FUTURES

Types of Ag Spreads

There are three basic types of spreads—interdelivery, intermarket, and intercommodity.

Interdelivery (or Intramarket) Spreads

The simultaneous purchase of one delivery month of a given futures contract and the sale of another delivery month of the same commodity on the same exchange—e.g., buy July wheat and sell December wheat at the Chicago Board of Trade.

Intermarket Spreads

The simultaneous sale of a given delivery month of a futures contract on one exchange and the purchase of the same delivery month and futures contract at another exchange—e.g., the sale of December wheat futures on the Chicago Board of Trade and the purchase of December wheat futures at the Kansas City Board of Trade.

Intercommodity Spreads

The simultaneous purchase of a given delivery month of one futures market and the sale of the same delivery month of a different, but related,

---

**Not all spreads may be less risky than outright positions. For example, if a trader is long July beans and short November beans, July bean prices might unexpectedly decrease and November bean prices might increase during the life of the spread. If so, a trader might lose on both sides of the spread.

futures market—e.g., the purchase of July wheat futures and the sale of July corn futures.

The interdelivery spread is one of the most common types of spreads. An interdelivery spread position attempts to take advantage of the price difference between two delivery months of a single futures market when the difference is abnormal. Traders can describe interdelivery spreads as either bull or bear spreads. In an ag bull spread, a trader buys the nearby[†] and sells the deferred[†] expecting the nearby to gain on the deferred. The ag bear spread is just the opposite of a bull spread—a trader sells the nearby and buys the deferred expecting the deferred to gain on the nearby.

Among storable commodities, such as grains and metals, carrying charges have the greatest effect on the underlying futures prices of different delivery months.

Carrying Charges

Carrying charges are the combined costs of storage, insurance, and interest. The storage cost is the least variable of these three elements. For instance, the cost to store wheat, corn, soybeans, or oats in Chicago Board of Trade approved elevators averaged 4.8 cents per bushel per month in 1988. This storage cost reflects general inflationary trends due to increased construction, labor, and energy costs.

Insurance costs vary with the price of the commodity. Obviously, it costs more to insure soybeans valued at $7.50 per bushel than it does for corn worth $2.50 per bushel. As an example, insurance per year for corn averaged about .5 cent per bushel and for soybeans averaged about 1.5 cents per bushel in 1988.

The most variable component of carrying charges has been interest rates. Historically, most agricultural production has been financed through loans based on deposits in savings and checking accounts from banks located in farm areas. For many years, the interest rate that local banks charged farmers was relatively insulated from fluctuations in the prime rate—the rate that the large money-center banks charge their most creditworthy corporate customers. This has changed since the mid-1970s, however, as smaller customers have shifted funds from savings accounts at local banks to forms of savings and investments offering greater yields. Because of this loss of funds, local banks have become more dependent upon larger money-center banks for funds to loan to farm clients. The rates at which local banks borrow funds to lend to farmers are directly affected by fluctuations in the prime rate.

[†]Nearby futures month refers to the contract month closest to expiration and a deferred futures month refers to a contract month further from expiration.

Full-Carry Markets

Theoretically, in a normal futures market—reflecting adequate supplies of the underlying cash commodity and sufficient storage capacity—the price of the nearby futures month and the price of the deferred futures month have a definite price relationship. The deferred futures price is usually more than the nearby futures price by approximately the amount of the cost of carrying the commodity from the nearby to the deferred month. Each futures delivery month price is usually higher than the previous month by the amount of the cost to store, insure, and finance the commodity from month to month. In the case of corn priced at $2.50 per bushel—with a base storage cost of 4.8 cents per bushel per month, insurance cost of .09 cent per bushel, and a prime rate of 10 percent—the carrying charge is 6.97 cents per bushel per month:

$$\frac{(\$2.50 \times 10\%)}{12} + \$0.048 + \$0.0009 = \$0.0697/\text{bu/month}$$

The theoretical spreads of futures prices at full carry are:

Dec	Mar	May	Jul
$2.50	$2.71	$2.85	$2.99

These prices reflect the corn crop year that begins September 1 and ends August 31. Consequently, December is considered the first new-crop futures delivery month, and July the last. Futures prices tend to be at their seasonal low right after harvest—October and November for corn. In a normal market, December futures (first contract month for the new corn marketing year) should be priced lower compared to deferred contract months as carrying charges accumulate in the deferred months.

Remember that these full-carry markets are theoretical. In practice, interdelivery futures price spreads only rarely attain the full cost of carry due to changing market conditions.

Let's take a look at the actual corn spreads at the Chicago Board of Trade from mid-November 1982. With the nearby December corn futures selling at $2.34½ per bushel and a prime rate of 11½ percent, the monthly carrying cost is about 7 cents.

Dec	Mar 1983	May	Jul	Sep
$2.34½	$2.45	$2.51½	$2.56¾	$2.60

These spreads are far from full carry. There are many different market variables that could have affected the spread between the delivery months:

♦ Expectations about the amount of corn planted by farmers during the next crop year

♦ Corn demand for animal feed, food, seed, and industrial uses
♦ Carryover expectations (remaining supplies of corn carried from one crop year to the next)
♦ Expected rate of inflation
♦ Interest rate fluctuations
♦ Availability of storage

Inverted Markets

Thus far, we have looked at interdelivery spreads in relatively normal carrying charge markets (in which the futures price of the nearby month is less than the futures price of the deferred month). In periods when a commodity is in short supply, the nearby futures contract trades at a premium to the deferred futures. Such a market is called an *inverted market*. The inversion represents, in effect, a negative return for holding inventories.

A common interdelivery spread is the intercrop—or old-crop/new-crop—spread. It involves buying futures in one crop year and selling futures in another crop year. Since prices are usually lowest at harvest, new-crop futures tend to be priced lower than futures from the previous crop year.

An Interdelivery or Carry Charge Spread

There are a number of factors to consider, however, when establishing an old-crop/new-crop spread. First, the trader should look at the price relationship—not absolute price levels—between the two contracts and determine whether the spread is expected to change. Then he should ask himself:

♦ How large are remaining supplies (carryover) from the last harvest?
♦ What is the outlook for the size of the next harvest?
♦ How does the rate of usage compare to previous forecasts?
♦ How strong is future demand expected to be?

Answering these questions will help a trader determine whether a spread will change over time. If he expects old-crop prices to rise relative to new-crop prices, the trader can buy the old-crop month and simultaneously sell the new-crop month. On the other hand, if he expects new-crop prices to gain relative to old-crop prices, the trader can buy the new-crop month and sell the old-crop month. Note that, in each case, both sides of the spread are usually executed in one step, not two.

A common intercrop spread is the July/December corn spread. July represents the old-crop month and December represents the new-crop month. The spread is calculated by subtracting the December futures price from the July futures price (July minus December).

As an example, assume in May 1986 a spread trader expects July prices to decline relative to December (i.e., spread to become less positive) because no new export business has developed during the month since the Chernobyl nuclear accident.

On May 28, the trader simultaneously sells one July 1986 corn futures contract at $2.37 and buys one December 1986 corn futures contract at $1.95. The spread on May 28 is 42 cents ($2.37 − $1.95). (This market position is considered a bear spread since he sold the nearby and bought the deferred.)

On July 2, the trader offsets both positions and closes out the spread. He buys one July 1986 corn futures contract at $2.05, for a gain on the July contract of 32 cents ($2.37 − $2.05). At the same time, the trader sells one December 1986 corn futures contract at $1.82, for a loss on the December contract of 13 cents ($1.95 − $1.82).

Jul Futures	Dec Futures	Spread
May 28 Sells 1 Jul corn futures at $2.37/bu	Buys 1 Dec corn futures at $1.95/bu	$0.42
Jul 2 Buys 1 Jul corn futures at $2.05/bu	Sells 1 Dec corn futures at $1.82/bu	$0.23
Result $0.32 gain/bu $950 on spread ($0.19 × 5,000 bu)	$0.13 loss/bu	$0.19

In this example, the spread became less positive moving from 42 cents to 23 cents, for a net gain of 19 cents per bushel ($0.42 − $0.23). Notice that this equals the 32-cent gain on the July contract less the 13-cent loss on the December contract. One futures contract equals 5,000 bushels, so this spread would have produced a $950 gain ($0.19 × 5,000 bushels) for the trader.

Intermarket Spreads

When a commodity is traded on two or more futures exchanges, price differences between contracts may reflect geographic relationships. Futures trading in wheat, for example, is conducted at the Chicago Board of Trade, the Kansas City Board of Trade, the MidAmerica Commodity Exchange, and the Minneapolis Grain Exchange. Spreading between markets might involve a long position in Kansas City wheat futures against a short position in Chicago Board of Trade wheat futures.

The intermarket spreader must analyze several factors that influence price differences between markets. Transportation costs are an important determining factor. Wheat prices are generally lowest in the primary producing areas and increase at least by the cost of transportation to areas where consumers are located.

A second factor influencing price differentials is the value of the class and grade of wheat deliverable on each exchange. While the different exchanges generally allow delivery of several classes of wheat (premiums and discounts allowed), each market has a tendency to reflect the prices of a particular wheat class. As an example, Chicago Board of Trade wheat futures prices tend to reflect the price of Soft Red Winter wheat, and Kansas City wheat futures prices tend to reflect the price of Hard Red Winter wheat. This is because the price at each market usually reflects the type of wheat grown nearby, i.e., Chicago and surrounding areas produce Soft Red Winter wheat, while Kansas and surrounding states produce Hard Red Winter wheat. It is also important for the spread trader to realize that different wheat classes tend to vary in price depending upon their use.

Market participants interested in spreading wheat watch the relationship between these two markets. When the price relationship becomes abnormal, spreaders tend to buy the underpriced contract and sell the overpriced contract. This occurred in October 1986 when Chicago wheat futures were trading nearly 40 cents higher than Kansas City wheat futures. The price discrepancy corresponded to a shortage of Soft Red Winter wheat in the cash market caused by a poor Soft Red Winter wheat crop coupled with heavy participation by wheat producers in the government programs.

In this market situation, spreaders bought Kansas City wheat futures and sold Chicago Board of Trade futures. When the price relationship reflected more normal market conditions, they closed their spreads by selling Kansas City wheat and buying Chicago Board of Trade wheat.

Opportunities for spreading between U.S. futures markets and foreign futures exchanges also exist. Some common international spread positions include New York versus London sugar, cocoa, or copper, and gold spreads between New York, Chicago, and London.

Intercommodity Spreads

An intercommodity spread is a spread between two different but related commodities. The two commodities can either be used interchangeably or have common supply and demand characteristics. Although it is not necessary in an intercommodity spread to spread the same months in both commodities, it is a common practice.

Wheat/Corn Spread

The wheat/corn spread is a popular intercommodity spread, and involves buying (selling) one or more wheat futures contracts and selling (buying) one or more corn futures contracts of the same delivery month. Since wheat prices are generally higher than corn prices, the spread is usually positive and quoted as wheat over corn—wheat minus corn.

Changes in the wheat/corn spread can be seasonal. The wheat/corn spread usually tends to become less positive sometime in May/June/July (following winter wheat harvest) when wheat prices are low and corn prices are high. On the other hand, a trader might expect the spread to become more positive in September/October/November during the corn harvest, when corn prices are low and wheat prices are high.

Given a "normal" spread relationship between wheat and corn, a trader can take advantage of an abnormal relationship returning to normal or a normal spread relationship becoming abnormal.

Suppose a trader anticipates a normal spread—wheat falling faster relative to corn until summer then wheat gaining on corn in the fall. On June 29, the trader buys one wheat futures contract at $4.15 per bushel and sells one corn futures contract at $3.42½ per bushel in anticipation of the spread becoming more positive. The spread difference is 72½ cents a bushel ($4.15 − $3.42½).

On November 2, the trader offsets the position by selling one wheat futures contract at $4.41 per bushel and buying one corn futures contract at $2.89 per bushel for a difference of $1.52 per bushel ($4.41 − $2.89).

In this example, the spread moved from 72½ cents to $1.52, and the trader profited from both legs of the spread. His net gain on the position was 79½ cents per bushel ($1.52 − $0.72½) or $3,975 per spread ($0.79½ × 5,000 bushels).

Wheat Futures	Corn Futures	Spread
Jun 29 Buys 1 Dec wheat futures at $4.15/bu	Sells 1 Dec corn futures at $3.42½/bu	$0.72½
Nov 2 Sells 1 Dec wheat futures at $4.41/bu	Buys 1 Dec corn futures at $2.89/bu	$1.52
Result $0.26 gain/bu $3,975 on the spread ($0.79½ × 5,000 bu)	$0.53½ gain/bu	$0.79½

Commodity Versus Product Spreads

A special type of intercommodity spread is the spread between a commodity and its products. The most common example, the spread between the soybean and its two products—soybean meal and soybean oil—is known as *putting on the crush* or a *crush spread*. This spread is often used by soybean-processing firms to hedge the purchase price of soybeans and the selling price of soybean oil and meal. It is established by purchasing soybean futures and selling soybean oil and soybean meal futures.

Putting on the Crush

The crush spread is used to minimize the financial risks of sudden increases in soybean costs and/or declining values of finished soybean oil and meal. To make a profit from soybean processing, soybeans must be purchased at a lower cost than the combined sales income from the finished oil and meal. The difference, or profit margin, is called the *gross processing margin (GPM)*. Application of the GPM to the soybean, soybean oil, and soybean meal futures markets makes it possible for processors to buy soybean futures to hedge later purchases of cash soybeans and, at the same time, sell soybean oil and meal futures to hedge later sales of meal and oil. (For more information on the GPM, see Chapter 13 on agricultural commodities.)

Given a favorable price relationship between soybean futures and soybean oil and meal futures, the processor buys soybean futures and simultaneously sells oil and meal futures. He holds the long soybean portion of his hedge until he actually buys the required cash soybeans.

Suppose, as the processor feared, the price of soybeans in the cash market has risen. He is still relatively unaffected because the futures price of soybeans also rose in response to the same economic factors. He buys soybeans in the cash market and offsets his long soybean position—at the higher price—by selling an equal number of soybean futures contracts. This approximately offsets the increased cost of his raw material.

The processor holds the short side of his crush hedge—the sale of oil and meal futures—until he is ready to sell his finished oil and meal. If the cash market values of oil and meal decline, the futures prices probably will decline also. Although the processor receives less income from his cash market sale of the oil and meal, this loss is roughly offset by his equal purchase of oil and meal futures contracts at lower prices.

The hedge works in the same way and for the same reasons as do all well-placed hedges—because of the tendency of cash and futures prices, which are influenced by the same economic factors, to move in the same direction. But the crush spread is a uniquely effective hedge because it affords the soybean processor protection in three related markets.

Reverse Crush

The opposite of a crush spread is called a *reverse crush*. This spreading opportunity results from distortions in normal price patterns when the cost of soybeans is higher than the combined sales value of soybean oil and meal. The resulting unfavorable gross processing margin makes it unprofitable for the soybean processor to manufacture meal and oil.

When the GPM drops below a profitable level, a soybean processor may slow down or even stop his manufacturing operation, and at the same time possibly initiate a reverse crush spread—selling soybean futures and buying oil and meal futures. Of course, this firm would not be alone in this action, and the concerted pressure of reduced soybean meal and oil manufacturing and a reverse crush spread in the futures market will gradually reverse the price relationships to a more normal level.

SPREADING IN FINANCIAL INSTRUMENT FUTURES

The differences between spreading in ag futures and in financial futures are slight. In fact, there is a strong similarity. As an example, the cost of carry becomes a dominant factor to consider in both grain and interest rate spreads.

With interest rate futures, the cost of carry is determined by the differential between the yield on the cash instrument under consideration and the cost of funds necessary to buy the instrument. For instance, if short-term rates are higher than long-term rates (an inverted yield curve), there is an actual cost associated with buying a financial instrument and holding it over time. Since a holder of cash bonds yielding 12 percent loses money when financing at 14 percent, he must receive a premium on resale at a later date just to recoup the cost of carry. (For more information on cost of carry and yield curves, see Chapters 8 and 17.)

The futures market tends to reflect this cash market scenario with the deferred months priced higher than the nearby, i.e., negative cost of carry. If a futures trader expected the market to normalize (short-term rates lower than long-term rates), he could initiate a spread. Financial traders watch the relationship between short- and long-term interest rates, and depending upon their market expectations will decide whether or not to put on a spread.

Types of Financial Instrument Spreads

Within the financial markets, the three primary types of spreads are interdelivery, intermarket, and intercommodity.

Interdelivery (or Intramarket) Spreads
Spreads between different delivery months of the same futures market on the same exchange—e.g., the sale (purchase) of December T-bonds and the purchase (sale) of March T-bonds.

Intermarket Spreads
Intermarket spreading involves taking opposite positions simultaneously in two similar markets at two different exchanges. Common intermarket spreads include the Major Market Index/S&P 500 futures—buying (selling)

Major Market Index futures and selling (buying) S&P 500 futures—and the LIFFE/CBOT bond spread—buying (selling) Chicago T-bond futures and selling (buying) London T-bond futures.

Intercommodity Spreads

An intercommodity spread consists of buying one commodity and selling a different, but related, commodity—e.g., selling (buying) Municipal Bond Index futures and buying (selling) T-bond futures (commonly called the MOB—Munis Over Bonds), or buying (selling) 10-Year T-note futures and selling (buying) T-bond futures (referred to as the NOB—Notes Over Bonds).

Interdelivery spreads can be divided into two groups: the bull spread and the bear spread. A bull spread can be referred to as *buying the spread* and a bear spread can be referred to as *selling the spread.*

Interdelivery or Intramarket Spreads

Bull Spread

In a financial bull spread, a trader is long the nearby contract and short the deferred contract. A trader holding a bull spread is looking for the price of the nearby contract to rise faster than the deferred futures contract in a bull market. Conversely, if the market prices are declining, the trader expects the nearby month to fall slower than the deferred month.

As an example, suppose a trader has been watching the T-bond futures market for several months. By mid-March, June T-bonds were at 70-10 and September bonds were at 70-03, making the June/September spread 00-07 (June minus September). He expects the spread to become more positive as the demand for credit is easing due to a softening of the economy. In other words, the trader anticipates the net cost of carry to become more positive with the nearby contract (June) rising faster than the deferred (September). So, he initiates a bull spread, purchasing the nearby month and selling the deferred month.

In April, as he expected, interest rates dropped and bond prices rose. By May 9, the June bonds rose to 75-16 and September bonds increased to 74-10 for a spread difference of 1-06. The trader then decided to unwind the spread by selling three June contracts and purchasing three September contracts:

Jun Futures	Sep Futures	Spread
Mar 14 Buys 3 Jun T-bond contracts at 70-10	Sells 3 Sep T-bond contracts at 70-03	00-07
May 9 Sells 3 Jun T-bond contracts at 75-16	Buys 3 Sep T-bond contracts at 74-10	01-06
Result 05-06 or $^{166}\!/_{32}$ gain $166 \times \$31.25 =$ $\$5,187.50 \times 3 =$ $\$15,562.50$	04-07 or $^{135}\!/_{32}$ loss $135 \times \$31.25 =$ $-\$4,218.75 \times 3 =$ $-\$12,656.25$	00-31

Net gain = $2,906.25 on the spread
$\qquad$ (31 × $31.25 × 3 contracts)

In this bull spread, the trader made a profit, since the price of the nearby contract (June) rose faster than the price of the deferred contract (September).

Bear Spread

The bear spread is the opposite of a bull spread. In a financial bear spread, a trader is short the nearby month and long the deferred month. A trader holding a bear spread anticipates the price of the deferred contract to rise faster than the nearby futures contract in a bull market. Conversely, if the market prices are declining, the trader expects the deferred month to fall slower than the nearby month.

For instance, a spread trader noticed that from May through August interest rates were fairly stable with short-term rates lower than long-term rates. Then, by the end of August, the market inverted as short-term interest rates rose above long-term rates. The futures market reflected this change with the nearby month (December) trading at a discount to the deferred (March). At the time, the spread difference was −00-14. The spread remained negative through October but rose to −00-05.

He expects the spread to become more negative as the demand for short-term credit is rising in conjunction with increased economic activity. In other words, the trader anticipates the cost of carry to become more negative with the deferred contract (March) gaining on the nearby contract (December). So, he initiates a bear spread buying two March contracts at 72-13 and selling two December contracts at 72-08.

Between October 17 and November 21, bond prices decreased and the December/March spread declined substantially. By November 18, the spread was −00-31, and by November 21 it had fallen to −1-01. With steadily declining open interest in the December contract one week ahead of the first delivery day, the trader decided to unwind the spread:

Dec Futures	Mar Futures	Spread
Oct 17		
Sells 2 Dec T-bond contracts at 72-08	Buys 2 Mar T-bond contracts at 72-13	−00-05
Nov 21		
Buys 2 Dec T-bond contracts at 67-30	Sells 2 Mar T-bond contracts at 68-31	−01-01
Result		
4-10 or $^{138}\!/_{32}$ gain	3-14 or $^{110}\!/_{32}$ loss	= −00-28
$138 \times \$31.25 =$	$110 \times \$31.25 =$	
$\$4,312.50 \times 2 =$	$−\$3,437.50 \times 2 =$	
$\$8,625$	$−\$6,875$	

Net gain = $1,750 on the spread
(28 × $31.25 × 2 contracts)

The spreader was correct in his market expectations: the cost of carry became more negative with the price of the deferred month (March) falling slower than the nearby month (December).

Another common interdelivery spread is a butterfly spread. A butterfly spread involves the placing of two interdelivery spreads in opposite directions with the center delivery month common to both spreads. Two examples of a butterfly spread are:

Butterfly Spread

♦ Long 3 Mar T-bonds/short 6 Jun T-bonds/long 3 Sep T-bonds
♦ Short 3 Mar T-bonds/long 6 Jun T-bonds/short 3 Sep T-bonds

A butterfly spread actually can be divided into two interdelivery spreads, e.g., long March T-bonds and short June T-bonds; short June T-bonds and long September T-bonds. The first example can be classified as a bull spread (long March bonds and short June bonds) together with a bear spread (short June bonds and long September bonds). The second example, on the other hand, is actually a bear spread (short March bonds and long June bonds) followed by a bull spread (long June bonds and short September bonds).

One reason a trader may be interested in establishing a butterfly spread is because he believes the price of the middle contract is out of line to the contract months on each side.

Intermarket Spreads

Intermarket spreading involves taking opposite positions simultaneouly in two similar markets at two different exchanges. As mentioned earlier in the chapter, there are a variety of financial intermarket spreads. An example of a stock index intermarket spread follows.

Stock Index Intermarket Spreads

All stock indexes reflect general market risk and, therefore, tend to move in the same direction over time. Because the indexes move in the same direction, spreaders base their trading strategies on the strength of one contract relative to another rather than speculating on overall market direction.

A stock index contract is strong relative to another if it advances faster during a bull market rally or declines slower in a bear market. For example, if a trader anticipates that the Major Market Index (MMI) will be strong relative to the NYSE Composite, he would buy the MMI and sell the NYSE Composite. Regardless of the direction of the market, the trader profits from this spread position as long as the MMI advances faster in a bull market or declines slower in a bear market.

The performance of different stock index futures contracts varies in certain phases of the market due to the nature of the underlying stocks. The MMI, for example, is a narrower-based, blue-chip composite, while the New York Stock Exchange (NYSE) Composite Index consists of all the stocks listed on the New York Stock Exchange. Historically, blue-chip stocks often tend to lead the rest of the market in the early stages of a bull market, and, as the bull market matures, individual investors often rush to buy the more affordable secondary and OTC issues, causing that segment to catch up to the blue chips. As the bull market nears its end, buying of blue chips levels off, while activity in secondary issues typically continues to increase. Because of these fundamental factors, the MMI tends to move first in a bull or bear market, and, as the market matures, NYSE Composite buying increases.

Stock index intermarket spread trades are usually done in one of two ways: (1) by matching total contract values (the dollar multiplier times the index point level) or (2) by equating just the dollar multipliers. An example of the latter would be spreading two MMIs ($250 multiplier) against one NYSE Composite ($500 multiplier). This 2:1 spread makes it easy for the trader to quickly determine the status of his position, since a one-point move in the spread equals $500.

As an example of an intermarket spread, assume a trader forecasts a bull stock market and expects the MMI to gain on the NYSE Composite.

He buys two MMI futures each at 461.85 and sells one NYSE Composite contract at 168.00, for a spread difference of 293.85. At a later date, the spread increases to 298.50, and the trader closes his positions by selling two MMI contracts at 471.45 and buying one NYSE Composite contract at 172.95.

MMI Futures	NYSE Composite Futures	Spread
Now		
Buys 2 Dec MMI contracts at 461.85	Sells 1 Dec NYSE Composite contract at 168.00	293.85
Later		
Sells 2 Dec MMI contracts at 471.45	Buys 1 Dec NYSE Composite contract at 172.95	298.50
Result		
9.60 point gain × $250 × 2 = $4,800 gain	4.95 point loss × $500 = $2,475 loss	4.65 point gain × $500 = $2,325

In this scenario, the trader made a profit because the MMI contract, which gained 9.60 points, rose faster in the bull market than did the NYSE Composite contract, which gained 4.95 points.

In the futures markets, intermarket spreading is often loosely referred to as *arbitrage*—the purchase and sale of similar commodities in two different markets to take advantage of a price discrepancy. By performing this economic function, arbitrageurs increase the efficiency of the markets by narrowing the gap between bid and offer prices and minimizing price distortions between similar markets.

Typical arbitrage trading examples include cash and futures spreads between similar instruments, spreads between futures of the same type of commodity or security trading at different exchanges (e.g., Chicago Board of Trade gold versus COMEX gold), and spreads between markets in different countries (e.g., Chicago Board of Trade T-bonds versus London International Financial Futures Exchange T-bonds).

Intercommodity spreads normally are traded between two different, but closely related, futures markets. These markets tend to have a strong price correlation because they respond to the same economic and financial factors, may have comparable terms to maturity, and generally have somewhat comparable risk/return relationships. Two of the most actively traded intercommodity spreads among financial instruments are the MOB

Arbitrage

Intercommodity Spreads

(Munis Over Bonds, i.e., Munis minus T-bonds) and the NOB (10-year Notes Over Bonds).

The MOB Spread

The MOB (Munis Over Bonds) spread takes advantage of price differences between the Municipal Bond Index futures contract and Treasury bond futures.

The strategy consists of buying muni-bond futures and selling T-bond futures (buying the MOB) when an investor expects municipal bonds to gain on government bonds. Conversely, an investor anticipating government bonds to gain on municipal bonds would sell muni-bond futures and buy T-bond futures (selling the MOB).

Assume a spreader expected the MOB spread to become less positive and decided to sell the MOB. With December muni futures at 87-18 and December T-bond futures at 79-15, the spreader sold one muni contract and bought one T-bond contract. As expected, both contracts rallied, but T-bonds rose faster than munis, so the trader decided it was time to offset his position by selling one T-bond contract and buying one muni-bond contract.

Muni-bond Futures	T-bond Futures	Spread
Now		
Sells 1 muni-bond contract at 87-18	Buys 1 T-bond contract at 79-15	08-03
Later		
Buys 1 muni-bond contract at 89-29	Sells 1 T-bond contract at 83-10	06-19
Result		
02-11 loss	03-27 gain	01-16

Net gain = $^{48}/_{32}$ or $1,500 on the spread
(48 × $31.25 × 1 contract)

The NOB

The NOB refers to the spread between 10-Year T-note futures and T-bond futures. Since intermediate-term note prices usually are higher than long-term bond prices, the spread is called the *NOB*—Notes Over Bonds (notes minus T-bonds).

NOB spread strategies take advantage of the different price sensitivities of 10-Year notes and T-bonds to changes in interest rates—that is, bond prices are more sensitive than note prices to changes in interest rates. Depending on interest rate expectations, a trader can either buy or sell the

NOB. For example, to take advantage of rising interest rates—the spread becoming more positive—a spreader would buy the NOB (purchasing T-note futures and selling T-bond futures). On the other hand, an investor can take advantage of falling interest rates and a spread becoming more negative by selling the NOB (selling T-notes and buying T-bond futures contracts).

The information presented in this chapter just scratches the surface regarding the topics of spreads. Keep in mind that the primary purpose of this chapter is to give the reader a basic understanding of how spreads are established, the advantages of trading spreads, and the price relationships between different futures contracts. (For more information about the different types of spreads and their price relationships, see the Sources of Information in the Appendix. Options spreads are covered in Chapter 12.)

Conclusion

> **Note:** The examples listed in this chapter are for the sole purpose of illustrating interdelivery, intermarket, and inter-commodity spreads and are not meant as recommendations for trading strategies.

Options on futures contracts have added a new dimension to futures trading. Like futures, options provide price protection against an adverse price move. But unlike futures hedgers, option hedgers are not locked in to a specific floor or ceiling price, and can take advantage of a market trend. In addition, the variety of trading strategies available with options or in combination with futures makes options attractive to a wide base of investors.

Options on futures contracts were introduced in October 1982 when the Chicago Board of Trade began trading options on Treasury bond futures. They were initially offered as part of a government pilot program, and the success of this contract opened the way for options on agricultural and other financial futures contracts.

Trading in options is not new. Options traditionally have been used with underlying cash securities, such as stocks, as well as with physicals, such as precious metals and real estate. There was over-the-counter trading in options on shares of common stock long before the creation in the mid-1970s of centralized exchange trading in stock options. Participants in the stock options markets are primarily investors seeking to profit, on a leveraged basis, from anticipated movements in common stock prices. Many of the principles that apply to options trading in the cash market can be used effectively with futures contracts.

OPTIONS ON FUTURES CONTRACTS

Risk-Management Alternatives

12

OPTION BASICS

What Is an Option?

An option provides a choice. The buyer of an option acquires the right, but not the obligation, to buy or sell an underlying commodity (whether it is a physical commodity, security, or futures contract) under specific conditions in exchange for the payment of a premium. Within the futures industry, the underlying instrument is a futures contract.

Calls and Puts

There are two types of options: calls and puts. A *call option* gives the buyer the right, but not the obligation, to *purchase* a particular futures contract at a specific price anytime during the life of the option. A *put option* gives the buyer the right, but not the obligation, to *sell* a particular futures contract at a specific price anytime during the life of the option.

The price at which the buyer of a call has the right to purchase a futures contract and the buyer of a put has the right to sell a futures contract is known as the *strike price* or *exercise price.*

In options trading, it is important to understand that trading in call options is completely distinct from trading in put options. For every call buyer, there is a call seller; for every put buyer, there is a put seller.

Offset and Exercise

If someone purchases a call option, the only way to offset the position is by selling the same call option contract. Conversely, if someone purchases a put option, the only way to offset the position is by selling the same put option. The same is true for an option seller. If an option seller wants to offset his short position, he buys back an option at the same strike price and expiration date—a specific day preceding the futures contract delivery month.

Both buyers and sellers may offset an open option position any time prior to its expiration. However, only option buyers may *exercise* the contract, i.e., acquire a futures position at the option strike price. An option can be exercised on any trading day up to and including its last day of trading, which is usually the day before the actual expiration day of the option.

Once the buyer of a put or call exercises the option, the exchange where the contract is traded records an open futures position for the designated contract month at the strike price in the accounts of the buyer and the seller. The table on the next page illustrates the positions assigned to an option buyer and seller after an option is exercised.

Premium

In the case of either a call or put, the option buyer (option holder) must pay the option seller (option writer) a premium. This is the only

Futures Positions After Option Exercise		
	Call Option	**Put Option**
Buyer Assumes	Long futures position	Short futures position
Seller Assumes	Short futures position	Long futures position

variable of the contract and is determined on the trading floor of an exchange depending on market conditions, such as supply, demand, and other economic and market variables.

Regardless of how much the market swings, the most an option buyer can lose is the option premium. He deposits the premium with his broker, and the money goes to the option seller. Because of this limited and known risk, option buyers are not required to maintain margin accounts.

Option sellers, on the other hand, face similar risks as participants in the futures market.

For example, since the seller of a call is assigned a short futures position if the option is exercised, his risk is the same as someone who initially sold a futures contract. Because no one can predict exactly how the market will move, the option seller posts margin to demonstrate his ability to meet any potential contractual obligations.

Marking-to-Market

Following the conclusion of each trading session, each seller's option position is marked-to-market to reflect the gains or losses from that particular trading session. If there is a significant adverse price move, the seller may have to post additional margin before the start of the next day's trading to maintain the open position.

Furthermore, option margins are set by the exchange where the contract is traded at a level high enough to guarantee the financial integrity of the marketplace without unduly increasing the cost of participation to the investor. During conditions of high price volatility, futures exchanges raise margins; as price volatility decreases, these margins are lowered.

Margins

OPTION PRICING

Even though the marketplace is the ultimate determinant of how much an option is worth, there are some basic guidelines traders use to calculate option premiums. In general, an option premium is the sum of intrinsic and time value, which are influenced by volatility, the difference between a strike price and the underlying price, and time to maturity.

Intrinsic Value

Intrinsic value is the difference, if any, between the market price of the underlying commodity and the strike price of an option. A call option has intrinsic value if its strike price is below the futures price. A put option has intrinsic value if its strike price is above the futures price. Any option that has intrinsic value is referred to as being *in-the-money*.

For example, if corn futures were trading at $3 a bushel, a corn call option with a $2.50 strike price gives the holder the right to purchase corn futures at $2.50 a bushel. If he exercises his call, the option holder realizes a 50-cent profit ($3 − $2.50). A call option with a strike price less than the current futures price is said to be *in-the-money*.

If corn futures were trading at $3 a bushel, a corn put option with a $3.50 strike price gives the holder the right to sell corn futures at $3.50. If he exercises his put, the option holder realizes a 50-cent profit ($3.50 − $3). A put option with a strike price greater than the current futures price is said to be *in-the-money*.

A call option with a strike price above the current market price is said to be *out-of-the-money*. For instance, if an option buyer is holding a $3.50 corn call option, he has the right to buy corn futures at $3.50. But, if the futures price is trading at $3, he would be better off to buy corn futures at the lower price of $3 a bushel rather than exercising his option to buy at $3.50.

A put option with a strike price below the current market price is said to be *out-of-the-money*. If an option buyer is holding a $2.50 corn put, he has the right to sell corn futures at $2.50. But, if corn futures are trading at $3, his put option is not worth exercising, since he can sell corn futures for a higher price in the futures market.

When the strike price of any put or call option equals the current market price, the option is said to be *at-the-money*. With corn futures at $3 a bushel, a $3 call or $3 put option has no intrinsic value.

A summary of the intrinsic value of different put and call options is listed in the table on the next page.

Delta and Gamma

Two sensitivity measures associated with an option premium are delta and gamma. Delta measures how much an option premium changes, given a unit change in the underlying futures. Delta often is interpreted as the

Calculating Intrinsic Value

	Call Option	Put Option
In-the-Money	Futures > Strike	Futures < Strike
At-the-Money	Futures = Strike	Futures = Strike
Out-of-the-Money	Futures < Strike	Futures > Strike

probability that the underlying futures price will move in-the-money by expiration. Gamma measures how fast delta changes and is defined as the change in delta, given a unit change in the underlying futures price.

The second major component of an option premium is time value. *Time value* is the amount of money that option buyers are willing to pay for an option in the anticipation that over time a change in the underlying futures price will cause the option to increase in value. Of course, since there are sellers as well as buyers in the market, time value also reflects the price that sellers are willing to accept for writing an option.

In general, the more time remaining until expiration, the greater the time value. That is because the right to purchase or sell something is more valuable to a market participant if he has a year to decide what to do with the option rather than just six months. Conversely, an option buyer is asking the seller to face the risk of exercise, and a year's worth of risk costs more than six months' worth.

Some parallels can be drawn between the time value of an option premium and the premium charged for a casualty insurance policy. The longer the term of the insurance policy, the greater the probability a claim will be made by the policyholder, thus, the greater the risk assumed by the insurance company. To compensate for this increased risk, the insurer will charge a greater premium. The same is true with options on futures—the longer the term until option expiration, the greater the risk to the option seller, hence, the higher the option premium.

Volatility

Volatility of the underlying commodity is one of the more important factors affecting the value of the option premium. Volatility measures the change in price over a given time period. It is often expressed as a percentage and computed as the annualized standard deviation of percentage changes in daily prices.*

Time Value

---

*Vega is a pricing variable that measures the net change in an option premium, given a 1 percent change in the volatility based on actual option prices.

Time Decay

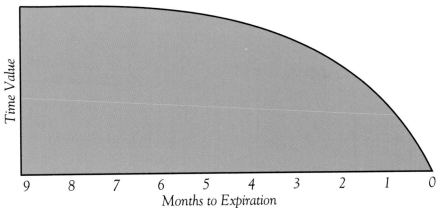

Months to Expiration

As the chart illustrates, when an option approaches expiration, its time value erodes faster (all else being equal) because there is less time for the option to move in-the-money. At expiration, an option has no time value; its only value, if any, is intrinsic value. One option pricing derivative, theta, measures the rate at which an option value decreases with the passage of time, i.e., how fast the slope in the time decay chart changes. Many traders use theta when they are selling options to gauge their potential profit or when they are buying options to measure their exposure to time decay.

While there are several mathematical models that compute volatility, the basic theory behind its influence on price is simple. Volatile prices of the underlying futures contract increase the probability that an option will move in-the-money, thereby increasing the option premium. The more volatile the price of the underlying commodity, the greater the chance of an adverse price move; thus, buyers are willing to pay more, and option sellers facing the risk of exercise require higher premiums.

For instance, if silver futures are trading for $6 an ounce and remain at that price for a year, there is little risk in selling a $6.50 call option. But, if silver futures trade between $5.25 and $6.75 an ounce during the same week, there is a greater risk that the $6.50 call will run in-the-money. The option seller must be paid for taking on the risk the option buyer requests, so the option premium should be greater than the same call in a less volatile market.

Option Pricing Models

There are many option pricing models that take these different variables—intrinsic value, time remaining to expiration, and volatility—into account (as well as other factors such as short-term interest rates) to calculate the theoretical value of an option. These theoretical values may or may not correspond to the actual market values in the pit, but are used by traders as a price gauge.

One of the most prominent option pricing models is the Black-Scholes, developed by Fischer Black and Myron Scholes in 1973. Different option pricing models also calculate the value of delta, gamma, vega, and other pricing variables. (While it is beyond the scope of this text to describe how the Black-Scholes or any other option pricing model works, there are several texts that cover this topic in depth and some of them are listed in the Appendix.)

Option Strategies

Options are used in all market environments—bullish, slightly bullish, bearish, slightly bearish, and neutral. In no way can all of them be covered in this chapter, but, in reviewing those that are discussed, the reader will gain a basic appreciation of why call and put options are bought and sold daily.

Since a call gives the buyer the right to buy a futures contract at a fixed price, a call option buyer believes futures prices will rise by at least enough to cover the premium he paid. In some situations, a trader might buy a call to establish a maximum price for the future purchase of a cash commodity or to cover a short futures position.

Buying Call Options

Using Calls for Protection Against Higher Prices
For example, a treasurer of an investment firm anticipates having funds available at a later date to purchase U.S. Treasury bonds. However, the treasurer is worried that between now and the time he purchases the bonds, interest rates may decline, raising bond prices. He would like to have temporary insurance against a sudden price increase, but also wants to avoid paying too much if bond prices decline. To achieve both price protection and an opportunity to purchase bonds at a lower rate, the treasurer decides to buy a call option.

Suppose in May the price of a specific cash Treasury bond is 87-00. A September 86-00 call is purchased by the treasurer for $1,500. By August, interest rates on long-term Treasury bonds have declined and the price of the cash bond is 96-00, and the September 86-00 call is priced at $10,100. He decides to offset his position by selling the September 86-00 call.

By selling back his call option for $10,100, the treasurer makes an $8,600 gain ($10,100 − $1,500) and offsets most of the increased cost in the price of T-bonds.

Cash	Options
May Price of T-bonds is 87-00	Buys Sep 86-00 call option for $1,500
Aug Price of T-bonds is 96-00	Sells Sep 86-00 call option for $10,100
Result $9,000 (or 9-00) loss	$8,600 gain

A major advantage of this strategy is that the treasurer established an interest rate floor, but not a ceiling. Had interest rates increased instead of decreased, the treasurer could have purchased T-bonds at a lower price and either let the option expire or offset his option position to earn any remaining time value. The only cost for this price protection was the option premium.

Buying Put Options

Bearing in mind that a put is an option to sell a futures contract at a fixed price, a put option buyer expects futures prices to decline by enough to cover the premium. In many cases, a market participant might buy a put to establish a minimum price for the future sale of a cash commodity or to cover a long futures position.

Using Puts for Protection Against Lower Prices

Assume a feed manufacturer expects soybean meal prices to rise, so he contracts ahead for all his soybean meal needs during the spring and summer months. Prices do trend higher for a short time, but after hitting $165 per ton in mid-April, it appears that prices could drop sharply.

Fearing that competitors might pass along any cost savings to their customers and gain market share, the manufacturer buys an August $160 soybean meal put option for $4.40. By mid-June, soybean meal prices have fallen to $148, so the company sells back the put for $12.50 and makes a profit of $8.10 per ton.

The feed manufacturer uses the $8.10 per ton profit from the put to keep his selling price for feed competitive. If soybean meal prices moved higher, the manufacturer could have let the put option expire or offset his option position to earn any remaining time value. The only cost for this price protection was the option premium.

Cash	Options
Mid-Apr	
Soybean meal price is $165	Buys Aug $160 put option for $4.40
Mid-June	
Soybean meal price is $148	Sells Aug $160 put option for $12.50
Result	
$17 loss	$8.10 gain

The primary reason for a trader to sell either a call or put option is to earn the option premium.

Selling Call and Put Options

Generally, call options are sold by individuals who anticipate either little price movement or a slight decrease in prices. In any case, they hope the underlying futures price will not rise to a level that will cause the option to be exercised and result in a loss greater than the premium received.

Those who sell put options, on the other hand, generally expect prices to stay the same or increase only slightly. Sellers of put options hope the underlying futures price will not fall to a level that will cause the option to be exercised and result in a loss greater than the premium received.

Market Expectations for Option Buyers and Sellers

	Call Option	Put Option
Buyer	Bullish	Bearish
Seller	Neutral to slightly bearish	Neutral to slightly bullish

Selling Calls to Earn the Option Premium

At a time when the futures price is 76-00 for Treasury bonds, an investor collects a premium of $3,000 by selling a six-month, at-the-money call. Since an at-the-money call, by definition, has no intrinsic value, the $3,000 premium is entirely time value. If the futures price at expiration is at or below 76-00, the option will expire worthless—with neither intrinsic value nor time value—and the investor's return will be the original $3,000 premium.

If the futures price at expiration is above 76-00, the option seller stands to realize some net return at expiration as long as the intrinsic value of the option is less than the premium received when the option was sold. Assume the futures price has risen to 78-00 by expiration. The option buyer exercises the call and the option seller incurs a $2,000 loss on the short futures position. However, since the initial premium received by the option seller was $3,000, his net gain is $1,000.

As stated earlier in the chapter, an option seller wishing to liquidate a position prior to exercise or expiration can make an offsetting option purchase at the prevailing premium. To whatever extent the erosion of the option's time value has reduced the cost of the offsetting purchase, the seller realizes a net profit.

What if three months after the investor sold the 76-00 call, the futures price is still 76-00, but the option's time value has declined to $2,000? By making an offsetting purchase at this price, the option seller realizes a net gain of $1,000. This purchase eliminates any further possibility of the option being exercised.**

Selling Puts for Limited Protection Against Higher Prices

When prices are likely to remain relatively stable, or when the expected price increase is fairly small, a hedger may find it worthwhile to sell a put option. By selling a put option, the seller receives a premium from the buyer and enters the hedge with a credit to his account. But the seller also faces the risk that the buyer may exercise the option if the futures price falls below the option strike price.

Suppose in late March a company that produces pet food and livestock feed expects soybean meal prices to move sideways in a fairly narrow range around the current price of $146 a ton. Wanting only limited protection against rising prices, the company sells a September $140 soybean meal put option and receives a premium of $8.55 a ton.

The market remains relatively quiet during the spring and summer months, with the price at $148 in early August. Therefore, the company pays 95 cents to buy back the put option for a gain of $7.60 a ton.

Since the market price of soybean meal rose slightly, the company is able to buy back the put option at a lower premium† and use the profit to partially offset the higher ingredient costs.

An option can be exercised **only by the option buyer any time before expiration. Although gains on in-the-money options are often realized through offsetting option sales, and the majority of exercises do not occur until at or near expiration, early exercise remains the prerogative of every option buyer.

†The premium for a put option tends to move in the opposite direction from the price of the underlying futures contract.

Cash	Options
Late Mar	
Price of soybean meal is $146	Sells Sep $140 put for $8.55
Early Aug	
Price of soybean meal is $148	Buys Sep $140 put for $0.95
Result	
$2 loss	$7.60 gain

If futures prices had fallen, the premium of the put option would have risen. In this case, the option seller who buys back the put option could have suffered a loss. But ingredient prices also would have fallen, partially offsetting the potential loss on the option position.

As the previous examples illustrate, there are a variety of ways options can be used to achieve either price protection or profits. While some option strategies can be as simple as either buying or selling one option, option strategies can become quite complicated and incorporate a combination of long and short options and/or futures and cash positions. Many of the more complicated option strategies fall under the category of spreads.

Other Option Strategies

An option spread is the simultaneous purchase and sale of one or more options contracts, futures, and/or cash positions. Since the prices of two different contracts for the same or related instruments have a tendency to move up or down together, spread trading can offer protection against losses that arise from unexpected or extreme price volatility.

Option Spreads

This occurs because losses from one side of a spread are more or less offset by gains from the other side of the spread. For example, if the short (sold) side of a spread results in a loss due to a price increase, the long (bought) side should produce a profit, offsetting much of the loss.

While option strategies allow a trader to limit the amount of risk he is carrying, other reasons for establishing option spreads are: to capitalize on a market environment where one option is overvalued or undervalued in relation to another; to hedge; or to enhance the return on investments.

Market participants have a variety of different option strategies at their fingertips to use in reaching their market objectives. These strategies can take into account different strike prices, futures prices, and expiration dates.

Vertical Spreads

Vertical spreads, sometimes referred to as *money spreads,* offer traders limited return with limited risk. They involve buying and selling puts or calls of the same expiration month but different strike prices. The four major types of vertical spreads are the bull put spread, the bull call spread, the bear put spread, and the bear call spread. Bull spreads are used when the trader expects a rising market, while bear spreads are used when the trader expects a declining market.

Bull call spread: Buying a call at one strike price and simultaneously selling a call at a higher strike price.

Example: Bull Call Spread for Moderate Price Protection

In late June, a baker is concerned that shortening prices might rise and reduce his expected profits from a cash contract he made to supply baked goods in December.

With the price of soybean oil at 17.2 cents a pound, he executes a bull call spread by purchasing a December 17-cent soybean oil call option for .96 cent a pound and simultaneously selling a December 18-cent soybean oil call option for .535 cent a pound.

By early September, soybean oil prices have risen to 17.8 cents, so he closes out the spread. He sells back the 17-cent call option for 1.285 cents, for a profit of .325 cent, and buys back the 18-cent call option for .55 cent, for a loss of .015 cent. When the results from both legs of the spread are combined, the hedger has a net gain of .31 cent a pound.

Cash	Options
Late Jun Soybean oil price is 17.2 cents	Buys Dec 17-cent call for .96 cent; sells Dec 18-cent call for .535 cent
Early Sep Soybean oil price is 17.8 cents	Sells Dec 17-cent call for 1.285 cents; buys Dec 18-cent call for .55 cent
Result .6-cent loss	.325-cent gain on Dec 17-cent call option; .015-cent loss on Dec 18-cent call; .31-cent net gain on spread

Bull put spread: Buying a put at one strike price and simultaneously selling a put at a higher strike price.

Bear call spread: Selling a call at one strike price and simultaneously buying a call at a higher strike price.

Bear put spread: Selling a put at one strike price and simultaneously buying a put with a higher strike price.

Horizontal Spreads

Horizontal spreads, also known as *calendar spreads*, offer traders the opportunity to profit from different time decay patterns associated with options of different maturities. Therefore, horizontal spreads involve the purchase of either a call or put option and the simultaneous sale of the same type of option with typically the same strike price but with a different expiration month. Because time value in a near-term option decays more rapidly than time value in a more distant option, a near-term option is often sold the same time a distant option is bought.

Horizontal spreads using calls often are employed when the long-term price expectation is stable to bullish, while horizontal spreads using puts often are employed when the long-term price expectation is stable to bearish.

Conversions

With a conversion, the trader buys a put option, sells a call option, and buys a futures contract. The put and call options have the same strike price and the same expiration month. The futures contract has the same expiration month as the options and its price should be as close as possible to the options' strike price. If the futures price is above the call strike price before expiration, the short call is exercised against the trader, which automatically offsets his long futures position; the long put option expires unexercised.

If the futures price falls below the put strike price before expiration, the long put option is exercised by the trader, which automatically offsets his long futures position; the short call option expires unexercised.

Example: Conversion Spread to Take Advantage of Price Discrepancies

Assume a 90-day $3 wheat put option is underpriced by a quarter of a cent at 10¼ cents, while a 90-day $3 wheat call option is correctly priced at 10½ cents, with the underlying futures at $3.

The trader establishes a conversion by purchasing an at-the-money put option for 10¼ cents, buying wheat futures at $3, and selling an at-the-money call option for 10½ cents. Under this market scenario, he is guaranteed a profit of a quarter of a cent a bushel, or $12.50 on the position (based on a 5,000-bushel contract). He retains this profit no matter what the price of the underlying futures contract is at expiration because the net debit[††] or net credit[††] from the conversion is always zero at expiration. See the calculations below.

		Credit (Debit)
Long 1 $3 put	$0.10¼	($512.50)
Short 1 $3 call	0.10½	525.00
Long 1 $3 futures	3.00	0
Net credit		$12.50

Futures price decreases to $2.50 at expiration:

		Credit (Debit)
Exercise 1 $3 put for 1 short futures	$0.50	$2,500
Abandon 1 $3 call	0.00	0
Offset 1 long futures by the exercise of the put option	2.50	(2,500)
Net debit/credit		0

Futures price remains at $3 at expiration:

		Credit (Debit)
Exercise 1 $3 put for 1 short futures	$0.00	0
Abandon 1 $3 call	0.00	0
Offset 1 long futures by the exercise of the put option	3.00	0
Net debit/credit		0

Futures price increases to $3.50 at expiration:

		Credit (Debit)
Exercise 1 $3 call for 1 short futures	$0.50	($2,500)
Abandon 1 $3 put	0.00	0
Offset 1 long futures by the call exercised against the trader	3.50	2,500
Net debit/credit		0

In this example, a conversion was initiated at a net credit. The return on a conversion can be calculated as follows:

Return on conversion = (call premium − put premium) − (futures price − strike price).

Reverse Conversions

In a reverse conversion, the trader buys a call option, sells a put option, and sells a futures contract. The put and call options have the same strike price and the same expiration month. The futures price also

[††]Net debit or net credit = (premium received − premium paid)

has the same expiration month and its price should be as close as possible to the options' strike price. If the futures price is above the strike price by expiration, the long call option is exercised by the trader, which automatically offsets his short futures position; the short put option expires unexercised. If the futures price falls below the strike price by expiration, the short put option is exercised against the trader, which automatically offsets his short futures position; the long call option expires unexercised.

Delta-neutral spreads, also known as *neutral* or *ratio hedges*, involve offsetting the profit/loss potential in one option position with that in one or more options/futures/cash positions.

Delta-Neutral Spreads

Ratio Hedge

Suppose an institution has scheduled several sales of Treasury bonds over the next few months even though bond prices are low and the weakness in the market is expected to continue.

The institution wants to obtain price protection against further declines in bond values that could sharply reduce proceeds from bond sales. In order to reach its market objective, the institution decides to employ a *ratio hedge*. In other words, put options are purchased and, subsequently, liquidated as cash bonds are sold and/or as bond prices change.

It should be recognized that this strategy requires continuous day-to-day management. As bonds are sold and as bond prices decrease or increase relative to the strike price of the options, the number of put options needed to maintain an effective hedge is subject to change. The complexity of the strategy can be justified, however, by its effectiveness when skillfully executed.

The management requirement consists of two components. The simpler and more obvious of these stems from the fact that once the institution no longer owns the assets, the institution no longer needs to protect its price. Thus, as bonds from a portfolio are sold, those put options purchased to provide protection can be sold. In effect, selling the puts cancels the protection.

Somewhat more involved are those adjustments required by changing bond prices. If bond futures prices decline, then fewer puts should be needed to maintain the hedge because the dollar value of the holdings is lower. Accordingly, some of the options can be sold.

The controlling variable (which an experienced options broker can explain in greater detail) is the option delta: the change in the option premium resulting from a one-unit change in the futures price. In general, the delta increases as an option moves in-the-money and decreases as an option moves out-of-the-money.

If the futures price decreases from 90-00 to 89-00 (a $1,000 decrease), it may be accompanied by a $500 increase in the premium of a put with a strike price of 90-00. The delta in this case is said to be .5. If there is a further decline in the futures price to 88-00 and the put option premium increases by $600, then the option delta would increase to .6.

The delta dictates the number of options needed to provide a "perfect" hedge, i.e., futures and options values move dollar for dollar. And as the delta changes, so does the necessary number of options for each bond being hedged. Specifically, the number needed to maintain a hedge at any given point in time is often calculated by dividing the conversion factor*** (for the particular bonds to be hedged) by the current option delta.

Assume the conversion factor for the bonds to be hedged (such as 10⅜ percent bonds of 2012) is 1.25 and that the option delta is .5. In this instance, 2.5 (1.25 divided by .5) puts per bond would be needed to provide a perfect hedge.

If a decline in the futures price results in an increase in the option delta to .7, then the number of options needed to maintain the hedge would be reduced to 1.8 (1.25 divided by .7). Some of the puts originally bought then could be sold.

A changing option delta in a delta-neutral hedge can work to the advantage of the institution, particularly if there is a significant movement in interest rates and bond prices. Reason: as bond prices fall below the strike price of the put options, an increase in the delta results in the options rising in value by an amount greater than the decrease in the value of the hedged bonds.

Assume the futures price is 90-00 and the delta for an at-the-money put is .5. To hedge against a decline in the value of ten 10⅜ percent bonds, an investor buys 25[†††] at-the-money puts. Under these assumptions, each $1,000 decrease in the value of the bonds should be offset by a $1,000 increase in the value of the options, i.e., a perfect hedge.

Suppose, however, that the decline in bond prices is sharper than expected and that the option delta becomes .7. Each $1,000 decrease in the value of the bonds then would be offset by more than a $1,000 increase in the value of the options.

More Information

It is not uncommon for those learning about options to be overwhelmed by their complexity. Keep in mind, then, that the primary purpose of including specific options strategies in this text is to give the reader an idea of the market possibilities available with options, and not to make anyone an options expert.

While this text gives the reader just a few examples of how options are used, there are many other textbooks devoted to options and their uses. (Some of these texts are listed in the Appendix.)

***The value of each cash market T-bond eligible for delivery against the T-bond futures contract is adjusted using a conversion factor to reflect a standard 8 percent coupon value.
[†††]Conversion factor of 1.25 divided by delta of .5 multiplied by 10 bonds equals 25.

This chapter explains some of the economic, political, and market factors affecting the price of a variety of agricultural commodities traded on U.S. futures exchanges. The information discussed is a general overview and should not be viewed as an all-inclusive study of agricultural commodities. (More information on particular commodities traded on U.S. futures exchanges, including contract specifications, is listed in the Appendix.)

AGRICULTURAL MARKETS

Grains,
Oilseeds,
Livestock

GRAINS

Several of the world's most important grains are traded on futures markets. They are commonly referred to as either *food* or *feed* grains. Grains such as corn and oats are used primarily as feed grains and, to a lesser extent, in manufactured foods. Rice is almost exclusively a food grain. Wheat also is generally grown and marketed for food uses, with a strong secondary demand as a feed grain.

Corn is unique among the grasses cultivated as grain cereals. It is used both for feed and as food, and is the only grain that originated in the Western Hemisphere. In fact, corn was unknown to the rest of the world until 1492, when Christopher Columbus returned to Europe with samples.

13

Within a generation, cultivation of corn spread to most farming areas of Europe; by the mid-1500s, corn was being grown in China. Worldwide, most corn is used for animal feed, but corn is a major part of the diet of the people of Mexico and Central America, and is raised by them mainly for food.

Corn	

Varieties of Corn

There are 100 to 150 corn varieties; farmers and commercial users have developed a grading system based on kernel tests.

Dent corn is the most common variety, accounting for 95 percent of U.S. corn production. Dent corn is named for the crease or trough that is formed in the top of the kernel by unequal shrinking of the starch components. Grain standards established for dent corn distinguish among Yellow, White, and Mixed. Yellow dominates all markets for livestock feed and for wet milling into flour and other products for human consumption and industrial uses. White corn is demanded by dry corn millers for flour production, for manufacturing hominy and grits, and for many industrial uses. Mixed corn—White and Yellow corn accidentally combined during storage—is seldom traded commercially and is used in livestock feed.

The other major American corn is Sweet corn; its kernels are predominately composed of starch, making it easy to chew. The chemical structure of still another type, Waxy corn, is well suited for certain wet milling processes. And, Squaw or Indian corn is used primarily for decorative purposes.

Corn Supply

Acreage and Yields

Acreage and yields are the major factors affecting corn production. The current practice by farmers of planting denser and narrower rows than in the past has resulted in a higher plant population per acre. The use of fertilizer, pesticides, and herbicides has helped minimize crop damage caused by insects and crop diseases. Also, hybrid seed has increased yields by about 20 percent.

Two of the chief factors governing yields are moisture and temperature. To bring a large corn crop to successful harvest, an even amount of moisture is needed throughout the summer months. July and August are the critical weather months for corn. Higher-than-normal rainfall favors high yields. Below-normal rainfall, especially during July, and higher-than-normal temperatures, particularly during August, tend to reduce yields.

Growing Season

The length of the growing season can be an important production factor. During spring, late frosts or exceptionally wet weather can delay planting and reduce potential yields. And, early fall frosts can critically stunt development of late-planted seedlings.

Most U.S. corn production is centered in the area known as the Corn Belt, which includes Illinois, Indiana, Iowa, Minnesota, Missouri, Nebraska, Ohio, and South Dakota. Corn planting in most of these key production states begins in early May, with Minnesota and the Dakotas planting later. The corn plant reaches maturity in late August with one or two developed ears; harvest usually begins about October 15, just after the first hard frost. By mid-November, most of the corn in the United States has been harvested. Each year more corn is harvested prior to October 1 due to earlier planting in March or April, so the United States Department of Agriculture (USDA) now designates September 1 to August 31 as the official corn crop year. Because October is the principal harvest month, December is the first futures contract month for the new-crop year.

U.S. Government Farm Programs

The structure of the U.S. agricultural program has remained the same since its inception as part of the Great Depression reforms in the 1930s. The major program tools for domestic grains remain: price supports, target price deficiency payments, and production control programs.

In the nonrecourse loan program (price supports), farmers place grain under loan for less than one year. The *loan rate* is the amount lent per unit of the commodity. If the local cash price rises enough to pay back the loan and cover the interest cost, the loan is likely repaid and the farmer redeems the grain for sale in the cash market. If it is not redeemed, the Commodity Credit Corporation (CCC)* takes title to the grain. Therefore, the CCC is a market of last resort, offering the farmer a guaranteed price.

In the case of target price deficiency payments, a target price above the loan rate is established for each commodity. If the market price fails to reach the target, the difference between the target and local cash prices (or between the target and the loan rate) is paid directly from the Treasury to the farmer. To become eligible for loan and deficiency payment programs, farmers may be required to set aside cropland.

Built into the government farm program is considerable discretionary authority for the Secretary of Agriculture and administering agencies. In many cases, the law establishes only minimum price levels for the most important programs, giving the Secretary of Agriculture authority to set higher price levels if warranted. Also, programs can be changed significantly from the original intent of the Congress. For example, the Payment-In-Kind (PIK) program of 1983 was not specifically authorized by the Farm Bill of 1981, but was implemented using discretionary authority.

To participate in PIK, farmers are required to comply with the voluntary acreage-control program and to set aside an additional percentage of acreage specified by the government. In return for not growing a

---

*The Commodity Credit Corporation (CCC) is a branch of the USDA that supervises the government's various farm loan and subsidy programs.

particular crop, the government pays the farmers with certificates that can be redeemed for government-owned stocks of grain.

The use of discretionary authority is a highly charged political issue. Typically, farm groups and segments of Congress pressure the Administration to make the programs more lucrative, while others exert pressure to use programs sparingly to hold down costs.

1985 *Farm Bill*

The current farm bill, The Food Security Act of 1985, attempts to support grain prices in ways that would avoid the costly buildup of huge supplies that depresses market prices and requires publicly financed storage. Loan rates and target prices have been scaled down, enhancing the ability of U.S. commodities to compete abroad. For 1987-90, the basic loan rates are 75 to 85 percent of the average of the season prices received by producers during the five preceding marketing years, dropping the years with the highest and lowest prices. In 1986-87, the target price for corn was $3.03 per bushel, and, for 1987-88, it was set at $2.97 per bushel.

Distribution of Corn in the United States
Millions of Bushels

Year Beg. Sept.	Wet-Milled Products					Dry-Milled Products		
	HFCS	Glucose & Dextrose	Starch	Alcohol Fuel	Alcohol Beverage	Alcohol Fuel	Alcohol Beverage	Alkaline Cooked Pdt's.
1982–3	215	188	127	100	30	40	10	170
1983–4	256	189	147	120	30	40	10	164
1984–5	310	187	143	140	30	90	10	160
1985–6	328	188	152	155	30	115	10	161
1986–7*	339	185	155	160	30	125	10	161

Year Beg. Sept.	Total Shipments	Seed	Feed	Exports	Total Use	Domestic Disappearance
1982–3	895	14.5	4,521	1,834	7,249	5,416
1983–4	975	19.1	3,818	1,902	6,694	4,793
1984–5	1,091	21.2	4,079	1,865	7,036	5,170
1985–6	1,160	19.5	4,095	1,241	6,496	5,255
1986–7*	1,191	15.6	4,717	1,504	7,412	5,908

*Preliminary
Source: Economics Research Service, USDA

Because of the discretionary nature of the U.S. farm bill and its myriad requirements, contact the USDA regarding the eligibility of corn for specific government programs.

Other countries also have specific policies regarding the production and price of agricultural commodities that ultimately affect the price of ag commodities worldwide.

Approximately 60 to 65 percent of the cash corn crop is used as livestock feed; in recent years, corn has accounted for 25 percent of all livestock feed. Because feed is typically the largest single cost item in raising livestock, the profitability of feeding corn is determined by its cost relative to the price of meat. When livestock-corn ratios are low, livestock feeders reduce their use of corn by adjusting the number of animals fed and the length of time livestock are kept on feed.

Two major factors account for the attractiveness of corn as an animal feed:

♦ It is generally good as a feed for fattening livestock and poultry because of its high starch content. In addition, it contains more oil than other cereal grains making it high in total energy.

♦ An acre of corn yields more animal feed in both grain and forage than any other crop, although it costs no more in labor to produce and harvest.

Because of the meat industry's traditional pattern of heavy corn consumption, any significant increase or decrease in animal production forces farmers to reevaluate their corn production.

Food and Industrial Uses

The manufacturing industry uses the entire corn plant to produce a variety of products. Paper and wallboard are made from the stalks. Husks are used as fillers. Cobs become fuel, charcoal, and industrial solvents. However, the grain kernel is the most valuable portion of the plant used commercially.

In wet milling, corn kernels are soaked in diluted sulfuric acid for 40 to 60 hours. Grinding and other operations then separate the hulls from the rest of the grain, which is further treated in various ways to produce corn oil, starches, dextrins, and syrups for human consumption, and adhesives, glues, textile fibers, soaps, sizings, paints, varnishes, explosives, and a host of other useful industrial products.

Dry milling, a process in which corn kernels are subjected to some spray or steam softening and then ground, is used largely for the production of cereals, flour, hominy, grits, feeds, and industrial products.

Consumption and Usage

Exports

Supply and demand factors in the principal exporting and importing nations have a significant impact on corn and its price. For instance, a bumper world corn crop might reduce foreign demand, lead to increased competition between U.S. and foreign corn producers, or both. On the other hand, a smaller world corn crop can cause increased demand for U.S. corn exports. Livestock price levels in other nations are another important factor affecting U.S. corn export demand. Low livestock prices abroad discourage feeding and lessen the demand for U.S. corn, conversely, higher livestock prices tend to increase demand.

The USDA estimated worldwide corn production in 1987-88 at over 440 million tons. The United States was the largest producer with an estimated production of 182 million tons in 1987-88—about 41 percent of the total world supply. U.S. corn exports were projected at nearly 2 billion bushels, up 13 percent from a year earlier—the highest level since 1984. Production in China, Brazil, and the Soviet Union follows the United States, however, China and the Soviet Union tend to also import large amounts of corn.

The fastest-growing markets for U.S. corn are South Korea, Mexico, and Japan, and sales to Eastern Europe have expanded.

Futures Markets

Corn futures and options on corn futures contracts are traded at the Chicago Board of Trade; the MidAmerica Commodity Exchange trades corn futures.

Wheat

Wheat is one of the world's oldest and most widely used food crops. First cultivated in Asia Minor nearly 9,000 years ago, wheat production gradually spread across much of Europe, Asia, and Africa. Wheat was introduced to the United States in the 1600s by early colonists who brought seeds with them from Europe. Wheat is now grown on every continent except Antarctica. World production for 1987-88 was estimated at 502 million metric tons.

Types of Wheat

Wheat is divided into two major types: winter and spring. Winter wheat is planted in the fall, becomes dormant during the winter, resumes growth in the spring, and is harvested in the summer. Spring wheat is planted in the spring and is harvested in the fall.

The five main classes of wheat grown in the United States are Hard Red Winter, Soft Red Winter, Hard Red Spring, Durum, and White. Each class is adapted to a particular set of growing conditions, is raised in a specific region, and has unique milling and baking properties.

The predominant class of wheat grown in the United States is Hard Red Winter—accounting for nearly half of all U.S. wheat produced in 1987-88. Hard Red Winter is grown in Kansas, Nebraska, Oklahoma, and the Texas Panhandle. The annual precipitation in this area of the country

Types of Wheat Grown in the United States

Soft Red Winter

Durum

Hard Red Spring

White

Hard Red Winter

Source: Wheat Flour Institute, Washington, D.C.

averages less than 25 inches, with frequent dry periods and winters that produce subzero temperatures. Flour from Hard Red Winter wheat is used primarily in bread.

The Soft Red Winter wheat belt extends from central Texas northeastward to the Great Lakes and then east to the Atlantic coast. Soft Red Winter wheat is generally grown in a subhumid climate, not conducive to the production of hard wheats. Soft Red Winter wheat production, estimated at 347 million bushels for 1987-88, accounted for 17 percent of total U.S. production. Flour from Soft Red Winter wheat is used in cakes, cookies, crackers, snack foods, and pastries.

Hard Red Spring wheat is grown principally in northern states where the winters are too severe for winter wheat production. The principal Hard Red Spring wheat districts have a fairly deep black soil and dry, hot summers, both important factors in the production of a high-grade wheat suitable for milling as bread flour. Hard Red Spring wheat production was estimated at 431 million bushels for 1987-88, approximately 20 percent of total U.S. production.

Durum, a spring wheat, is produced primarily in North Dakota and Montana. Durum kernels are extremely hard and contain the highest percentage of protein of any of the wheat classes.

Durum flour is used to make spaghetti, macaroni, and other pasta products and is not suitable for bread, cakes, or pastries. U.S. production of Durum wheat was estimated at nearly 93 million bushels or 5 percent of total production for 1987-88.

White wheat can be either spring or winter type, and is grown mainly in southern Michigan, western New York, and the Pacific Northwest. It is used much like Soft Red Winter wheat and is available in both winter and spring varieties. Estimated U.S. White wheat production for 1987-88 was 19 million bushels, almost 1 percent of total U.S. production.

Wheat Supply

Production Factors

The crop year in the United States for wheat is June 1 to May 31. Winter wheat usually is seeded in September or early October, whenever the soil has sufficient moisture to germinate the seed. At this time of the year, the danger of the seed being damaged from insects such as the Hessian fly is considerably less than in late summer.

At freezing temperatures, winter wheat enters a period of dormancy that lasts until warm weather returns. Ideally, a blanket of snow should cover the fields to insulate and protect the plants. If adequate snow cover is not present, wheat sometimes heaves, i.e., the stem is severed from the root system, due to alternate thawing and freezing of the soil.

In the spring, the head, which contains the kernels, develops on top of the stem. After the kernels have fully developed and filled, the color of the plant begins to change from green to gold. When the heads are sufficiently dried, the fields are ready to be harvested; this begins in late May and is usually completed by the middle of July.

In the northern United States, where winters are too severe for winter wheat, spring wheat is planted as early as possible in the spring. The dormancy period is eliminated, the crop matures in August, and harvesting is usually completed by early September.

Yield

Wheat yields can vary substantially from one class to another and from one country or state to another. During the 1987-88 crop year, winter wheat produced an average yield of almost 40 bushels to the acre, spring wheat varieties yielded an average of about 34 bushels an acre, and Durum wheat yielded an average of 28 bushels an acre.

U.S. Farm Policy and Programs

As with other agricultural commodities, U.S. government programs—price support targets, acreage set-aside programs, and loan programs—can have a major influence on wheat production and price levels. (For more information on this topic, see U.S. Government Farm Programs under the Corn section in this chapter.)

Consumption and Usage

Wheat Demand

Approximately 35 percent of the U.S. wheat crop is milled domestically for flour; about 55 percent is exported. Since 1970, less than 5 percent of each year's crop has been set aside for subsequent crop plantings. The balance is used for animal feeds and in industrial products.

During the past decade, domestic wheat millers have produced over 350 million bags of flour annually. A 100-pound bag of white flour requires the milling of a little more than two 60-pound bushels of wheat. (This conversion factor varies according to wheat quality and flour type.)

Since World War II, domestic flour consumption has declined at the retail level. However, escalating standards of living have caused consumer demand for commercially prepared products using wheat flours to increase. In recent years, per capita flour consumption has leveled at about 109 pounds annually; per capita cereal consumption has remained steady at less than 3 pounds.

World Production

U.S. wheat production for 1987-88 was estimated at 2.2 billion bushels, approximately 11 percent of the world's total. One half to two thirds of U.S. production is exported to other countries. Japan is one of the largest customers for U.S. wheat and buys consistent quantities each year; the Soviet Union also makes huge but irregular purchases.

Other major wheat-producing countries are the Soviet Union, followed by the People's Republic of China, India, Canada, and Australia.

Futures Markets

Wheat futures and options on wheat futures contracts are traded at the Chicago Board of Trade (Soft Red Winter wheat), the MidAmerica Commodity Exchange (Soft Red Winter wheat), the Minneapolis Grain Exchange (Soft White wheat (futures only) and Northern Spring wheat), and the Kansas City Board of Trade (Hard Red Winter wheat). While exchanges may designate a specific type and grade of wheat to be delivered against a futures contract, most will allow substitutions at differentials.

Oats

Oats, like other grains, belong to the grass family. Early records of oats indicate that they were first harvested as straw and used in mud bricks for Egyptian temples.

The ancient Romans used oats as a forage crop for grazing livestock nearly 3,000 years ago. However, it was not until the Middle Ages that oats were raised for their grain. During much of the intervening period, they were considered little more than weeds that infested fields of barley and other small grains.

Over the centuries, oats were recognized as an excellent grain for feeding livestock and poultry. They were introduced in the United States around 1600 by English settlers, who raised oats throughout the northern colonies. As the nation was settled and animal numbers increased, U.S. oat production also expanded.

Oat Varieties

Oats are divided into five major classes: White, Red, Gray, Black (including Brown), and Yellow. White oats comprise most of the U.S. production.

Oat Production Factors

Oats are less exacting in soil requirements than any other cereal grain except rye. To produce top yields, oats need at least medium levels of the essential nutrients—nitrogen, phosphate, and potash. Oats grow best in temperate climates that have plentiful moisture and cool weather at maturity time.

Most domestically grown oats are sown in the spring—early April and late May—and harvested between mid-July and late August. The leading oat-producing states are South Dakota, Minnesota, and North Dakota.

The official U.S. crop year for oats is July 1 through June 30. U.S. oat production in 1987-88 was projected to be 369 million bushels—the smallest in many decades. This represents a 6 percent drop in oat production compared to 1986, and a 29 percent decline since 1985.

In fact the number of acres planted to oats has decreased steadily since about 1920. During the early 1900s, oat production declined rapidly when horses and mules, which eat oats as a primary feed, were replaced by automobiles, trucks, and tractors. In later years, oat production fell again as rising milk production per cow led to a steady reduction in the number of dairy cattle.

Government Programs

The government programs available to oat producers are similar to those available to other grain producers. To participate in the 1988 price supports and target price deficiency payments, oat producers were required to reduce their base acreage by 20 percent. Because of the wide administrative latitude of the 1985 Farm Bill, commodity eligibility depends heavily on assumptions about how programs will be managed from year to year. (For more information on this topic, see U.S. Government Farm Programs under the Corn section in this chapter.)

Approximately 85 to 90 percent of the total oat crop is used as feed for livestock and poultry. About 6 to 7 percent is used for rolled oats, meal, ready-to-eat breakfast cereals, and oat flour; 7 to 8 percent is used as seed for upcoming crops.

Consumption and Usage

In recent years, U.S. production has amounted to approximately 15 to 20 percent of the world total of 48 million tons; exports account for 3 to 4 percent of the U.S. oat crop. Oats are grown in most regions of the world. The Soviet Union produces the greatest amount, followed by North America and Western Europe.

World Production

Oat futures contracts are traded at the Chicago Board of Trade, the MidAmerica Commodity Exchange, and the Minneapolis Grain Exchange.

Futures Markets

Rice, an annual cereal grain, was probably first cultivated 5,000 years ago in China. Rice culture gradually spread westward and was introduced to southern Europe during medieval times. Since then, rice has been the most important food staple for most of the world's population.

Rice

Rice is produced throughout the world in climates ranging from temperate to tropical. It is cultivated on wetlands that provide the necessary uniform moisture. Rice thrives under sunny, warm conditions and is highly vulnerable to either drought or unusually cool and overcast weather conditions. Cultivation practices vary widely among major rice-producing nations, reflecting differences in climate, other growing conditions, and levels of agricultural technology.

Factors Affecting Rice Production

The harvested rice kernel, known as *paddy* or *rough rice*, is enclosed by the hull, or husk. Long, medium, and short grain are the three types of rice grown in the United States, and account for 60, 34, and 6 percent of total U.S. production, respectively. The 1987-88 U.S. rice production was estimated at 129 million hundredweights. Rice is grown in Arkansas, California, Texas, Louisiana, Mississippi, and Missouri. Arkansas is, by far, the largest rice producer, accounting for some 36 percent of total U.S.

output. The marketing year for rice in the United States is August 1 through July 31.

Government Programs

Rice production and marketing are covered by various government programs. One new government rice program, established under the 1985 Farm Bill, was designed to make U.S. rice competitive in world markets and to lower stockpiles. Under the rules of the program, rice farmers are allowed to borrow money from the government, using their crop as collateral, just as they have done under past government programs. When it is time to pay back the loan, they only need to repay an amount equal to the prevailing world price of rice (calculated by the USDA).

Demand for Rice	The uses of rice in the United States fall into three major categories: table rice (regular milled, parboiled, precooked, and brown rice); rice in processed foods (breakfast cereals, snacks, etc.); and brewers' rice. Approximately 41 percent of U.S. rice is consumed domestically.

Rice Milling and Processing

Following harvest, rice is cleaned, sorted, and dried for further processing. Milling usually removes both the hull and bran layers of the kernel, and a coating of glucose and talc is sometimes applied to give the kernel a glossy finish. Rice that is processed to remove only the hulls is called *brown rice*. Rice that is milled to remove the bran as well is called *white rice* and is greatly diminished in nutrients. Parboiled white rice is processed before milling to retain most of the nutrients; enriched rice has iron and B vitamins added.

The processing of precooked or quick-cooking rice is more complex and involves one of several methods, the most basic known as the *freeze-thaw process*. Raw milled rice is steeped, immersed briefly in boiling water, drenched in chilled water, slowly frozen, and then thawed. This results in a porous kernel that readily absorbs water and reduces the required cooking time.

By-products of rice milling (including bran and rice polish, a finely powdered bran and starch resulting from polishing) are used in a variety of manufactured goods. For example, broken rice is used in brewing, distilling, and in the manufacturing of starch and rice flour. Hulls are used for fuel, packing material, industrial grinding, and fertilizer manufacturing. Rice straw is used for feed, livestock bedding, roof thatching, mats, garments, packing material, and broomstraws.

World Production and Exports

World rice production was estimated at 442 million metric tons for the 1987-88 crop year. China, India, and Indonesia were the three largest rice producers, accounting for an estimated 35, 18, and 8 percent of total world production, respectively. Other major producers include Bangladesh, Burma, Japan, South Korea, Pakistan, Thailand, Vietnam, the Philippines,

Brazil, and the United States. U.S. rice production in 1987-88 was 6.3 million metric tons, and nearly 50 percent was exported. Major importers of U.S. rice are South Korea, Indonesia, Nigeria, Liberia, the Ivory Coast, South Africa, and Middle Eastern countries including Saudi Arabia, Iraq, Iran, and North Yemen. Middle Eastern imports of U.S. rice have more than doubled since 1971.

Futures Markets

A futures contract in rough rice is traded at the Chicago Rice & Cotton Exchange.

Canadian Grain Futures Markets

Two other important grains—barley and rye—have futures contracts trading on the Winnipeg Commodity Exchange. Both barley and rye are hardy and are grown around the world. In Canada, the planting of barley occurs during May and harvest occurs during August. On the other hand, most of Canada's rye crop is sown in September and October, lies dormant throughout winter, and is harvested in late July and August.

The amount of barley planted and its price are related to the level of production and the price of other feed grains, such as corn and sorghum. Barley is used chiefly as an animal feed for hogs and cattle. Another major use of barley is as a malt in beer.

Rye also has several uses. It is the only cereal grass other than wheat that can be used to make bread. In Canada and the United States, rye is used for human food, animal feed, industrial applications, and seed. The milling and baking industries consume about 20 percent of the rye produced; approximately 35 percent is used for animal feed, although in the United States rye is not regarded as a primary livestock feed; and about 10 percent is used to manufacture whiskey.

The Soviet Union is the world's largest producer of rye followed by Poland, West Germany, and East Germany. Canada is a modest producer of rye but is the largest exporter, as 60 percent of its production is exported.

OILSEEDS

Soybean Complex

It is nearly impossible to discuss soybeans without talking about soybean meal and soybean oil. The interrelationship between the soybean and its two principal by-products exists throughout the production, processing, and marketing phases. The term *soybean complex* refers to this interrelationship. This section presents the development of the soybean crop, its processing, and the intertwined supply and demand relationships of the soybean complex.

Soybeans

Soybeans were grown by the Chinese 5,000 years ago. Through cooking, fermentation, germination, and other methods, the ancient Chinese developed a wide variety of soy foods. The development of these foods encouraged the spread of soybean production across much of the Pacific Basin.

Historians believe Marco Polo may have introduced many of these soy foods to Europe, upon returning from his travels through China in the 13th century. During the next few centuries, limited quantities of these foods were carried west over the trade routes between Asia and Europe.

Until the early 1900s, there was little soybean production outside the Orient. At that time, the unique value of the soybean as a source of edible oil and high-protein meal, with secondary industrial and chemical applications, began to be recognized in the Western world.

Large-scale production of soybeans in the United States dates only from the mid-1930s. The rapid growth of soybeans as a crop in the United States was a result of the trade embargo by China in the 1930s that cut off soybean supplies. Acreage restrictions in cotton, corn, and wheat to curb oversupply in those commodities also stimulated increased soybean plantings. The production of less cotton reduced the supply of cottonseed oil—once the preferred domestic edible oil—and soybean oil became a logical substitute.

At the time of World War II, trade restrictions necessitated the development of a domestic oilseed industry, and this further stimulated soybean production. During the postwar recovery period, population growth and increased affluence in the United States, Western Europe, and Japan led to increased demand for meats, and, therefore, for animal feeds, which increased soybean meal demand. These same factors were instrumental in the rising demand for both soybean oil and soybean meal from the 1950s to the present. Since the 1970s, U.S. soybean production has accounted for approximately 60 to 70 percent of the world total.

The 1987-88 U.S. soybean production was nearly 2 billion bushels. Soybeans are the third largest crop, following corn and wheat, in the United States, and the leading dollar-earner among U.S. agricultural exports.

Factors Affecting Soybean Production

There are more than 150 varieties of soybeans grown in the United States, which vary according to soil and climate conditions from Arkansas to the Canadian border. The dominant class of soybeans in commercial markets is the Yellow soybean.

The soybean is a bushlike plant that grows to heights ranging from 12 inches to 6 feet. An extensive root system gives the soybean notable resistance to drought. After flowering, the plant develops several pods, each of which normally carries three seeds, or beans.

Soybeans grow best on fertile, sandy loam suitable for cotton or corn. Planting takes place in late May or June following corn planting, and harvest usually runs from early September through October.

World Production of Soybeans
1985-1986

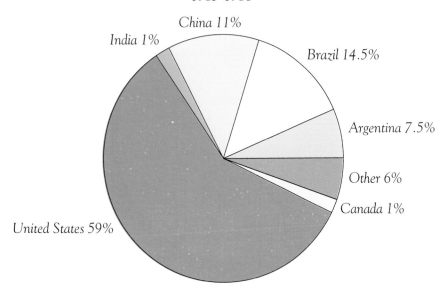

Source: U.S. Department of Agriculture

The soybean plant is photoperiodic, which means that the flowering and opening of the pods is controlled by the length of daylight. Also, because of this photoperiodic growth habit, the soybean plant will mature within a few days of a given calendar date, regardless of planting time. Increased worldwide demand and higher overhead costs have prompted farmers in many cereal- and cotton-producing areas to double-crop using a short-term soybean hybrid. Illinois and Iowa are the two major soybean-producing states, followed by Indiana, Missouri, Minnesota, and Arkansas. The important growing areas are more concentrated, and roughly coincide with the central and southern sections of the Corn Belt. As a result, soybeans must compete with corn and cotton acreage.

Farm Programs
Although there is a loan program for soybeans, it is used to a much lesser extent than those for most other commodities. (For more information on the loan program, see U.S. Government Farm Programs under the Corn section in this chapter.) In addition, there is no target price for soybeans and therefore no deficiency payment. There also is no acreage-diversion program for soybeans.

Whole soybeans have limited uses. They are held as seed for the coming crop, or baked, puffed, roasted, or steamed for dairy animal feed. The greatest demand for soybeans is as meal and oil.

Soybean Demand

Soybean Meal

Feed

Approximately 90 percent of soybean meal is used as animal feed to satisfy basic protein and amino acid requirements.

Therefore, demand for soybean meal is closely related to the number of livestock and poultry on feed.

An attempt to forecast consumption of soybean meal focuses on the demand for animal protein—meat and poultry products—which is influenced by such factors as consumer preferences.

Soybean meal faces competition from various animal and vegetable products. In the animal category, fish meal and tankage—dried by-products of meat packing—compete with soybean meal. Vegetable oilseed meals include those produced from rapeseed, cottonseed, flaxseed, and sunflower seeds. There is a tendency to substitute them for soybean meal when they are priced more favorably.

Food and Industrial Uses

Approximately 10 percent of the soybean meal consumed in the United States is used directly in food and industrial production. The food uses are the more significant of the two categories, and include high-protein derivatives of soybean meal consumed in relatively small amounts in cake mixes, waffles, cereals, breads, snack foods, blended meat products, soups, and baby foods. Higher concentrations of soybean meal products are found in dietetic, health, and hypoallergenic foods and cosmetics, and in antibiotics.

Soybean Oil

The greatest demand for soybean oil is in the form of edible oil products—such as shortening, margarines, salad oils, and cooking oils. To a lesser extent, soybean oil is used to manufacture chemicals, paints, varnishes, sealants, lubricants, and adhesives.

In food and industrial markets, soybean oil faces competition from a variety of animal and vegetable oils. Soybean oil competes with such animal oil products as butter, lard, and fish oils, and with vegetable oil products such as cottonseed oil, rapeseed oil, sunflowerseed oil, flaxseed oil, olive oil, coconut oil, and palm oil. Because of the competition among these fat and oil products, soybean oil accounts for only one fifth of the total world oil consumption.

Processing Methods

Oil

Over the years, there has been a radical change in the technology of soybean processing methods—a shift from mechanical extraction to chemical extraction. Oil and meal were originally extracted from soybeans by hydraulic crushing, a method that left about 4 to 15 percent of the oil and solvent in the soybean flake or cake. (The cake is what remains after the extraction of the oil and solvent.)

Today, nearly all U.S. and foreign processing plants use a chemical extraction method that leaves only 1 percent of the oil in the cake. In this hexane-solvent extraction method, the soybeans are first crushed and flaked. The oil is then extracted, and the solvent removed from it by evaporation and saved for reuse. In the refining process, crude oil can be degummed, refined, bleached, deodorized, or hydrogenated, depending on the end use.

Meal

After extraction, the soybean flake is toasted and ground into soybean meal containing 44 percent protein. If the hull is removed before processing, the percentage of protein meal increases to 49 percent. Approximately half of all U.S. soybean meal is 49 percent protein, and is used primarily for high-performance feeds.

Soybean Processing

The average weight of a bushel of soybeans is 60 pounds. It yields approximately 11 pounds of crude oil and 47 to 48 pounds of meal, with the remaining 1 to 2 pounds of weight primarily composed of hulls. These yield rates are relatively constant, but vary slightly with changes in soybean quality and variations in processing efficiency. However, this constant yield relationship makes it possible to have a very exact measurement of costs versus income in the soybean-processing industry.

Gross Processing Margin

Profitability is critical in determining the rate at which domestic soybeans are processed. It is estimated using the Gross Processing Margin (GPM) formula, which measures the difference in the cost of soybeans and the value of processed soybean oil and meal.

Calculating the Gross Processing Margin

To calculate the GPM, the first step is to determine the oil and meal dollar value in one bushel of soybeans. It is customary to use standard conversion factors: 11 pounds of oil and 48 pounds of meal. Oil prices are converted to a bushel equivalent by multiplying the oil price by 11. If soybean oil is selling at $18.69 per hundredweight, or $0.1869 per pound, the value of oil in a bushel of soybeans would be $0.1869 × 11 or $2.0559.

Similarly, the value of meal per ton is converted to the bushel equivalent by multiplying the price per ton by the conversion factor of .024 (48 pounds divided by 2,000 pounds (one ton) = .024). With meal selling at $155.70 per ton, the meal conversion would be $155.70 × .024 = $3.7368, the value of soybean meal per bushel of soybeans.

If the price of soybeans is $5.30¼ per bushel, and given the above values for soybean oil and soybean meal, the gross processing margin would be computed as follows:

$ Amount × Conversion Factor	
Oil value ($0.1869 x 11)	= $2.0559/bu
Meal value ($155.70 × .024)	= +3.7368
Combined sales value	$5.7927
Less soybean cost	−5.3025
Gross processing margin	$0.4902/bu

Economics of Soybean Processing

Frequently, there is a seasonal pattern in processing margins, reflecting a favorable GPM after the fall harvest when soybeans are in abundance and priced low. During this same period, there tends to be a growing demand for feed in anticipation of colder weather, lack of grazing, and heavier livestock feeding requirements. Thus, the combination of lower soybean prices and strengthening soybean meal demand tends to increase the processing margin.

Processing margins tend to decline later in the crop year for two primary reasons. First, as demand for feed declines, soybean meal prices drop. Second, soybean prices tend to rise as the crop year progresses, due to lower supplies and the accumulation of carrying costs.

Reverse Crush Pattern

Occasionally, the market will be confronted with higher than usual soybean prices. This usually reflects tightening supplies and a processing margin that is unfavorable or negative. In this situation, the return on sales of oil and meal in relation to the cost of soybeans is insufficient to allow for profitable processing.

A decline in soybean processing eases the drain on tight supplies and tends to curb rising soybean prices. At the same time, reduced processing tends to lead to tighter supplies of oil and meal, increasing their price levels. As the soybean price is held down, the cost/price relationship tends to reverse, and favorable processing margins are reestablished.

World Markets

Global exports for 1987-88 were estimated at 29 million tons, with the U.S. market share equaling 72 percent of the world total. Other major exporters, particularly Brazil and Argentina, have reduced soybean exports and, instead, process the soybeans, then later export the oil and meal. The leading soybean importers are West Germany, the Netherlands, Spain, and Japan.

Futures Markets

The Chicago Board of Trade trades contracts for soybean, soybean oil, and soybean meal futures, and options on all three contracts. The MidAmerica Commodity Exchange trades soybean and soybean meal futures and options on soybean futures.

Rapeseed and flaxseed are two oilseeds, that like, soybeans can be crushed into meal and oil. The Winnipeg Commodity Exchange trades futures contracts in both commodities.

The largest producer of flaxseed is Argentina, followed by Canada, India, the Soviet Union, and the United States. Flaxseed is grown in temperate climates in drained sandy loam. Canadian flaxseed is generally sown in May and June and harvested in September and October. Most flaxseed is crushed to produce linseed oil and meal. Linseed oil is used as an industrial oil—as a drying oil in outside paints, printing inks, and varnishes. Linseed meal is a valuable supplement in livestock and poultry feed.

In the case of rapeseed, China is the world's largest producer, followed by India and Canada. France also has become a major producer and exports a significant portion of its crop. In the last decade, world production of rapeseed has doubled. This trend can be attributed to the increased use of rapeseed as an edible oil. Rapeseed oil is used for margarine, shortening, salad and cooking oil, and to some extent as an industrial lubricant. Rapeseed meal is a valuable supplement in livestock and poultry feed.

Rapeseed competes in the world market with 12 other vegetable oils, and its price is influenced by these vegetable oils and six other animal or marine sources of oil, including soybeans, peanuts, sunflower, tallow, fish, and whale.

LIVESTOCK

Meat is the major source of protein in the diet of Americans and persons of other developed nations. It is also a growing source of protein in the diet of those living in developing nations. In 1987, Americans spent nearly $346 billion on food and beverages; approximately 21 percent of this—$73 billion—was spent on beef and pork products.

The public's attitude toward pork and its consumption has changed over the years. Pork was once regarded as part of the rich man's diet. Now, increased production efficiency has made pork readily available. A shift away from the fat-type hog—reflecting a decline in the use of lard—and a corresponding emphasis on production of a lean, meat-type hog has boosted demand for pork.

Federally inspected slaughter of hogs averaged about 81 million head annually during 1983-87. In 1987, the commercial slaughter of hogs was 78 million head, yielding over 13 billion pounds of pork.

Pork Production

Pork production is concentrated in the Corn Belt; Iowa, Illinois, Indiana, and Missouri account for more than 50 percent of total U.S. pork production. Other major producing states include Minnesota, Nebraska, Ohio, Wisconsin, South Dakota, Georgia, Kansas, and North Carolina.

Historic price patterns and current price trends are among the most important influences on the level of pork production. Hog producers, as do producers of most other commodities, tend to cut back on production when the price outlook is bearish. However, cutbacks in periods of weakening prices are not as pronounced as they were previously. Hog-feeding operations tend to be larger than they once were; therefore, operators attempt to feed at or near capacity to offset the higher fixed costs of automated feeding facilities.

Feeding Costs

Feed is the primary cost in livestock production operations. Feed cost, in relation to the sales value of finished market-weight hogs, is the primary determinant of how much pork will be produced. In addition, feed prices may influence the producer's decision of when and at what weight to market hogs. Generally, when feed costs are high relative to the sales value of finished hogs, producers tend to breed, feed, and market fewer hogs, at lighter weights, than they would in periods of lower feed costs. When the cost-to-sales-price ratio is more favorable, breeding, feeding, marketing, and average market weights of hogs increase.

Hog/Corn Ratio

The hog/corn ratio is used to express the relationship of feeding costs to the dollar value of hogs. It is measured by dividing the price of hogs ($/hundredweight) by the price of corn ($/bushel). For instance, if the price of hogs in Omaha was $49.50 per hundredweight and the Omaha price of #2 Yellow corn was $3.20¼ per bushel, the hog/corn ratio would be 15.5 ($49.5000 divided by $3.2025 = 15.5). In other words, 15.5 bushels of corn has the same dollar value as 100 pounds of live pork.

When corn prices are high relative to pork prices, fewer units of corn equal the dollar value of 100 pounds of pork. Conversely, when corn prices are lower in relation to pork prices, more units of corn are required to equal the value of 100 pounds of pork. A hog/corn ratio of 13.3 would indicate higher corn costs and perhaps weaker hog prices than a ratio of 22.5. Thus, the higher the ratio, the more profitable it is to feed hogs.

Production-Marketing Schedule

By closely controlling breeding and feeding operations, hog producers can be relatively certain about the number and weight of hogs they will have ready for market at a given date. The producer's first decision is how many sows to breed. In making this decision, he takes into account the gestation period of nearly four months and the average yield of 7.3 pigs per litter. By knowing the number of sows bred and then multiplying that number by the average litter size, the producer is able to accurately project feeding requirements and develop a marketing plan. Depending on his feed plan and seasonal factors that can affect weight gain, the producer normally can bring newly born pigs to market weight in five to seven months.

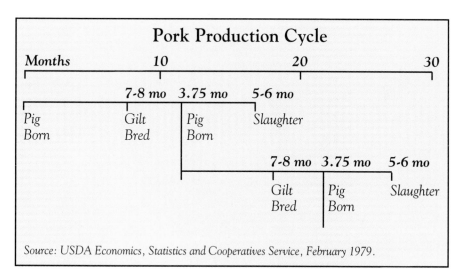

Pork Production Cycle

Source: USDA Economics, Statistics and Cooperatives Service, February 1979.

He makes this kind of calculation not only in terms of his own production but, based on reports from the USDA, applies it as well to total U.S. hog production in an attempt to get a reasonably sound picture of total production, available market supply, and probable price outlook.

Seasonal Pattern

Hog production usually follows a seasonal pattern, however, seasonal production trends are now of less importance than they once were. The largest number of farrowings (pig births) occurs during March, April, and May, and, ordinarily, the smallest number occurs during December, January, and February. Since it takes five to six months to bring newly born pigs to market, spring pigs farrowed in March, April, and May come to market from August through December. Because the hog supply is greatest during this period, pork commodities are traditionally at the lowest price level of the year from August through December.

In the past, most sows were bred only twice a year; now they are commonly bred three times a year, which tends to even out the number of hogs coming to market throughout the year. Better management, improved feeding programs, and higher fixed costs (such as heated production facilities) make it desirable to maintain production at near-capacity level throughout the year.

Long-term Price Cycles

Along with the historic seasonal trends in production, there are long-term cycles in hog prices, which may last up to five or six years. They occur chiefly because of producers' reactions to price levels. Relatively high prices stimulate hog production for several years thereafter. Increased production then leads to depressed prices; this then influences producers to cut production. Volatile feed prices have affected these patterns also. As in the beef industry, hog price cycles now tend to be shorter in duration than in the past as a result of better price forecasting, greater production planning, and the trend toward more even production levels.

Supply Factors for Pork Products

Various long- and short-term factors affect the supply situation for both pork bellies and other pork products—hams, loins, and butts. Some factors have greater impact upon the supply and price level of pork bellies than they do on other cuts of pork. The most important long-term factors affecting supplies include the current livestock situation—feed costs and profitability considerations—general consumer-income levels, the number of hogs and pigs on farms, and the birth of new pigs.

In the short run, the current rate of weekly hog marketings at major markets tends to be the strongest influence on both the supply and price of pork products. In addition to current hog marketings, weekly bacon slicings and cold storage figures are most important in forecasting pork belly supplies and price levels.

Demand for Pork

The demand for pork—such as chops, hams, bacon, and in prepared meat products—is most strongly affected by the price relative to general income and to the price of competitive meat products. The trend to greater weight consciousness has increased the demand for leaner pork products, particularly those made from hams and loins. Hams and loins account for 20 percent and 16.9 percent of carcass weight, respectively.

Pork bellies, the end product of which is cured sliced bacon, account for 15 percent of the carcass weight of hogs. The demand for bacon has risen due to increasing demand for pork in general, and increases in population and per capita consumption. Bacon is rather unique among meat products in that it has relatively few substitutes. Consumption tends to remain stable from one year to the next, except in situations of major price changes.

Demand for pork, particularly bacon and processed meats, reaches its peak in the summer and early fall. The convenience of these items is particularly well suited to vacationing families; and their lower seasonal prices tend to stimulate consumption.

Futures Markets

The Chicago Mercantile Exchange trades futures in live hogs and pork bellies, and options on both contracts. The MidAmerica Commodity Exchange trades futures on live hogs.

The U.S. cattle/calf inventory peaked in the mid-1970s, and was 132 million head on January 1, 1975. By 1980, it had decreased to about 111 million head. It then gained about 4 million head during the early 1980s. Liquidation resumed in the mid-1980s, because of volatile financing costs and shifts in consumer tastes. The January 1, 1987, cattle/calf inventory of 102 million was the lowest in 25 years. And in 1987, cattle feedlots in the United States marketed 23 million head of cattle, yielding 18 billion pounds of beef.

Beef Commodities

U.S. Beef Production

The production of beef involves breeding and raising cattle. At specific stages of development, cattle are sent through the three sectors of the cattle industry. The first sector is the cow-calf operation, which produces calves, or feeder cattle. The second is the feedlot or cattle-feeding system. A cattle feeder buys calves and feeder cattle from Western ranchers and commercial breeders and then feeds them to a desired market weight in the surplus feed grain production areas of the Corn Belt and the Great Plains. The third is the meat packer, who slaughters cattle for beef.

Factors Affecting
Beef Supply

The major beef-producing states are Texas, Iowa, Nebraska, Kansas, Oklahoma, South Dakota, California, Missouri, Illinois, and Montana. The level of beef production is affected by many interrelated factors, the most influential of which are current and recent-past price levels. When prices are high, commercial breeders increase their breeding programs in anticipation of increased demand for feeder cattle. When prices are low, feeders cut back their production, and breeders reduce the number of feeder cattle produced. In periods of extremely low prices, breeders may liquidate some of their breeding stock.

Drought and crop failure in the Corn Belt may reduce feed-grain production and cut back cattle feeding. Sustained periods of excessively hot, cold, or rainy weather slow the rate of weight gain and increase feeding costs. Conversely, less extreme weather generally results in better feed-grain yields, creating cheaper feed supplies and improved profits for the cattle feeder.

Feeding Costs

The cost of feed in relation to the market price of beef is an important influence on the level of production, and is determined by the steer/corn ratio. The ratio, released monthly by the USDA, is calculated by dividing the price of cattle ($/hundredweight) by the price of corn ($/bushel). For instance, if the price of Choice steers in Omaha is $66.69 per hundredweight and the Omaha price of #2 Yellow corn is $3.20¼ per bushel, the steer/corn ratio would be 20.8 ($66.690 divided by $3.2025 = 20.8). In other words, 20.8 bushels of corn are equal in dollar value to 100 pounds of Choice steer beef.

When the value of corn is high in relation to the sales value of beef, fewer units of corn equal the dollar value of 100 pounds of beef. Conversely, when corn prices are lower in relation to beef prices, more units of corn are required to equal the value of 100 pounds of beef. A steer/corn ratio of 17.6 would indicate higher corn costs and weaker beef prices than a ratio of 22.5. Thus, the higher the ratio, the more profitable it is to feed the cattle.

Production Cycles

Beef production requires a lengthy start-up time. A heifer, a female that has not yet produced a calf, is normally not bred until it is 14 to 18 months old, and the gestation requires another nine months. At 6 to 8 months of age, calves are weaned from their mothers and are either sent directly to a feedlot or to an intermediate stage wherein they are fed roughage. This phase lasts 6 to 10 months at which time cattle are sent to feedlots. Both steers and heifers are placed in feedlots, although fewer heifers are placed because their retention is necessary to maintain cow herds. To bring feeder cattle to a desired market weight requires another six to nine months. Because of the time required from breeding to finished market weight, adjustments in beef breeding and feeding to meet demand and price changes are difficult.

Cattle Cycle

The cattle cycle—a cyclical change in the size of the cattle herd—arises from several factors including a lengthy start-up time, changes in demand for beef, and the availability and cost of feed. Since 1896, there have been seven cattle cycles. The length of the cycles averages about 12 years, but ranges from 9 to 16 years. On average, 7 years of the cycle are herd expansion and 5 years are herd reduction.

The expansion phase of a typical cattle cycle begins when producers decide to expand their breeding stock in response to rising prices or expectations that prices will rise. Breeding stock is held back to expand herds and, as a result, prices rise. Rising prices also keep calves, yearlings, and steers out of the market and on feed to an older age and a heavier weight. When the large number of new calves from the expanded herds matures, slaughter begins to increase because fully finished steers must be marketed. Prices then start to drop because of the oversupply of cattle. The slaughter of cows and calves is then increased, because herd expansion is no longer desirable, thus depressing prices further. Eventually, herds become so small that prices go up, and cattle producers realize that the bottom of the cycle has been reached.

Seasonal Effects

Despite the seasonal breeding and feeding patterns, beef production has only a small seasonal trend, tending to rise slightly from the second to the fourth quarter, after declining slightly from the first to the second quarter.

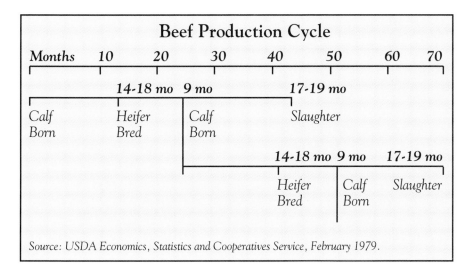

Beef Production Cycle

Source: USDA Economics, Statistics and Cooperatives Service, February 1979.

Similarly, there is a fairly weak seasonal trend in prices, tending to reach a low in February and peak in August.

Government Influences

Various government regulations, programs, and information, particularly from the USDA, impact the production and marketing of beef. The effect of the government is first felt in the overall annual farm program, which may use acreage controls or crop-production incentives to influence the amount of feed grain raised during a given crop production/marketing year. The dairy program also can greatly affect beef supply. For instance, if the government initiates a program to reduce milk production, farmers participating in the program will be required to reduce dairy cattle numbers. In turn, more dairy cattle will be slaughtered, increasing beef supplies. This action ultimately forces beef prices down.

Other government actions are aimed directly at beef production. In periods of depressed meat prices, for example, the government has attempted to stimulate demand through subsidized school lunches and other donation programs. At other times, the government uses export or import quotas of beef products to influence domestic beef production and price levels.

The USDA also provides information on cattle and livestock inventories, the number of cattle and calves on feed, and production and stocks data on competitive meat and poultry. This information is watched closely by the cattle-breeding, feedlot, and meat-packing segments of the industry to enable them to anticipate future beef demand and price trends.

Demand Considerations

The amount of U.S. beef produced depends on domestic demand factors. Meat consumption tends to increase as a result of population growth and rising affluence. Production has barely kept pace with the demand for Choice beef and has never exceeded demand for any significant time period. In inflationary periods and in times of steeper feed costs, however, consumers tend to avoid the more expensive beef varieties in favor of cheaper cuts. At such times, a change in diet—the substitution of poultry or pasta products—is not uncommon.

Competitive Meat Products

Since 1976, the annual per capita consumption of beef has declined from 127.5 pounds to 106.1 pounds in 1987, while the annual per capita demand for pork and chicken has increased from 58.6 to 65.2 pounds, and from 43.3 to 54.8 pounds, respectively.

One reason for the decrease in beef consumption is consumers' preference toward white meat products—fish and poultry. Another reason for the increase in chicken consumption is the development of more convenience foods that include chicken.

Price Considerations

Although beef historically has commanded higher prices than either pork or poultry, price movements for the three commodities are somewhat parallel, as they are all affected by the general availability and cost of feeds, chiefly corn. However, when beef supplies are scarce, higher beef prices tend to lead to greater consumption of lower-priced meat products—pork, poultry, and fish.

Import, Export Trade

Except for the relatively small number of live cattle imported and exported to improve breeding herds, most beef in international trade is either frozen or canned. Imports and exports tend to be of the lesser grades of beef—Standard, Utility, Cutter, and Canner.

Futures Markets

Live cattle futures and options on futures, as well as feeder cattle futures and options are traded on the Chicago Mercantile Exchange. Live cattle futures are traded on the MidAmerica Commodity Exchange.

Futures contracts in gold, silver, copper, aluminum, platinum, and palladium are traded on various commodity exchanges throughout the United States. The following chapter covers the supply, demand, current production, known reserves, and U.S. policies for these metals.

GOLD

Gold is primarily used for jewelry and monetary investment purposes. It is therefore regarded as a precious metal rather than an industrial metal. However, gold has industrial qualities—durability, electrical conductivity, and indestructibility. It also is used to a small extent in electronic applications.

For centuries, gold has been used for domestic and international exchange, but it was not until the mid-1800s that gold became the formal standard of exchange. In modern history, the first formal monetary role for gold was established when England made the gold sovereign the primary monetary unit in 1816. By the mid-1800s, the economies of many nations were based on the gold standard, including the United States, as provided for by the United States Coinage Act of 1873.

The gold standard system, in its pure form, specified that payments

METALS
FUTURES
AND
OPTIONS

Gold,
Silver,
Copper,
Aluminum,
Platinum,
Palladium

14

between nations be made in gold, either bullion or coins. This system worked until World War I when Britain suspended payments in gold. The United States, however, sought to continue the gold standard; but, later, the economic strains of war caused the United States to abandon gold as its means for international settlement.

Gold Exchange Standard

In 1922, the United States modified the pure gold standard by creating the *gold exchange standard*, which allowed international payments in both gold and U.S. dollars. This was possible because the United States continued to honor its commitment to redeem the dollar in gold on demand.

By 1931, in the midst of worldwide economic depression, Britain came off the gold standard. Two years later, to lend stability to U.S. banks, Franklin Roosevelt broke the link between the dollar and gold by banning gold hoarding and public exporting of gold bullion. In 1933, the official price of gold was changed from $20 an ounce—a level at which it had been since 1869—to $35 an ounce, the level at which it remained until 1971.

Changing Economic Policies

Bretton Woods Agreement

The world's major trading nations, anticipating the severe economic and financial problems that would follow World War II, met at Bretton Woods, New Hampshire, in 1943, to deal with separate proposals by the United States, Britain, Canada, and France for a new international system of payments. A compromise between U.S. and British plans resulted in the Articles of Agreement International Monetary Fund (IMF), signed in July 1944. Central to this system, which functioned until 1972, was the concept that each IMF member nation's currency would have a par value relation to the gold content of the U.S. dollar.

Throughout most of the 1950s, the Bretton Woods system worked comparatively well, despite the economic disruption of the Korean War and the Suez crisis. A general problem on the part of less-developed nations was the shortage of money because they tended to spend more for imports than was generated from their exports.

In the 1960s, the economies of the less-developed nations strengthened. At this time, the United States began to experience a slight balance-of-payments deficit rather than a surplus, and U.S. foreign expenditures outdistanced export income. (A balance-of-payments deficit occurs when a nation's foreign purchases exceed its foreign sales.)

Two-Tier Gold and SDRs

In 1968, a two-tier gold market was developed. Gold had an official price of $35 an ounce to be used in all international settlements and a free market price to be used in all other transactions.

At the same time, the Special Drawing Right (SDR) was created as a new international medium of exchange. The SDR was based on the weighted values of 16 member-nation currencies according to their daily fluctuations. Issued by the IMF to its member nations, SDRs are used to meet international payments between central banks. SDRs were and still are priced at 35 SDRs per ounce of gold, reflecting the official dollar price of gold when the SDRs were created.

New U.S. Economic Policies

U.S. inflation and balance-of-payments deficits continued to worsen, and, in the spring of 1971, the United States announced the suspension of converting dollars to gold bullion, along with an anti-inflationary effort using wage and price controls. At the same time, a formal devaluation of the dollar to $\frac{1}{38}$ ounce of gold raised the official price of gold to $38 an ounce.

With the balance-of-payments deficit approaching $6 billion in 1973, the United States again devalued the dollar to $\frac{1}{42}$ ounce of gold; the resulting official value of gold applied to international payments between central banks. On December 31, 1974, the U.S. ban on the ownership of gold bullion by private citizens was lifted, and the first gold futures contract began trading.

From 1975 through 1979, the IMF and U.S. Treasury continued efforts to eliminate the use of gold as a monetary standard. Both, for example, increased gold sales significantly during this period. In 1978, official gold sales accounted for 20 percent of total world gold supplies, compared to 1971 when official gold sales accounted for only 7 percent of total sales.

In 1982, the question of the role of gold in the international monetary system received attention once more with the formation of the Gold Commission by President Reagan. But, this panel voted against any move to return to the gold standard.

Investments

Investments in gold take many forms—gold bullion, coins, mine stocks, to name a few. A popular means of investing in gold today is the purchase of official coins. Among those most in demand are the American Eagle, Chinese Panda, Canadian Maple Leaf, Australian Nugget, and the Mexican 50 Peso.

Sales of gold coins skyrocketed in 1987, amounting to 12 million ounces of gold. The United States began minting its own gold bullion in October 1987 and by the end of the year produced 3.4 million coins containing nearly 2 million ounces of gold. In addition, a Statue of Liberty commemorative gold coin program started in 1985 consumed 42,000 ounces of the yellow metal in 1987.

Another form of gold investment is hoarding. This involves purchasing gold as a means of protection against inflation and eroding currency values. In 1987, the Japanese were the largest investors of bar hoarding,

Gold and Its Uses

accounting for four fifths of all hoarding outside of Europe and North America.

Jewelry

The total amount of gold made into jewelry during 1987 was 1,589 metric tons, over 70 percent of the total manufactured. Seventy-five percent of this gold came from new supplies. Europe, led by Italy, was the main jewelry fabrication center; the Far East, with Taiwan and Thailand in the lead, also manufactured large amounts of gold into jewelry.

Industrial Demand

Even though gold is a precious metal, it has several different industrial applications. The electronics industry, for instance, uses gold in various products because it is an excellent conductor of electricity and is quite durable. In 1987, the electronics industry consumed 124 metric tons of gold.

There is a growing use of gold in the making of plate glass for large office buildings. This is due to the reflective qualities of gold, which reduce the cost of air-conditioning.

World Supply

Total supply figures include mine production, sales from the centrally planned economies, old gold scrap, and the net result of all dealings by central banks and other bodies that comprise the official sector. In 1987, the total supply of gold to the noncommunist private sector, estimated at 2,008 metric tons, remained virtually unchanged from its 1986 level.

Mine Production

In 1987, world mine production grew by 6 percent from the 1986 level to 1,373 metric tons, the highest level ever recorded. South Africa is the largest gold producer in the world, mining 607 metric tons in 1987 despite a strike by the National Union of Mineworkers.

The USSR is the world's second largest gold producer, although the Soviet Union has not released any production statistics since 1936. Bureau of Mines data estimate Soviet gold production for 1987 at 276 metric tons.

Once again, the United States, Canada, and Australia were the leaders of Western world mining, accounting for 383 metric tons. Gold production in the United States continued to rise strongly, increasing 31 percent in 1987 to 155 metric tons. Of this total, 80 metric tons, or 52 percent, was produced in Nevada. The second largest producing state was California, accounting for 21 metric tons, up from 13 metric tons in 1986.

Canadian mine output, taking into account undeclared production from placer deposits (glacial deposits that contain particles of valuable minerals) in the Yukon, increased by 14 percent to 120 metric tons in 1987. Australia followed Canada, producing 108 million metric tons in 1987.

World Gold Supply and Private Investment
1983-1987

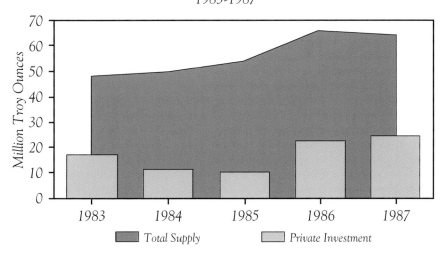

Source: CPM Group, New York

Note: All gold statistics in the previous section refer to the manufacturing of gold in the country where it is processed, not in the country where the product is eventually sold.

Gold Scrap

In 1987, production of old gold scrap, which is derived from jewelry and industrial products, reached 471 metric tons, the highest level since 1980.

Official Reserves

Large supplies of gold are still held as reserves by most central banks and the IMF. As of October 1987, when the average gold price was selling at roughly $444 per fine troy ounce, free-world stocks were estimated at 1.44 billion ounces, with an approximate value of $621.6 billion.

Futures markets in gold are conducted at the Chicago Board of Trade, the Commodity Exchange, Inc. (COMEX), and the MidAmerica Commodity Exchange. Options on gold futures are traded at COMEX and the MidAm.

Futures Markets

SILVER

For centuries, silver has been used in coins, ornaments, and jewelry. But, recently, these uses have accounted for less than 15 percent of total world silver consumption.

Today, the electronics and photography industries have taken the lead, consuming the majority of the world's silver. Silver is highly attractive to these industries due to its technical and industrial properties—malleability, ductility, high electrical and thermal conductivity, and resistance to corrosion.

World Production

Estimated total world production for silver reached nearly 430 million ounces in 1987. More than half of all silver is produced in the Western Hemisphere. In recent years, Canada, Peru, Mexico, and the United States have emerged as the leading silver producers. Outside the Western Hemisphere, the two leading silver producers are Australia and the Soviet Union.

Silver Supply

The supply of silver comes from mine production, scrap production, and hoarding. The primary source of silver, approximately 70 percent, is as a by-product from the mining of other metals, such as nickel, copper, lead, zinc, and gold. As a result, the demand and price of these metals directly influence the amount of silver produced and, in turn, the demand and the price of raw silver.

An important, but smaller, percentage of silver comes directly from silver mining operations. In 1987, world mine production of silver, excluding communist countries, amounted to nearly 340 million ounces. Mexico, the world's leading silver producer, increased its output to 68 million ounces—approximately 20 percent of the world total. Peru was second at 66 million ounces, followed by Canada and the United States at 38 and 37 million ounces, respectively.

While mining is a primary source of silver, secondary sources include government stocks, private holdings, and silver particles recovered by reclamation and recycling of scrap and silver-bearing waste solutions.

Demand

Free-world consumption of silver in 1987 was estimated at more than 415 million ounces (384 million ounces for industrial uses and 31 million ounces for coinage).

The United States was the world's largest consumer of silver, followed by Canada, Mexico, the United Kingdom, France, West Germany, Italy,

World Total Silver Supply
1987

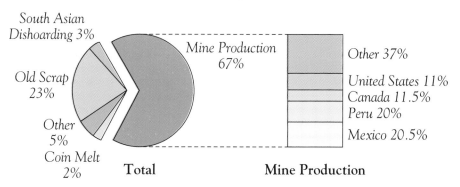

Source: CPM Group, New York

Japan, and India. Total 1987 imports of silver by the United States were nearly 82 million ounces, a decline of 43 percent from the previous year.

Monetary

Historically, silver has been used for monetary purposes. In the United States, silver, like gold, has been used in coins and its price has been supported by the government. However, its uses and value for monetary purposes have decreased significantly since 1968.

In 1965, the U.S. Coinage Act stopped the use of silver in quarters and dimes and cut back the amount of silver in half-dollars from 90 to 40 percent. Two years later, the U.S. Treasury stopped selling silver at $1.2929 per fine ounce, and the price of silver immediately increased to $1.87 per ounce. The coins became worth more than their face value, and a ban on melting down coins was issued. In the middle of 1967, Congress authorized the Secretary of the Treasury to rule that outstanding silver certificates worth about $150 million were either lost, destroyed, or privately held and would not be redeemed. And, by 1968, holders of U.S. silver certificates could no longer redeem them for silver. The international demand for silver also has declined and Britain, Canada, and Australia no longer use silver coinage.

In today's markets, the price of silver is determined primarily by its industrial applications, and to a lesser extent by its use in jewelry; its value is not based on monetary purposes.

Industrial Applications

In 1987, industrial purposes accounted for about 90 percent of U.S. silver consumption; the remaining 10 percent was used for coinage and medallion purposes.

Uses of Silver

Factors Affecting Price

As mentioned earlier, the photography film, plate, sensitized paper, and photocopying machine industries comprise the largest single market for silver in the United States today. In 1987, more than 61 million ounces were used by the photographic industry, which also is the leader in reclamation and recycling of silver, primarily from waste solutions from film development.

Because silver is a thermal and electrical conductor with high heat resistance, the electrical and electronic industries are major silver consumers. Silver electrical contacts are used in practically every on-off switch and electrical appliance. Silver also is used in computer, telephone, and aviation systems. In 1987, these industries accounted for 23.5 million ounces of the total U.S. silver consumption.

Silver is used largely as a solder and brazing alloy to join metallic surfaces. In 1987, over 6 million ounces were used as a solder and brazing alloy in the manufacturing of sterling and electroplate. Manufacturers of air conditioners, refrigerators, and aircraft are other major users of silver as a solder and brazing alloy, averaging 5.5 million ounces in 1987.

Other Uses

Collection of commemorative coins and medallions in recent years has created an additional demand for silver, reaching more than 4 million ounces in 1987. The dental and medical professions consume more than 1 million ounces of silver each year.

Substitutable Commodities

Stainless steel, pewter, and aluminum are popular substitutes for silver tableware. Aluminum and rhodium are used as substitutes for silver in reflectors, and tantalum is substituted in surgical sutures, plates, and pins.

Substitutes for silver in the electrical and electronic fields are available, but at the moment are costly and somewhat inferior to silver.

Futures Markets

Silver futures are traded at the Chicago Board of Trade, the Commodity Exchange, Inc. (COMEX), and the MidAmerica Commodity Exchange. Options on silver futures are traded at the Chicago Board of Trade and COMEX.

COPPER

Geological evidence shows that open-pit mining of copper and the use of copper in primitive weapons, tools, and utensils dates back to prehistoric times. Copper was probably first discovered and used by people living in a European region.

A nonferrous metal, copper is a highly versatile substance valued for its excellent conductivity, noncorrosiveness, and heat resistance. It has many applications in automotive, electrical/electronic, communications, and construction products, as well as lesser uses in jewelry, decorative arts, and housewares.

Mining and Processing

Copper is obtained from mining and from secondary recovery of scrap. Approximately 80 to 90 percent of copper is mined in open pits; the remainder is mined by various underground methods. Most mined copper comes from base-metal sulfide ores that contain varying amounts of other metals, including gold, silver, nickel, lead, zinc, platinum, and palladium. As a result, a rather complex processing that includes milling, smelting, and refining is necessary to obtain pure, refined copper. The milling process involves crushing the ore and using water, chemicals, and air to concentrate the copper and isolate it from other metals and waste.

In the smelting process, the copper concentrate that results from milling is roasted, melted, and treated with air. Prior to smelting, the concentrate is only 20 to 30 percent copper. At the end of the three-part smelting operation, the resulting product, called *blister copper*, is 98.5 percent pure.

Refining

Copper can be refined by two different methods—electrolysis and firing. Electrolytic refining is used to produce nearly 90 percent of all refined copper. In this process, the blister copper is melted in a furnace and cast into anodes (positive terminals of an electrolytic cell). The anodes are then placed in tanks of electrolytic solution with thin sheets of copper called *cathodes*. When an electrical charge is run through the electrolyte solution, pure copper is deposited onto the cathodes, leaving impurities behind in the tank and solution. The pure copper cathodes can then be melted and cast into ingots.

Manufacturing

To manufacture finished copper products, ingots of various kinds and sizes are normally rolled to produce sheets, melted and extruded for wire products, or melted and recast to make parts of many shapes and sizes.

Throughout the world, there are only a few large companies that mine, refine, and manufacture copper; they vary greatly in the type of functions they perform. Some firms are involved in all stages of copper production, from mining copper through the manufacturing process, while others specialize in refining or manufacturing.

Supply

World and U.S. Production

The world mine production of copper in 1987 totaled nearly 8.5 million metric tons, and total refined copper, which is close to 99 percent pure copper, was almost 10 million metric tons. The leading copper-producing countries in 1987 were the United States and Chile.

Since 1983, the United States has been the world's largest copper producer. In 1987, the United States accounted for 15 percent of world mined copper production and 16 percent of refined copper production. Arizona totaled 61 percent of the 1.2 million metric tons mined in the United States in 1987. Other copper mining states include Utah, New Mexico, Montana, and Nevada.

The United States also imports copper, with total imports reaching 568,470 metric tons in 1987. Of this total, 469,181 metric tons were refined.

Newly refined copper, however, is not the only source of supply. In 1987, secondary recovery—the reclamation of old and new copper scrap—accounted for 40 percent of the total U.S. consumption of copper.

U.S. Copper Exports
1987

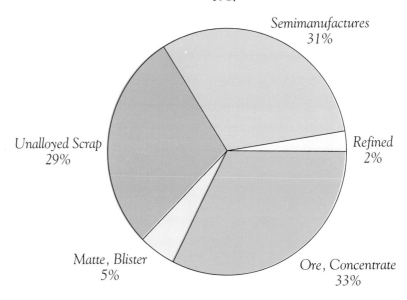

Source: U.S. Bureau of the Census

Demand

The United States is the largest copper consumer, followed by the Soviet Union and Japan. Together, these three countries consume approximately one half of the world's total production.

Uses

Copper is used in a wide range of products. The electrical and electronic industries are the primary users of copper, accounting for 70 percent of U.S. demand. Also consuming large amounts of copper are the construction, industrial machinery, and transportation industries.

Because copper is resistant to corrosion and has the ability to conduct heat, it is used in motors, power generators, batteries, fans, and heating and refrigeration equipment. Copper also is used in a variety of communications equipment, such as telephones, telegraphs, televisions, radio receivers, and communications satellites.

The construction industry accounts for 15 percent of total U.S. demand and uses it in roofs, plumbing fixtures and pipes, hardware, and decorative products. However, copper faces some competition from aluminum for use in roof construction, and plastic, which is used in place of copper pipes.

The transportation industry consumes copper to manufacture motors and turbines in automotive, rail, and aircraft applications, and in steering, air-conditioning, switching, and signal devices.

Copper also is used in jewelry and coins. These uses of copper account for approximately 9 percent of total copper demand.

Because copper is used in a variety of products, its price is highly sensitive to fluctuations in supply and demand.

Copper futures and options on copper futures are traded on the Commodity Exchange, Inc. (COMEX).

Futures Market

ALUMINUM

Aluminum is one of the most popular industrial metals used today because of its unique chemical and physical properties. Not only is it lightweight and strong, aluminum has high levels of thermal and electrical conductivity, and is resistant to corrosion, heat, and light. It is also malleable, nonmagnetic, and nontoxic.

Despite its popularity and usefulness, large-scale production and significant usage of aluminum did not occur until the turn of the century. A major reason for the delay was that aluminum, unlike other metals, is not found free in nature. It is found combined with oxygen in an ore called *bauxite*. And, the scientific knowledge to separate the two elements was not discovered until the late 1800s.

The production of aluminum from bauxite is a two-step process. Bauxite is first refined into a nonmetallic intermediate product called *alumina*. This white powder is then converted into primary aluminum by a smelting process during the second step. Primary aluminum is about 99.8 percent aluminum and .2 percent other elements. Further refining can produce metal that is 99.9 percent pure.

While pure aluminum is noncorrosive and an excellent conductor of electricity, it lacks strength and hardness. Because of this, aluminum is

Supply

alloyed (mixed with other metals like copper, manganese, and zinc) to improve its properties. Molten aluminum can be cast into many shapes—ingots, T-bars, sows—and used for a variety of different metal products.

Bauxite Reserves

World bauxite reserves, estimated at about 23 billion tons, are adequate to supply the world demand for aluminum well into the 21st century. Among the countries with the largest bauxite reserves are Australia, Guinea, Brazil, and Jamaica. Greece, Hungary, Yugoslavia, and France also have significant reserves. The United States, on the other hand, does not have sizable enough bauxite reserves to produce aluminum and must rely on imports for its raw material needs.

World Production

World aluminum production in 1987 was about 16 million tons. The United States is the world's leading aluminum producer; total 1987 production was estimated at 3 million tons. Other major producers, in descending order, were the Soviet Union, Canada, Australia, Brazil, West Germany, and Norway.

Demand

Aluminum is used in containers and packaging, construction, transportation, electrical applications, machinery and equipment, and consumer items such as air conditioners, refrigerators, portable appliances, and cooking utensils. In 1987, the packaging industry accounted for an estimated 28 percent of U.S. consumption; building and construction, 19 percent; transportation, 19 percent; electrical, 9 percent; consumer durables, 8 percent; machinery equipment, 5 percent; and 12 percent was for other uses.

The United States consumed 92 percent of the aluminum it produced in 1987; the remaining 8 percent was exported.

Futures Market

An aluminum futures contract is traded on the Commodity Exchange, Inc. (COMEX).

PLATINUM AND PALLADIUM

Six metals comprise the platinum group: platinum, palladium, iridium, osmium, rhodium, and ruthenium. Of these, platinum and palladium are the most important, accounting for 90 percent of the total metal produced from this group of platinum ores.

Platinum and palladium have many similarities and common metallurgical characteristics; often they are used in combination with one another. Both have excellent electrical conductivity and are noncorrosive. Platinum, particularly, is used in settings for fine jewelry.

Supply

Nearly 4 million ounces of platinum and 4 million ounces of palladium were produced worldwide in 1987. Approximately 97 percent of the total was mined and the remainder came from scrap.

South African-mined platinum and palladium totaled 3.7 million ounces in 1987, accounting for 46 percent of the world supply of the two metals. Soviet sales of platinum and palladium on the world market also constitute an important source of world supply. Soviet platinum and palladium production was approximately 3.5 million ounces in 1987. Canada, a smaller producer of the platinum-group metals, produced 381,000 ounces in 1987—approximately 4 percent of the world supply.

World Production

Known reserves of platinum-group ores are relatively small. At present, world reserves of platinum-group ores are estimated at nearly 2 billion troy ounces. These reserves are believed to be five to eight times the projected demand for the next quarter century.

Platinum-group ores are found either in placers (glacial deposits that contain particles of valuable minerals), loose rock formations shifted by glacial movements, or in deposits in rock fissures.

Both South Africa and the Ural Mountain region of the Soviet Union are rich in platinum-group ores, estimated at 1.6 billion ounces and 190 million ounces, respectively. There are smaller, but significant, reserves of platinum-group ores in Canada and Colombia.

The United States had reserves of platinum-group ores of 8 million ounces in 1987.

Reserves

Platinum-group metals are used primarily in the automotive industry. In 1987, production of catalytic converters created the largest demand for platinum and palladium, equaling 1.14 million ounces of total world demand.

Properties of platinum, used in the catalytic converter, help break down poisonous carbon monoxide and hydrocarbon emissions into harmless oxygen and hydrogen. The use of platinum metals by the auto industry has grown in recent years due to the strict government exhaust-emission standards.

Platinum and palladium can be used in combination or singly as catalysts in the production of nitric acid, an important element used to make fertilizers and explosives. In addition, both platinum and palladium are used as catalysts in the production of pharmaceuticals, high-octane gasoline, and other petroleum products.

Demand

U.S. Platinum-Palladium Consumption
1987

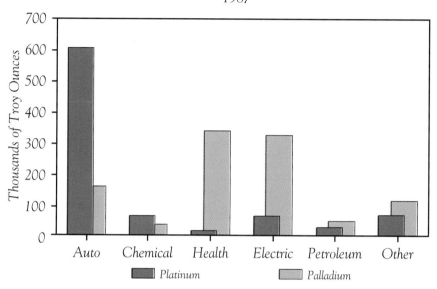

Source: U.S. Bureau of Mines

Platinum, in particular, is used in the manufacturing of blown glass, pressed glass, and glass and synthetic fibers. The use of palladium in low-voltage electrical contacts is far greater than the use of platinum in these products. Due to their excellent electrical conductivity, both platinum and palladium are important products used in the manufacturing of telephones, other telecommunications equipment, and industrial controls.

Though highly valued as precious metals in settings for jewelry and other decorative pieces, use of platinum and palladium for these purposes is small, representing less than 1 percent of total world demand.

U.S. Production and Consumption

As a major consumer of platinum and palladium with only light domestic mine production—100,000 ounces in 1987—the United States relies heavily on secondary refining and imports.

In 1987, the United States consumed 825,000 ounces of platinum and 995,000 ounces of palladium. U.S.-mined and secondary refined platinum and palladium accounted for only 7 and 19 percent, respectively, of reported consumption. The remaining amount came from imports.

Price History

Large supplies of platinum in the mid-1970s decreased prices and stimulated cutbacks by major producing nations. In addition, the Soviet Union reduced platinum sales in 1978. The sales reduction was believed to reflect the channeling of domestically produced platinum by the Soviets toward the production of commemorative coins for the 1980 Moscow Olympics. It also reflected delays in increasing platinum-group metal production and related nickel mining and refining.

The reduced Soviet sales, coupled with an approximate 18 percent increase in the world industrial demand, were major factors behind the world supply deficit of 400,000 to 500,000 ounces in 1979, which sent platinum prices sharply higher.

Part of the sharp rise was caused by increased gold prices related to inflation and currency considerations. Prices continued to climb through 1980 and 1981. In early 1980, for example, platinum exceeded $1,000 an ounce, and palladium was over $300. More recently, prices of both metals have fallen. By 1987, the average price of platinum was estimated at $553 per ounce, and palladium was estimated at $130 per ounce. Palladium prices are significantly lower than platinum prices mainly because palladium is a less effective catalyst in industrial applications.

Futures markets for platinum are conducted on the MidAmerica Commodity Exchange, and palladium and platinum futures trade on the New York Mercantile Exchange.

Futures Markets

This chapter covers the basic economic and political factors that affect the price of lumber, cotton, orange juice, sugar, cocoa, and coffee. All of these commodities are traded on U.S. futures exchanges and specific contract specifications are listed in the Appendix.

The information presented here is a general overview and is not meant to cover all the factors affecting commodity prices. (For additional information on these commodities, see the Sources of Information listed in the Appendix.)

FOREST

Forests are among the country's most valuable national resources. Timber provides a wide variety of wood products that are used in housing, nonresidential construction, furniture, packaging, transportation, and paper products.

Although timber is regarded as an agricultural commodity, a renewable resource, it differs greatly from crops that have annual growing seasons; timber grows for years before it is ready to harvest and mill into wood and paper products.

FOREST,
FIBER,
AND
FOOD
CONTRACTS

Lumber,
Cotton,
Orange Juice,
Sugar,
Cocoa,
Coffee

15

The first section of this chapter discusses two-by-four lumber—a commonly used timber product.

Lumber

Forestlands

Ownership of commercial forestland is divided among private individuals, lumber firms, local and state governments, and the federal government. There are three major forest areas in the United States—the Pacific Northwest, the Rocky Mountain, and the Southern regions. A variety of hardwood and softwood timber is grown in the Pacific Northwest and Rocky Mountain regions, while nearly all timber produced in the Southern region is southern yellow pine. The Pacific Northwest and the Rocky Mountain regions are sometimes referred to as the coastal and inland regions, respectively. The primary species of timber grown in the Pacific Northwest are the Douglas fir and hemlock pine. The Rocky Mountain region forests are populated by white fir, Douglas fir, larch pine, Engelmann spruce, and lodgepole pine. In 1987, these forestlands produced about 35 billion feet of lumber.

Lumber Production

The production of lumber is generally not affected by seasonal considerations; levels are determined primarily by the rate of demand and price. Most lumber mills operate five days a week, two shifts a day, as long as prices are sufficient to produce a profit. This puts a continuous supply of lumber into the distribution pipeline. To produce two-by-four lumber, sawlogs are fed through the automated sawmills onto planing machinery. From there, the lumber is transferred to boxcars and flatcars and transported to where it is sold.

The sawmills that make two-by-fours also produce other lumber products. When prices for two-by-four lumber production are weak, sawmill equipment can be realigned to produce lumber products of other dimensions with better profit potential.

Price Factors

Demand for Lumber

Approximately 40 percent of all dimensional lumber produced in the United States is used in residential construction—framing applications, including external and internal walls, rafters, roofing, and floor joists.

The second highest demand for dimensional lumber, about 30 percent, is in repairs and remodeling followed by nonresidential construction applications, approximately 14 percent. The remainder of dimensional lumber is used in material handling, furniture manufacturing, and other wood products.

Housing Starts and Mortgage Rates

Because lumber is used primarily in residential construction, the monthly housing starts report, compiled by the U.S. Department of

U.S. Timberland Ownership

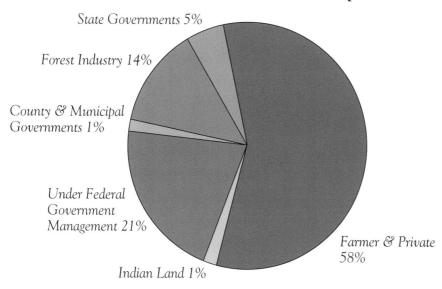

State Governments 5%

Forest Industry 14%

County & Municipal
Governments 1%

Under Federal
Government
Management 21%

Indian Land 1%

Farmer & Private
58%

Source: U.S. Department of Agriculture

Commerce, is the most critically watched indicator of lumber demand. In 1986, new housing starts were estimated at 1.8 million and declined to 1.6 million units in 1987.

In addition to housing starts, a variety of other economic factors indicate lumber demand. In particular, mortgage interest rates, which increased in 1980, caused construction of single-family housing to decrease with a corresponding decrease in lumber demand.

Substitutes, such as steel and aluminum, which are being used more and more in place of lumber for residential construction, also influence lumber demand.

Lumber Exports

In recent years, the export level of U.S. lumber products has been a major factor in the overall demand and price for two-by-four lumber. This was particularly true in the mid-1970s when Japan imported large quantities of U.S. lumber.

Although U.S. exports have declined somewhat, there is still significant foreign demand for plywood, lumber, and sawlogs. This is partly due to the dollar exchange rate in 1987-88, which caused lumber to become more competitive in the world market.

The Chicago Mercantile Exchange trades a futures contract on two-by-four lumber of random lengths from 8 feet to 20 feet and options on two-by-four lumber futures.

Futures Markets

Fiber

Cotton

Cotton, one of the oldest fibers known to man, is the world's leading natural textile fiber. For the past 20 years, the demand for cotton has grown significantly because of population increases and the desire for quality fabrics.

While world cotton consumption has continued to grow over the years, the introduction of synthetics such as rayon and polyester has affected U.S. demand. As a matter of fact, in 1982, U.S. cotton consumption was at its lowest point since 1911. More recently, U.S. consumers have begun to value the superior quality of cotton as a textile, and U.S. demand has begun to rise.

Production

World Cotton

Cotton is produced in more than 75 countries and on every continent in the world except Antarctica. World cotton production in 1987 was at 80 million bales. (One bale of cotton weighs 480 pounds.)

The People's Republic of China, the leading cotton producer during the 1987-88 marketing year, produced more than 19 million bales of cotton. The United States followed China with an estimated production of nearly 15 million bales. The Soviet Union, India, Brazil, Pakistan, Turkey, Egypt, Mexico, and Australia also are leading cotton producers.

U.S. Production

The cotton crop year in the United States begins on August 1 and ends on July 31. Planting begins in March and continues through mid-June depending on the area of the country where cotton is grown. Cotton is grown in four major regions: the Southwest produces approximately 34 percent, followed by the Delta at 32 percent, the West at 27 percent, and the Southeast at 7 percent.

The U.S. Department of Agriculture (USDA) releases a cotton planted acreage intentions report in the spring and an actual planted acreage report during mid-July. Production estimates are published monthly, August through January, or until harvest is completed.

Factors Affecting Production

The price of cotton and the number of acres planted to other crops each year have a great effect on cotton production. For instance, when cotton is priced low and other crops are priced high, fewer acres of cotton are planted. On the other hand, when cotton is priced high and other crops are priced low, more acres of cotton are planted.

Cotton production also is sensitive to weather and insects. Extremes in temperature and rainfall during planting, growing, and harvesting can affect the quantity and quality of cotton.

Government Policies

Government policies play an important role in the supply and price level of cotton.

U.S. government production and price programs for cotton began in 1929 when the Agricultural Marketing Act established a loan rate for cotton. During the 1940s, 1950s, and 1960s, U.S. cotton carryover grew under government programs. Basically, farmers were producing cotton for the government, and artificially high price levels made U.S. cotton unattractive on the world market.

In the 1970s, the government moved toward a free-market system but several government-support programs for cotton continue today including acreage-reduction, Payment-In-Kind, and export programs.

One new government cotton program, established under the 1985 Farm Bill, was designed to make U.S. cotton competitive in world markets and lower stockpiles. Under the rules of the program, cotton farmers are allowed to borrow money using their crop as collateral, just as they have done under past government programs. But when it comes time to pay back the loan, they only need to repay an amount equal to the prevailing world price for cotton (calculated by the USDA).

This marketing program has made U.S. cotton prices competitive in foreign markets and, as a result, U.S. cotton carryover has fallen drastically. The USDA reported that cotton carryover stocks dropped from over 9 million bales in 1985 to 5 million bales in 1987.

The marketing route for cotton starts with the farmer. He sells his crop to the local gin, uses it to redeem a government loan, or sells it to cotton merchants or large textile mills where it is eventually processed into fiber and oilseed.

Marketing Chain

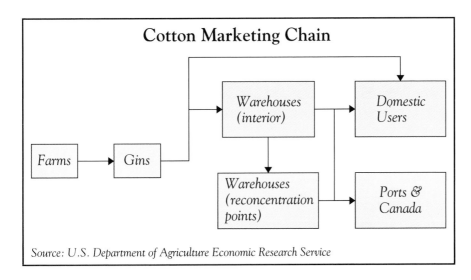

Cotton Marketing Chain

Farms → Gins → Warehouses (interior) → Domestic Users

Warehouses (interior) → Warehouses (reconcentration points)

Warehouses (reconcentration points) → Ports & Canada

Source: U.S. Department of Agriculture Economic Research Service

Cotton Processing

At a gin, the cotton is cleaned, and fiber, called *lint*, is removed from the seed and pressed into 480-pound gross weight bales. The cottonseed is usually sold to oil mills where it is processed into a variety of edible and industrial oil products and cottonseed meal, an animal feed ingredient.

After cotton is processed, its quality and grade are determined. Quality is established by the grade, staple length, and fiber fineness. Merchants then classify the cotton and price it according to similar types.

Cotton is graded according to color, brightness, foreign matter, and the ginning preparation that determines the smoothness of cotton. Actual grading and classifying are done by trained classers, who are licensed and supervised by the USDA.

Both the grade and class tell a buyer how a specific lot of cotton will perform under further manufacturing.

Cotton Uses

Cotton represents approximately 30 percent of the U.S. fiber market. The greatest use of cotton is for clothing, followed by household items such as linen goods, upholstery, draperies, and carpeting.

Futures Market

Cotton futures and options are traded on the New York Cotton Exchange.

FOOD

Orange Juice

Oranges are grown in several countries, and the United States and Brazil are among the top producers.

The popularity of frozen concentrated orange juice (FCOJ) has skyrocketed since World War II, causing orange production and the development of frozen concentrated orange juice to increase significantly.

Factors Affecting Yield

The U.S. crop year for oranges runs from December through November. Florida is the dominant orange-producing state and its production runs from January through mid-June or July, with a break in late February and early March. Frozen concentrated orange juice (also known as *pack*) is processed from mid-December through mid-July.

Orange juice production is directly related to the number of oranges each tree yields. Yield is measured in gallons of juice per box, and one box equals 1.55 gallons of Florida FCOJ.

Yield varies according to the age of the tree and weather conditions. An orange tree requires more than four years of intensive care before it begins to bear fruit. A 5-year-old tree, for example, can be expected to yield only one box of oranges per year, while a mature tree (20 to 45 years old) yields about six boxes each year. Weather affects yield; cold spells, sudden heat, dryness, and strong winds all can damage orange growth and production. The sweetness depends on the length of time the fruit remains on the tree—the longer an orange is on the tree, the sweeter it will be. Processors measure sweetness by the yield of pounds solids. Solids, which are mostly sugar, are what remain when the water is evaporated from the orange juice.

U.S. Orange Production
1987-1988

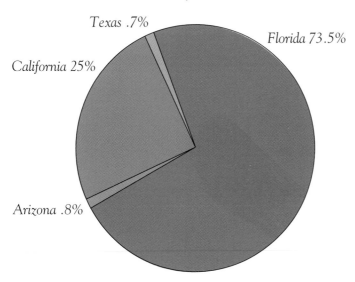

Texas .7%

Florida 73.5%

California 25%

Arizona .8%

Source: U.S. Department of Agriculture

Production
World production of oranges has doubled in the last 20 years reaching 40 million metric tons during the 1985-86 crop year. The United States produced about 16 percent of the world's oranges that year, an estimated 6.8 million metric tons.

In 1986-87, the United States produced more than 7 million metric tons of oranges. Florida produced the most oranges with more than 119 million boxes.* California followed with 58.5 million boxes, and the remainder were grown in Texas and Arizona.

Other Sources of Supply
Supply is influenced not only by current production, but by the number of stocks on hand and the movement of FCOJ to retail outlets.

*The size of one box of oranges varies per state. Florida: one box = 90 pounds; Texas: one box = 85 pounds; Arizona and California: one box = 75 pounds.

Demand

Ninety-three percent of Florida oranges is processed into various food products and 80 percent of that is made into frozen concentrated orange juice and consumed domestically. While the FCOJ market has been primarily a domestic market, it appears it could become more international in the future as more oranges are imported from Brazil to meet U.S. consumer demand.

The best measure of demand is found in the movement of pack (FCOJ) from Florida processors to wholesalers, supermarket chains and other distributors, and manufacturers of food products that use the concentrate as an ingredient. This figure is released every Thursday by the Florida Citrus Processors.

The federal government also is a large consumer of frozen concentrated orange juice because of its purchases for school-lunch and various food programs.

U.S. exports are another measure of demand. In 1987, U.S. exports accounted for 8 percent of the total FCOJ with Canada and the United Kingdom being the largest customers.

Although it has become a staple breakfast item over the years, FCOJ has not escaped competition from market competitors such as artificial orange juice products, other pure fruit juices, and diluted fruit drinks.

Futures Markets

A futures contract in frozen concentrated orange juice and options on that contract are traded by the Citrus Associates of the New York Cotton Exchange, Inc.

Sugar

Historically, sugar has been an important item of international trade because it is considered a luxury item and produced in many countries throughout the world.

Production of sugar has tripled in the last 25 years; much of the growth has taken place in wealthy countries, which consume most of their own production. Seventy percent of the world's sugar is consumed in the same country where it is grown. In 1986-87, more than 103 million metric tons of sugar were produced worldwide.

Largest Producers

During most of the past decade, the United States has been among the top five sugar producers, generally following the Soviet Union, Cuba, Brazil, and India. Other major producing nations include China, Mexico, France, the Philippines, West Germany, and Australia.

Sugarcane and Sugar Beets

Sugar is produced from both sugarcane and sugar beets. Except for the United States, which raises both sugarcane and sugar beets, most areas of the world produce sugar from only one type of plant. Although the nature and location of production as well as the processing techniques for sugarcane and sugar beets are different, refined sugar from each is indistinguishable.

Sugarcane, a bamboolike grass that grows in tropical and semitropical climates, can be harvested approximately 18 months after planting and continues to produce for several years. Sugarcane is usually harvested from fall through spring.

Brazil, India, and Cuba are large sugarcane producers. In the United States, sugarcane is grown predominantly in Hawaii, Louisiana, and Florida.

Sugar beets are white, tapering roots that are about 12 inches long and weigh approximately 2 pounds. They are planted in early spring and harvested before the first winter freeze. The sugar beet plant produced about 38 percent of all sugar in 1986. Sugar beets are grown in temperate zones; 80 percent is produced in the Soviet Union and Europe. The United States produces about 8 percent of the world's sugar beets. California and Minnesota are the major sugar beet-producing states.

There are several economic and political factors that affect the supply and demand of sugar, which, in turn, affect price.

Supply/Demand

Income, Population Growth

On the demand side, per capita income and population are two important economic factors influencing price. Increases in the level of income and population growth in Third World countries, for example, have led to an increase in sugar demand. In recent years, however, sugar demand has fallen slightly due to the use of corn sweeteners.

Production

Variables affecting production and, eventually, the supply of sugar include weather, the number of acres of sugar beets and sugarcane planted, and disease problems.

Among the other variables that affect sugar prices are government stocks, protective agreements, and government policies. Reports of sugar stocks, which measure the balance between supply and demand, are an important indication of total supply and expected price levels.

Most of the world production remaining after domestic consumption is sold internationally under special protective agreements. This accounts for most of the sugar sold to major importers, such as the United States, the Soviet Union, Great Britain, and France.

Marketing Agreements

Since most sugar is either consumed domestically or sold through protective agreements, only about 20 percent is available for trade in the free market. This sugar, referred to as *world sugar*, is monitored by the International Sugar Organization (ISO), a voluntary alliance of sugar exporting and importing countries. The ISO was formed in 1937 to maintain a stable, orderly, free world sugar market.

U.S. Refined Sugar Deliveries
Thousands of Short Tons

Year	Bakery & Cereal Products	Beverages	Confectionery	Institutions	Dairy Products	Processed Foods
1983	1,387	1,248	1,087	195	385	454
1984	1,404	908	1,115	209	408	433
1985	1,494	340	1,059	204	456	428
1986	1,432	266	1,051	142	447	387
1987	1,513	212	1,146	163	449	398

Year	Other Food Uses	Retail Grocers	Wholesalers	Other Uses	Total Deliveries
1983	431	1,168	1,713	131	8,199
1984	416	1,100	1,744	127	7,864
1985	441	1,045	1,874	131	7,472
1986	443	1,066	1,867	138	7,239
1987	534	996	2,040	149	7,600

Source: U.S. Department of Agriculture, Sugar Market Statistics

U.S. Quota System

U.S. sugar supplies are governed by a quota system, established by the USDA, wherein domestic production is supplemented by imports. Each exporting nation is given a quota for which the United States will pay a certain price, usually above the world market price.

The top four sugar exporting nations are Cuba, Australia, Brazil, and the Philippines. The United States exports virtually no raw sugar, but is a significant exporter of edible syrups refined from sugar.

Futures Markets

World sugar, domestic sugar, and world white sugar futures and options on world sugar futures are traded on the Coffee, Sugar & Cocoa Exchange, Inc.

Cocoa

Cocoa is produced from the cocoa or cacao tree, a tropical plant that bears cantaloupe-sized pods. The pods contain cocoa beans, which are processed into cocoa, cocoa butter, and various sweetened and unsweetened chocolate products.

The cocoa plant was originally cultivated in Central and South America and introduced to the European explorers of the Western Hemisphere in the 16th century. Until the 20th century, most cocoa production continued to come from Central and South American countries. Since then, various African nations have become major cocoa producers, and Asian and Oceanian nations have begun production.

World cocoa bean production in 1986-87 was almost 2 million metric tons, down by less than 1 percent from the previous crop-marketing year.

In 1986-87, Africa produced more than 1 million metric tons, or 56 percent of the total world cocoa bean production, with the largest crop coming from the Ivory Coast. South America was the second largest cocoa producer, with 512,800 metric tons, or 26 percent of world production. Brazil and Ecuador grew the most cocoa of the South American countries. Brazil alone accounted for 18.5 percent of world cocoa production. Asia and Oceania raised slightly more than 13 percent of the world's cocoa in 1986-87; Malaysia and Papua New Guinea were the two largest producing nations.

World Cocoa Production

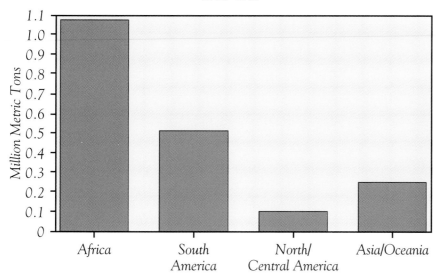

World Cocoa Production
1986-1987

Source: U.S. Department of Agriculture

It takes several years to produce cocoa, because the cocoa tree does not produce enough beans to harvest until it is at least 5 years old. After that, the amount of beans produced increases until the tree reaches its peak

Production Process

yield at 15 years and maintains that yield for another 15 years. A tree's production begins to decline after 40 or 50 years until the tree can no longer be used for commercial production.

Harvest

Beans ripen from October through August with two crops being harvested. The main crop runs from October through March and produces approximately 80 percent of the world total. The mid-crop runs from May to August and produces the balance of the world's total.

After the cocoa pods ripen, they are cut from the trees, opened, and the beans are removed. The beans are fermented, dried, packed into bags, and transported to a processing plant.

In processing, beans are roasted, separated from the husks, and ground into a liquid known as *chocolate liquor*. As the liquor cools, it hardens into a cake. To produce cocoa, most of the fat or cocoa butter is removed from the liquor by hydraulic presses. In the manufacturing of chocolate, however, additional cocoa butter is mixed with the cocoa.

Consumers/ Producers

Brazil, the United States, the Netherlands, West Germany, the Soviet Union, the United Kingdom, and France are among the largest consumers of cocoa. Of these countries, Brazil is the only one that grows cocoa domestically.

Supply

Virtually all of the major bean producers—the African and South American countries, Malaysia, Papua New Guinea, and Oceania—are exporters of cocoa.

Government Policies

Governments of the countries that produce the largest quantities of cocoa designate the amount of cocoa to export. However, the marketing and sales policies of these nations differ considerably. In Ghana, Nigeria, and other West African countries, for instance, government marketing agencies purchase cocoa from farmers and then sell the exports to buyers at predetermined prices. Announcements of the size of the holdings by the marketing agencies, especially those by the Ghana Cocoa Marketing Board, are important indicators of the current crop size and of available supplies for export.

By contrast, Brazilian cocoa is sold through free markets, although the government may establish minimum selling prices and export quotas.

Visible and Invisible Supplies

Cocoa bean stocks are either visible or invisible. Visible stocks are held in public warehouses and these supply figures are available to the public. However, a larger portion of cocoa bean stocks is invisible and held in private warehouses. Because these stocks are privately held, invisible supply figures are difficult to estimate.

Cocoa futures and options on cocoa futures are traded at the Coffee, Sugar & Cocoa Exchange, Inc.

The Ethiopians were probably the first people to use coffee during ancient times. Its popularity spread from Ethiopia to various Arabian countries and into Europe in the Middle Ages. In the 1600s, coffee was the main nonalcoholic drink of most of Europe and the Americas. As coffee demand continued to grow in the United States and Western countries before World War II, coffee was mainly imported from South and Central America. Since then, several African countries have become major producers.

Coffee is one of the most internationally traded commodities. A primary reason for this is that coffee production is concentrated in subtropical and tropical climates while the major consumers live in the United States, Canada, and Europe.

There are two types of coffee: high and low quality. The high-quality group includes the mild coffees of Brazil, Colombia, and other South and Central American countries. The low-quality coffees are lower priced and are grown primarily in Africa.

Coffee trees, or bushes, are grown from hybrid seeds, and they begin to produce fruit about five years after planting. They thrive in subtropical climates at altitudes from 500 feet to more than 2,000 feet above sea level.

Mature trees, 8 to 30 years old, produce about 1 pound of marketable coffee per year. Yield is adversely affected by frost, high wind, drought, excessive rain, and various insects and diseases.

Harvest and Processing

To harvest the coffee berries, which are the seeds of coffee beans, they are picked by hand and soaked in water. The coffee beans are removed from the pulp by friction and fermentation. Beans are then dried and peeled before being sized and packed in 60-kilogram bags to protect the coffee from foreign odors and moisture.

Coffee that is processed and ready for shipment and storage is known as *green coffee*. Green coffee can be stored for long periods of time with little change in quality. At a later time, the coffee beans are blended, roasted, and packaged for consumer sales.

The United States produces very little coffee, but consumes and imports more than any other country in the world. In 1987, U.S. green

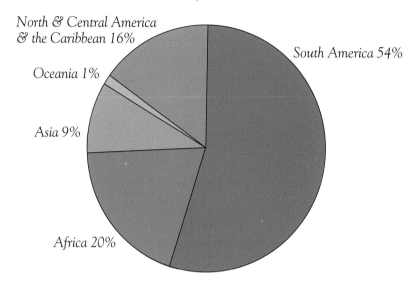

World Green Coffee Production
1987-1988

North & Central America & the Caribbean 16%

Oceania 1%

Asia 9%

Africa 20%

South America 54%

Source: U.S. Department of Agriculture

coffee imports totaled nearly 20 million bags—more than 18 percent of the world coffee production.

Coffee is consumed almost entirely as a beverage in the United States, but also is used as a flavoring in food products. U.S. coffee is sold as beans or ground into a variety of processed forms, such as instant, decaffeinated, or freeze-dried. Coffee bean oil, extracted during processing, is used to manufacture soaps, paints, shoe polish, and medicine. Coffee also is used to produce a type of plastic called *cafelite*.

Other major coffee-importing countries include Canada, Belgium, Luxembourg, Denmark, France, West Germany, United Kingdom, Italy, the Netherlands, and Sweden.

Imports are largely from Central and South America. During the late 1980s, they have produced approximately 70 percent of the world's total.

Marketing

The International Coffee Organization (ICO), a voluntary alliance of coffee exporting and importing countries, sets export and import quotas in an effort to maintain market stability. The ICO evaluates current world supply and demand, and determines production and marketing policies.

Futures Markets

The Coffee, Sugar & Cocoa Exchange, Inc. trades coffee futures and options on coffee futures.

This chapter covers some of the basic supply and demand factors that affect the price of crude oil, heating oil, gasoline, and propane. (To find out more about each, see the Sources of Information listed in the Appendix.)

ENERGY
FUTURES
AND
OPTIONS

Crude Oil,
Heating Oil,
Gasoline,
Propane

CRUDE OIL

Crude oil is petroleum in its natural state. The word *petroleum*, derived from Latin and Greek, means *rock oil*. Petroleum is a generic term applied to oil and oil products in all forms, such as crude oil and petroleum products.

Petroleum probably was used 5,000 years ago to coat the hulls of wooden ships and for religious and medical applications. It was not until approximately 2,000 years ago that its value as a source of light and heat began to be understood. And, the first oil well dug deliberately to obtain crude oil, in Titusville, Pennsylvania, dates only from 1859. In less than 130 years, crude oil exploration has spread around the world to the Middle East, North and South America, Europe, and Africa.

16

World Market

A number of changes occurred during the last decade regarding crude oil pricing and supply. These changes, resulting from political and economic factors, increased competition and limited profits throughout the petroleum marketing chain.

In the early 1970s, the price structure of crude oil changed dramatically due to the Organization of Petroleum Exporting Countries (OPEC).* OPEC emerged as the major pricing power in 1973, when the ownership of oil production in the Middle East transferred from the operating companies to the governments of the oil-producing countries or their national oil companies.

At the same time, OPEC, led by the world's largest oil producer, Saudi Arabia, was the major supplier to the United States, Western Europe, and Japan. Due to increased oil demand, by the mid-1970s, OPEC was supplying two thirds of the free world's oil and more than half of U.S. petroleum imports.

With OPEC's new authority came tremendous price increases and supply changes influenced by political and economic events within the OPEC countries. For example, the Arab oil embargo in 1973 and the Iranian revolution in 1979 had a great effect on oil prices and supply. The price of crude oil rose from about $7 per barrel in 1973 to $34 per barrel in 1982—an increase of almost 400 percent.

However, OPEC's influence decreased as new suppliers emerged following price increases throughout the late 1970s. By 1985, the OPEC share of U.S. petroleum imports declined to 36 percent and the Arab OPEC** share slipped to 9 percent, primarily due to a Presidential order in 1982 prohibiting crude oil imports from Libya. By 1987, however, U.S. imports from Saudi Arabia and Nigeria had increased. As a result, the OPEC and Arab OPEC shares of petroleum imported by the United States increased to 46 and 19 percent, respectively.

Production

In December 1987, world production of crude oil averaged more than 55 million barrels per day. (Barrels per day are the maximum number of barrels of crude oil that can be processed during a 24-hour period. One barrel equals 42 U.S. gallons.) The Soviet Union was the world's leading producer of crude oil in 1987 with about 12 million barrels, approximately 21 percent of the world total.

U.S. Policies and Practices

Producing more than 8 million barrels of crude oil per day, approximately 15 percent of the world's total in 1987, the United States

---

*OPEC members: Algeria, Ecuador, Gabon, Indonesia, Iran, Iraq, Kuwait, Libya, Nigeria, Qatar, Saudi Arabia, the United Arab Emirates, and Venezuela

**Arab OPEC members: Algeria, Iran, Iraq, Kuwait, Libya, Qatar, Saudi Arabia, and the United Arab Emirates

U.S. Petroleum Imports by Source
1986-1987

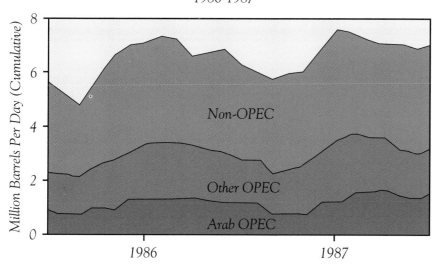

Source: Energy Information Administration, Monthly Energy Review December 1987

was the third largest oil producer and the largest oil importer in the world. In 1987, the United States consumed an average of over 16 million barrels of crude oil per day because of its great energy demands, especially for heavy industry, manufacturing, and transportation. However, the 1987 figure marks a decline from the amount of oil consumed during the 1970s. In 1978, for instance, U.S. oil use peaked at 19 million barrels per day.

This decline in consumption was the result of changes in the world's economy and U.S. policies and practices to conserve more oil. As a result, increased consumer awareness, conservation programs, and alternative sources of energy enabled greater conservation of oil products. The United States became more energy independent, which eventually led to decreases in petroleum imports.

Demand

The demand for energy from crude oil and its refined products is generally broken down into three sectors: residential/commercial, transportation, and industrial, which includes electrical utilities. In addition, petrochemical ingredients are used to manufacture various products, such as plastics, fertilizers, insecticides, waxes, adhesives, foods, cosmetics, pharmaceuticals, and textiles.

The New York Mercantile Exchange trades crude oil futures and options.

Futures Markets

HEATING OIL

Petroleum is refined into six basic product groups—kerosene, jet fuel, diesel fuel, motor gasolines, and residual and distillate fuels.

Distillate fuels are primarily used as fuels for heating, diesel engines, railroads, and agricultural machinery. Heating oil, used to heat homes, accounts for about 40 percent of total distillate fuel production.

Demand for Heating Oil

Heating oil prices are relatively volatile. For example, in 1976, U.S. distributors paid an average price of 32 cents per gallon and consumers an average of 40 cents per gallon for heating oil. In 1987, distributors paid about 53 cents while consumers paid 80 cents per gallon. Much of the cost increase was due to the amount of crude petroleum imported and to inflationary pressures.

While the short-run demand for heating oil is relatively inelastic,[†] several factors influence heating oil demand and price such as the types and sizes of homes, conservation habits, regional differences in climate, and availability and price of alternative home-heating sources.

As an example, if heating oil prices increase significantly, home-owners may be prompted to convert to cheaper fuel sources such as natural gas, electricity, coal, or wood. This occurred during the 1980s when, due to rising costs, consumers reduced their use of heating oil and switched to less expensive fuels.

Weather also plays a major role in demand for heating oil. A particularly harsh, cold winter can increase demand substantially, leading to large price increases. On the other hand, a particularly mild winter can result in lower demand and lead to a price decline.

Futures Markets

Heating oil futures and options are traded on the New York Mercantile Exchange.

GASOLINE

Gasoline includes premium and regular grades, both leaded and unleaded, gasohol, and other refinery products.

For more than 10 years, gasoline has been the largest petroleum product refined in the United States. Nearly 75 percent of gasoline is used by individuals, peaking during the summer when people travel more, and reaching lows during the winter. Total U.S. motor gasoline

[†]Inelastic: Buyers are slow to respond to a change in price.

U.S. Consumption of Energy by End-Use Sector
1973-1987

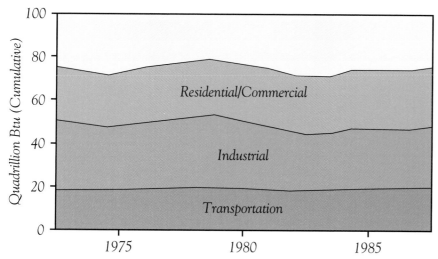

Source: Energy Information Administration, Monthly Energy Review December 1987

consumption for 1987 averaged about 7.2 million barrels a day. More than 90 percent of that total was used for transportation, and the remaining 10 percent was used for construction and agricultural purposes.

The introduction of unleaded gasoline has heralded an important change in the gasoline market over the past decade. Production of unleaded gasoline increased as more and more cars using unleaded fuel were sold. In 1983, leaded gasoline comprised nearly 45 percent of the total U.S. gasoline production, down from 72 percent in 1977. But, by 1987, leaded gasoline declined to 24 percent of the total U.S. gasoline production.

Supply and Demand

Gasoline demand is influenced by summer driving conditions, winter heating oil needs, and governmental fuel efficiency regulations such as pollution-control devices.

In 1987, demand for motor gasoline was strong; prices paralleled those of crude oil, which increased from January through August and then began to decline. The price of unleaded regular motor gasoline averaged 95 cents a gallon in 1987. It rose from 86 cents in January 1987 to almost $1 in August before falling off during the last four months of the year. Leaded regular and unleaded premium gasoline followed the same price movements.

Factors that affect the supply of gasoline include refiners' production ratios, storage capacity, cost of crude oil imports, international events, and government regulations.

U.S. Energy Overview
1973-1987

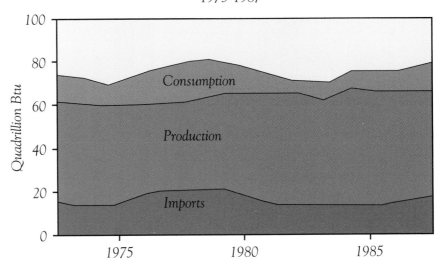

Source: Energy Information Administration, Monthly Energy Review December 1987

Refining	Because gasoline and heating oil demands are inversely related—heating oil demand is greatest during the winter months and gasoline demand is highest during the summer—refineries can alter their production to meet changes in demand.

Gasoline is refined from lighter molecules of crude oil, and distillate fuels from heavier molecules. The heavier molecules can be transformed into lighter-end gasoline products by a catalytic cracking process. If gasoline demand increases, then refiners can run the catalytic cracking at higher levels, increasing the production of lighter-end gasoline products. |
| **Futures Market** | Unleaded regular gasoline futures contracts are traded on the New York Mercantile Exchange. |

PROPANE

Propane is used both as an energy source and to make ethylene and propylene. Propane is a liquid under high pressures and low temperatures and a gas under normal atmospheric conditions. Propane accounts for about 40 percent of all liquefied gases used domestically and represents a broad group of products, including butane, butane-propane, and ethane-propane mixtures.

Propane can be produced in two ways—as a by-product of petroleum refining operations or via a gas-processing plant. If propane is produced at a refinery, it is sometimes labeled *liquid refinery gas (LRG)*; if produced at a gas-processing plant, propane is called *liquefied petroleum gas (LPG)*. In 1986, some 70 percent of all propane was produced at a gas-processing plant.

Production

Propane usage tends to follow the seasonal pattern of heating oil use. This is because propane and other types of liquefied gases compete with heating oil as a heating source in residential and commercial markets. Distribution of propane and other liquid propane gases is different than other refined products for two reasons: (1) to remain liquid, propane must be cooled and subjected to high pressure, and (2) a greater proportion of propane is sold wholesale in comparison to other refined products.

Usage

Propane offers significant advantages over other types of fuel because it is clean burning, highly portable, and easily adaptable to a wide variety of energy needs. In 1986, residential and commerical heating markets accounted for about 40 percent of all propane consumed domestically.

Another important area of propane fuel demand is agriculture. Propane is used in crop drying, flame weeding, poultry brooding, and hog farrowing operations.

Industries such as glass manufacturing and welding use propane because it is portable and provides steady, clean heat. It is also used to manufacture plastics, polyester, and polyvinyl, and to operate floor-cleaning machines, ice rink machines, forklifts for trucks, generators, and refrigerators in vacation and motor homes.

The New York Mercantile Exchange trades a propane futures contract.

Futures Market

Financial instrument futures have gained widespread acceptance as hedging vehicles and have experienced dynamic growth in volume since the first contracts were introduced in the early 1970s. The variety of financial-related futures contracts ranges from interest rate instruments and foreign currencies to stock indexes and Eurodollars. This chapter reviews the history of these contracts and some of the economic factors that affect their price.

FOREIGN CURRENCY FUTURES

The first financial futures contracts began trading in 1972. That year, the Chicago Mercantile Exchange organized the International Monetary Market (IMM) to trade foreign currency futures—the British pound, the Canadian dollar, the Deutsche mark, the Italian lira, the Japanese yen, the Swiss franc, and the Mexican peso.

The birth of foreign currency futures was the result of a changing economic world following World War II. In 1944 at Bretton Woods, New Hampshire, the leaders of the Western world met and created the International Monetary Fund (IMF), a new international monetary system designed to cope with the economic and financial problems

FINANCIAL
FUTURES
AND
OPTIONS

*Currencies,
Interest
Rate
Instruments,
Stock
Indexes*

17

resulting from the Great Depression and World War II.

Under the Bretton Woods agreement, the U.S. dollar was valued at ⅓₅ ounce of gold. In addition, values of other nations' currencies were fixed in relation to the gold content of the U.S. dollar. The Bretton Woods agreement called for central banks of the world to keep the exchange rates of their currencies fixed to the dollar's gold content, with variations limited to plus or minus 1 percent. In practice, however, the central banks kept even tighter margins of parity, allowing variations of only plus or minus one half to three fourths of 1 percent.

As long as there was confidence that official exchange rates would remain stable, the Bretton Woods agreement remained effective. During the 1960s and early 1970s, these fixed exchange rates began to unravel and eventually fell apart in August 1971 when President Richard M. Nixon announced several measures to control inflation: wage and price controls, a dollar devaluation, and the suspension of the dollar's convertibility to gold. The resulting devaluation set the value of the dollar at ⅓₈ ounce of gold. During the following weeks, the exchange rates of the Deutsche mark, the Canadian dollar, the Japanese yen, and other currencies were allowed to float on international currency markets.

By December 1971, during a meeting at the Smithsonian Institution in Washington, D.C., finance ministers of the world's major industrialized nations readjusted the value of both the Japanese yen and the Deutsche mark and attempted to hold down currency fluctuations by allowing them to trade within a 2¼ percent band of par, instead of 1 percent. But it didn't work. Gold prices and inflation rose, and the dollar continued to lose value.

The Smithsonian agreement collapsed in March 1973, which led to a free float of all currencies, and contributed greatly to the volatility of foreign currencies and, ultimately, to the further development of currency futures contracts.

Currency Valuations

The value of a nation's currency fluctuates daily based on a variety of economic factors. These include:

♦ Relative rates of inflation

♦ Comparative interest rates

♦ Growth of domestic money supply

♦ Size and trend of balance of payments

♦ Economic growth as measured by the Gross National Product

♦ Dependency on outside energy sources

♦ Central bank intervention

♦ Government policy and political stability

♦ World perception of a currency's strength

Depending on how a nation's economic environment is viewed by the world's market forces, its currency may be stronger and trade at a premium compared to that of another nation viewed as economically weak. The price relationship between two currencies is known as the *exchange rate*, i.e., the price at which one nation's currency is converted into another nation's currency.

How Exchange Rates Are Quoted

The rates of exchange between the U.S. dollar and foreign currencies are generally quoted in foreign currency units per dollar—e.g., 1.5 Swiss francs per dollar or 1.8 Deutsche marks per dollar.* This is known as the *European terms* and measures the amount of foreign currency needed to buy or sell one U.S. dollar.

Another method used to measure the value of different currencies is the *reciprocal of the European terms.* This measures the dollar value of one foreign currency unit. (This method is used on U.S. futures exchanges where foreign currency futures are traded.)

For example, if the dollar is valued at 125.28 Japanese yen, the value of one Japanese yen is 1 divided by 125.28, or 0.0079821 U.S. dollars. In the case of the British pound, one pound might equal 1.8783 dollars whereas one U.S. dollar equals 0.5324 pound (1 divided by 1.8783).

Exchange Rates

Foreign currency futures—Australian dollar, British pound, Canadian dollar, Deutsche mark, French franc, Japanese yen, Swiss franc—are traded at the International Monetary Market, a division of the Chicago Mercantile Exchange. The Index and Option Market, a division of the Chicago Mercantile Exchange, trades options on Australian dollar, British pound, Canadian dollar, Deutsche mark, Japanese yen, and Swiss franc futures. The MidAmerica Commodity Exchange trades British pound, Canadian dollar, Deutsche mark, Japanese yen, and Swiss franc futures. French franc, British pound, Canadian dollar, Australian dollar, Japanese yen, Swiss franc, Deutsche mark, and European Currency Unit futures are traded at the Philadelphia Board of Trade. The Financial Division of the New York Cotton Exchange (FINEX®) trades European Currency Unit futures and U.S. Dollar Index^sm futures and options.

Futures Markets

A Eurodollar is any U.S. dollar on deposit outside of the United States. This generally refers to dollar balances on the books of London branches of major world banks.

Eurodollars

---

*The only exception is the British pound in which quotes are made in the opposite manner—$1.65 per pound.

History

The growth and development of these financial markets is the result of political tension during the 1950s and 1960s. At that time, the Soviet Union, its Eastern European satellites, and the People's Republic of China feared that, due to Cold War tensions, the U.S. might someday freeze their accounts and confiscate the dollar balances they held in New York City banks. In anticipation of this possibility, the Soviets transferred their dollar balances from New York to London and other European financial centers. Because this transfer of funds was accomplished via the Banque Commerciale pour l'Europe du Nord—the Soviet bank in Paris, also known as *Eurobank*—the term *Eurodollar* emerged.

Several factors were instrumental in developing a demand for dollar financing outside the United States. These included regulatory and capital controls instituted during the 1960s, such as the Interest Equalization Tax of 1964, the Foreign Credit Restraint Program of 1965, and the Foreign Investment Program and Regulation Q in 1968. These controls were later discontinued. Oil price increases in 1974 and 1979 resulted in large dollar transfers into the accounts of nations belonging to the Organization of Petroleum Exporting Countries (OPEC). These petrodollars were deposited in the Euromarket and, in turn, were loaned to oil-importing nations to finance their imports.

The Eurodollar market has become an international capital market outside the jurisdiction of the Federal Reserve System. Consequently, non-U.S. banks accepting dollar-denominated deposits face no reserve requirements. This enables them to loan funds to interested institutions at lower interest rates as well as pay higher interest rates on Eurodollar deposits than domestic money markets of the same maturities.

The Eurodollar market is not without risk. Because Eurodollar deposits are not guaranteed by any government, there are no safeguards to guarantee the depositors' funds. Moreover, a government could establish regulations that would affect the movement of bank deposits into or out of that country. This typically occurs when a country's currency is under pressure. There also is a risk that a government could block the payment of dollar liabilities of its domestic banks during a time of crisis. Nevertheless, an increasing number of banks and corporations use the Eurodollar market to fund foreign debt.

Futures Markets

Eurodollar futures are traded at the International Monetary Market Division of the Chicago Mercantile Exchange, and options on Eurodollar futures are traded at the Index and Option Market Division of the Chicago Mercantile Exchange.

INTEREST RATE INSTRUMENTS

One of the most prominent changes in the marketplace, which has spurred the use of financial futures and options on futures, has been the change from a relatively stable interest rate environment to one that is more volatile. This volatility, in effect, has made not only money, but other financial assets (such as Treasury bonds and Treasury notes) more vulnerable to change.

Following the collapse of the Smithsonian agreement in 1973 and in an effort to curb the rising inflation of the mid-1970s and early 1980s, the Federal Reserve, under Chairman Paul Volcker, moved toward a policy of controlling the nation's money supply rather than controlling the level of interest rates. With this major shift in policy in October 1979, interest rate levels and prices of U.S. debt instruments became a function of the marketplace.

The Federal Reserve, through its network of regional Federal Reserve Banks, acts as a central bank. The Fed is able to control U.S. money supply by regulating the amount of reserves within the banking system.

Money supply has three components:

Federal Reserve

◆ M-1, which consists of currency in circulation, traveler's checks, checking account funds, NOW and super-NOW accounts, automatic transfer service accounts, and balances in credit unions.

◆ M-2, which consists of M-1 plus savings and small time deposits (less than $100,000) at depository institutions, overnight repurchase agreements at commercial banks, and money market mutual fund accounts.

◆ M-3, which consists of M-2 plus large time deposits ($100,000 or more) at depository institutions, repurchase agreements with maturities longer than one day at commercial banks, and institutional money market accounts.

The three tools the Fed uses to control the supply of money are reserve requirements, discount rate, and open market operations.

Reserve Requirements

Member banks of the Federal Reserve are required to maintain a minimum amount of reserves (cash and liquid assets) as a percentage of demand deposits and time deposits. By adjusting the required ratio of reserves to deposits, the Federal Reserve determines how much money banks can lend, thereby setting the pace at which the country's economy and money supply grow.

The lower the reserve requirement, the looser the money supply and the faster the economic growth. By raising the reserve requirement, the money supply is tightened, and economic growth is slowed.

When member banks fall short on their reserve requirements, they may borrow funds from other banks that have excess reserve balances. The rate of interest charged by banks with excess reserves to banks desiring overnight loans to meet reserve requirements is known as the *federal funds rate.*

Discount Rate

The discount rate is the interest rate the Fed charges member banks for loans. The Federal Reserve has the authority to establish the discount rate at whatever level it chooses. By lowering the discount rate, borrowing

Organization of the Federal Reserve System

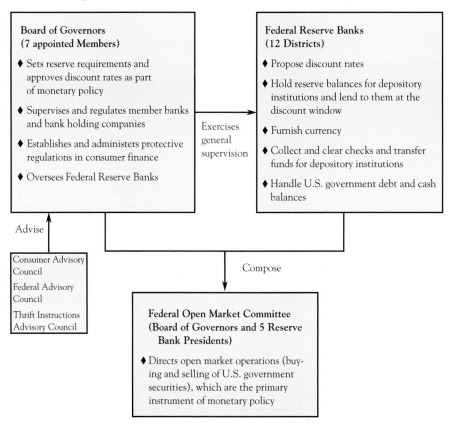

The Federal Reserve System was created in 1913 following the passage of the Federal Reserve Act. The Federal Reserve was formed to provide a safer, more flexible banking and monetary system.

Source: The Federal Reserve System Purposes & Functions, 1984

is less expensive and banks tend to make more loans to their customers. This has the effect of loosening the supply of money.

An increase in the discount rate makes borrowing more expensive, and less attractive to commercial banks. These banks then usually raise interest rates to customers, which causes the demand for credit to decrease.

Open Market Systems

One of the most powerful and flexible monetary policy tools of the Federal Reserve is the open market operation. This involves the purchase and sale of government securities—Treasury bills, notes, and bonds.

When the Federal Reserve buys securities, it adds money in its member bank reserves, thereby increasing the money supply. When it sells securities, it collects money from its member banks, which lowers member bank reserves, thus reducing the supply of money available for lending.

With these three tools—discount rate, reserve requirements, open market operation—the Federal Reserve attempts to control U.S. money supply and influence the U.S. economy. Decisions made by the Federal Reserve do not have to be ratified by the President or by one of his appointees in the executive branch. However, the Federal Reserve must report to Congress, and thereby to the people as a whole, on its policies.

(The information presented in this chapter on the Federal Reserve summarizes its role in the economy and how it controls U.S. money supply. To learn more about the U.S. monetary policies and the Federal Reserve, there are several good texts published by the Federal Reserve listed in the Appendix.)

Another major factor contributing to the rising trading volume in financial futures, particularly interest rate futures, has been the surge in the supply of the underlying commodity—government-issued debt. In 1977, when U.S. Treasury bond futures began trading, U.S. government interest-bearing debt totaled slightly more than $697 billion. By the end of 1988, however, total government-issued, interest-bearing debt had skyrocketed more than 261 percent to more than $2.6 trillion.

| Explosion of Government-Issued Debt |

This explosion of government-issued debt has whetted the appetites of both domestic and foreign investors. Since these securities are backed by the U.S. government, they are considered risk-free because there is virtually no danger of the government defaulting on the timely payment of interest and repayment of principal. Furthermore, the interest rate on U.S. government-issued debt is generally high, which attracts foreign investors. Consequently, U.S. government securities have become global commodities.

Government debt instruments as well as other interest rate instruments are marketable in active secondary markets where investors sell to buyers anytime, anyplace. However, the resale value of securities is determined by prevailing interest rates. To hedge against any undesired changes that could adversely affect the potential resale price of their cash market instruments, a rising number of institutional investors have turned to the financial futures markets.

| **What Is a Debt Instrument?** | Some basic terms and concepts can be applied to debt-instrument markets. A debt instrument is a legally binding promise, sometimes documented through a certificate, in which the debtor promises to repay a loan made by an individual, corporation, or government. In U.S. financial markets, debt instruments are issued by thousands of entities, which are generally categorized into three groups: central governments including the United States, cities and states (collectively known as *municipalities*), and corporations. |

Regardless of whether the issuer is the U.S. government, a municipality, or a corporation, all debt instruments have several common features. These include the rate of interest paid, the face value of the debt instrument, the maturity date, and the terms on which interest is to be paid on the funds loaned.

The interest rate is the cost of loanable funds. It represents the rate of payment a borrower is willing to sustain over a period of time to use the lender's money now. Viewed from the lender's perspective, the interest rate is the rate of return the lender is willing to accept over time for loaning funds.

The lender considers several factors when loaning funds: the amount of money demanded by the borrower, the amount of money the lender has available, the creditworthiness of the borrower, the period of time the borrower wishes to use the money, and whether there are other ways to use the same funds more profitably. The borrower, on the other hand, also evaluates several factors before requesting a loan: the minimum amount of funds needed, the length of time involved, and how the rate compares with other interest rates for comparable loans.

Coupon

The rate of interest (earned or paid) on a debt instrument is typically expressed as an annualized percentage. In the debt market, it is common for this interest rate to be called the *coupon*. Before the advent of computer and electronic fund transfers, debt instruments that were issued by corporations as well as state and local governments had small coupons that detached from the certificate. These coupons stated the dollar amount the bank was to pay the bearer when they were presented at local banks or banks designated by the issuer of the debt.

Book Entry

Due to the cost of printing and distributing certificates to investors, and the risks involved with keeping them in inventory, there has been an acceleration in the issuance of book-entry securities during the 1980s. With book-entry securities, no certificates are issued to bond holders. Instead, the issuer of debt asks its transfer agent, generally a bank or trust company, to electronically record on computer each creditor's name, address, Social Security or tax identification number, and dollar amount loaned. At a later date, the transfer agent electronically transfers interest payments to each creditor's bank account on a designated date.

This process began at the U.S. Treasury Department in 1979 when T-bills were first offered in book-entry form. By July 1986, all marketable Treasury securities (bills, notes, and bonds) were issued in electronic book-entry form. Individuals or corporations purchasing Treasury securities receive a statement showing their holdings. Interest payments are electronically forwarded to the designated bank account. At maturity, the creditor receives a final interest payment and the face value.

Term

Between the time a debt instrument is issued and the time it matures, a period known as the *term*, the holder of the debt instrument may sell that instrument to any interested buyer. A misconception about the debt market is that once a debt instrument is purchased it must be retained until maturity. That is not the case. Most fixed-income instruments, especially those issued by the U.S. government and large corporations, can be sold at almost any time the purchaser desires. However, the price received by the holder of the debt instrument at resale is influenced by several factors, including the current level of interest rates for comparable debt instruments, the economic outlook, the perceived credit risk of the issuer, and the demand for the specific debt instrument being sold.

Interest Rates, Bond Prices

The price of a specific bond with a fixed coupon fluctuates to compensate for changes in current interest rates. For instance, when interest rates rise above the fixed-rate coupon, the market value of the bond declines since investors are less likely to invest funds in an instrument offering a lower return. When interest rates fall below a fixed-rate coupon, the market value of the bond rises since investors are more likely to invest in an instrument offering a higher return. For these reasons, an inverse relationship exists between bond prices and interest rates: when interest rates rise, the market value of debt instruments declines; when interest rates fall, the market value of debt instruments rises.

Dramatic examples of the relationship were provided on different occasions during the 1980s. As interest rates on long-term government bonds rose to 14 and 15 percent, holders of long-term government bonds receiving 8 or 9 percent interest from their investment saw the value of their debt instruments fall dramatically. On the other hand, as interest rates on long-term Treasury bonds subsequently retreated to single-digit

Interest Rates, Bond Prices, and Yield

levels in the mid-1980s, investors holding government bonds paying 13 or 14 percent interest saw the market value of their investments soar.

Current Yield

The rate of return on invested funds can be determined using two different calculations. The simpler of the two calculations is current yield: the ratio of the coupon to the current price of the instrument.

Current yield can be determined by the following formula:

$$\text{Current yield} = \frac{\text{dollar amount of interest received annually}}{\text{current market price}}$$

Assume an individual invests $10,000 in a U.S. Treasury bond paying 10 percent annual interest. Because the rate of interest paid remains constant, the investor receives $1,000 annually, or semiannual installments of $500. Under this market scenario, the current yield (return on invested funds) is identical to the coupon rate of 10 percent.

$$\text{Current yield} = \frac{\$1,000 \text{ annual interest received}}{\$10,000 \text{ current market price}} = 10\%$$

Current yield changes when interest rates fluctuate. For instance, if interest rates rise above the 10 percent coupon rate on the bond, the market price of the bond falls, thus increasing the current yield. Assume the market price of the bond fell to $8,700 due to higher interest rates. In this case, the current yield would be approximately 11.5 percent.

$$\text{Current yield} = \frac{\$1,000 \text{ in interest received}}{\$8,700 \text{ market value}} = 11.5\%$$

On the other hand, if interest rates fall below 10 percent, the current market value of the bond increases thus lowering the current yield. Suppose the market price of the bond rose to $11,000 due to lower interest rates. Under this scenario, the current yield would be approximately 9 percent.

$$\text{Current yield} = \frac{\$1,000 \text{ in interest received}}{\$11,000 \text{ market value}} = 9\%$$

Yield to Maturity

Despite its wide use, current yield only draws a relationship between coupon payments and market prices; it does not take into account the principal to be paid at maturity. To account for this cash flow, investors use another formula to calculate the return on a bond called *yield to maturity*. Yield to maturity is the rate of interest an investor would have to earn if an investment equal to the price of a bond was capable of generating the coupon payments and the principal of the bond in exactly the yearly pattern promised by the issuer. For instance, assume a bond is selling at $961.60 and has an annual coupon of $80 for the next 20 years and $1,000 at the end of the twentieth year. What interest rate on a $961.60 investment could generate those funds and leave nothing after the payment of the $1,000? A yearly compounding rate of 8.4 percent, which is the yield to maturity of this bond.

Yield-to-maturity calculations are complex because they include the purchase price of the debt instrument, the value received at maturity, the interest received, and the timing of the cash flows between the purchase of the debt instrument and maturity. Because of their complexity, these calculations are not shown here. (For more information on yield to maturity, refer to the texts listed in the Sources of Information.)

Interest rates vary according to the risk, creditworthiness of the borrower, and term of the loan. Repayment risk and creditworthiness are rated by financial agencies. Two of the most prominent agencies are Moody's and Standard & Poor's. After careful analysis of all financial factors as well as the issuer's previous record, if any, in making timely

Interest Rates and Rating Risk

Bond Ratings

		Moody's	Standard & Poor's
Investment Grade	Highest Quality	Aaa	AAA
	High Quality	Aa	AA
	Upper Medium Grade	A	A
	Medium Grade	Baa	BBB
High Yield or **Junk Bonds**	Predominately Speculative	Ba	BB
	Low Grade	B	B
	Default Likely	Caa	CCC
	Very Speculative	Ca	CC
	Lowest Quality	C	C
	Default		DDD

interest and principal payments, each agency assigns a letter grade to the issuer's debt. The rule of thumb is simple: the higher the rating, the greater the likelihood the issuer will pay interest on time and repay the principal at maturity. Generally, issuers with high credit ratings can issue debt at a lower cost (interest rate) than issuers with poor credit ratings.

The letter ratings assigned by Moody's and Standard & Poor's are listed on the previous page.

The broken line in the chart is an important threshold, especially for institutional money managers. Debt instruments listed above the line are rated *investment grade,* meaning they are suitable for purchase by the institutional money manager in accordance with his obligation to be a prudent investor.

On the other hand, bonds rated Ba/BB or lower are classified as high yield, or junk bonds. Junk bonds are generally issued by recently incorporated businesses with little or no financial history that need financing to continue their operations. Well-established companies that have recently encountered severe financial problems or are using debt to finance the acquisition of another corporation also issue junk bonds.

Yield Curve

The relationship between interest rates and the maturities (short-term to long-term) of debt instruments with the same rating can be graphed in a yield curve. In U.S. financial markets, the yield curve is based on U.S. government debt instruments.

The most common shape of the yield curve is an upward slope. In this instance, the yield curve is termed *positive* because long-term interest rates are higher than short-term interest rates. Investors who commit their money for a longer time period are compensated with a higher interest rate.

Positive Yield Curve

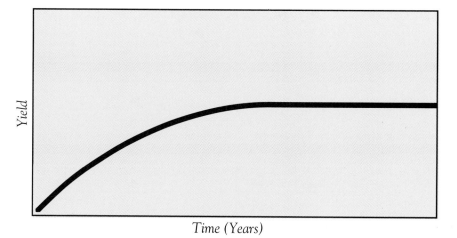

Time (Years)

On the other hand, if short-term interest rates exceed long-term interest rates, then the yield curve slopes generally downward and is referred to as a *negative yield curve*. A negative yield curve can occur during a period of pronounced inflation, such as the late 1970s and early 1980s, when heavy demand for credit forced short-term rates well above the levels of long-term rates. Interest rate levels depicted on yield curves are usually yields to maturity.

Negative Yield Curve

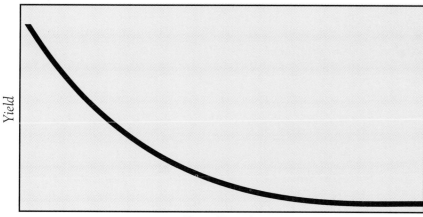

Time (Years)

While individual and corporate taxes help meet the U.S. government's demands for credit, much government spending is financed through borrowing conducted at auctions of U.S. Treasury bills, notes, and bonds. These debt instruments, which are direct, legal obligations of the United States government, have maturities ranging from 90 days to 30 years.	**The U.S. Government**

Debt instruments with maturities of less than a year are known as *bills*; those with maturities from 1 to 10 years are known as *notes*; those with maturities ranging from 10 to 30 years are called *bonds*.

T-bills are among the most widely used money market (short-term) instruments. First issued in December 1929, U.S. Treasury bills are extremely popular investments because of their liquidity and backing by the U.S. government. These interest-bearing instruments are offered in maturities of one year or less: 13 weeks, 26 weeks, or 52 weeks. Unlike other U.S. government debt instruments that pay interest semiannually, T-bills are issued at a discount to their redemption value. The rate of return is reflected in the difference between the discount price and the face value of the bill paid at maturity.	**U.S. Treasury Bills**

T-bills are widely used by banks, corporations, state and local governments, Federal Reserve Banks, pension funds, and individual investors. Commercial banks have special liquidity needs and use T-bills in managing deposits and portfolios as collateral for loans from the Federal Reserve. Corporations use T-bills to earn interest on temporarily idle funds, such as those set aside against future tax liabilities. State and local governments commonly invest tax revenues in T-bills until they are needed for expenditures. The largest ownership of T-bills is by Federal Reserve member banks and U.S. government trust funds.

T-bill Primary Market

As direct obligations of the U.S. government, T-bills are sold to finance the short-term needs of the federal government. The U.S. Treasury Department determines the dollar amount of T-bills to be issued in any given week. The number of bills to be issued is affected by the number of maturing T-bills to be refunded, current interest rate levels, the Treasury's short-term financing needs, and the legal debt limit of the U.S. government.

The Federal Reserve System functions as an agent for the Treasury Department in selling T-bills in the primary market. The Treasury Department is not bound to its auction schedules.

The 13-week and 26-week T-bills are the most widely issued. Both are auctioned every Monday (except holidays) and issued three days later. The 52-week Treasury bills are auctioned every fourth Thursday and issued the following Thursday.

Yields on Treasury bills are quoted on a discount basis using a 360-day calendar year. Consider the auction of 13-week T-bills issued at 6 percent, on December 14, 1987. (The bills were dated December 7, 1987, and matured March 17, 1988.) At the 6 percent rate, the 13-week T-bills were issued at a discount price of $9,848.33.

$$\text{Face value} \times \left(\frac{\text{days to maturity}}{360} \times \text{annual rate}\right) = \text{discount amount}$$

$$\$10,000 \times \left(\frac{91}{360} \times .06\right) = \text{discount amount}$$

$$\$10,000 \times 0.0151666 \quad = \$151.67$$

Once the discount amount is known, the discount price can be calculated:

$$\text{Face value} - \text{discount amount} = \text{discount price}$$

$$\$10,000 \quad - \$151.67 \quad\quad = \$9,848.33$$

Because T-bills are issued at a discount to their redemption value, discounted yields on T-bills cannot be considered on an equivalent basis to yields on term instruments that pay interest semiannually. To make a proper yield-equivalent comparison, the discounted amount of the Treasury bill is divided by the discounted price of the T-bill using a 365-day year.

$$\frac{\$151.67}{\$9,848.33} \times \frac{365 \text{ days}}{91 \text{ days}} = \text{yield equivalent}$$

$$.0154005 \times 4.010989 = \text{yield equivalent}$$

$$6.18\% = \text{yield equivalent}$$

As this example illustrates, using the discounted T-bill yield of 6 percent considerably understates the true yield of the T-bill (6.18 percent) in comparison to other interest-bearing debt instruments.

T-bill Secondary Market

The secondary, or cash market, for T-bills is very active, reflecting the appeal of their variety of maturities and government guarantee. Cash market operations are conducted by 44 primary bank and nonbank securities dealers approved by the New York Federal Reserve Bank. The main function of the dealers is to help the Federal Reserve conduct its open market operations and repo and reverse repo transactions. Along the way, they create ready markets for T-bills and other government securities. These primary dealers receive income through differences in bid/ask spreads. Primary dealers also sell T-bills and other government securities to their customers.

The International Monetary Market Division of the Chicago Mercantile Exchange trades Treasury bill futures, and the Index and Option Market Division of the Chicago Mercantile Exchange trades options on T-bill futures. The MidAmerica Commodity Exchange trades T-bill futures.

Futures Markets

U.S. Treasury notes are intermediate-term debt instruments of the government with maturities ranging from 1 to 10 years.

U.S. Treasury Notes

Because interest rates have been so volatile in recent years, there has been a discernible shift by investors from long-term government debt instruments to intermediate-term government debt instruments. As the chart on the next page illustrates, U.S. Treasury notes accounted for nearly 60 percent of all marketable Treasury debt by the end of 1986, up sharply from over 42 percent in 1972.

Investors in U.S. Treasury notes include the federal government, the Federal Reserve System, banks, insurance companies, savings and loan associations, corporations, state and local governments, private and public pension and trust funds, and individuals.

U.S. Treasury notes are part of a larger group of investment vehicles commonly referred to as *fixed-income investments*, which include U.S. government and federal agency issues, corporate bonds of various

Marketable Treasury Debt

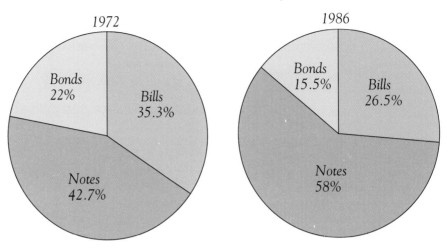

maturities, tax-exempt bonds of state and local governments, and international bonds.

U.S. Treasury notes, unlike U.S. Treasury bills, are not issued on a discounted basis. Furthermore, unlike U.S. Treasury bills, which pay interest at maturity, interest on U.S. Treasury notes is paid semiannually. The semiannual payment is determined when the note is issued. At maturity, a final interest payment is made along with payment of the face value of the note.

As with Treasury bills, U.S. Treasury notes are direct obligations of the federal government, and the Federal Reserve System functions as an agent for the Treasury Department by auctioning T-notes in the primary market. The secondary market for Treasury notes is quite similar to that for Treasury bills and is conducted by essentially the same group of primary dealers and nonbank securities dealers approved by the Federal Reserve System.

Futures Markets

Ten-year T-note futures and options, and five-year T-note futures are traded at the Chicago Board of Trade. Ten-year notes are traded at the MidAmerica Commodity Exchange. The Financial Division of the New York Cotton Exchange (FINEX®) trades five-year T-note futures and options.

U.S. Treasury Bonds

U.S. Treasury bonds are long-term debt instruments of the U.S. government with maturities ranging from 10 to 30 years.

Ownership of U.S. Treasury bonds includes holdings by U.S. government agencies, the Federal Reserve, commercial banks, savings and loan associations, insurance companies, state and local governments, individuals, and foreign investors. As cited earlier, foreign investment in

U.S. Treasury bonds has increased considerably in recent years.

One reason for the increased investment in U.S. Treasury bonds by foreign concerns has to do with the interest rate differential between T-bonds and some foreign issues. For example, in late March 1988, the yield on long-term U.S. Treasury bonds was 8.54 percent, versus 4.46 percent for the long-term Japanese government bond—a difference of 4.08 percent. Competitive interest rates, guarantees of timely payment of interest and repayment of principal, and liquidity have made U.S. Treasury bonds an attractive investment for foreign governments and corporations.

Primary and Secondary Markets for T-bonds

The primary and secondary markets for T-bonds are similar to those for T-bills and T-notes. The Federal Reserve functions as an agent for the Treasury Department in selling T-bonds in the primary market. The secondary market for T-bonds is conducted by the same group of primary dealers and nonbank securities dealers approved by the Federal Reserve.

Because of the effects on the reinvestment value of its coupons among all government-issued debt, U.S. Treasury bonds are typically the most price sensitive to yield changes. Increased interest rate volatility during the 1970s and 1980s has contributed to the growth of the secondary market for T-bonds.

Treasury bond futures and options are traded at the Chicago Board of Trade. The MidAmerica Commodity Exchange also trades T-bond futures. In addition to T-bill, T-note, and T-bond futures and options, there are futures based on the overnight federal funds rate, 30-day interest rate futures, that are traded at the Chicago Board of Trade.

Futures Markets

Municipal bonds are securities issued by state and local governments, and special districts and counties. Although some investors purchase municipal bonds to help fund the many developments and improvements within a municipality, the majority of investors buy them because interest earned from municipal bonds is usually exempt from U.S. federal and sometimes state income taxes.

Municipal Bonds

There are a variety of municipal bond securities with different credit risks, redemption features, and marketability. Consequently, the holder of municipal bonds is exposed to the same risks—changing interest rates, reinvestment risk, credit risk—as the holder of other debt instruments, such as T-bonds and T-notes.

There are basically two different kinds of municipal bonds: general obligation bonds and revenue bonds.

General obligation bonds are debt instruments secured by the general taxing power of the issuer. Revenue bonds, on the other hand, are not backed by the taxing power of a municipality and are issued to fund special building projects like bridges, highways, airports, hospitals, and other structures that serve the general public. The funds collected from these facilities go toward retiring the bond issue.

As industry, finance, and commerce have grown and expanded nationwide, the need for municipal bonds has increased. In fact, newly issued municipal debt has more than doubled since the mid-1970s and has increased by more than 80 percent from 1980 to 1987.

This rapid growth, coupled with a multitude of changing socioeconomic factors, has complicated the municipal bond marketplace and led to the introduction of Municipal Bond Index futures in 1985 at the Chicago Board of Trade.

Futures Markets

Municipal Bond Index futures and options on muni-bond futures are traded at the Chicago Board of Trade.

Mortgage-Backed Certificates

The U.S. mortgage lending and investment process involves securing housing credit from public and private lending institutions for those wanting to borrow funds to purchase a home. However, the number of institutions that may come between borrowers and investors as well as the characteristics of the mortgage asset can change many times as different insurers and guarantors are included and as securities replace the original loan.

Primary Market

The mortgage finance system can be broken into a primary and secondary market. The primary market consists of borrowers who obtain mortgage credit primarily from depository institutions or mortgage banking companies. The repayment of mortgage loans made in primary markets may be guaranteed or insured by third parties. The federal government underwrites fixed-rate residential mortgages under the Federal Housing Administration (FHA) insurance programs and guarantees loans under its Veterans Administration (VA) programs. Since the 1970s, private mortgage insurance companies have become an important factor in the primary market, and in recent years these companies have insured roughly the same number of home mortgage loans as the FHA and VA combined.

Secondary Market

Institutions operating in the primary mortgage markets may hold the mortgages they originate, but, in most cases, the mortgages are sold in the secondary market thereby replenishing their loanable funds.

If a mortgage originator decides to sell its loans in the secondary market, it has three alternatives. First, it may sell whole loans or portions of mortgage loans to private investors, with or without another institution serving as intermediary or broker. Second, a mortgage originator may sell fixed- or adjustable-rate loans to municipal or federal government agencies that either resell the mortgages to private investors or issue debt and hold mortgages in their portfolios. Third, the originator of a mortgage may sell its loans through the secondary market for pass-through securities. By using this technique, lenders pool like groups of loans and sell shares in these pools by issuing pass-through securities. These securities entitle holders to portions of the principal and interest payments on the underlying mortgages in the pools. The payments to securities holders ordinarily are guaranteed by government or private institutions.

The secondary market was first used in the 1930s to provide a market for VA and FHA loans. Today, the secondary market has expanded beyond FHA/VA and conventional loans to include a variety of alternate mortgage instruments, including second mortgages, homeowner loans, and mortgages for multifamily and nonresidential properties. The secondary market has been able to expand since the 1970s due to the introduction of federally regulated pass-through securities issued against pools of government-underwritten and conventional residential mortgage loans. Such securities are issued and guaranteed by the Government National Mortgage Association, the Federal National Mortgage Association, and the Federal Home Loan Mortgage Corporation.

Major securities dealers make primary and secondary cash markets in pass-through securities, providing both immediate and forward delivery. Today's cash market for mortgage-backed securities exceeds the 10- and 30-year Treasury market in terms of annual issuance. Managing the price of originating, securitizing, dealing, and investing in mortgage-backed securities has become paramount. Because of this, futures and options markets in mortgage-backed securities have been organized.

Futures on mortgage-backed securities and options on those contracts are traded at the Chicago Board of Trade.

Futures Markets

STOCK INDEX FUTURES

A major innovation in the application of futures trading occurred on February 24, 1982, when the Kansas City Board of Trade introduced the first futures contract based on a stock index, the Value Line Composite Average. Following the introduction of futures on the Value Line Composite Average, other stock index futures contracts were launched April 21, 1982, at the Chicago Mercantile Exchange on the Standard & Poor's 500 Index; at the New York Futures Exchange (a division of the New York Stock Exchange) May 6, 1982, on the NYSE Composite Index; and at the Chicago Board of Trade on July 23, 1984, on the Major Market Index.

When the futures industry introduced stock index futures in 1982, they received an immediate and impressive response from the U.S.

investment community. Portfolio managers saw stock index futures as a tool to assist in managing the overall market risk of their portfolios.

The investment community found it was valuable to use stock index futures due to the changing nature of the stock market. For example, in 1978, average daily volume on the New York Stock Exchange (NYSE) was just over 22 million shares; the number of block trades (10,000 shares or more) averaged 215 a day; and the Dow Jones Industrial Average (DJIA) traded between 800 and 1000. By 1987, however, average NYSE daily volume was 163 million shares; block trades averaged 3,700 daily; and the DJIA closed above the 2000 level.

Not only does the volume in today's stock market exceed the volume of a decade ago, but the mix of investors active in the stock market and the pattern of investments also have changed considerably.

Institutional investors have been more active in the stock market in recent years. Corporate pension funds and state and federal employee funds as well as insurance companies and banks have increased funds under management. It should be noted that the monies invested in these various equity funds, including mutual funds, are the collective investments of ordinary people. The various funds pool their money and reap economies of scale that benefit members.

What Is a Stock Index?

A stock index is an indicator used to measure and report value changes in a selected group of stocks. There are a variety of stock indexes that track the movement of a specific segment of the stock market or the general movement of the market. How a particular stock index tracks the market depends on its composition—the sampling of the stocks, weighting of the individual stocks, and the method of averaging used to establish an index.

Sampling

When selecting a sample of stocks for an index, the aim is to choose stocks whose aggregate price movement reflects price movements as close as possible to those of the overall market or some desired segment of the market. Studying the performance of stock indexes through the years reveals that a relatively small number of carefully chosen stocks experience price movements similar to those of the entire stock market or of a particular segment of the market.

Weighting

The weighting of individual stocks in the sample is done so the index reflects the relative importance of each stock consistent with the purpose of the index. Some indexes are capitalization weighted (also known as *market value weighted*). With a capitalization-weighted index, component stocks are weighted according to the total market value of their outstanding shares. The impact of a component's price change is proportional to the issue's overall market value, which is the share price times the number of outstanding shares.

Other indexes are price weighted, i.e., component stocks are weighted by their price. Higher-priced stocks therefore have a greater impact on the index than lower-priced stocks.

Averaging

Most stock indexes are computed using the arithmetic mean of stock prices. This means the sum of the prices, or capitalization, is divided by a divisor that is specifically computed and periodically revised to reflect stock splits, mergers, and stock dividends. The divisor maintains the comparability of one day's index level to another day's index level even as the composition of the index changes.

There are a variety of stock indexes and descriptions of some of them follow.

Specific Stock Indexes

Amex Major Market Index

The Amex Major Market Index is a price-weighted (high-priced issues have more influence than low-priced issues) average of 20 blue-chip industrial stocks. It is designed to track the Dow Jones Industrial Average. The index is composed of 20 blue-chip stocks, 17 of which are DJIA-listed companies.

Standard & Poor's Composite Index of 500 Stocks

The S&P 500 Index is capitalization weighted so that a change in a stock's price influences the index in proportion to the stock's relative market value. It is composed of 500 stocks, mostly NYSE-listed companies together with some Amex and over-the-counter stocks. The market value of this index equals approximately 80 percent of the value of all stocks listed on the NYSE.

New York Stock Exchange Composite Index

The New York Stock Exchange Composite Index includes more than 1,500 common stocks traded on the NYSE. The NYSE Composite is a capitalization-weighted index, which means that a change in a stock's price influences the index in proportion to the stock's relative market value.

Value Line Composite Index

The Value Line Composite Average is an arithmetically averaged index of approximately 1,700 stocks that trade on the New York Stock Exchange, the American Stock Exchange, and the over-the-counter market. This index is designed to reflect price changes of a wide range of stocks including many small capitalization issues.

Futures Markets

Futures on the Major Market Index are traded at the Chicago Board of Trade.

S&P 500 futures and options on S&P 500 futures are traded at the Index and Option Market Division of the Chicago Mercantile Exchange.

The New York Futures Exchange trades NYSE Composite Index futures and options.

Value Line Composite Index and Mini Value Line Composite Index futures are traded at the Kansas City Board of Trade.

National Over-the-Counter Index™ futures are traded at the Philadelphia Board of Trade.

Directory of U.S. Futures Exchanges

Chicago Board of Trade
LaSalle at Jackson
Chicago, IL 60604
(312) 435-3500

Chicago Mercantile Exchange
(Index & Option Market)
(International Monetary Market)
30 South Wacker Drive
Chicago, IL 60606
(312) 930-8200

Chicago Rice & Cotton Exchange
141 West Jackson Boulevard
Chicago, IL 60604
(312) 341-3078

Coffee, Sugar & Cocoa Exchange
Four World Trade Center
8th Floor
New York, NY 10048
(212) 938-2800

Commodity Exchange Inc.
Four World Trade Center
New York, NY 10048
(212) 938-2900

Kansas City Board of Trade
4800 Main Street, Suite 303
Kansas City, MO 64112
(816) 753-7500

MidAmerica Commodity Exchange
141 West Jackson Boulevard
Chicago, IL 60604
(312) 341-3000

Minneapolis Grain Exchange
400 South Fourth Street
150 Grain Exchange Building
Minneapolis, MN 55415
(612) 338-6212

New York Cotton Exchange
(Citrus Associates)
(Financial Instrument Exchange
FINEX®)
Four World Trade Center
New York, NY 10048
(212) 938-2650

New York Futures Exchange
20 Broad Street
10th Floor
New York, NY 10005
(212) 656-4949

New York Mercantile Exchange
Four World Trade Center
New York, NY 10048
(212) 938-2222

Philadelphia Board of Trade
1900 Market Street
Philadelphia, PA 19103
(215) 496-5000

CONTRACT SPECIFICATIONS*

CBOT Corn Futures

Trading Unit	5,000 bushels
Tick Size	¼ cent per bushel ($12.50 per contract)
Daily Price Limit	10 cents per bushel ($500 per contract) above or below the previous day's settlement price. No limit in the spot month.
Contract Months	December, March, May, July, September
Trading Hours	9:30 a.m. to 1:15 p.m. (Chicago time), except on the last trading day of an expiring contract, when trading closes at noon
Last Trading Day	Seven business days before the last business day of the delivery month
Deliverable Grades	No. 2 Yellow corn at par and substitutions at differentials established by the exchange

Chicago Board of Trade (CBOT)

Options on CBOT Corn Futures

Trading Unit	One CBOT corn futures contract of 5,000 bushels
Tick Size	⅛ cent per bushel ($6.25 per contract)
Strike Prices	Integral multiples of 10 cents per bushel
Daily Price Limit	10 cents per bushel ($500 per contract) above or below the previous day's settlement premium
Contract Months	December, March, May, July, September
Trading Hours	9:30 a.m. to 1:15 p.m. (Chicago time), except on the last trading day of an expiring contract, when trading closes at noon
Last Trading Day	The last Friday preceding the first notice day of the corresponding corn futures contract by at least five business days
Expiration	10 a.m. (Chicago time) on the first Saturday following the last trading day

*The information in this section is taken from sources believed to be reliable, but it is not guaranteed by the Chicago Board of Trade as to accuracy or completeness, and is intended for purposes of information only. The Rules and Regulations of the individual exchanges should be consulted as the authoritative sources on all current contract specifications.

CBOT *Oat Futures*

Trading Unit	5,000 bushels
Tick Size	¼ cent per bushel ($12.50 per contract)
Daily Price Limit	10 cents per bushel ($500 per contract) above or below the previous day's settlement price. No limit in the spot month.
Contract Months	July, September, December, March, May
Trading Hours	9:30 a.m. to 1:15 p.m. (Chicago time), except on the last trading day of an expiring contract, when trading closes at noon
Last Trading Day	Seven business days before the last business day of the delivery month
Deliverable Grades	No. 2 Heavy and No. 1 oats at par and substitutions at differentials established by the exchange

CBOT *Soybean Futures*

Trading Unit	5,000 bushels
Tick Size	¼ cent per bushel ($12.50 per contract)
Daily Price Limit	30 cents per bushel ($1,500 per contract) above or below the previous day's settlement price. No limit in the spot month.
Contract Months	September, November, January, March, May, July, August
Trading Hours	9:30 a.m. to 1:15 p.m. (Chicago time), except on the last trading day of an expiring contract, when trading closes at noon
Last Trading Day	Seven business days before the last business day of the delivery month
Deliverable Grades	No. 2 Yellow soybeans at par and substitutions at differentials established by the exchange

Options on CBOT Soybean Futures

Trading Unit	One CBOT soybean futures contract of 5,000 bushels
Tick Size	⅛ cent per bushel ($6.25 per contract)
Strike Prices	Integral multiples of 25 cents per bushel
Daily Price Limit	30 cents per bushel ($1,500 per contract) above or below the previous day's settlement premium
Contract Months	September, November, January, March, May, July, August
Trading Hours	9:30 a.m. to 1:15 p.m. (Chicago time), except on the last trading day of an expiring contract, when trading closes at noon
Last Trading Day	The last Friday preceding the first notice day of the corresponding soybean futures contract by at least five business days
Expiration	10 a.m. (Chicago time) on the first Saturday following the last trading day

CBOT Soybean Meal Futures

Trading Unit	100 tons (200,000 lbs.)
Tick Size	10 cents per ton ($10 per contract)
Daily Price Limit	$10 per ton ($1,000 per contract) above or below the previous day's settlement price. No limit in the spot month.
Contract Months	January, March, May, July, August, September, October, December
Trading Hours	9:30 a.m. to 1:15 p.m. (Chicago time), except on the last trading day of an expiring contract, when trading closes at noon
Last Trading Day	Seven business days before the last business day of the delivery month
Deliverable Grades	One grade of meal only with minimum protein of 44 percent; see exchange regulations for exact specifications

Options on CBOT Soybean Meal Futures

Trading Unit	One CBOT soybean meal futures contract of 100 tons
Tick Size	5 cents per ton ($5 per contract)
Strike Prices	Integral multiples of $5 per ton when futures price is less than $200 per ton; integral multiples of $10 per ton when futures price is equal to or greater than $200 per ton
Daily Price Limit	$10 per ton ($1,000 per contract) above or below the previous day's settlement premium
Contract Months	October, December, January, March, May, July, August, September
Trading Hours	9:30 a.m. to 1:15 p.m. (Chicago time), except on the last trading day of an expiring contract, when trading closes at noon
Last Trading Day	The last Friday preceding the first notice day of the corresponding soybean meal futures contract by at least five business days
Expiration	10 a.m. (Chicago time) on the first Saturday following the last trading day

CBOT Soybean Oil Futures

Trading Unit	60,000 pounds
Tick Size	$0.0001 per pound ($6 per contract)
Daily Price Limit	1 cent per pound ($600 per contract) above or below the previous day's settlement price. No limit in the spot month.
Contract Months	January, March, May, July, August, September, October, December
Trading Hours	9:30 a.m. to 1:15 p.m. (Chicago time), except on the last trading day of an expiring contract, when trading closes at noon
Last Trading Day	Seven business days before the last business day of the delivery month
Deliverable Grades	One grade of crude soybean oil only; see exchange regulations for exact specifications

Options on CBOT Soybean Oil Futures

Trading Unit	One CBOT soybean oil futures contract of 60,000 pounds
Tick Size	$.00005 per pound ($3 per contract)
Strike Prices	Integral multiples of 1 cent per pound
Daily Price Limit	1 cent per pound ($600 per contract) above or below the previous day's settlement premium
Contract Months	January, March, May, July, August, September, October, December
Trading Hours	9:30 a.m. to 1:15 p.m. (Chicago time), except on the last trading day of an expiring contract, when trading closes at noon
Last Trading Day	The last Friday preceding the first notice day of the corresponding soybean oil futures contract by at least five business days
Expiration	10 a.m. (Chicago time) on the first Saturday following the last trading day

CBOT Wheat Futures

Trading Unit	5,000 bushels
Tick Size	¼ cent per bushel ($12.50 per contract)
Daily Price Limit	20 cents per bushel ($1,000 per contract) above or below the previous day's settlement price. No limit in the spot month.
Contract Months	July, September, December, March, May
Trading Hours	9:30 a.m. to 1:15 p.m. (Chicago time), except on the last trading day of an expiring contract, when trading closes at noon
Last Trading Day	Seven business days before the last business day of the delivery month
Deliverable Grades	No. 2 Soft Red, No. 2 Hard Red Winter, No. 2 Dark Northern Spring, No. 1 Northern Spring wheat at par, and substitutions at differentials established by the exchange

Options on CBOT Wheat Futures

Trading Unit	One CBOT wheat futures contract of 5,000 bushels
Tick Size	⅛ cent per bushel ($6.25 per contract)
Strike Prices	Integral multiples of 10 cents per bushel
Daily Price Limit	20 cents per bushel ($1,000 per contract) above or below the previous day's settlement premium
Contract Months	July, September, December, March, May
Trading Hours	9:30 a.m. to 1:15 p.m. (Chicago time), except on the last trading day of an expiring contract, when trading closes at noon
Last Trading Day	The last Friday preceding the first notice day of the corresponding wheat futures contract by at least five business days
Expiration	10 a.m. (Chicago time) on the first Saturday following the last trading day

CBOT 5,000-ounce Silver Futures

Trading Unit	5,000 troy ounces
Tick Size	¹⁄₁₀ of a cent per troy ounce ($5 per contract)
Daily Price Limit	$1 per troy ounce ($5,000 per contract)
Contract Months	Current month and the next two calendar months and February, April, June, August, October, December
Trading Hours	7:25 a.m. to 1:25 p.m. (Chicago time), Monday through Friday. Evening trading hours are from 5 to 8:30 p.m. (Chicago time), or from 6 to 9:30 p.m. (central daylight saving time), Sunday through Thursday
Last Trading Day	The fourth to last business day of the delivery month
Deliverable Grades	Refined silver in the form of four or five bars and assaying not less than 999 fineness. Each bar must weigh 1,000 or 1,100 troy ounces with a 10 percent tolerance. The total pack cannot vary from a 5,000-troy-ounce weight by more than 6 percent.
Delivery	By vault receipt issued by a CBOT-approved vault in Chicago or New York

CBOT Kilo Gold Futures

Trading Unit	One kilogram (32.15 troy ounces)
Tick Size	10 cents per troy ounce ($3.22 per contract)
Daily Price Limit	$50 per troy ounce ($1,607.50 per contract) above or below the previous day's settlement price
Contract Months	Current month and the next two calendar months and February, April, June, August, October, December
Trading Hours	7:20 a.m. to 1:40 p.m. (Chicago time)
Last Trading Day	The fourth to last business day of the delivery month
Deliverable Grades	One bar of refined gold (995 fineness) weighing at least one kilogram (32.15 troy ounces) and bearing brands and markings approved by the exchange
Delivery	By vault receipt issued by a CBOT-approved vault in Chicago or New York

CBOT 100-ounce Gold Futures

Trading Unit	100 troy ounces
Tick Size	10 cents per troy ounce ($10 per contract)
Daily Price Limit	$50 per troy ounce ($5,000 per contract) above or below the previous day's settlement price
Contract Months	Current month and the next two calendar months and February, April, June, August, October, December
Trading Hours	7:20 a.m. to 1:40 p.m. (Chicago time), Monday through Friday. Evening trading hours are from 5 to 8:30 p.m. (Chicago time), or from 6 to 9:30 p.m. (central daylight saving time), Sunday through Thursday
Last Trading Day	The fourth to last business day of the delivery month
Deliverable Grades	Refined gold in the form of one 100-ounce bar or three 1-kilo gold bars assaying not less than 995 fineness. The total pack cannot vary from a 100-troy-ounce weight by more than 5 percent.
Delivery	By vault receipt issued by a CBOT-approved vault in Chicago or New York

CBOT 1,000-ounce Silver Futures

Trading Unit	1,000 troy ounces
Tick Size	¹⁄₁₀ of a cent per troy ounce ($1 per contract)
Daily Price Limit	$1 per troy ounce ($1,000 per contract) above or below the previous day's settlement price
Contract Months	Current month and the next two calendar months and February, April, June, August, October, December
Trading Hours	7:25 a.m. to 1:25 p.m. (Chicago time)
Last Trading Day	The fourth to last business day of the delivery month
Deliverable Grades	Refined silver, assaying not less than 999 fineness and made up of one or more brands and markings officially listed by the exchange, in bars cast in basic weights of 1,000 troy ounces (each bar may vary not more than 12 percent more or less)
Delivery	By vault receipt drawn on deposits made in exchange-approved vaults in Chicago

Options on CBOT 1,000-ounce Silver Futures

Trading Unit	One CBOT silver futures contract of 1,000 troy ounces
Tick Size	¹⁄₁₀ of a cent per troy ounce ($1 per contract)
Strike Prices	Integral multiples of 25 cents per troy ounce for strike prices less than $8; 50 cents per ounce for strike prices from $8 to $20; $1 per troy ounce for strike prices of $20 or more
Daily Price Limit	$1 per troy ounce ($1,000 per contract) above or below the previous day's settlement premium
Contract Months	Current month and the next two calendar months, and February, April, June, August, October, December
Trading Hours	7:25 a.m. to 1:25 p.m. (Chicago time)
Last Trading Day	The last Friday preceding the first notice day of the corresponding silver futures contract by at least five business days
Expiration	10 a.m. (Chicago time) on the first Saturday following the last trading day

CBOT *Major Market Index Futures*

Trading Unit	$250 times the value of the Major Market Index, e.g., at 472.00, the value of the MMI futures contract is $118,000 ($250 times 472.00)
Tick Size	.05 of an index point ($12.50 per contract)
Daily Price Limit	80 index points above the previous day's settlement price; initial limit of 50 index points below the previous day's settlement price*
Contract Months	The first three consecutive months and the next three months in the March, June, September, December cycle
Trading Hours	8:15 a.m. to 3:15 p.m. (Chicago time)
Last Trading Day	Third Friday of the delivery month
Delivery	Major Market Index futures are marked-to-market daily according to closing MMI futures prices and are settled in cash at the closing value of the Major Market Index on the last trading day

*For prices below the previous day's settlement price, coordinated price limits and trading halts will be based on 250- and 400-point declines in the Dow Jones Industrial Average. See CBOT Rules and Regulations for detailed plan.

CBOT Mortgage-Backed Futures

Trading Unit	$100,000 par value
Coupons Traded	Each month, the exchange will list a new coupon four months in the future. The coupon for that month will be the current Government National Mortgage Association coupon; trading nearest to par (100) but not greater than par.
Tick Size	⅟₃₂ of a point ($31.25 per contract)
Daily Price Limit	Three points ($3,000 per contract) above or below the previous day's settlement price (expandable to 4½ points)
Contract Months	Four consecutive months
Trading Hours	7:20 a.m. to 2 p.m. (Chicago time)
Last Trading Day	At 1 p.m. on the Friday preceding the third Wednesday of the month
Delivery	In cash on the last trading day based on the mortgage-backed Survey Price; the Survey Price shall be the median price obtained from a survey of dealers

Options on CBOT Mortgage-Backed Futures

Trading Unit	One CBOT mortgage-backed futures contract of a specified delivery month and coupon
Tick Size	⅟₆₄ of a point ($15.625 or $15.63 per contract)
Strike Prices	Multiples of one point ($1,000)
Daily Price Limit	Three points ($3,000 per contract)
Contract Months	Four consecutive months
Trading Hours	7:20 a.m. to 2 p.m. (Chicago time)
Last Trading Day	Options cease trading at 1 p.m. (Chicago time) on the last day of trading in mortgage-backed futures in the corresponding delivery month
Expiration	8 p.m. (Chicago time) on the last day of trading; in-the-money options are exercised automatically

CBOT Municipal Bond Index Futures

Trading Unit	$1,000 times *The Bond Buyer*™ Municipal Bond Index.* A price of 90-00 reflects a contract size of $90,000.
Tick Size	¹⁄₃₂ of one point ($31.25 per contract)
Daily Price Limit	Three points ($3,000 per contract) above or below the previous day's settlement price
Contract Months	March, June, September, December
Trading Hours	7:20 a.m. to 2 p.m. (Chicago time)
Last Trading Day	The eighth to last business day of the delivery month
Delivery	Municipal Bond Index futures settle in cash on the last day of trading. Settlement price on the last trading day equals *The Bond Buyer*™ Municipal Bond Index* value on that day.

*Copyright 1983, *The Bond Buyer*™ and the Chicago Board of Trade. All rights reserved.

Options on CBOT Municipal Bond Index Futures

Trading Unit	One CBOT Municipal Bond Index futures contract deliverable during the months of March, June, September, December
Tick Size	¹⁄₆₄ of a point ($15.63 per contract)
Strike Prices	Integral multiples of two points ($2,000) to bracket the current muni-bond futures price
Daily Price Limit	Three points ($3,000) per contract above or below the previous day's settlement premium
Contract Months	March, June, September, December
Trading Hours	7:20 a.m. to 2 p.m. (Chicago time)
Last Trading Day	Options on Municipal Bond Index futures cease trading at 2 p.m. (Chicago time) on the last day of trading in the Municipal Bond Index futures of the corresponding month
Expiration	8 p.m. (Chicago time) on the last trading day

CBOT 30-Day Interest Rate Futures

Trading Unit	$5 million
Tick Size	In .01 of 1 percent of $5 million on a 30-day basis ($41.67 per basis point)
Price Basis	100 minus the monthly average overnight fed funds rate
Daily Price Limit	150 basis points
Contract Months	First seven calendar months and the first two months in the March, June, September, December cycle following the last spot month
Trading Hours	7:20 a.m. to 2 p.m. (Chicago time)
Last Trading Day	Last business day of the delivery month
Delivery	The contract is cash settled against the average daily fed funds rate for the delivery month. The daily fed funds rate is calculated and reported by the Federal Reserve Bank of New York.

CBOT U.S. 5-Year Treasury Note Futures

Trading Unit	$100,000 face value U.S. Treasury notes
Tick Size	Prices are quoted in increments of $\frac{1}{32}$ of a point; minimum price fluctuation is $\frac{1}{2}$ of $\frac{1}{32}$ ($15.625 per contract)
Daily Price Limit	Three points ($3,000 per contract) above or below the previous day's settlement price (expandable to 4½ points)
Contract Months	March, June, September, December
Trading Hours	7:20 a.m. to 2 p.m. (Chicago time)
Last Trading Day	The eighth to last business day of the delivery month
Deliverable Grades	Any of the four most recently auctioned five-year Treasury notes. Specifically, U.S. Treasury notes that have an original maturity of not more than 5 years and 3 months and remaining maturity of not less than 4 years and 3 months as of the first day of the delivery month.
Delivery	Federal Reserve book-entry wire-transfer system

CBOT U.S. 10-Year Treasury Note Futures

Trading Unit	$100,000 face value U.S. Treasury notes
Tick Size	½₂ of a point ($31.25 per contract)
Daily Price Limit	Three points ($3,000) per contract above or below the previous day's settlement price
Contract Months	March, June, September, December
Trading Hours	7:20 a.m. to 2 p.m. (Chicago time), Monday through Friday Evening trading hours are from 5 to 8:30 p.m. (Chicago time), or 6 to 9:30 p.m. (central daylight saving time), Sunday through Thursday
Last Trading Day	Seven business days prior to the last business day of the delivery month
Deliverable Grades	U.S. Treasury notes maturing at least 6½ years, but not more than 10 years, from the first day of the delivery month. Coupon based on an 8 percent standard.
Delivery	Federal Reserve book-entry wire-transfer system

Options on CBOT U.S. 10-Year Treasury Note Futures

Trading Unit	One $100,000 face value CBOT U.S. Treasury note futures contract
Tick Size	¼₄ of a point ($15.63 per contract)
Strike Prices	Integral multiples of one point ($1,000) per T-note futures contract to bracket the current T-note futures price. If T-note futures are at 92-00, strike prices may be set at 89, 90, 91, 92, 93, 94, 95, etc.
Daily Price Limit	Three points ($3,000) per contract above or below the previous day's settlement premium
Contract Months	March, June, September, December
Trading Hours	7:20 a.m. to 2 p.m. (Chicago time), Monday through Friday Evening trading hours are from 5 to 8:30 p.m. (Chicago time), or from 6 to 9:30 p.m. (central daylight saving time), Sunday through Thursday
Last Trading Day	Options cease trading prior to the delivery month of the underlying futures contract. Options cease trading at noon on the first Friday preceding by at least five business days the first notice day for the corresponding T-note futures contract. For example, the last trading day for December 1988 T-note options is November 18, 1988.
Expiration	10 a.m. (Chicago time) on the first Saturday following the last trading day

CBOT U.S. Treasury Bond Futures

Trading Unit	$100,000 face value U.S. Treasury bonds
Tick Size	1/32 of a point ($31.25 per contract)
Daily Price Limit	Three points ($3,000) per contract above or below the previous day's settlement price
Contract Months	March, June, September, December
Trading Hours	7:20 a.m. to 2 p.m. (Chicago time), Monday through Friday Evening trading hours are from 5 to 8:30 p.m. (Chicago time), or 6 to 9:30 p.m. (central daylight saving time), Sunday through Thursday
Last Trading Day	Seven business days prior to the last business day of the delivery month
Deliverable Grades	U.S. Treasury bonds maturing at least 15 years from the first business day of the delivery month, if not callable; if callable, not so for at least 15 years from the first day of the delivery month. Coupon based on an 8 percent standard.
Delivery	Federal Reserve book-entry wire-transfer system

Options on CBOT U.S. Treasury Bond Futures

Trading Unit	One $100,000 face value CBOT U.S. Treasury bond futures contract
Tick Size	1/64 of a point ($15.63 per contract)
Strike Prices	In integral multiples of two points ($2,000) per T-bond futures contract to bracket the current T-bond futures price. For example, if T-bond futures are at 86-00, strike prices may be set at 80, 82, 84, 86, 88, 90, 92, etc.
Daily Price Limit	Three points ($3,000) per contract above or below the previous day's settlement premium
Contract Months	March, June, September, December
Trading Hours	7:20 a.m. to 2 p.m. (Chicago time), Monday through Friday Evening trading hours are from 5 to 8:30 p.m. (Chicago time), or from 6 to 9:30 p.m. (central daylight saving time), Sunday through Thursday
Last Trading Day	Options cease trading prior to the delivery month of the underlying futures contract. Options cease trading at noon on the first Friday preceding by at least five business days the first notice day for the corresponding T-bond futures contract. For example, the last trading day for December 1988 T-bond options is November 18, 1988.
Expiration	10 a.m. (Chicago time) on the first Saturday following the last trading day

CME Feeder Cattle Futures

Trading Unit	44,000 pounds of 600- to 800-pound feeder steers
Tick Size	$0.00025 per pound ($11 per contract)
Daily Price Limit	1½ cents per pound ($660 per contract) above or below the previous day's settlement price
Contract Months	January, March, April, May, August, September, October, November
Trading Hours	9:05 a.m. to 1 p.m. (Chicago time), except on the last trading day of an expiring contract, when trading closes at noon
Last Trading Day	The last Thursday of the contract month (with exceptions)
Delivery	Cash settled. Settled at the U.S. Feeder Steer Price as calculated by Cattle-Fax.

Options on CME Feeder Cattle Futures

Trading Unit	Option to buy, in the case of the call, or to sell, in the case of the put, one feeder cattle futures contract
Tick Size	$0.00025 per pound ($11 per contract). A trade may occur at a price of $0.000125 per pound ($5.50) if it results in the liquidation of positions for both parties to the trade.
Strike Prices	Stated in terms of cents per pound
Daily Price Limit	None
Contract Months	January, March, April, May, August, September, October, November
Trading Hours	9:05 a.m. to 1 p.m. (Chicago time)
Last Trading Day	The same date and time as the underlying futures contract
Exercise Days	Any business day that the option is traded
Delivery	A long or short position in the underlying futures contract

CME Frozen Pork Bellies Futures

Trading Unit	40,000 pounds of frozen pork bellies, cut and trimmed
Tick Size	$0.00025 per pound ($10 per contract)
Daily Price Limit	2 cents per pound ($800 per contract) above or below the previous day's settlement price
Contract Months	February, March, May, July, August
Trading Hours	9:10 a.m. to 1 p.m. (Chicago time), except on the last trading day of an expiring contract, when trading closes at noon
Last Trading Day	The business day immediately preceding the last five business days of the contract month
Delivery Days	Any business day of the contract month

Options on CME Frozen Pork Bellies Futures

Trading Unit	Option to buy, in the case of the call, or to sell, in the case of the put, one frozen pork bellies futures contract
Tick Size	$0.00025 per pound ($10 per contract). A trade may occur at a price of $0.000125 per pound ($5) if it results in the liquidation of positions for both parties to the trade.
Strike Prices	Stated in terms of cents per pound
Daily Price Limit	None
Contract Months	February, March, May, July, August
Trading Hours	9:10 a.m. to 1 p.m. (Chicago time)
Last Trading Day	The last Friday that is more than three business days prior to the first business day of the delivery month of the underlying futures contract. If that Friday is not a business day, then trading shall terminate on the immediately preceding business day.
Exercise Days	Any business day that the option is traded
Delivery	A long or short position in the underlying futures contract

CME *Live Cattle Futures*

Trading Unit	40,000 pounds of choice grade or better live steers
Tick Size	$0.00025 per pound ($10 per contract)
Daily Price Limit	1½ cents per pound ($600 per contract) above or below the previous day's settlement price
Contract Months	February, April, June, August, September, October, December
Trading Hours	9:05 a.m. to 1 p.m. (Chicago time), except on the last trading day of an expiring contract when trading closes at noon
Last Trading Day	The 20th calendar day of the contract month (with exceptions)
Delivery	Delivery of live cattle must take place on the third business day that is also a delivery day following the initial tender of the certificate
Transfer of Notices	The contract contains some major innovations in the delivery procedure, including a tenderable and retenderable certificate of delivery, demand notices, reclaims
Delivery Papers Due	1. A certificate of delivery no later than 1 p.m. on the third business day prior to any delivery day. 2. A demand notice between 1:30 and 2:30 p.m. on any business day on which certificates are tendered or retendered. 3. A retender notice by 1 p.m. on the business day following assignment. 4. A reclaim notice between 1:30 and 2:30 p.m. on the day the certificate is retendered.

Options on CME Live Cattle Futures

Trading Unit	Option to buy, in the case of the call, or to sell, in the case of the put, one live cattle futures contract
Tick Size	$0.00025 per pound ($10 per contract). A trade may occur at a price of $0.000125 per pound ($5) if it results in the liquidation of positions for both parties to the trade.
Strike Prices	Stated in terms of cents per pound
Daily Price Limit	None
Contract Months	February, April, June, August, September, October, December
Trading Hours	9:05 a.m. to 1 p.m. (Chicago time)
Last Trading Day	The last Friday that is more than three business days prior to the first business day of the delivery month of the underlying futures contract. If that Friday is not a business day, then trading shall terminate on the immediately preceding business day.
Exercise Days	Any business day that the option is traded
Delivery	A long or short position in the underlying futures contract

CME Live Hog Futures

Trading Unit	30,000 pounds of hogs (barrows and gilts)
Tick Size	$0.00025 per pound ($7.50 per contract)
Daily Price Limit	1½ cents per pound ($450 per contract) above or below the previous day's settlement price
Contract Months	February, April, June, July, August, October, December
Trading Hours	9:10 a.m. to 1 p.m. (Chicago time), except on the last trading day of an expiring contract, when trading closes at noon
Last Trading Day	The 20th calendar day of the contract month (with exceptions)
Delivery Days	Monday, Tuesday, Wednesday, Thursday of the contract month, provided such days are not holidays nor the day preceding a holiday
Delivery Papers Due	Notice of Intent no later than 1 p.m. (Chicago time) one business day prior to actual delivery

Options on CME Live Hog Futures

Trading Unit	Option to buy, in the case of the call, or to sell, in the case of the put, one live hog futures contract
Tick Size	$0.00025 per pound ($7.50 per contract). A trade may occur at a price of $0.000125 per pound ($3.75) if it results in the liquidation of positions for both parties to the trade.
Strike Prices	Stated in terms of cents per pound
Daily Price Limit	None
Contract Months	February, April, June, July, August, October, December
Trading Hours	9:10 a.m. to 1 p.m. (Chicago time)
Last Trading Day	The last Friday that is more than three business days prior to the first business day of the delivery month of the underlying futures contract. If that Friday is not a business day, then trading shall terminate on the immediately preceding business day.
Exercise Days	Any business day that the option is traded
Delivery	A long or short position in the underlying futures contract

CME Random Length Lumber Futures

Trading Unit	150,000 bd. ft. of random length 2 × 4s (8 feet to 20 feet)
Tick Size	10 cents per 1,000 bd. ft. ($15 per contract)
Daily Price Limit	$5 per 1,000 bd. ft. ($750 per contract) above or below the previous day's settlement price; no limit in the spot month
Contract Months	January, March, May, July, September, November
Trading Hours	9:10 a.m. to 1:05 p.m. (Chicago time), except the last day of an expiring contract, when trading closes one hour earlier
Last Trading Day	Business day immediately preceding the 16th calendar day of the contract month
Delivery	A seller intending to make delivery must give to the clearinghouse a written "Notice of Intent to Delivery" in a form provided by the exchange, and such notice shall be delivered to the clearinghouse prior to 7 a.m. (Chicago time) on any business day after the termination of trading in the contract month except that on the last business day of the month, the notice shall be given prior to noon

Options on CME Random Length Lumber Futures

Trading Unit	Option to buy, in the case of the call, or to sell, in the case of the put, one random length lumber futures contract
Tick Size	10 cents per 1,000 bd. ft. ($15 per contract). A trade may occur at a price of 5 cents per thousand board feet ($7.50) if it results in the liquidation of positions for both parties to the trade.
Strike Prices	Stated in terms of cents per pound
Daily Price Limit	None
Contract Months	January, March, May, July, September, November
Trading Hours	9 a.m. to 1:05 p.m. (Chicago time)
Last Trading Day	The last Friday of the month prior to the delivery month of the underlying futures contract. If that Friday is not a business day, then trading shall terminate on the immediately preceding business day.
Exercise Days	Any business day that the option is traded
Delivery	A long or short position in the underlying futures contract

International Monetary Market (IMM)
Division of the CME

IMM Australian Dollar Futures

Trading Unit	100,000 Australian dollars
Tick Size	.0001 per Australian dollar ($10 per contract)
Daily Price Limit	Opening price limit between 7:20 and 7:35 a.m. of 150 points. There are no price limits after 7:35 a.m.
Contract Months	January, March, April, June, July, September, October, December, spot month
Trading Hours	7:20 a.m. to 2 p.m. (Chicago time), except on the last trading day of an expiring contract, when trading closes at 9:16 a.m. The market will close earlier on or preceding certain holidays. Contact the exchange for further details.
Last Trading Day	9:16 a.m. on the second business day immediately preceding the third Wednesday of the contract month
Delivery	Delivery shall be made on the third Wednesday of the contract month
Delivery Points	Delivered in the country of issuance at a bank designated by the clearinghouse

IMM Canadian Dollar Futures

Trading Unit	100,000 Canadian dollars
Tick Size	.0001 per Canadian dollar ($10 per contract)
Daily Price Limit	Opening price limit between 7:20 and 7:35 a.m. of 100 points. There are no price limits after 7:35 a.m.
Contract Months	January, March, April, June, July, September, October, December, spot month
Trading Hours	7:20 a.m. to 2 p.m. (Chicago time), except on the last trading day of an expiring contract, when trading closes at 9:16 a.m. The market will close earlier on or preceding certain holidays. Contact the exchange for further details.
Last Trading Day	9:16 a.m. on the second business day immediately preceding the third Wednesday of the contract month
Delivery	Delivery shall be made on the third Wednesday of the contract month
Delivery Points	Delivered in the country of issuance at a bank designated by the clearinghouse

IMM Deutsche Mark Futures

Trading Unit	125,000 Deutsche marks
Tick Size	.0001 per mark ($12.50 per contract)
Daily Price Limit	Opening price limit between 7:20 and 7:35 a.m. of 150 points. There are no price limits after 7:35 a.m.
Contract Months	January, March, April, June, July, September, October, December, spot month
Trading Hours	7:20 a.m. to 2 p.m. (Chicago time), except on the last trading day of an expiring contract, when trading closes at 9:16 a.m. The market will close earlier on or preceding certain holidays. Contact the exchange for further details.
Last Trading Day	9:16 a.m. on the second business day immediately preceding the third Wednesday of the contract month
Delivery	Delivery shall be made on the third Wednesday of the contract month
Delivery Points	Delivered in the country of issuance at a bank designated by the clearinghouse

IMM French Franc Futures

Trading Unit	250,000 French francs
Tick Size	.00005 per franc ($12.50 per contract)
Daily Price Limit	Opening price limit between 7:20 and 7:35 a.m. of 500 points. There are no price limits after 7:35 a.m.
Contract Months	January, March, April, June, July, September, October, December, spot month
Trading Hours	7:20 a.m. to 2 p.m. (Chicago time), except on the last trading day of an expiring contract, when trading closes at 9:16 a.m. The market will close earlier on or preceding certain holidays. Contact the exchange for further details.
Last Trading Day	9:16 a.m. on the second business day immediately preceding the third Wednesday of the contract month
Delivery	Delivery shall be made on the third Wednesday of the contract month
Delivery Points	Delivered in the country of issuance at a bank designated by the clearinghouse

IMM Japanese Yen Futures

Trading Unit	12,500,000 Japanese yen
Tick Size	.000001 per yen ($12.50 per contract)
Daily Price Limit	Opening price limit between 7:20 and 7:35 a.m. of 150 points. There are no price limits after 7:35 a.m.
Contract Months	January, March, April, June, July, September, October, December, spot month
Trading Hours	7:20 a.m. to 2 p.m. (Chicago time), except on the last trading day of an expiring contract, when trading closes at 9:16 a.m. The market will close earlier on or preceding certain holidays. Contact the exchange for further details.
Last Trading Day	9:16 a.m. on the second business day immediately preceding the third Wednesday of the contract month
Delivery	Delivery shall be made on the third Wednesday of the contract month
Delivery Points	Delivered in the country of issuance at a bank designated by the clearinghouse

IMM Pound Sterling Futures

Trading Unit	62,500 pounds sterling (British pounds)
Tick Size	.0002 per pound ($12.50 per contract)
Daily Price Limit	Opening price limit between 7:20 and 7:35 a.m. of 400 points. There are no price limits after 7:35 a.m.
Contract Months	January, March, April, June, July, September, October, December, spot month
Trading Hours	7:20 a.m. to 2 p.m. (Chicago time), except on the last trading day of an expiring contract, when trading closes at 9:16 a.m. The market will close earlier on or preceding certain holidays. Contact the exchange for further details.
Last Trading Day	9:16 a.m. on the second business day immediately preceding the third Wednesday of the contract month
Delivery	Delivery shall be made on the third Wednesday of the contract month
Delivery Points	Delivered in the country of issuance at a bank designated by the clearinghouse

IMM Swiss Franc Futures

Trading Unit	125,000 Swiss francs
Tick Size	.0001 per franc ($12.50 per contract)
Daily Price Limit	Opening price limit between 7:20 and 7:35 a.m. of 150 points. There are no price limits after 7:35 a.m.
Contract Months	January, March, April, June, July, September, October, December, spot month
Trading Hours	7:20 a.m. to 2 p.m. (Chicago time), except on the last trading day of an expiring contract, when trading closes at 9:16 a.m. The market will close earlier on or preceding certain holidays. Contact the exchange for further details.
Last Trading Day	9:16 a.m. on the second business day immediately preceding the third Wednesday of the contract month
Delivery	Delivery shall be made on the third Wednesday of the contract month
Delivery Points	Delivered in the country of issuance at a bank designated by the clearinghouse

IMM Three-Month Eurodollar Futures

Trading Unit	Eurodollar Time Deposit having a principal value of $1 million with a three-month maturity
Tick Size	Multiples of .01 ($25 per contract)
Daily Price Limit	No limit
Contract Months	March, June, September, December, spot month
Trading Hours	7:20 a.m. to 2 p.m. (Chicago time), except on the last trading day of an expiring contract, when trading closes at 9:30 a.m. (3:30 p.m. London time). The market will close earlier on or preceding certain holidays. Contact the exchange for further details.
Last Trading Day	The second London bank business day immediately preceding the third Wednesday of the contract month
Delivery Days	The last trading day. Cash settled.

IMM Three-Month U.S. Treasury Bill Futures

Trading Unit	Three-month (13-week) U.S. Treasury bills having a face value at maturity of $1 million
Tick Size	Multiples of .01 ($25 per contract)
Daily Price Limit	No limit
Contract Months	March, June, September, December
Trading Hours	7:20 a.m. to 2 p.m. (Chicago time), except on the last trading day of an expiring contract, when trading closes at 10 a.m. The market will close earlier on or preceding certain holidays. Contact the exchange for further details.
Last Trading Day	Futures trading in the lead month shall terminate on the business day immediately preceding the first delivery day
Delivery	Delivery shall be made on three successive business days. The first delivery day shall be the first day of the spot month on which a 13-week Treasury bill is issued and a 1-year Treasury bill has 13 weeks remaining to maturity.

IOM Options on Australian Dollar Futures

Trading Unit	Option to buy, in the case of the call, or to sell, in the case of the put, one Australian dollar futures contract
Tick Size	One point, or $0.0001 per Australian dollar ($10 per contract). A trade may occur at a price of .00005 ($5) if it results in the liquidation of positions for both parties to the trade.
Strike Prices	Stated in terms of U.S. dollars per Australian dollar at intervals of 1 cent
Daily Price Limit	Option ceases trading when corresponding futures lock limit at the opening price limit
Contract Months	Serial month listings include options in the March quarterly cycle (March, June, September, December) and options not in the March quarterly cycle (January, February, April, May, July, August, October, November)
Trading Hours	7:20 a.m. to 2 p.m. (Chicago time). The market will close earlier on or preceding certain holidays. Contact the exchange for further details.
Last Trading Day	Second Friday immediately preceding the third Wednesday of the contract month. If this date is an exchange holiday, trading shall terminate on the immediately preceding business day.
Exercise Days	Any business day that the option is traded
Delivery	A long or short position in the underlying futures contract

Index and Option Market (IOM)
Division of the CME

IOM *Options on Canadian Dollar Futures*

Trading Unit	Option to buy, in the case of the call, or to sell, in the case of the put, one Canadian dollar futures contract.
Tick Size	One point, or $0.0001 per Canadian dollar ($10 per contract). A trade may occur at a price of .00005 ($5) if it results in the liquidation of positions for both parties to the trade.
Strike Prices	Stated in terms of U.S. dollars per Canadian dollar at intervals of ½ cent
Daily Price Limit	Option ceases trading when corresponding future locks limit at the opening price limit
Contract Months	Serial month listings include options in the March quarterly cycle (March, June, September, December) and options not in the March quarterly cycle (January, February, April, May, July, August, October, November)
Trading Hours	7:20 a.m. to 2 p.m. (Chicago time). The market will close earlier on or preceding certain holidays. Contact the exchange for further details.
Last Trading Day	Second Friday immediately preceding the third Wednesday of the contract month. If this date is an exchange holiday, trading shall terminate on the immediately preceding business day.
Exercise Days	Any business day that the option is traded
Delivery	A long or short position in the underlying futures contract

IOM Options on Deutsche Mark Futures

Trading Unit	Option to buy, in the case of the call, or to sell, in the case of the put, one Deutsche mark futures contract
Tick Size	One point, or $0.0001 per Deutsche mark ($12.50 per contract). A trade may occur at a price of .00005 ($6.25) if it results in the liquidation of positions for both parties to the trade.
Strike Prices	Stated in terms of U.S. dollars per Deutsche mark at intervals of 1 cent
Daily Price Limit	Option ceases trading when corresponding future locks limit at the opening price limit
Contract Months	Serial month listings include options in the March quarterly cycle (March, June, September, December) and options not in the March quarterly cycle (January, February, April, May, July, August, October, November)
Trading Hours	7:20 a.m. to 2 p.m. (Chicago time). The market will close earlier on or preceding certain holidays. Contact the exchange for further details.
Last Trading Day	Second Friday immediately preceding the third Wednesday of the contract month. If this date is an exchange holiday, trading shall terminate on the immediately preceding business day.
Exercise Days	Any business day that the option is traded
Delivery	A long or short position in the underlying futures contract

IOM *Options on Japanese Yen Futures*

Trading Unit	Option to buy, in the case of the call, or to sell, in the case of the put, one Japanese yen futures contract
Tick Size	One point, or $0.000001 per Japanese yen ($12.50 per contract). A trade may occur at a price of .0000005 ($6.25) if it results in the liquidation of positions for both parties to the trade.
Strike Prices	Shall be stated in terms of U.S. dollars per Japanese yen at intervals of $0.0001
Daily Price Limit	Option ceases trading when corresponding futures lock limit at the opening price limit
Contract Months	Serial month listings include options in the March quarterly cycle (March, June, September, December) and options not in the March quarterly cycle (January, February, April, May, July, August, October, November)
Trading Hours	7:20 a.m. to 2 p.m. (Chicago time); the market will close earlier on or preceding certain holidays. Contact the exchange for further details.
Last Trading Day	Second Friday immediately preceding the third Wednesday of the contract month. If this date is an exchange holiday, trading shall terminate on the immediately preceding business day.
Exercise Days	Any business day that the option is traded
Delivery	A long or short position in the underlying futures contract

IOM Options on Pound Sterling Futures

Trading Unit	Option to buy, in the case of the call, or to sell, in the case of the put, one pound sterling futures contract
Tick Size	Two points, or $0.0002 per pound sterling ($12.50 per contract). A trade may occur at a price of .0001 ($6.25) if it results in the liquidation of positions for both parties to the trade.
Strike Prices	Stated in terms of U.S. dollars per pound sterling at intervals of 2½ cents
Daily Price Limit	Option ceases trading when corresponding future locks limit at the opening price limit
Contract Months	Serial month listings include options in the March quarterly cycle (March, June, September, December) and options not in the March quarterly cycle (January, February, April, May, July, August, October, November)
Trading Hours	7:20 a.m. to 2 p.m. (Chicago time). The market will close earlier on or preceding certain holidays. Contact the exchange for further details.
Last Trading Day	Second Friday immediately preceding the third Wednesday of the contract month. If this date is an exchange holiday, trading shall terminate on the immediately preceding business day.
Exercise Days	Any business day that the option is traded
Delivery	A long or short position in the underlying futures contract

IOM Options on Swiss Franc Futures

Trading Unit	Option to buy, in the case of the call, or to sell, in the case of the put, one Swiss franc futures contract
Tick Size	One point, or $0.0001 per Swiss franc ($12.50 per contract). A trade may occur at a price of .00005 ($6.25) if it results in the liquidation of positions for both parties to the trade.
Strike Prices	Stated in terms of U.S. dollars per Swiss franc at intervals of 1 cent
Daily Price Limit	Option ceases trading when corresponding future locks limit at the opening price limit
Contract Months	Serial month listings include options in the March quarterly cycle (March, June, September, December) and options not in the March quarterly cycle (January, February, April, May, July, August, October, November)
Trading Hours	7:20 a.m. to 2 p.m. (Chicago time). The market will close earlier on or preceding certain holidays. Contact the exchange for further details.
Last Trading Day	Second Friday immediately preceding the third Wednesday of the contract month. If this date is an exchange holiday, trading shall terminate on the immediately preceding business day.
Exercise Days	Any business day that the option is traded
Delivery	A long or short position in the underlying futures contract

IOM Options on Three-Month Eurodollar Futures

Trading Unit	Option to buy, in the case of the call, or to sell, in the case of the put, one Eurodollar time deposit futures contract
Tick Size	One basis point, or .01 IMM Index point ($25 per contract). A trade may occur at a price of .005 IMM Index point ($12.50) if it results in the liquidation of positions for both parties to the trade.
Strike Prices*	Stated in terms of the IMM Index for the Eurodollar time deposit futures contract that is deliverable upon exercise of the option and shall be at intervals of .50 for IMM Index levels below 88.00 and at intervals of .25 for IMM Index levels above 88.00
Daily Price Limit	None
Contract Months	March, June, September, December
Trading Hours	7:20 a.m. to 2 p.m. (Chicago time), except on the last day of an expiring contract, when trading closes at 9:30 a.m. The market will close earlier on or preceding certain holidays. Contact the exchange for further details.
Last Trading Day	Same date and time as the underlying futures contract
Exercise Days	Any business day that the option is traded

*The CME has proposed rules specifying exercise price intervals of .25 for all IMM Index points. The proposed rules are pending CFTC approval.

IOM Options on Three-Month U.S. Treasury Bill Futures

Trading Unit	Option to buy, in the case of the call, or to sell, in the case of the put, one three-month U.S. Treasury bill futures contract
Tick Size	One basis point, or .01 IMM Index point ($25 per contract). A trade may occur at a price of .005 IMM Index point ($12.50) if it results in the liquidation of positions for both parties to the trade.
Strike Prices	Stated in terms of the IMM Index for the three-month Treasury bill futures contract that is deliverable upon exercise of the option and shall be at intervals of .50 for IMM Index levels below 91.00 and at intervals of .25 for IMM Index levels above 91.00
Daily Price Limit	None
Contract Months	March, June, September, December
Trading Hours	7:20 a.m. to 2 p.m. (Chicago time). The market will close earlier on or preceding certain holidays. Contact the exchange for further details.
Last Trading Day	The business day nearest the underlying futures contract that meets the following two criteria: 1) the last day of trading shall be the last business day of the week; and 2) the last trading day shall precede by at least six business days the first business day of the underlying futures contract month
Exercise Days	Any business day that the option is traded

IOM *Standard & Poor's 500 Stock Price Index Futures*

Trading Unit	$500 times the Standard and Poor's 500 Stock Price Index
Tick Size	.05 index points ($25 per contract)
Daily Price Limit and Trading Halts	Coordinated with trading halts of the underlying stocks listed for trading in the securities markets. For complete details of this rule, contact the Chicago Mercantile Exchange Research Division.
Opening Price Limit	During the opening range, there shall be no trading at a price more than five index points above or below the previous day's settlement price. If the primary futures contract is limit bid or offered at the five index point limit at the end of the first 10 minutes of trading, trading shall terminate for a period of two minutes, then reopen with a new opening range.
Contract Months	March, June, September, December
Trading Hours	8:30 a.m. to 3:15 p.m. (Chicago time)
Last Trading Day	The business day immediately preceding the day of determination of the final settlement price
Delivery	Cash settlement to the final settlement price, determined by a special quotation of the Standard and Poor's Stock Price Index based on the opening prices of the component stocks in the index on the third Friday of the contract month

IOM Options on Standard & Poor's 500 Stock Price Index Futures

Trading Unit	Option to buy, in the case of the call, or to sell, in the case of the put, one Standard & Poor's 500 Stock Price Index futures contract
Tick Size	.05 index points ($25 per contract), except that trades may occur at a price of .025 index points ($12.50) if such trades result in the liquidation of positions for both parties to the trade
Daily Price Limit	All S&P 500 options series close when the S&P 500 futures lock limit
*Strike Prices**	Stated in terms of Standard & Poor's 500 Stock Price Index futures contract, which is deliverable upon exercise of the option and shall be an integer divisible by 5 without remainder, e.g., 110, 115, 120, etc.
Contract Months	Serial month listings include options in the March quarterly cycle (March, June, September, December) and options not in the March quarterly cycle (January, February, April, May, July, August, October, November)
Trading Hours	8:30 a.m. to 3:15 p.m. (Chicago time)
Last Trading Day	The same date and time as the underlying futures contract for March quarterly months and on the third Friday of the contract month in those months other than those in the March quarterly cycle
Exercise Days	Any business day that the option is traded
Delivery	A long or short position in the underlying futures contract. In the absence of contrary instructions to the clearinghouse, expiring March quarterly cycle in-the-month options are automatically exercised and settled in cash to the final settlement price of the underlying futures contract.

*The CME has proposed 10.00 index point exercise price intervals for the third-nearest contract month in the March quarterly cycle, e.g., 110, 120, 130, etc. Proposed rule is pending CFTC approval.

CRCE Rough Rice Futures

Trading Unit	2,000 hundredweight (200,000 lbs.)
Tick Size	$0.005 per hundredweight ($10 per contract) above or below the previous day's settlement price
Daily Price Limit	30 cents per hundredweight ($600 per contract) above or below previous day's settlement price
Contract Months	September, November, January, March, May, July
Trading Hours	9:15 a.m. to 1:30 p.m. (Chicago time), except on the last trading day of an expiring contract, when trading closes at noon
Last Trading Day	The eighth to last business day of the delivery month
Deliverable Grades	No. 2 or better long grain rough rice with a total milling yield of not less than 65 percent, including head rice of not less than 48 percent. Premiums and discounts are provided for each percent of head rice over or below 55 percent and for each percent of broken rice over or below 15 percent.

CSCE Cocoa Futures

Trading Unit	10 metric tons (22,046 pounds)
Tick Size	$1 per metric ton ($10 per contract)
Daily Price Limit	$88 above or below the previous day's settlement price; limits are expandable to $132; limits do not apply to the first two delivery months
Contract Months	December, March, May, July, September
Trading Hours	9:30 a.m. to 2:15 p.m. (New York time)
Deliverable Growths	The growths of any country or clime, including new or yet unknown growths. Growths are divided into three classifications. Group A, deliverable at a premium of $160 per ton, includes Ghana, Nigeria, Ivory Coast, among others. Group B, deliverable at a premium of $80 per ton, includes Bahia, Central America, Venezuela, among others. Group C, deliverable at par, includes Sanchez, Haiti, Malaysia, and all others. Grades are established by the exchange-licensed graders in accordance with specified tolerances for defects, bean count, bean size, and other standards.
Delivery Points	At licensed warehouses in the Port of New York District, Delaware River Port District, or Port of Hampton Roads; optional ex-dock/bulk delivery at discounts from the contract price, subject to agreement of the receiver

Options on CSCE Cocoa Futures

Trading Unit	One CSCE cocoa futures contract
Tick Size	$1 per metric ton ($10 per contract)
Strike Prices	*Futures Contract Price All Months* Less than $3,600 $100 Above $3,600 $200
Daily Price Limit	None
Contract Months	March, May, July, September, December
Trading Hours	9:30 a.m. to 2:15 p.m. (New York time)
Last Trading Day	First Friday of the month preceding the delivery month of the underlying futures contract
Expiration	9 p.m. (New York time) on the last trading day; notification of intention to exercise must be made by option holders to member firms by 4 p.m. (New York time) on such day

CSCE Coffee "C" Futures

Trading Unit	37,500 pounds in approximately 250 bags
Tick Size	$0.0001 per pound ($3.75 per contract)
Daily Price Limit	Six cents (600 points) above or below the previous day's settlement price. Limits are expandable to 9 cents (900 points). Limits do not apply to the two nearest months.
Contract Months	March, May, July, September, December
Trading Hours	9:15 a.m. to 1:58 p.m. (New York time); closing call commences at 2 p.m.
Deliverable Grades	Testing of the quality of the coffee is determined on the basis of the grade of the beans and by cup tasting for flavor. If the coffee is found deliverable, a certification of grade and quality is issued. Since all coffees are not of equal value, the exchange has established certain differentials when delivery occurs. Certain coffees are used to establish the "basis." Coffees judged to be better than the basis are deliverable at a premium. Those judged to be inferior are deliverable at a discount.
Delivery Points	By grading certificate at exchange-licensed warehouses in Port of New York and New Jersey, and the Port of New Orleans

Options on CSCE Coffee "C" Futures*

Trading Unit	One coffee "C" futures contract
Tick Size	$0.0001 per pound ($3.75 per contract)
Strike Prices	*Futures Contract Price* *All Months* Less than 200 cents 5 cents Above 200 cents 10 cents
Daily Price Limit	None
Contract Months	March, May, July, September, December
Trading Hours	9:15 a.m. to 2:13 p.m. (New York time); closing call commences at 2:15 p.m.
Last Trading Day	First Friday of the month preceding the delivery month of the underlying futures contract
Expiration	9 p.m. (New York time) on the last trading day; notification of intention to exercise must be made by option holder to member firm by 4 p.m. (New York time) on such day

*Options contract specifications on those that have been approved by the CFTC as of July 22, 1986. Current specifications may be different and are subject to change. Verify current specifications with your broker.

CSCE Sugar No. 11 (World) Futures

Trading Unit	50 long tons (112,000 lbs.)
Tick Size	$0.0001 per pound ($11.20 per lot)
Daily Price Limit	$0.005. Variable limits go into effect under certain conditions. No price limits are put on the first two delivery months on or after the first business day immediately succeeding the last trading day of the preceding delivery month.
Contract Months	January, March, May, July, October
Trading Hours	10 a.m. to 1:43 p.m. (New York time); closing call commences at 1:45 p.m.
Last Trading Day	Last business day of the month preceding the delivery month
Deliverable Grades	Raw centrifugal cane sugar based on 96 degrees average polarization. Deliverable growths: growths of Argentina, Australia, Barbados, Belize, Brazil, Colombia, Costa Rica, Dominican Republic, El Salvador, Ecuador, Fiji Islands, French Antilles, Guatemala, Honduras, India, Jamaica, Malawi, Mauritius, Mexico, Nicaragua, Peru, Republic of the Philippines, South Africa, Swaziland, Taiwan, Thailand, Trinidad, United States, Zimbabwe delivered f.o.b. and stowed in bulk.
Delivery Points	A port in the country of origin or in the case of landlocked countries, at a berth or anchorage in the customary port of export, f.o.b. and stowed in bulk

Options on CSCE Sugar No. 11 (World) Futures

Trading Unit	One CSCE sugar No. 11 (world) futures contract; the underlying futures contract for the December delivery month is March
Tick Size	$0.0001 per pound ($11.20 per contract)
Strike Prices	*Futures Contract Price* *Two Nearby Months* Less than 10 cents ½ cent-50 points Between 10 and 40 cents 1 cent-100 points Above 40 cents 2 cents-200 points *Futures Contract Price* *Deferred Months* Less than 16 cents 1 cent-100 points Between 16 and 40 cents 2 cents-200 points Equal to or above 40 cents 4 cents-400 points
Daily Price Limit	None
Contract Months	March, May, July, October, December, and first of these months in next year for which futures trading has begun as well as an option that expires in December and calls for delivery of March futures
Trading Hours	10 a.m. to 1:58 p.m. (New York time); closing call commences at 2 p.m.
Last Trading Day	Second Friday of the month preceding the delivery month of the underlying futures contract
Expiration	9 p.m. (New York time) on the last trading day; notification of intention to exercise on the last trading day must be made by option holders to member firms by 3 p.m. (New York time) on such day

CSCE Sugar No. 14 (Domestic) Futures

Trading Unit	50 long tons (2,240 pounds per long ton); 112,000 pounds per lot
Tick Size	$0.0001 per pound ($11.20 per lot)
Daily Price Limit	½ cent (50 points) above or below previous day's settlement price. Limits are expandable in increments of ½ cent (50 points) to a maximum of 2 cents (200 points). Limits do not apply to the nearest two months.
Contract Months	January, March, May, July, September, November
Trading Hours	9:40 a.m. to 1:43 p.m. (New York time); closing call commences upon completion of the white sugar closing call
Deliverable Grades	Raw centrifugal cane sugar based on 96 degrees average polarization; cane sugars of the United States duty free; foreign origin, duty paid, delivered in bulk
Delivery Points	New York, NY (including Yonkers); Baltimore, MD; New Orleans, LA (including Grammercy, Burnside, and Reserve); Savannah and Port Wentworth, GA; Galveston, TX

CSCE World White Sugar Futures

Trading Unit	50 metric tons of white refined crystal beet or cane sugar in new jute bags of 50 kg net weight with polythene liners
Tick Size	20 cents per ton ($10 per contract)
Daily Price Limit	$10 per metric ton; variable limits go into effect under certain conditions. Check with your broker or any exchange member for more information. No price limits are put on the first two delivery months on or after the first business day immediately succeeding the last trading day of the preceding delivery month.
Contract Months	January, March, May, July, October traded in an 18-month cycle
Trading Hours	9:45 a.m. to 1:43 p.m. (New York time); plus a closing call that commences at the conclusion of the No. 11 call
Last Trading Day	The 15th of the month prior to the delivery month; if the 15th is not an exchange business day, then the last trading day is the next exchange business day; notice day is the next exchange business day after the last trading day
Deliverable Grades	Refined or white, beet or cane sugar based on minimum 99.8 degrees polarization
Delivery Points	Rotterdam and Flushing, Netherlands; Antwerp, Belgium; Hamburg, West Germany; Dunkirk and Rouen, France; Immingham, United Kingdom; Galveston, TX; New Orleans, LA; Savannah, GA; Baltimore, MD; New York, NY (including Yonkers); Recife/Maceio, Imbituba/Itajai, and Santos, Brazil; Pusan, Inchon, and Ulsan, Republic of South Korea; Gdansk/Gdynia, Poland

Commodity Exchange, Inc. (COMEX)	

COMEX *Aluminum Futures*

Trading Unit	40,000 pounds; as of September 1989, 44,000
Tick Size	$0.0005 of a cent per pound ($20 per contract)
Daily Price Limit	None
Contract Months	Current month, next two calendar months and any January, March, May, July, September, December falling within a 23-month period beginning with the current calendar month
Trading Hours	9:30 a.m. to 2:15 p.m. (New York time)
Deliverable Grades	Primary aluminum grade P1020A from approved smelter; 40,000 pounds (2 percent more or less) in one and only one of ingot, sow, or T-bar shape; primary aluminum grade P1535A deliverable at discount of 1 cent per pound
Delivery	By negotiable warehouse receipt issued by an exchange-licensed warehouseman, properly endorsed, and including weight certificate returns and producer's certificate of assay and declaration of grade and quality issued by the first clearing member; delivery without any allowance for freight

COMEX *Copper Futures*

Trading Unit	25,000 pounds
Tick Size	$0.0005 per pound ($12.50 per contract)
Daily Price Limit	Subject to change; consult latest official notices from the exchange
Contract Months	January, March, May, July, September, October, December, plus the current month and the next two calendar months
Trading Hours	9:25 a.m. to 2 p.m. (New York time)
Deliverable Grades	Grade 2 electrolytic copper cathodes (full plate or cut); other specified grades and shapes may be tendered, some at contract price and others at premiums established by the exchange

Options on COMEX Copper Futures

Trading Unit	One COMEX copper futures contract
Tick Size	$0.0005 per pound ($12.50 per contract)
Strike Prices	1-cent per pound increments for strike prices below 40 cents; 2-cent per pound increments for strike prices between 40 cents and $1; 5-cent per pound increments for strike prices above $1
Daily Price Limit	None
Contract Months	The nearest four of the following months: March, May, July, September, December
Trading Hours	9:25 a.m. to 2 p.m. (New York time)
Last Trading Day	Second Friday of the month prior to the delivery month of the underlying futures contract

COMEX High Grade Copper Futures

Trading Unit	25,000 pounds
Tick Size	$0.0005 per pound ($12.50 per contract)
Contract Months	Current month, next two calendar months and any January, March, May, July, September, December falling within a 23-month period beginning with the current calendar month
Trading Hours	9:25 a.m. to 2 p.m. (New York time)*
Last Trading Day	Third last business day of the maturing delivery month
Delivery	25,000 pounds (2 percent more or less) of Grade 1 electrolytic copper cathode

*Temporary trading hours for high grade copper futures and options contracts will be 9:28 a.m. to 2 p.m. (New York time). The currently traded contract (standard) will continue to trade from 9:25 a.m. to 2 p.m. (New York time). This will be done on a temporary basis to facilitate price discovery and will cease when trading activity in the standard contract permits. At that time, market opening will return to 9:25 a.m.

Options on COMEX High Grade Copper Futures

Trading Unit	One COMEX high grade copper futures contract
Tick Size	$0.0005 per pound ($12.50 per contract)
Strike Prices	Increments of 1 cent per pound apart for strike prices below 40 cents; 2 cents per pound apart for strike prices between 40 cents and $1; 5 cents per pound apart for strike prices above $1
Contract Months	The nearest four of the following contract months: March, May, July, September, December
Trading Hours	9:25 a.m. to 2 p.m. (New York time)*
Last Trading Day	Second Friday of the month prior to the delivery month of the underlying futures contract
Exercise	Until 3 p.m. (New York time) on any business day for which the option is listed for trading. Upon exercise, option holders receive the appropriate short or long COMEX high grade copper futures contract by way of book entry. Writers of options who receive a notice of exercise are assigned the opposite futures position.

*Temporary trading hours for high grade copper futures and options contracts will be 9:28 a.m. to 2 p.m. (New York time). The currently traded contract (standard) will continue to trade from 9:25 a.m. to 2 p.m. (New York time). This will be done on a temporary basis to facilitate price discovery and will cease when trading activity in the standard contract permits. At that time, market opening will return to 9:25 a.m.

COMEX Gold Futures

Trading Unit	100 troy ounces
Tick Size	10 cents per troy ounce ($10 per contract)
Daily Price Limit	None
Contract Months	February, April, June, August, October, December, plus the current month and the next two calendar months
Trading Hours	8:20 a.m. to 2:30 p.m. (New York time)
Deliverable Grades	100 troy ounces (5 percent more or less) of refined gold assaying not less than 995 fineness, cast either in one bar or in three one-kilogram bars by an approved refiner; the weight, fineness, bar number, and identifying stamp of the refiner must be clearly incised on each bar by an approved refiner
Delivery	By negotiable warehouse receipt issued by and signed on behalf of a licensed depository, properly endorsed and accompanied by a weight certificate

Options on COMEX Gold Futures

Trading Unit	One COMEX gold futures contract
Tick Size	10 cents per troy ounce ($10 per contract)
Strike Prices	$10 per oz. apart for strike prices below $500; $20 per oz. apart for strike prices between $500 and $1,000; $50 per oz. apart for strike prices above $1,000. On the first trading day for any option, there will be nine strike prices each for puts and calls. Strike prices will be added as required according to a predetermined formula.
Daily Price Limit	None
Contract Months	The nearest four of the following contract months: February, April, June, August, October, December
Trading Hours	8:20 a.m. to 2:30 p.m. (New York time)
Last Trading Day	Second Friday of the month prior to the expiration of the underlying futures contract

COMEX Silver Futures

Trading Unit	5,000 troy ounces
Tick Size	1⁄10 of a cent per troy ounce ($5 per contract)
Daily Price Limit	None
Contract Months	January, March, May, July, September, December, plus the current month and the next two calendar months
Trading Hours	8:25 a.m. to 2:25 p.m. (New York time)
Deliverable Grades	Refined silver cast in bars of 1,000 or 1,100 troy ounces with customary trade tolerances above or below said basic weights, weighing in the aggregate 5,000 troy ounces (6 percent more or less), assaying not less than 999 fineness, and made up of one or more brands and markings officially listed by the exchange
Delivery	By negotiable warehouse or vault receipts issued and signed by exchange-licensed warehousemen, properly endorsed and accompanied by (i) invoice, and (ii) itemized bar list showing brand, bar numbers, and weight as stamped on bars

Options on COMEX Silver Futures

Trading Unit	One COMEX silver futures contract
Tick Size	¹⁄₁₀ of a cent per troy ounce ($5 per contract)
Strike Prices	25-cent increments for strike prices below $8; 50-cent increments for strike prices between $8 and $15; $1 increments for strike prices above $15. On the first trading day for any option contract month, there will be nine strike prices available each for puts and calls. Strike prices will be added based on futures price movements.
Daily Price Limit	None
Contract Months	The nearest four of the following contract months: March, May, July, September, December
Trading Hours	8:25 a.m. to 2:25 p.m. (New York time)
Last Trading Day	Second Friday of the month prior to the delivery month of the underlying futures contract

Kansas City Board of Trade (KCBT)

KCBT Wheat Futures

Trading Unit	5,000 bushels
Tick Size	¼ cent per bushel ($12.50 per contract)
Daily Price Limit	25 cents per bushel ($1,250 per contract) above or below the previous day's settlement price
Contract Months	March, May, July, September, December
Trading Hours	9:30 a.m. to 1:15 p.m. (Kansas City time)
Deliverable Grades	No. 2 Hard Red Winter; No. 1 and No. 3 wheat deliverable at differentials established by the exchange
Delivery	Registered warehouse receipts issued by regular elevators

Options on KCBT Wheat Futures

Trading Unit	One KCBT wheat futures contract of 5,000 bushels Hard Red Winter wheat
Tick Size	⅛ cent per bushel ($6.25 per contract)
Strike Prices	Consult exchange for current information
Daily Price Limit	25 cents per bushel ($1,250 per contract) above or below the previous day's settlement price (same as underlying futures contract)
Contract Months	March, May, July, September, December
Trading Hours	9:30 a.m. to 1:20 p.m. (Kansas City time)
Last Trading Day	1 p.m. (Kansas City time) on the Friday that is at least five business days prior to the first notice day of the underlying futures. (The first notice day for Kansas City wheat futures is the last business day of the month preceding the contract month.)
Expiration	10 a.m. (Kansas City time) on the first Saturday following the last trading day

KCBT Mini Value Line Average Stock Index Futures

Trading Unit	$100 times the Value Line Arithmetic Index
Tick Size	.05 point ($5 per contract)
Daily Price Limit	Consult the exchange for current information
Contract Months	March, June, September, December
Trading Hours	8:30 a.m. to 3:15 p.m. (Kansas City time)
Delivery	Settlement: actual Value Line Arithmetic Index at the close on the last trading day of the contract month

KCBT Value Line Average Stock Index Futures

Trading Unit	$500 times the Value Line Arithmetic Index
Tick Size	.05 point ($25 per contract)
Daily Price Limit	Consult the exchange for current information
Contract Months	March, June, September, December
Trading Hours	8:30 a.m. to 3:15 p.m. (Kansas City time)
Delivery	Settlement: actual Value Line Arithmetic Index at the close on the last trading day of the contract month

**MidAmerica
Commodity
Exchange (MidAm)**

MidAm Corn Futures

Trading Unit	1,000 bushels
Tick Size	⅛ cent per bushel ($1.25 per contract)
Daily Price Limit	10 cents per bushel ($100 per contract) above or below the previous day's settlement price
Contract Months	December, March, May, July, September
Trading Hours	9:30 a.m. to 1:45 p.m. (Chicago time), except on the last trading day of an expiring contract, when trading closes at 12:15 p.m.
Deliverable Grades	No. 2 Yellow corn is deliverable at par; No. 1 Yellow corn is deliverable at a ½ cent per bushel premium; and No. 3 Yellow corn is deliverable at a 1½ cent per bushel discount

MidAm Live Cattle Futures

Trading Unit	20,000 pounds
Tick Size	$0.00025 per pound ($5 per contract)
Daily Price Limit	1½ cents per pound ($300 per contract) above or below the previous day's settlement price
Contract Months	February, April, June, August, September, October, December
Trading Hours	9:05 a.m. to 1:15 p.m. (Chicago time), except on the last trading day of an expiring contract, when trading closes at 12:15 p.m.
Last Trading Day	The 20th calendar day of the contract month (see special provisions in contract)
Deliverable Grades	USDA Choice steers, Yield Grades 1,2,3, and 4 with the weight range between 1,050 and 1,200 pounds. See exchange rules for details.

MidAm Live Hog Futures

Trading Unit	15,000 lbs.
Tick Size	$0.00025 per pound ($3.75 per contract)
Daily Price Limit	1½ cents per pound ($225 per contract) above or below the previous day's settlement price
Contract Months	February, April, June, July, August, October, December
Trading Hours	9:10 a.m. to 1:15 p.m. (Chicago time), except on the last trading day of an expiring contract, when trading closes at 12:15 p.m.
Last Trading Day	The 20th calendar day of the contract month (see special provision in contract)
Deliverable Grades	U.S. No. 1, No. 2, No. 3 Grade hogs (barrows and gilts) in the weight range of 210 to 240 pounds are deliverable at par. See exchange rules for details.

MidAm Oat Futures

Trading Unit	1,000 bushels
Tick Size	⅛ cent per bushel ($1.25 per contract)
Daily Price Limit	10 cents per bushel ($100 per contract) above or below the previous day's settlement price
Contract Months	March, May, July, September, December
Trading Hours	9:30 a.m. to 1:45 p.m. (Chicago time), except on the last trading day of an expiring contract, when trading closes at 12:15 p.m.
Deliverable Grades	No. 2 Heavy oats and No. 1 oats are deliverable at par; other grades are deliverable at differentials

MidAm Soybean Futures

Trading Unit	1,000 bushels
Tick Size	⅛ cent per bushel ($1.25 per contract)
Daily Price Limit	30 cents per bushel ($300 per contract) above or below the previous day's settlement price. Limit is increased by 50 percent after one limit day in three or more contract months in a contract year.
Contract Months	January, March, May, July, August, September, November
Trading Hours	9:30 a.m. to 1:45 p.m. (Chicago time), except on the last trading day of an expiring contract, when trading closes at 12:15 p.m.
Deliverable Grades	No. 2 Yellow soybeans are deliverable at par; other grades deliverable at differentials

Options on MidAm Soybean Futures

Trading Unit	One MidAm soybean futures contract
Tick Size	⅛ cent per bushel ($1.25 per contract)
Strike Prices	Integral multiples of 25 cents per bushel
Daily Price Limit	30 cents per bushel ($300 per contract) above or below the previous day's settlement price
Contract Months	January, March, May, July, August, September, November
Trading Hours	9:30 a.m. to 1:45 p.m. (Chicago time), except on the last trading day of an expiring contract, when trading closes at 12:15 p.m.
Expiration	10 a.m. (Chicago time) on the first Saturday following the last day of trading

MidAm Soybean Meal Futures

Trading Unit	20 tons (40,000 lbs.)
Tick Size	10 cents per ton ($2 per contract)
Daily Price Limit	$10 per ton ($200 per contract) above or below the previous day's settlement price; no daily limits in the spot month
Contract Months	January, March, May, July, August, September, October, December
Trading Hours	9:30 a.m. to 1:45 p.m. (Chicago time), except on the last trading day of an expiring contract, when trading closes at 1:15 p.m.
Delivery	Cash settlement

MidAm Wheat Futures

Trading Unit	1,000 bushels
Tick Size	⅛ cent per bushel ($1.25 per contract)
Daily Price Limit	20 cents per bushel ($200 per contract) above or below previous day's settlement price
Contract Months	March, May, July, September, December
Trading Hours	9:30 a.m. to 1:45 p.m. (Chicago time), except on the last trading day of an expiring contract, when trading closes at 12:15 p.m.
Deliverable Grades	No. 2 Soft Red, No. 2 Hard Red Winter, No. 2 Dark Northern Spring, and No. 1 Northern Spring wheat are deliverable at par; other grades deliverable at differentials

Options on MidAm Wheat Futures

Trading Unit	One MidAm 1,000-bushel wheat futures contract
Tick Size	⅛ cent per bushel ($1.25 per contract)
Strike Prices	Integral multiples of 10 cents per bushel
Daily Price Limit	20 cents per bushel ($200 per contract) above or below the previous day's settlement price
Contract Months	March, May, July, September, December
Trading Hours	9:30 a.m. to 1:45 p.m. (Chicago time), except on the last trading day of an expiring contract, when trading closes at 12:15 p.m.
Expiration	10 a.m. (Chicago time) on the first Saturday following the last day of trading

MidAm New York Gold Futures

Trading Unit	33.2 fine troy ounces
Tick Size	10 cents per fine troy ounce ($3.32 per contract)
Daily Price Limit	See rules and regulations
Contract Months	The current month and any subsequent months
Trading Hours	7:20 a.m. to 1:40 p.m. (Chicago time)
Last Trading Day	The business day prior to the last business day of the delivery month
Deliverable Grades	A single bar within 10 percent (plus or minus) the contract weight is deliverable, assaying not less than 995 fineness and bearing one of the brands and markings officially listed by the exchange

Options on MidAm New York Gold Futures

Trading Unit	One MidAm 33.2 fine troy ounce futures contract
Tick Size	10 cents per fine troy ounce ($3.32 per contract)
Strike Prices	Integral multiples of $10 when futures price is less than or equal to $500; integral multiples of $20 when futures price is greater than $500 but less than $1,000; integral multiples of $50 when futures price is greater than $1,000
Daily Price Limit	None
Contract Months	February, April, June, August, October, December
Trading Hours	7:20 a.m. to 1:40 p.m. (Chicago time), except on the last trading day in an option class, when trading closes at noon
Expiration	Unexercised options expire at 10 a.m. (Chicago time) on the first Saturday following the last day of trading

MidAm New York Silver Futures

Trading Unit	1,000 troy ounces
Tick Size	1/10 cent per troy ounce ($1 per contract)
Daily Price Limit	See rules and regulations
Contract Months	Current month and any subsequent months
Trading Hours	7:25 a.m. to 1:40 p.m. (Chicago time)
Last Trading Day	The business day prior to the two last business days of the delivery month
Deliverable Grades	Refined silver in a bar cast in a basic weight of either 1,000 troy ounces or 1,100 troy ounces (varying in weight no more than plus or minus 10 percent), assaying not less than 999 fineness, and bearing one of the brands and markings officially listed by the exchange

MidAm Platinum Futures

Trading Unit	25 fine troy ounces
Tick Size	10 cents per fine troy ounce ($2.50 per contract)
Daily Price Limit	$25 per troy ounce ($625 per contract); no limit in the spot month
Contract Months	The current month and any subsequent months, up to 24 months in the future
Trading Hours	7:20 a.m. to 1:40 p.m. (Chicago time)
Deliverable Grades	Ingot or plate containing not less than 23.5 fine troy ounces nor more than 27.5 fine troy ounces of platinum, assaying not less than 999 fineness as attested by a certificate from an assayer officially listed by the exchange

MidAm British Pound Futures

Trading Unit	12,500 British pounds
Tick Size	$0.0002 per British pound ($2.50 per contract)
Daily Price Limit	None
Contract Months	March, June, September, December
Trading Hours	7:20 a.m. to 2:15 p.m. (Chicago time), except on the last trading day of an expiring contract, when trading closes at 9:31 a.m.
Delivery	The currency shall be deliverable in the country of issuance at a bank approved by the clearinghouse

MidAm Canadian Dollar Futures

Trading Unit	50,000 Canadian dollars
Tick Size	$0.0001 per Canadian dollar ($5 per contract)
Daily Price Limit	None
Contract Months	March, June, September, December
Trading Hours	7:20 a.m. to 2:15 p.m. (Chicago time), except on the last trading day of an expiring contract, when trading closes at 9:31 a.m.
Delivery	The currency shall be deliverable in the country of issuance at a bank approved by the clearinghouse

MidAm Deutsche Mark Futures

Trading Unit	62,500 Deutsche marks
Tick Size	$0.0001 per Deutsche mark ($6.25 per contract)
Daily Price Limit	None
Contract Months	March, June, September, December
Trading Hours	7:20 a.m. to 2:15 p.m. (Chicago time), except on the last trading day of an expiring contract, when trading closes at 9:31 a.m.
Delivery	The currency shall be deliverable in the country of issuance at a bank approved by the clearinghouse

MidAm Japanese Yen Futures

Trading Unit	6,250,000 Japanese yen
Tick Size	$0.000001 per Japanese yen ($6.25 per contract)
Daily Price Limit	None
Contract Months	March, June, September, December
Trading Hours	7:20 a.m. to 2:15 p.m. (Chicago time), except on the last trading day of an expiring contract, when trading closes at 9:31 a.m.
Delivery	The currency shall be deliverable in the country of issuance at a bank approved by the clearinghouse

MidAm Swiss Franc Futures

Trading Unit	62,500 Swiss francs
Tick Size	$0.0001 per Swiss franc ($6.25 per contract)
Daily Price Limit	None
Contract Months	March, June, September, December
Trading Hours	7:20 a.m. to 2:15 p.m. (Chicago time), except on the last trading day of an expiring contract, when trading closes at 9:31 a.m.
Delivery	The currency shall be deliverable in the country of issuance at a bank approved by the clearinghouse

MidAm U.S. Treasury Bill Futures

Trading Unit	$500,000 face value U.S. Treasury bills with 90 days until maturity
Tick Size	One basis point ($12.50 per contract)
Daily Trading Limit	None
Contract Months	March, June, September, December
Trading Hours	7:20 a.m. to 2:15 p.m. (Chicago time), except on the last trading day of an expiring contract, when trading closes at 10:15 a.m.
Last Trading Day	The second day following the third weekly Treasury bill auction in the contract month
Delivery	Settled in cash at the settlement price of the corresponding International Monetary Market T-bill contract

MidAm U.S. Treasury Bond Futures

Trading Unit	$50,000 face value U.S. Treasury bonds
Tick Size	$\frac{1}{32}$ of a point ($15.62 per tick)
Daily Price Limit	$\frac{96}{32}$ ($1,500 per contract) above or below the previous day's settlement price
Contract Months	March, June, September, December
Trading Hours	7:20 a.m. to 3:15 p.m. (Chicago time), except on the last trading day of an expiring contract, when trading closes at noon
Last Trading Day	The business day prior to the last seven business days of the delivery month
Deliverable Grades	U.S. Treasury bonds with a nominal 8 percent coupon maturing at least 15 years from delivery date if not callable; if callable, not so for at least 15 years from delivery date
Delivery	Federal Reserve book-entry wire-transfer system. Invoice price on delivery is adjusted for coupon rates and term to maturity or call.

MidAm U.S. Treasury Note Futures

Trading Unit	$50,000 face value U.S. Treasury notes
Tick Size	In percentage of par in minimum increments of ⅟32 of a point, or $15.62 per tick (e.g., 91-01, or 91 points and ⅟32 of a point)
Daily Price Limit	96⁄32 ($1,500 per contract) above or below the previous day's settlement price
Contract Months	March, June, September, December
Trading Hours	7:20 a.m. to 3:15 p.m. (Chicago time), except on the last trading day of an expiring contract, when trading closes at noon
Last Trading Day	The eighth to last business day of the delivery month
Deliverable Grades	U.S. Treasury notes maturing not less than 6½ years, nor more than 10 years, from the first day of the delivery month
Delivery	Federal Reserve book-entry wire-transfer system. Invoice price on delivery is adjusted to a standard 8 percent and actual term to maturity.

MGE High Fructose Corn Syrup Futures

Trading Unit	37,000 pounds dry basis (one tank truck)
Tick Size	2 cents
Daily Price Limit	$1 per hundredweight ($370 per contract)
Contract Months	March, May, July, September, December, next two months in this same cycle
Trading Hours	9 a.m. to 1:25 p.m. (Minneapolis time)
Deliverable Grades	Second generation HFCS-55 conforming to quality standards specified in contract following SSDT Quality Guidelines and Analytical Procedure Bibliography for Bottlers High Fructose Corn Syrup 42 and 55

Minneapolis Grain Exchange (MGE)

MGE Oat Futures

Trading Unit	5,000 bushels
Tick Size	¼ cent per bushel
Daily Price Limit	20 cents per bushel ($1,000 per contract)
Contract Months	March, May, July, September, December
Trading Hours	9:30 a.m. to 1:15 p.m. (Minneapolis time)
Deliverable Grades	No. 1 oats or No. 2 Heavy oats at contract price, with premiums and discounts set by the exchange for other grades

MGE Spring Wheat Futures

Trading Unit	5,000 bushels (job lots of 1,000 bushels permitted)
Tick Size	⅛ cent per bushel
Daily Price Limit	20 cents per bushel ($1,000 per contract)
Contract Months	March, May, July, September, December
Trading Hours	9:30 a.m. to 1:15 p.m. (Minneapolis time)
Deliverable Grades	No. 2 Northern Spring, 13.50 protein or higher, with premiums and discounts for deviations as established by the exchange

Options on MGE Spring Wheat Futures

Trading Unit	One MGE Spring wheat futures contract of 5,000 bushels
Tick Size	⅛ cent
Strike Prices	a) Intervals: increments of 10 cents per bushel; b) Initial listing: nearest strike price to prior day's settlement and the next three intervals higher and lower in 10-cent increments for each option month listed; c) Additional listings: when a trade in the Spring wheat futures contract occurs at a price that causes there to be fewer than three strike prices above or below such futures transaction, sufficient new strike prices shall be added to ensure at least three strike prices above or below the price of such futures transaction. Each contract month is treated independently. No new strike prices can be added during the expiration month.
Daily Price Limit	20 cents above and/or below the previous day's settlement premium for each put or call option, subject to variable price fluctuation limits
Contract Months	September, December, March, May, July
Trading Hours	9:35 a.m. to 1:25 p.m. (Minneapolis time)
Last Trading Day	1 p.m. (Minneapolis time) on the Friday that precedes by at least 10 business days the first notice day of the underlying futures contract
Expiration	10 a.m. (Minneapolis time) on the first Saturday following the last trading day

MGE White Wheat Futures

Trading Unit	5,000 bushels (job lots of 1,000 bushels permitted)
Tick Size	¼ cent per bushel
Daily Price Limit	20 cents per bushel ($1,000 per contract)
Contract Months	March, May, July, September, December
Trading Hours	9:30 a.m. to 1:15 p.m. (Minneapolis time)
Deliverable Grades	No. 2 or better Soft White wheat as described by the USDA Official Grain Standards with a maximum of 0.5 percent sprout damage allowed. Total dockage shall not exceed 2 percent and shall be subtracted from the total weight. (No free dockage is allowed.)

NYCE® Cotton (No. 2) Futures

Trading Unit	50,000 pounds net weight (approximately 100 bales)
Tick Size	$0.0001 per pound
Daily Price Limit	2 cents above or below previous day's settlement price; higher limits can take effect under certain market conditions. Spot month: no limit on or after first notice day.
Contract Months	Current month plus 17 succeeding months; active trading months: March, May, July, October, December
Trading Hours	10:30 a.m. to 3 p.m. (New York time)
Deliverable Grades	Strict Low Middling 1¹⁄₁₆ inch U.S.-grown white cotton
Delivery	Galveston and Houston, TX; New Orleans, LA; Memphis, TN; Greenville, SC

New York Cotton Exchange (NYCE®)

Options on NYCE® Cotton Futures

Trading Unit	One NYCE cotton futures contract
Tick Size	$0.0001 per pound
Strike Prices	Nearest three delivery months: 1-cent increments up to 74 cents; 2 cents at 75 cents and above. Distant four delivery months always 2 cents.
Daily Price Limit	None
Contract Months	March, May, July, October, December; the nearest seven delivery months will be trading at all times
Trading Hours	10:30 a.m. to 3 p.m. (New York time)
Last Trading Day	First Friday of the month preceding futures delivery month

Frozen Concentrated Orange Juice Futures

Trading Unit	15,000 pounds of orange solids (3 percent more or less)
Tick Size	$0.0005 per pound ($7.50 per contract)
Daily Price Limit	5 cents above or below previous day's settlement price; higher limits can take effect under certain market conditions. Spot month: 10 cents.
Contract Months	January, March, May, July, September, November
Trading Hours	10:15 a.m. to 2:45 p.m. (New York time)
Deliverable Grades	Grade A, with Brix value of not less than 57 degrees, having a Brix value to acid ratio of not less than 13 to 1 nor more than 19 to 1, with the factors of color and flavor each scoring 37 points or higher and 19 for defects, with a minimum score of 94
Delivery	Exchange-licensed warehouses in Florida

Options on Frozen Concentrated Orange Juice Futures

Trading Unit	One frozen concentrated orange juice futures contract
Tick Size	$0.0005 per pound ($7.50 per contract)
Strike Prices	2½-cent increments for all contract months
Daily Price Limit	None
Contract Months	January, March, May, July, September, November; the nearest six delivery months will be trading at all times
Trading Hours	10:15 a.m. to 2:45 p.m. (New York time)
Last Trading Day	First Friday of the month preceding futures delivery month
Exercise	Until 2:45 p.m. (New York time) or until 4 p.m. on last trading day

**Financial
Instrument
Exchange
(FINEX®)**
Division
of the NYCE®

FINEX® European Currency Unit Futures

Trading Unit	ECU 100,000
Tick Size	$0.0001 per ECU ($10 per contract)
Daily Price Limit	None
Contract Months	March, June, September, December
Trading Hours	8:20 a.m. to 3 p.m. (New York time)
Last Trading Day	Two business days prior to the third Wednesday of an expiring contract month
Delivery	Physical delivery of ECU

FINEX® U.S. Dollar Index^SM Futures

Trading Unit	$500 times the U.S. Dollar Index^SM
Tick Size	.01 of one U.S. Dollar Index^SM point ($5 per futures contract)
Daily Price Limit	None
Contract Months	March, June, September, December
Trading Hours	8:20 a.m. to 3 p.m. (New York time)
Last Trading Day	Third Wednesday of the expiring contract month
Delivery	Cash settlement

Options on FINEX® U.S. Dollar Index^SM Futures

Trading Unit	U.S. Dollar Index^SM futures contract
Tick Size	.01 of one U.S. Dollar Index^SM point ($5 per contract)
Strike Prices	Intervals of two U.S. Dollar Index^SM trading points (200 ticks)
Daily Price Limit	None
Contract Months	March, June, September, December
Trading Hours	8:20 a.m. to 3 p.m. (New York time)
Last Trading Day	Two Fridays before the third Wednesday of the expiring contract month

FINEX® U.S. 5-Year Treasury Note Futures

Trading Unit	U.S. Treasury notes with a face value at maturity of $100,000
Tick Size	Percentage of par in increments of ½ of 1⁄32 of a point ($15.625 per contract)
Daily Price Limit	None
Contract Months	March, June, September, December
Trading Hours	8:20 a.m. to 3 p.m. (New York time)
Last Trading Day	1 p.m. (New York time) on the eighth last business day of the delivery month
Delivery	Federal Reserve book-entry system

Options on FINEX® U.S. 5-Year Treasury Note Futures

Trading Unit	One FINEX® five-year Treasury note futures contract
Tick Size	1/64 of one point
Strike Prices	Intervals of 1/2 of one FINEX® five-year Treasury note futures point
Daily Price Limit	None
Contract Months	March, June, September, December
Trading Hours	8:20 a.m. to 3 p.m. (New York time)
Last Trading Day	The Friday that is at least the fifth business day prior to the first notice day of the expiring month

New York Futures Exchange (NYFE)

NYFE CRB Index Futures

Trading Unit	$500 times index futures level (e.g., futures at 225.00 are valued at $112,500: $500 times 225.00)
Tick Size	Five basis points, or .05 ($25 per contract)
Daily Price Limit	None
Contract Months	March, May, July, September, December
Trading Hours	9 a.m. to 3:15 p.m. (New York time)
Last Trading Day	Third Friday of the expiration month; beginning with the March 1989 contract, the last trading day will be the third business day of the expiration month
Delivery	Settlement at contract maturity is by cash payment

Options on NYFE CRB Index Futures

Trading Unit	One CRB Index futures contract
Tick Size	Five basis points, or .05 ($25 per contract); however, if an option transaction liquidates an existing position, the minimum fluctuation can be one point ($5) if the price is less than five points
Strike Prices	5.00 intervals at exercise values less than 300.00 and 10.00 intervals at exercise values greater than 300.00. Minimum of five exercise prices at all times: two in-the-money, one at-the-money, two out-of-the-money.
Daily Price Limit	None
Contract Months	March, May, July, September, December (three options months traded at all times)
Trading Hours	9 a.m. to 3:15 p.m. (New York time)
Last Trading Day	Third Friday of the expiration month; beginning with the March 1989 contract, the last trading day will be the third business day of the month

NYFE NYSE Composite Index Futures

Trading Unit	$500 times NYSE Composite Index (e.g., $500 times 135.00 = $67,500; 135.00 represents recent index level)
Tick Size	Five basis points, or .05, e.g., 135.05, 135.10 135.15 ($25 per contract)
Daily Price Limit	None
Contract Months	March, June, September, December cycle (four months traded at all times)
Trading Hours	9:30 a.m. to 4:15 p.m. (New York time)
Last Trading Day	The Thursday preceding the third Friday of the month; if that day is not a NYFE and NYSE business day, the last trading day will be the preceding such business day
Delivery	Settlement at contract maturity is by cash payment; final settlement is based upon a special calculation of the third Friday's opening prices of all the stocks listed in the NYSE Composite Index

Options on NYFE NYSE Composite Index Futures

Trading Unit	One NYSE Composite Index futures contract
Tick Size	Five basis points, or .05 ($25 per contract); however, if an option transaction liquidates an existing position, the minimum fluctuation can be one point ($5) if the price is less than five points
Strike Prices	Integers that are evenly divisible by two (e.g., 152.00, 154.00). Minimum of nine exercise prices at all times: four in-the-money, one at-the-money, four out-of-the-money.
Daily Price Limit	None
Contract Months	The current calendar month, the two months following the current calendar month, the next month in the calendar quarterly cycle (four options months traded at all times). The futures contract underlying the noncalendar quarterly cycle months is the next futures contract following the option expiration.
Trading Hours	9:30 a.m. to 4:15 p.m. (New York time)
Last Trading Day	For the calendar quarterly cycle months (March, June, September, December), the last day of trading is the last trading day of the underlying futures contract (the business day preceding the third Friday of the expiration month; except that if the third Friday is not a NYFE and NYSE business day, the last trading day shall be the business day preceding the business day immediately preceding the third Friday). For the noncalendar quarterly cycle months, the last day of trading is the third Friday of the expiration month; except that if the third Friday is not a NYFE and NYSE business day, the last trading day shall be the business day immediately preceding the third Friday.

<table>
<tr><td rowspan="7">New York
Mercantile
Exchange
(NYMEX)</td></tr>
</table>

New York Mercantile Exchange (NYMEX)

NYMEX Light "Sweet" Crude Oil Futures

Trading Unit	1,000 barrels
Tick Size	1 cent per barrel ($10 per contract)
Daily Price Limit	$1 per barrel ($1,000 per contract)
Contract Months	18 consecutive months, beginning with the current month
Trading Hours	9:45 a.m. to 3:10 p.m. (New York time)
Deliverable Grades	West Texas Intermediate 4 percent sulphur, 40 degrees API gravity, light "sweet" crude oil with 5 percent or less sulphur by weight, not less than 34 degrees API gravity, not more than 45 degrees API gravity; light sweet crudes with .5 percent or less sulphur by weight and with API gravity of not less than 34 degrees but not greater than 45 degrees are also deliverable

Options on NYMEX Light "Sweet" Crude Oil Futures

Trading Unit	One NYMEX crude oil futures contract
Tick Size	1 cent per barrel ($10 per contract)
Strike Prices	In increments of $1 per barrel; at all times at least seven strike prices are available for puts and calls on the underlying futures contracts. The middle strike price is closest to the previous day's close of the underlying futures contract. Strike price boundaries are adjusted according to the futures price movements.
Daily Price Limit	None
Contract Months	Six consecutive months
Trading Hours	9:45 a.m. to 3:10 p.m. (New York time)
Last Trading Day	Second Friday of the month prior to the delivery month of the underlying crude oil futures contract
Exercise	By 4:30 p.m. (New York time) on any day up to and including the option's expiration. Call buyers acquire a long position in the underlying futures contract, put buyers a short position. Call writers are assigned a short position in the underlying futures contract, put writers a long position.

NYMEX New York Harbor No. 2 Heating Oil Futures

Trading Unit	42,000 U.S. gallons
Tick Size	$0.0001 per gallon
Daily Price Limit	2 cents per gallon ($840 per contract) above or below the preceding day's settlement price; no maximum price fluctuations during month preceding the delivery month
Contract Months	15 consecutive months, beginning with the current month
Trading Hours	9:50 a.m. to 3:10 p.m. (New York time)
Deliverable Grades	No. 2 heating oil; consult the exchange for specifications

Options on NYMEX New York Harbor No. 2 Heating Oil Futures

Trading Unit	One NYMEX heating oil futures contract
Tick Size	$0.0001 per gallon
Strike Prices	Increments of 2 cents per gallon. Strike prices are listed only as even numbers, for example, $0.4800, $0.5000, etc. At all times, at least seven strike prices are available for puts and calls on the underlying futures contracts. The middle strike price is closest to the previous day's close of the underlying futures contract. Strike price boundaries are adjusted according to the futures price movements.
Daily Price Limit	None
Contract Months	Six consecutive months
Trading Hours	9:50 a.m. to 3:10 p.m. (New York time)
Last Trading Day	Second Friday of the month prior to the delivery month of the underlying heating oil futures contract
Exercise	By 4:30 p.m. on any day up to and including the option's expiration. Call buyers acquire a long position in the underlying futures contract, put buyers a short position. Call writers are assigned a short position in the underlying futures contract, put writers a long position.

NYMEX *New York Harbor Unleaded Regular Gasoline Futures*

Trading Unit	42,000 U.S. gallons
Tick Size	$0.0001 per gallon
Daily Price Limit	2 cents per gallon ($840 per contract) above or below the preceding day's settlement price; no maximum price fluctuations during month preceding the delivery month
Contract Months	15 consecutive months, beginning with the current month; listing of each month shall be submitted to the CFTC
Trading Hours	9:50 a.m. to 3:10 p.m. (New York time)
Deliverable Grades	Unleaded regular gasoline; consult the exchange for specifications

NYMEX *Propane Futures*

Trading Unit	42,000 gallons
Tick Size	$0.0001 per gallon
Daily Price Limit	2 cents per gallon ($840) above or below the preceding day's settlement price; no maximum price fluctuations during the month preceding the delivery month
Contract Months	15 consecutive months, beginning with the current month; listing of each month shall be submitted to the CFTC
Trading Hours	9:40 a.m. to 3:10 p.m. (New York time)
Deliverable Grades	Generally conforms to industry standards for fungible liquefied propane gas as determined by the Gas Processors Association

NYMEX *Palladium Futures*

Trading Unit	100 troy ounces
Tick Size	5 cents per ounce ($5 per contract)
Daily Price Limit	$6 per troy ounce ($600 per contract); no maximum daily limit during current delivery month and three business days preceding it
Contract Months	March, June, September, December, including current three months
Trading Hours	8:10 a.m. to 2:20 p.m. (New York time)
Deliverable Grades	Minimum 99.9 percent pure palladium

NYMEX *Platinum Futures*

Trading Unit	50 troy ounces
Tick Size	10 cents per troy ounce ($5 per contract)
Daily Price Limit	$25 per troy ounce; no maximum daily limit during current delivery month and three business days preceding it
Contract Months	January, April, July, October, including current three months
Trading Hours	8:20 a.m. to 2:30 p.m. (New York time)
Deliverable Grades	Minimum 99.9 percent pure platinum

PBOT *Australian Dollar Futures*

Trading Unit	100,000 Australian dollars
Tick Size	$0.0001 per Australian dollar, commonly referred to as one point ($10 per contract)
Contract Months	March, June, September, December, two additional near months
Trading Hours	4:30 a.m. to 2:30 p.m. (Philadelphia time), Monday through Friday Evening trading hours are from 6 to 10 p.m. (Philadelphia time), or from 7 to 11 p.m. (daylight saving time), Sunday through Thursday
Last Trading Day	Friday before the third Wednesday of the month

PBOT *British Pound Futures*

Trading Unit	62,500 British pounds sterling
Tick Size	$0.0001 per British pound ($6.25 per contract)
Contract Months	March, June, September, December, two additional near months
Trading Hours	4:30 a.m. to 2:30 p.m. (Philadelphia time), Monday through Friday Evening trading hours are from 6 to 10 p.m. (Philadelphia time), or from 7 to 11 p.m. (daylight saving time), Sunday through Thursday
Last Trading Day	Friday before the third Wednesday of the month

PBOT *Canadian Dollar Futures*

Trading Unit	100,000 Canadian dollars
Tick Size	$0.0001 per Canadian dollar, commonly referred to as one point ($10 per contract)
Contract Months	March, June, September, December, two additional near months
Trading Hours	4:30 a.m. to 2:30 p.m. (Philadelphia time)
Last Trading Day	Friday before the third Wednesday of the month

Philadelphia Board of Trade Inc. (PBOT)

PBOT Deutsche Mark Futures

Trading Unit	125,000 Deutsche marks
Tick Size	$0.0001 per Deutsche mark, commonly referred to as one point ($12.50 per contract)
Contract Months	March, June, September, December, two additional near months
Last Trading Day	Friday before the third Wednesday of the month
Trading Hours	4:30 a.m. to 2:30 p.m. (Philadelphia time), Monday through Friday Evening trading hours are from 6 to 10 p.m. (Philadelphia time), or from 7 to 11 p.m. (daylight saving time), Sunday through Thursday

PBOT European Currency Unit Futures

Trading Unit	125,000 European Currency Units
Tick Size	$0.0001 per European Currency Unit, commonly referred to as one point ($12.50 per contract)
Contract Months	March, June, September, December, two additional near months
Trading Hours	4:30 a.m. to 2:30 p.m. (Philadelphia time)
Last Trading Day	Friday before the third Wednesday of the month

PBOT French Franc Futures

Trading Unit	500,000 French francs
Tick Size	$0.00005 per French franc, commonly referred to as five points ($25 per contract)
Contract Months	March, June, September, December, two additional near months
Trading Hours	4:30 a.m. to 2:30 p.m. (Philadelphia time)
Last Trading Day	Friday before the third Wednesday of the month

PBOT Japanese Yen Futures

Trading Unit	12,500,000 Japanese yen
Tick Size	$0.000001 per Japanese yen, commonly referred to as one point ($12.50 per contract)
Contract Months	March, June, September, December, two additional near months
Trading Hours	4:30 a.m. to 2:30 p.m. (Philadelphia time), Monday through Friday Evening trading hours are from 6 to 10 p.m. (Philadelphia time), or from 7 to 11 p.m. (daylight saving time), Sunday through Thursday
Last Trading Day	Friday before the third Wednesday of the month

PBOT Swiss Franc Futures

Trading Unit	125,000 Swiss francs
Tick Size	$0.0001 per Swiss franc, commonly referred to as one point ($12.50 per contract)
Contract Months	March, June, September, December, two additional near months
Trading Hours	4:30 a.m. to 2:30 p.m. (Philadelphia time), Monday through Friday Evening trading hours are from 6 to 10 p.m. (Philadelphia time), or from 7 to 11 p.m. (daylight saving time), Sunday through Thursday
Last Trading Day	Friday before the third Wednesday of the month

PBOT National Over-the-Counter Index™ Futures

Trading Unit	$500 times futures price
Tick Size	.05 point ($25 per contract)
Daily Price Limit	None
Contract Months	Consecutive and cycle months, such as February, March, April, June, September
Trading Hours	9:30 a.m. to 4:10 p.m. (Philadelphia time), except on the last trading day of an expiring contract, when trading closes at 4 p.m.
Last Trading Day	At 4 p.m. (Philadelphia time) on the third Friday of the contract month
Delivery	Cash settled: OX futures contracts will be settled in cash based on the difference between the value of the XOC Index as disseminated by the exchange at 4 p.m. on the last trading day of the OX futures contract and the closing value of the OX futures contract on the day preceding the last trading day
Final Settlement	On the first business day following the last trading day in the contract month

SOURCES OF INFORMATION*

The following list includes just a few of the many possible resources on futures trading. Many of the books listed are available directly from the publisher or the library system.

Book
Hieronymus, Thomas A. *Economics of Futures Trading for Commercial and Personal Profit*, 2d ed. New York: Commodity Research Bureau, 1977.

Chicago Board of Trade Publication
Education and Marketing Services Department:
Action in the Marketplace, 1987.

Books
Goss, Barry A., and B.S. Yamey, eds. *Economics of Futures Trading*. New York: John Wiley & Sons, 1976.

Peck, Anne E., ed. *Futures Markets: Their Economic Role*. Washington, DC: American Enterprise Institute for Public Policy Research, 1985.

Williams, Jeffrey. *The Economic Function of Futures Markets*. New York: Cambridge University Press, 1986.

Books
Marasco, M.C., ed. *The Complete Commodity Futures Directory*, 3d ed. rev. Frankfort, IL: Christopher Resources, 1987.

Traders Directory of Foreign Exchange Futures and Options Dealers. Philadelphia: International Publications Service, 1986.

Chicago Board of Trade Publication
Education and Marketing Services Department:
Action in the Marketplace, 1987.

Book
Maxwell, Joseph R., Sr. *Commodity Futures Trading Orders*. Red Bluff, CA: Speer Books, 1975.

Chapter 1

Chapter 2

Chapter 3

Chapter 5

*The sources listed in this section are believed to be accurate as of the date of publication but are not guaranteed or endorsed by the Chicago Board of Trade as to accuracy or completeness. The textbooks, periodicals, and other sources are given for information and education purposes only.

Pamphlet
An Application Guide: NFA Membership and CFTC Registration. Chicago: National Futures Association, 1987.

Chicago Board of Trade Publications
Education and Marketing Services Department:
Margins for Options on T-Bond & T-Note Futures, 1987.

Secretary's Office:
Board of Trade of the City of Chicago Rules and Regulations.

Chapter 6	**Chicago Board of Trade Publications** Education and Marketing Services Department: *CRCE Rough Rice Delivery Manual,* 1988. *The Delivery Process in Brief: Treasury Bond and Treasury Note Futures,* 1987.
Chapter 7	**Book** Peck, Anne E., ed. *Futures Markets: Regulatory Issues.* Washington, DC: American Enterprise Institute for Public Policy Research, 1985. *Pamphlet* *An Introduction to the National Futures Association.* Chicago: National Futures Association, 1986. **Chicago Board of Trade Publication** Secretary's Office: *Board of Trade of the City of Chicago Rules and Regulations.*
Chapter 8	**Books** Figlewski, Stephen, et al. *Hedging with Financial Futures for Institutional Investors: From Theory to Practice.* Cambridge, MA: Ballinger Publishing, 1985. Fischer, Donald E., ed. *Options and Futures: New Route to Risk-Return Management.* Homewood, IL: Dow Jones-Irwin, 1984. Noddings, Thomas C. *Super Hedging.* Chicago: Probus Publishing, 1985. Platt, Robert B. *Controlling Interest Rate Risk: New Techniques and Applications for Money Management.* New York: John Wiley & Sons, 1986. Sennholz, Lyn M., et al. *Interest Rate Futures Hedging Course.* Spring Mills, PA: Center for Futures Education, 1984. ————. *Livestock Hedging Course.* Spring Mills, PA: Center for Futures Education, 1984.

_____. *Stock Index Futures Hedging Course.* Spring Mills, PA: Center for Futures Education, 1983.

Chicago Board of Trade Publications
Education and Marketing Services Department:
A Marketing Handbook for Producers, 1988.

Chicago Board of Trade Conversion Factors, rev. ed. Boston: Financial Publishing, 1989.

Understanding Basis: The Economics of Where and When, 1988.

Books

Chapter 9

Ainsworth, Ralph M. *Basic Principles of Successful Commodity Futures Speculation.* Albuquerque, NM: Institute for Economics and Financial Research, 1983.

Belveal, L. Dee. *Speculation in Commodity Contracts and Options,* 2d ed. Homewood, IL: Dow Jones-Irwin, 1985.

Ghosh, S., et al. *Stabilizing Speculative Commodity Markets.* Miami Beach, FL: Oxford Press, 1987.

Harper, Henry H. *The Psychology of Speculation: The Human Element in Stock Market Transactions.* Burlington, VT: Fraser Publishing, 1978.

Huff, Charles, and Barbara Marinacci. *Commodity Speculation for Beginners: A Guide to the Futures Market.* New York: McGraw-Hill, 1982.

Books

Chapter 10

Arnold, Curtis M. *Timing the Market: How to Profit in Bull and Bear Markets with Technical Analysis.* Chicago: Probus Publishing, 1986.

Bernstein, Jacob. *Handbook of Commodity Cycles: A Window on Time.* New York: John Wiley & Sons, 1982.

_____. *Short-Term Trading in Futures: A Manual of Systems, Strategies and Techniques.* Chicago: Probus Publishing, 1987.

Cadogan, Georges. *Kondratieff and the Mastery of the Future Through the Theory of Cycles.* Albuquerque, NM: Institute for Economic and Financial Research, 1983.

Edwards, Robert D., and John Magee. *Technical Analysis of Stock Trends,* 5th ed. Springfield, MA: John Magee, 1984.

Elliot, Ralph N. *The Wave Principle.* Albuquerque, NM: Institute for Economic and Political World Strategic Studies, 1979.

Frost, Alfred J., and Robert R. Prechter. *Elliot Wave Principle: Key to Stock Market Profits,* 5th ed. Chappaqua, NY: New Classics Library, 1985.

Grushcow, Jack, and Courtney Smith. *Profits Through Seasonal Trading.* New York: John Wiley & Sons, 1980.

Hadady, R. Earl. *Contrary Opinion: How to Use It for Profit in Trading Commodity Futures.* Pasadena, CA: Key Books Press, 1983.

Hill, John R. *Stock and Commodity Market Trend Trading by Advanced Technical Analysis.* Hendersonville, NC: Commodity Research Institute, 1977.

Hurst, J.M. *The Profit Magic of Stock Transaction Timing.* Englewood Cliffs, NJ: Prentice-Hall, 1970.

Kaufman, Perry J. *New Commodity Trading Systems and Methods.* New York: John Wiley & Sons, 1987.

_____, ed. *Technical Analysis in Commodities.* New York: John Wiley & Sons, 1980.

Maxwell, Joseph R. *Commodity Futures Trading with Moving Averages.* Red Bluff, CA: Speer Books, 1975.

_____. *Commodity Futures Trading with Point and Figure Charts.* Red Bluff, CA: Speer Books, 1978.

Murphy, John J. *Study Guide for Technical Analysis of the Futures Markets: A Self-Training Manual.* New York: New York Institute of Finance, 1987.

_____. *Technical Analysis of the Futures Markets: A Comprehensive Guide to Trading Methods and Applications.* New York: New York Institute of Finance, 1986.

Pring, Martin J., ed. *Historical Chart Book, Vol. 1.* Washington Depot, CT: International Institute for Economic Research, 1986.

_____. *Technical Analysis Explained: An Illustrated Guide for the Investor.* New York: McGraw-Hill, 1980.

Schwager, Jack D. *A Complete Guide to the Futures Markets: Fundamental Analysis, Technical Analysis, Trading, Spreads, and Options.* New York: John Wiley & Sons, 1984.

Schwarz, Edward W., Joanne M. Hill, and Thomas Schneeweis. *Financial Futures: Fundamentals, Strategies, and Applications.* Homewood, IL: Dow Jones-Irwin, 1986.

Sklarew, Arthur. *Techniques of a Professional Commodity Chart Analyst,* rev. ed. New York: Commodity Research Bureau, 1980.

Smith, Courtney. *Seasonal Charts for Futures Traders: A Sourcebook.* New York: John Wiley & Sons, 1987.

Taylor, William T. *Trader's and Investor's Guide to Commodity Trading Systems, Software, and Data Bases.* Chicago: Probus Publishing, 1986.

Books

Bernstein, Jacob. *How to Profit from Seasonal Commodity Spreads: A Complete Guide.* New York: John Wiley & Sons, 1983.

Goldberg, Harold. *Advanced Commodity Spread Trading.* Brightwaters, NY: Windsor Books, 1985.

Hadady, R. Earl. *Historical Commodity Spread Charts.* Pasadena, CA: Key Books Press, 1984.

Kallard, Thomas. *Commodity Spreads: Year-Round Trading Strategies to Beat Inflation and Build Capital.* New York: Optosonic Press, 1982.

Schwager, Jack D. *A Complete Guide to the Futures Markets: Fundamental Analysis, Technical Analysis, Trading, Spreads, and Options.* New York: John Wiley & Sons, 1984.

Smith, Courtney. *Commodity Spreads: Techniques and Methods for Spreading Financial Futures, Grains, Meats, and Other Commodities.* New York: John Wiley & Sons, 1982.

Weisweiller, Rudi, ed. *Arbitrage: Opportunities and Techniques in the Financial and Commodity Markets.* New York: John Wiley & Sons, 1986.

Chicago Board of Trade Publications
Education and Marketing Services Department:
CBOT Financial Instruments Guide, 1987.

CBOT Handbook Series on Agricultural Spreads: July/November Soybean Spread 1966-1986, 1986; *July/December Corn Spread 1972-1987,* 1987; *Wheat/Corn Spread 1977-1988,* 1989.

CBOT Handbook Series on Metals Markets: Gold/Silver Ratio Spread, 1988.

Chapter 11

Books

Angell, George. *Agricultural Options: Trading Puts and Calls in the New Grain and Livestock Futures Market.* New York: AMACOM, 1986.

Ansbacher, Max G. *The New Options Market.* New York: Walker, 1987.

Bookstaber, Richard M. *Option Pricing and Strategies in Investing.* Reading, MA: Addison-Wesley Publishing, 1981.

Catania, Patrick J., et al. *Agricultural Options: A Primer for Producers.* Bloomington, MN: Doane Information Services, 1984.

Cleeton, Claud Edwin. *Strategies for the Options Trader.* New York: John Wiley & Sons, 1979.

Fischer, Donald E., ed. *Options and Futures: New Route to Risk-Return Management.* Homewood, IL: Dow Jones-Irwin, 1984.

Gastineau, Gary. *The Stock Options Manual,* 3d ed. New York: McGraw-Hill, 1988.

Kramer, Samuel L., et al. *Options Hedging Handbook.* Spring Mills, PA: Center for Futures Education, 1985.

Labuszewski, John W., and Jeanne Cairns Sinquefield. *Inside the Commodity Option Markets.* New York: John Wiley & Sons, 1985.

Labuszewski, John W., and John E. Nyhoff. *Trading Options on Futures.* New York: John Wiley & Sons, 1988.

Mayer, Terry S. *Commodity Options: A User's Guide to Speculating and Hedging.* New York: New York Institute of Finance, 1983.

McMillan, Lawrence G. *Options as a Strategic Investment: A Comprehensive Analysis of Listed Option Strategies,* 3d ed. New York: New York Institute of Finance, 1980.

Natenberg, Sheldon. *Option Volatility and Pricing Strategies: Advanced Trading Techniques for Professionals.* Chicago: Probus Publishing, 1988.

Trester, Kenneth R. *The Compleat Option Player: Winning Strategy and Tactics in the New Options Game,* 2d ed. Costa Mesa, CA: Investrek Publishing, 1981.

Chicago Board of Trade Publications
Education and Marketing Services Department:
Options on Agricultural Futures: A Home Study Course, 1986.

Options on U.S. Treasury Bond Futures for Institutional Investors, 1987.

Strategies for Buying and Writing Options on Treasury Bond Futures, 1987.

Wheat Options Trading Manual, 1987.

Chapter 13

Books
Aldrich, Samuel R., and Walter O. Scott. *Modern Soybean Production,* 2d ed. Champaign, IL: S&A Publications, 1983.

Aldrich, Samuel R., Robert G. Hoeft, and Walter O. Scott. *Modern Corn Production,* 3d ed. Champaign, IL: S&A Publications, 1986.

Ensminger, M.E. *Beef Cattle Science,* 6th ed. Danville, IL: Interstate Printers & Publishers, 1987.

Ferris, William G. *The Grain Traders: The Story of the Chicago Board of Trade.* East Lansing, MI: Michigan State University Press, 1988.

From Wheat to Flour. Washington DC: Wheat Flour Institute, 1976.

Galston, William A. *A Tough Row to Hoe: The 1985 Farm Bill and Beyond.* Washington, DC: Hamilton Press, 1985.

Glaser, Leverne K. *Provisions of the Food Security Act of 1985.* Washington, DC: U.S. Department of Agriculture, 1985.

McCoy, John H. *Livestock and Meat Marketing,* 3d ed. Westport, CT: AVI, 1979.

Morgan, Daniel. *Merchants of Grain.* New York: Penguin Books, 1980.

Nosker, Dean. *Futures Handbook for Farmers.* Bloomington, MN: Doane Information Services, 1980.

Prior-Willeard, Christopher. *Farming Futures: A Guide to the Agricultural Commodity Futures Markets.* Wolfeboro, NH: Longwood Publishing Group, 1985.

Sennholz, Lyn M., et al. *Livestock Hedging Course.* Spring Mills, PA: Center for Futures Education, 1984.

Teweles, Richard J., and Frank J. Jones. *The Commodity Futures Game: Who Wins? Who Loses? Why?,* 2d ed. New York: McGraw-Hill, 1987.

Timmer, C. Peter. *Getting Prices Right: The Scope and Limits of Agricultural Price Policy.* Ithaca, NY: Cornell University Press, 1986.

Wills, Walter J. *An Introduction to Grain Marketing.* Danville, IL: Interstate Printers & Publishers, 1972.

Government Publications

U.S. Department of Agriculture:
  Cattle
  Crop Production
  Hogs and Pigs
  Livestock and Poultry Situation and Outlook
  Livestock Slaughter
  Outlook for U.S. Agricultural Exports
  Rice Situation and Outlook
  Wheat

USDA Foreign Agricultural Service:
  Oilseeds and Products

U.S. Agricultural Marketing Service:
  Grain and Feed Market News

U.S. Department of Commerce:
  Fats and Oils
  Oilseed Crushings

Chicago Board of Trade Publications
Education and Marketing Services Department:
CBOT Handbook Series on Agricultural Markets: Weather and the Corn Market; Weather and the Soybean Market; Weather and the Wheat Market, 1987.

Grains: Production, Processing, Marketing, rev. ed., 1982.

Chapter 14

Books
Bernstein, Jacob. *An Investor's Guide to Using Cycles in the Precious Metals and Copper.* New York: John Wiley & Sons, 1985.

Rapson, W.S., and T. Groenewald. *Gold Usage.* New York: Academic Press, 1978.

Teweles, Richard J., and Frank J. Jones. *The Commodity Futures Game: Who Wins? Who Loses? Why?,* 2d ed. New York: McGraw-Hill, 1987.

Periodicals and Reports
Metals Week. New York: McGraw-Hill.

The Silver Market. New York: Handy and Harman.

Government Publications
U.S. Bureau of Mines:
   Mineral Industry Surveys, Copper
   Mineral Industry Surveys, Gold and Silver Monthly
   Mineral Industry Surveys, Platinum-Group Metals
   Minerals Yearbook

U.S. Bureau of the Mint:
   Annual Report of the Director

Chapter 15

Books
Dean, William, and David S. Evans, eds. *Terms of the Trade: A Handbook for the Forest Products Industry.* Eugene, OR: Random Lengths Publications, 1978.

Duerr, William A., ed. *Timber! Problems, Prospects, Policies.* Ames, IA: Iowa State University, 1973.

Savaiko, Bernard C. *Trading in Soft Commodity Futures.* New York: John Wiley & Sons, 1986.

Teweles, Richard J., and Frank J. Jones. *The Commodity Futures Game: Who Wins? Who Loses? Why?,* 2d ed. New York: McGraw-Hill, 1987.

Periodicals and Reports
Crow's Weekly Letter. Portland, OR: C.C. Crow Publications.

Florida Agricultural Statistics: Citrus Summary. Florida Crop and Livestock Reporting Service.

Statistical Annual. Portland, OR: Western Wood Products Association.

Government Publications
U.S. Bureau of the Census:
   Housing Starts
   Lumber Production and Mill Stocks

U.S. Department of Agriculture:
   Cold Storage
   Cotton and Wool Situation and Outlook
   Crop Production
   Fruit and Tree Nuts Situation and Outlook
   Sugar and Sweetener Situation and Outlook

USDA Foreign Agricultural Service:
   World Cocoa Situation
   World Coffee Situation
   World Sugar and Molasses Situation and Outlook

U.S. Forest Service:
   Production, Prices, Employment, and Trade in Northwest Forest Industries

Books
Brown, Stewart L., and Steven Errera. *Trading Energy Futures: A Manual for Energy Industry Professionals.* Westport, CT: Quorum Books, 1987.

Prast, William G., and Howard L. Lax. *Oil-Futures Markets: An Introduction.* Lexington, MA: Lexington Books, 1983.

Stobaugh, Robert, and Daniel Yergin, eds. *Energy Futures: The Report of the Harvard Business School Energy Project.* New York: Random House, 1982.

Teweles, Richard J., and Frank J. Jones. *The Commodity Futures Game: Who Wins? Who Loses? Why?,* 2d ed. New York: McGraw-Hill, 1987.

Treat, John E. *Energy Futures Trading Opportunities for the 1980s.* Tulsa, OK: PennWell Books, 1984.

Periodical
Oil and Gas Journal. Tulsa, OK: PennWell Publishing.

Government Publications
U.S. Department of Energy:
   Monthly Energy Review
   Petroleum Supply Monthly
   Weekly Petroleum Status Report

Chapter 16

| Chapter 17 | |

Books

Aliber, Robert Z. *The International Money Game*, 5th ed. New York: Basic Books, 1987.

Ansbacher, Max G. *The New Stock-Index Market, Strategies for Profit in Stock Index Futures and Options*. New York: Walker, 1983.

Bookstaber, Richard. *The Complete Investment Book: Trading Stocks, Bonds and Options with Computer Applications*. Glenview, IL: Scott Foresman, 1985.

Cooner, James J. *Investing in Municipal Bonds: Balancing Risks and Rewards*. New York: John Wiley and Sons, 1987.

Darst, David. *The Complete Bond Book: A Guide to All Types of Fixed Income Securities*. New York: McGraw-Hill, 1975.

————. *The Handbook of the Bond and Money Markets*. New York: McGraw-Hill, 1981.

Downes, John, and Jordan Elliot Goodman. *Dictionary of Finance and Investment Terms*. Woodbury, NY: Barron's, 1985.

Fabozzi, Frank J., ed. *Handbook of Mortgage-Backed Securities*, rev. ed. Chicago: Probus Publishing, 1988.

Fabozzi, Frank J., and Irving M. Pollack, eds. *Handbook of Fixed Income Securities*, 2d ed. Homewood, IL: Dow Jones-Irwin, 1986.

Federal Reserve System: Its Purposes and Functions, 7th ed. Washington, DC: Board of Governors of the Federal Reserve System, 1984.

Feldstein, Sylvan G., and Frank J. Fabozzi. *The Dow Jones-Irwin Guide to Municipal Bonds*. Homewood, IL: Dow Jones-Irwin, 1986.

Figlewski, Stephen, et al. *Hedging with Financial Futures for Institutional Investors: From Theory to Practice*. Cambridge, MA: Ballinger Publishing, 1985.

Greider, William. *Secrets of the Temple: How the Federal Reserve Runs the Country*. New York: Simon & Schuster, 1987.

Kaufman, Perry J. *Handbook of Futures Markets: Commodity, Financial, Stock Index and Options*. New York: John Wiley & Sons, 1984.

Loosigian, Allan M. *Interest Rate Futures*. Homewood, IL: Dow Jones-Irwin, 1980.

Lorie, James H., and Mary T. Hamilton. *The Stock Market: Theories and Evidence*, 2d ed. Homewood, IL: Dow Jones-Irwin, 1985.

Luskin, Donald L. *Index Options and Futures: The Complete Guide*. New York: John Wiley & Sons, 1987.

Platt, Robert B. *Controlling Interest Rate Risk: Techniques and Applications for Money Management*. New York: John Wiley & Sons, 1986.

Powers, Mark, and David Vogel. *Inside the Financial Futures Market*, 2d ed. New York: John Wiley & Sons, 1984.

Rebell, Arthur L., and Gail Gordon. *Financial Futures and Investment Strategy*. Homewood, IL: Dow Jones-Irwin, 1984.

Rothstein, Nancy, and James M. Little. *The Handbook of Financial Futures: A Guide for Investors and Professional Financial Managers*. New York: McGraw-Hill, 1983.

Sennholz, Lyn M., et al. *Interest Rate Futures Hedging Course*. Spring Mills, PA: Center for Futures Education, 1984.

———. *Stock Index Futures Hedging Course*. Spring Mills, PA: Center for Futures Education, 1983.

Stigum, Marcia. *The Money Market*, rev. ed. Homewood, IL: Dow Jones-Irwin, 1983.

Van Horne, James C. *Financial Market Rates and Flows*, 2d ed. Englewood Cliffs, NJ: Prentice-Hall, 1984.

Weiner, Neil S. *Stock Index Futures: A Guide for Traders, Investors, and Analysts*. New York: John Wiley & Sons, 1983.

Periodicals and Reports
American Banker. New York: American Banker.

Bank Credit Analyst. Hamilton, Bermuda: Monetary Research.

Bank Credit Analyst Interest Rate Forecast. Hamilton, Bermuda: Monetary Research.

Euromoney. London, UK: Euromoney Publications.

Federal Reserve Bulletin. Washington, DC: U.S. Board of Governors of the Federal Reserve System.

Pick's Currency Yearbook. New York: Pick Publishing.

Real Estate Review. Boston: Warren, Gorham & Lamont.

Government Publication
U.S. Treasury Department:
  Treasury Bulletin

Chicago Board of Trade Publications
Education and Marketing Services Department:
CBOT Financial Instruments Guide, 1987.

Chicago Board of Trade Treasury Bond Futures Yield Calculator, 1987.

Chicago Board of Trade Treasury Note Futures Yield Calculator, 1987.

General

Books

Erickson, Rosemary, and George Steinbeck. *Language of Commodities: A Commodity Glossary.* New York: New York Institute of Finance, 1985.

Geczi, Michael L. *Futures, the Anti-inflation Investment.* New York: Avon Books, 1980.

Gold, Gerald. *Modern Commodity Futures Trading,* 7th ed. New York: Commodity Research Bureau, 1975.

Herbst, Anthony F. *Commodity Futures: Markets, Methods of Analysis, and Management of Risk.* New York: John Wiley & Sons, 1986.

Horn, Frederick F., and Victor W. Farah. *Trading in Commodity Futures,* 2d ed. New York: New York Institute of Finance, 1979.

Kolb, Robert W. *Understanding Futures Markets.* Glenview, IL: Scott Foresman, 1985.

Powers, Mark J. *Getting Started in Commodity Futures Trading.* Waterloo, IA: Investor Publications, 1983.

Teweles, Richard J., and Frank J. Jones. *The Commodity Futures Game: Who Wins? Who Loses? Why?,* 2d ed. New York: McGraw-Hill, 1987.

Williams, Larry. *Definitive Guide to Futures Trading, Vol. 1.* Brightwaters, NY: Windsor Books, 1988.

Periodicals and Reports

Commitments of Traders in Commodity Futures. Commodity Futures Trading Commission.

CRB Commodity Yearbook. New York: Commodity Research Bureau.

Journal of Futures Markets. New York: John Wiley & Sons.

Government Publications

U.S. Bureau of the Census:
Statistical Abstract of the United States

U.S. Printing Office:
Monthly Catalog of U.S. Government Publications

Chicago Board of Trade Publications

Education and Marketing Services Department:
Readings in Futures Markets, Book 1: Selected Writings of Holbrook Working.
Anne E. Peck, ed. 1977.

Readings in Futures Markets, Vol. 2: Selected Writings on Futures Markets: Basic Research in Commodity Markets. Anne E. Peck, ed. 1983.

Readings in Futures Markets, Book 3: Views from the Trade. Anne E. Peck, ed. 1978.

Readings in Futures Markets, Book 4: Selected Writings on Futures Markets: Research Directions in Commodity Markets, 1970-1980. Anne E. Peck, ed. 1984.

Readings in Futures Markets, Book 5: Selected Writings on Futures Markets: Explorations in Financial Futures Markets. Anne E. Peck, ed. 1985.

Review of Research in Futures Markets, Vols. 1-7, 1982-88.

Note: Chicago Board of Trade publications listed in the Sources of Information are generally available from the exchange. For more information on ordering specific publications, contact the appropriate Chicago Board of Trade departments.

GLOSSARY

Actuals: See **Cash Commodity.**

Adjusted Futures Price: The cash-price equivalent reflected in the current futures price. This is calculated by taking the futures price times the conversion factor for the particular financial instrument (e.g., bond or note) being delivered.

Afloat: Physical commodity in harbor or in transit in a vessel.

Against Actuals: See **Exchange For Physicals.**

Arbitrage: The simultaneous purchase and sale of similar commodities in different markets to take advantage of a price discrepancy.

Arbitration: The procedure of settling disputes between members, or between members and customers.

Assign: To make an option seller perform his obligation to assume a short futures position (as a seller of a call option) or a long futures position (as a seller of a put option).

Associated Person (AP): An individual who solicits orders, customers, or customer funds (or who supervises persons performing such duties) on behalf of a Futures Commission Merchant, an Introducing Broker, a Commodity Trading Adviser, or a Commodity Pool Operator.

Associate Membership (CBOT): A Chicago Board of Trade membership that allows an individual to trade financial instrument futures and other designated markets.

At-the-Money Option: An option with a strike price that is equal, or approximately equal, to the current market price of the underlying futures contract.

A

Balance of Payment: A summary of the international transactions of a country over a period of time including commodity and service transactions, capital transactions, and gold movements.

Bar Chart: A chart that graphs the high, low, and settlement prices for a specific trading session over a given period of time.

Basis: The difference between the current cash price and the futures price of the same commodity. Unless otherwise specified, the price of the nearby futures contract month is generally used to calculate the basis.

Bear: Someone who thinks market prices will decline.

Bear Market: A period of declining market prices.

Bear Spread: In most commodities and financial instruments, the term refers to selling the nearby contract month, and buying the deferred contract, to profit from a change in the price relationship.

Bid: An expression indicating a desire to buy a commodity at a given price; opposite of offer.

Board of Trade Clearing Corporation: An independent corporation that settles all trades made at the Chicago Board of Trade acting as a guarantor

B

for all trades cleared by it, reconciles all clearing member firm accounts each day to ensure that all gains have been credited and all losses have been collected, and sets and adjusts clearing member firm margins for changing market conditions. Also referred to as **clearing corporation.** See **Clearinghouse.**

Book Entry Securities: Electronically recorded securities that include each creditor's name, address, Social Security or tax identification number, and dollar amount loaned, (i.e., no certificates are issued to bond holders, instead, the transfer agent electronically credits interest payments to each creditor's bank account on a designated date).

Broker: A company or individual that executes futures and options orders on behalf of financial and commercial institutions and/or the general public.

Brokerage Fee: See **Commission Fee.**

Bull: Someone who thinks market prices will rise.

Bull Market: A period of rising market prices.

Bull Spread: In most commodities and financial instruments, the term refers to buying the nearby month, and selling the deferred month, to profit from the change in the price relationship.

Butterfly Spread: The placing of two interdelivery spreads in opposite directions with the center delivery month common to both spreads.

Buying Hedge: See **Purchasing Hedge.**

C

Calendar Spread: See **Horizontal Spread.**

Call Option: An option that gives the buyer the right, but not the obligation, to purchase (go "long") the underlying futures contract at the strike price on or before the expiration date.

Canceling Order: An order that deletes a customer's previous order.

Carrying Charge: For physical commodities such as grains and metals, the cost of storage space, insurance, and finance charges incurred by holding a physical commodity. In interest rate futures markets, it refers to the differential between the yield on a cash instrument and the cost of funds necessary to buy the instrument. Also referred to as **cost of carry** or **carry.**

Carryover: Grain and oilseed commodities not consumed during the marketing year and remaining in storage at year's end. These stocks are "carried over" into the next marketing year and added to the stocks produced during that crop year.

Cash Commodity: An actual physical commodity someone is buying or selling, e.g., soybeans, corn, gold, silver, Treasury bonds, etc. Also referred to as **actuals.**

Cash Contract: A sales agreement for either immediate or future delivery of the actual product.

Cash Market: A place where people buy and sell the actual commodities, i.e., grain elevator, bank, etc. See **Spot** and **Forward Contract.**

Cash Settlement: Transactions generally involving index-based futures contracts that are settled in cash based on the actual value of the index on the last trading day, in contrast to those that specify the delivery of a commodity or financial instrument.

Certificate of Deposit (CD): A time deposit with a specific maturity evidenced by a certificate.

Charting: The use of charts to analyze market behavior and anticipate future price movements. Those who use charting as a trading method plot such factors as high, low, and settlement prices; average price movements; volume; and open interest. Two basic price charts are bar charts and point-and-figure charts. See **Technical Analysis.**

Cheap: Colloquialism implying that a commodity is underpriced.

Cheapest to Deliver: A method to determine which particular cash debt instrument is most profitable to deliver against a futures contract.

Clear: The process by which a clearinghouse maintains records of all trades and settles margin flow on a daily mark-to-market basis for its clearing member.

Clearing Corporation: See **Board of Trade Clearing Corporation.**

Clearinghouse: An agency or separate corporation of a futures exchange that is responsible for settling trading accounts, clearing trades, collecting and maintaining margin monies, regulating delivery, and reporting trading data. Clearinghouses act as third parties to all futures and options contracts—acting as a buyer to every clearing member seller and a seller to every clearing member buyer.

Clearing Margin: Financial safeguards to ensure that clearing members (usually companies or corporations) perform on their customers' open futures and options contracts. Clearing margins are distinct from customer margins that individual buyers and sellers of futures and options contracts are required to deposit with brokers. See **Customer Margin.**

Clearing Member: A member of an exchange clearinghouse. Memberships in clearing organizations are usually held by companies. Clearing members are responsible for the financial commitments of customers that clear through their firm.

Closing Price: See **Settlement Price.**

Closing Range: A range of prices at which buy and sell transactions took place during the market close.

COM Membership (CBOT): A Chicago Board of Trade membership that allows an individual to trade contracts listed in the commodity options market category.

Commission Fee: A fee charged by a broker for executing a transaction. Also referred to as **brokerage fee.**

Commission House: See **Futures Commission Merchant (FCM).**

Commodity: An article of commerce or a product that can be used for commerce. In a narrow sense, products traded on an authorized commodity exchange. The types of commodities include agricultural products, metals, petroleum, foreign currencies, and financial instruments and indexes, to name a few.

Commodity Credit Corporation (CCC): A branch of the U.S. Department of Agriculture, established in 1933, that supervises the government's farm loan and subsidy programs.

Commodity Futures Trading Commission (CFTC): A federal regulatory agency established under the Commodity Futures Trading Commission Act, as amended in 1974, that oversees futures trading in the United States. The commission is comprised of five commissioners, one of whom is designated as chairman, all appointed by the President subject to Senate confirmation, and is independent of all cabinet departments.

Commodity Pool: An enterprise in which funds contributed by a number of persons are combined for the purpose of trading futures contracts or commodity options.

Commodity Pool Operator (CPO): An individual or organization that operates or solicits funds for a commodity pool.

Commodity Trading Adviser (CTA): A person who, for compensation or profit, directly or indirectly advises others as to the value or the advisability of buying or selling futures contracts or commodity options. Advising indirectly includes exercising trading authority over a customer's account as well as providing recommendations through written publications or other media.

Computerized Trading Reconstruction (CTR) System: A Chicago Board of Trade computerized surveillance program that pinpoints in any trade the traders, the contract, the quantity, the price, and time of execution to the nearest minute.

Consumer Price Index (CPI): A major inflation measure computed by the U.S. Department of Commerce. It measures the change in prices of a fixed market basket of some 385 goods and services in the previous month.

Contract Grades: See **Deliverable Grades.**

Controlled Account: See **Discretionary Account.**

Convergence: A term referring to cash and futures prices tending to come together (i.e., the basis approaches zero) as the futures contract nears expiration.

Conversion Factor: A factor used to equate the price of T-bond and T-note futures contracts with the various cash T-bonds and T-notes eligible for delivery. This factor is based on a static relationship of various coupons to an 8 percent bond or note, the coupon underlying the contract of the same first call date.

Cost of Carry (or Carry): See **Carrying Charge.**

Coupon: The interest rate on a debt instrument expressed in terms of a percent on an annualized basis that the issuer guarantees to pay the holder until maturity.

Crop (Marketing) Year: The time span from harvest to harvest for agricultural commodities. The crop marketing year varies slightly with each ag commodity, but it tends to begin at harvest and end before the next year's harvest, e.g., the marketing year for soybeans begins September 1 and ends August 31. The futures contract month of November represents the first major new-crop marketing month, and the contract month of July represents the last major old-crop marketing month for soybeans.

Crop Reports: Reports compiled by the U.S. Department of Agriculture on various ag commodities that are released throughout the year. Information in the reports includes estimates on planted acreage, yield, and expected production, as well as comparison of production from previous years.

Cross-Hedging: Hedging a cash commodity using a different but related futures contract when there is no futures contract for the cash commodity being hedged and the cash and futures markets follow similar price trends (e.g., using soybean meal futures to hedge fish meal).

Crush: The purchase of soybean futures (or cash soybeans) and the simultaneous sale of soybean oil and meal futures (or cash soybean oil and meal). This spread is used to minimize the financial risks of sudden increases in soybean costs and/or declining values of finished soybean oil and meal.

Current Yield: The ratio of the coupon to the current market price of the debt instrument.

Customer Margin: Within the futures industry, financial guarantees required of both buyers and sellers of futures contracts and sellers of options contracts to ensure fulfillment of contract obligations. FCMs are responsible for overseeing customer margin accounts. Margins are determined on the basis of market risk and contract value. Also referred to as **performance-bond margin.** See **Clearing Margin.**

D

Daily Trading Limit: The maximum price range set by the exchange each day for a contract.

Day Traders: Speculators who take positions in futures or options contracts and liquidate them prior to the close of the same trading day.

Deferred (Delivery) Month: The more distant month(s) in which futures trading is taking place, as distinguished from the nearby (delivery) month.

Deliverable Grades: The standard grades of commodities or instruments listed in the rules of the exchanges that must be met when delivering cash commodities against futures contracts. Grades are often accompanied by a schedule of discounts and premiums allowable for delivery of commodities of lesser or greater quality than the standard called for by the exchange. Also referred to as **contract grades.**

Delivery: The transfer of the cash commodity from the seller of a futures contract to the buyer of a futures contract. Each futures exchange has specific procedures for delivery of a cash commodity. Some futures contracts, such as stock index contracts, are cash settled.

Delivery Day: The third day in the delivery process at the Chicago Board of Trade, when the buyer's clearing firm presents the delivery notice with a certified check for the amount due at the office of the seller's clearing firm.

Delivery Points: The locations and facilities designated by a futures exchange where stocks of a commodity may be delivered in fulfillment of a futures contract, under procedures established by the exchange.

Delta: A measure of how much an option premium changes, given a unit change in the underlying futures price. Delta often is interpreted as the probability that the underlying futures price will move in-the-money by expiration.

Demand, Law of: The relationship between product demand and price.

Differentials: Price differences between classes, grades, and delivery locations of various stocks of the same commodity.

Discount Basis: A method of quoting securities wherein the price is expressed as an annualized discount from maturity value.

Discount Rate: The interest rate charged on loans by the Federal Reserve to member banks.

Discretionary Account: An arrangement by which the holder of the account gives written power of attorney to another person, often his broker, to make trading decisions. Also known as a **controlled** or **managed account.**

E

Econometrics: The application of statistical and mathematical methods in the field of economics to test and quantify economic theories and the solutions to economic problems.

Equilibrium Price: The market price at which the quantity supplied of a commodity equals the quantity demanded.

Eurodollars: U.S. dollars on deposit with a bank outside of the United States and, consequently, outside the jurisdiction of the United States. The bank could be either a foreign bank or a subsidiary of a U.S. bank.

Exchange For Physicals (EFP): A transaction generally used by two hedgers who want to exchange futures for cash positions. Also referred to as **against actuals** or **versus cash.**

Exercise: The action taken by the holder of a call option if he wishes to purchase the underlying futures contract or by the holder of a put option if he wishes to sell the underlying futures contract.

Exercise Price: See **Strike Price.**

Expanded Trading Hours: Additional trading hours of specific futures and options contracts at the Chicago Board of Trade that overlap with business hours in other time zones.

Expiration Date: Options on futures generally expire on a specific date during the month preceding the futures contract delivery month. For example, an option on a March futures contract expires in February but is referred to as a March option because its exercise would result in a March futures contract position.

Extrinsic Value: See **Time Value.**

Face Value: The amount of money printed on the face of the certificate of a security; the original dollar amount of indebtedness incurred.

Federal Funds: Member bank deposits held by the Federal Reserve; these funds are loaned by the Federal Reserve to other member banks.

Federal Funds Rate: The rate of interest charged for the use of federal funds.

Federal Housing Administration (FHA): A division of the U.S. Department of Housing and Urban Development that insures residential mortgage loans and sets construction standards.

Federal Reserve System: A central banking system in the United States, created by the Federal Reserve Act in 1913, designed to assist the nation in attaining its economic and financial goals. The structure of the Federal Reserve System includes a Board of Governors, the Federal Open Market Committee, and 12 Federal Reserve Banks.

Feed Ratio: A ratio used to express the relationship of feeding costs to the dollar value of livestock. See **Hog/Corn Ratio** and **Steer/Corn Ratio.**

Fill-or-Kill: A customer order that is a price limit order that must be filled immediately or canceled.

Financial Analysis Auditing Compliance Tracking System (FACTS): The National Futures Association's computerized system of maintaining financial records of its member firms and monitoring their financial conditions.

First Notice Day: According to Chicago Board of Trade rules, the first day on which a notice of intent to deliver a commodity in fulfillment of a given month's futures contract can be made by the clearinghouse to a buyer. The clearinghouse also informs the sellers who they have been matched up with.

Forward (Cash) Contract: A contract in which a seller agrees to deliver a specific cash commodity to a buyer sometime in the future. Forward contracts, in contrast to futures contracts, are privately negotiated and are not standardized.

Full Carrying Charge Market: A futures market where the price difference between delivery months reflects the total costs of interest, insurance, and storage.

Full Membership (CBOT): A Chicago Board of Trade membership that allows an individual to trade all futures and options contracts listed by the exchange.

Fundamental Analysis: A method of anticipating future price movement using supply and demand information.

Futures Commission Merchant (FCM): An individual or organization that solicits or accepts orders to buy or sell futures contracts or options on futures and accepts money or other assets from customers to support such orders. Also referred to as **commission house** or **wire house.**

Futures Contract: A legally binding agreement, made on the trading floor of a futures exchange, to buy or sell a commodity or financial instrument sometime in the future. Futures contracts are standardized according to the quality, quantity, and delivery time and location for each commodity. The

F

only variable is price, which is discovered on an exchange trading floor.

Gamma: A measurement of how fast delta changes, given a unit change in the underlying futures price.

GIM Membership (CBOT): A Chicago Board of Trade membership that allows an individual to trade all futures contracts listed in the government instrument market category.

Grain Terminal: Large grain elevator facility with the capacity to ship grain by rail and/or barge to domestic or foreign markets.

Gross National Product (GNP): The total value of final goods and services produced in the United States over a specific time period.

Gross Processing Margin (GPM): The difference between the cost of soybeans and the combined sales income of the processed soybean oil and meal.

Hedger: An individual or company owning or planning to own a cash commodity—corn, soybeans, wheat, U.S. Treasury bonds, notes, bills, etc.—and concerned that the cost of the commodity may change before either buying or selling it in the cash market. A hedger achieves protection against changing cash prices by purchasing (selling) futures contracts of the same or similar commodity and later offsetting that position by selling (purchasing) futures contracts of the same quantity and type as the initial transaction.

Hedging: The practice of offsetting the price risk inherent in any cash market position by taking an equal but opposite position in the futures market. Hedgers use the futures markets to protect their businesses from adverse price changes. See **Selling (Short) Hedge** and **Purchasing (Long) Hedge.**

High: The highest price of the day for a particular futures contract.

Hog/Corn Ratio: The relationship of feeding costs to the dollar value of hogs. It is measured by dividing the price of hogs ($/hundredweight) by the price of corn ($/bushel). When corn prices are high relative to pork prices, fewer units of corn equal the dollar value of 100 pounds of pork. Conversely, when corn prices are low in relation to pork prices, more units of corn are required to equal the value of 100 pounds of pork. See **Feed Ratio.**

Holder: See **Option Buyer.**

Horizontal Spread: The purchase of either a call or put option and the simultaneous sale of the same type of option with typically the same strike price but with a different expiration month. Also referred to as a **calendar spread.**

IDEM Membership (CBOT): A Chicago Board of Trade membership of trading privileges for futures contracts in the index, debt, and metals markets category (gold, silver, and stock index futures).

Initial Margin: The amount a futures market participant must deposit into his margin account at the time he places an order to buy or sell a futures contract.

Intercommodity Spread: The purchase of a given delivery month of one futures market and the simultaneous sale of the same delivery month of a different, but related, futures market.

Interdelivery Spread: The purchase of one delivery month of a given futures contract and simultaneous sale of another delivery month of the same commodity on the same exchange. Also referred to as an **intramarket spread.**

Intermarket Spread: The sale of a given delivery month of a futures contract on one exchange and the simultaneous purchase of the same delivery month and futures contract on another exchange.

In-the-Money Option: An option having intrinsic value. A call option is in-the-money if its strike price is below the current price of the underlying futures contract. A put option is in-the-money if its strike price is above the current price of the underlying futures contract. See **Intrinsic Value.**

Intramarket Spread: See **Interdelivery Spread.**

Intrinsic Value: The amount by which an option is in-the-money. See **In-the-Money Option.**

Introducing Broker (IB): A person or organization that solicits or accepts orders to buy or sell futures contracts or commodity options but does not accept money or other assets from customers to support such orders.

Inverted Market: A futures market in which the relationship between two delivery months of the same commodity is abnormal.

Invisible Supply: Uncounted stocks of a commodity in the hands of wholesalers, manufacturers, and producers that cannot be identified accurately; stocks outside commercial channels but theoretically available to the market.

L

Lagging Indicators: Market indicators showing the general direction of the economy and confirming or denying the trend implied by the leading indicators.

Last Trading Day: According to the Chicago Board of Trade rules, the final day when trading may occur in a given futures or options contract month. Futures contracts outstanding at the end of the last trading day must be settled by delivery of the underlying commodity or securities or by agreement for monetary settlement (in some cases by EFPs).

Leading Indicators: Market indicators that signal the state of the economy for the coming months. Some of the leading indicators include: average manufacturing workweek, layoff rate of manufacturing workers, inflation-adjusted new orders for consumer goods and material, speed of delivery of new goods, rate of net business formation, contracts for plant and equipment, change in inventories on hand, change in crude material prices, prices of stocks, change in total liquid assets, change in money supply.

Leverage: The ability to control large dollar amounts of a commodity with a comparatively small amount of capital.

Limit Order: An order in which the customer sets a limit on the price and/or time of execution.

Limits: See **Position Limit, Price Limit, Variable Limit.**

Linkage: The ability to buy (sell) contracts on one exchange (such as the Chicago Mercantile Exchange) and later sell (buy) them on another exchange (such as the Singapore International Monetary Exchange).

Liquid: A characteristic of a security or commodity market with enough units outstanding to allow large transactions without a substantial change in price. Institutional investors are inclined to seek out liquid investments so that their trading activity will not influence the market price.

Liquidate: Selling (or purchasing) futures contracts of the same delivery month purchased (or sold) during an earlier transaction or making (or taking) delivery of the cash commodity represented by the futures contract. See **Offset.**

Liquidity Data Bank® (LDB®): A computerized profile of CBOT market activity, used by technical traders to analyze price trends and develop trading strategies. There is a specialized display of daily volume data and time distribution of prices for every commodity traded on the Chicago Board of Trade.

Loan Program: A federal program in which the government lends money at preannounced rates to farmers and allows them to use the crops they plant for the upcoming crop year as collateral. Default on these loans is the primary method by which the government acquires stocks of agricultural commodities.

Loan Rate: The amount lent per unit of a commodity to farmers.

Long: One who has bought futures contracts or owns a cash commodity.

Long Hedge: See **Purchasing Hedge.**

Low: The lowest price of the day for a particular futures contract.

M

Maintenance Margin: A set minimum margin (per outstanding futures contract) that a customer must maintain in his margin account.

Managed Account: See **Discretionary Account.**

Margin: See **Clearing Margin** and **Customer Margin.**

Margin Call: A call from a clearinghouse to a clearing member, or from a brokerage firm to a customer, to bring margin deposits up to a required minimum level.

Market Information Data Inquiry System (MIDIS-Touch): Daily Chicago

Board of Trade price, volume, and open interest data accessible by telephone.

Market Order: An order to buy or sell a futures contract of a given delivery month to be filled at the best possible price and as soon as possible.

Market Price Reporting and Information System (MPRIS): The Chicago Board of Trade's computerized price-reporting system.

Market Reporter: A person employed by the exchange and located in or near the trading pit who records prices as they occur during trading.

Mark-to-the-Market: To debit or credit on a daily basis a margin account based on the close of that day's trading session. In this way, buyers and sellers are protected against the possibility of contract default.

Minimum Price Fluctuation: See **Tick.**

Money Supply: The amount of money in the economy, consisting primarily of currency in circulation plus deposits in banks: **M-1**—U.S. money supply consisting of currency in circulation, traveler's checks, checking account funds, NOW and super-NOW accounts, automatic transfer service accounts, and balances in credit unions. **M-2**—U.S. money supply consisting of M-1 plus savings and small time deposits (less than $100,000) at depository institutions, overnight repurchase agreements at commercial banks, and money market mutual fund accounts. **M-3**—U.S. money supply consisting of M-2 plus large time deposits ($100,000 or more) at depository institutions, repurchase agreements with maturities longer than one day at commercial banks, and institutional money market accounts.

Moving-Average Charts: A statistical price analysis method of recognizing different price trends. A moving average is calculated by adding the prices for a predetermined number of days and then dividing by the number of days.

Municipal Bonds: Debt securities issued by state and local governments, and special districts and counties.

National Futures Association (NFA): An industrywide, industry-supported, self-regulatory organization for futures and options markets. The primary responsibilities of the NFA are to enforce ethical standards and customer protection rules, screen futures professionals for membership, audit and monitor professionals for financial and general compliance rules, and provide for arbitration of futures-related disputes.

N

Nearby (Delivery) Month: The futures contract month closest to expiration. Also referred to as **spot month.**

Negative Yield Curve: See **Yield Curve.**

Notice Day: According to Chicago Board of Trade rules, the second day of the three-day delivery process when the clearing corporation matches the buyer with the oldest reported long position to the delivering seller and notifies both parties. See **First Notice Day.**

O

Offer: An expression indicating one's desire to sell a commodity at a given price; opposite of bid.

Offset: Taking a second futures or options position opposite to the initial or opening position. See **Liquidate.**

OPEC: Organization of Petroleum Exporting Countries, emerged as the major petroleum pricing power in 1973, when the ownership of oil production in the Middle East transferred from the operating companies to the governments of the producing countries or to their national oil companies. Members are: Algeria, Ecuador, Gabon, Indonesia, Iran, Iraq, Kuwait, Libya, Nigeria, Qatar, Saudi Arabia, the United Arab Emirates, and Venezuela.

Opening Range: A range of prices at which buy and sell transactions took place during the opening of the market.

Open Interest: The total number of futures or options contracts of a given commodity that have not yet been offset by an opposite futures or option transaction nor fulfilled by delivery of the commodity or option exercise. Each open transaction has a buyer and a seller, but for calculation of open interest, only one side of the contract is counted.

Open Market Operation: The buying and selling of government securities—Treasury bills, notes, and bonds—by the Federal Reserve.

Open Outcry: Method of public auction for making verbal bids and offers in the trading pits or rings of futures exchanges.

Option: A contract that conveys the right, but not the obligation, to buy or sell a particular commodity at a certain price for a limited time. Only the seller of the option is obligated to perform.

Option Buyer: The purchaser of either a call or put option. Option buyers receive the right, but not the obligation, to assume a futures position. Also referred to as the **holder.**

Option Premium: The price of an option—the sum of money that the option buyer pays and the option seller receives for the rights granted by the option.

Option Seller: The person who sells an option in return for a premium and is obligated to perform when the holder exercises his right under the option contract. Also referred to as the **writer.**

Option Spread: The simultaneous purchase and sale of one or more options contracts, futures, and/or cash positions.

Option Writer: See **Option Seller.**

Out-of-the-Money Option: An option with no intrinsic value, i.e., a call whose strike price is above the current futures price or a put whose strike price is below the current futures price.

P

P&S (Purchase and Sale) Statement: A statement sent by a commission house to a customer when his futures or options on futures position has changed, showing the number of contracts bought or sold, the prices at which the contracts were bought or sold, the gross profit or loss, the commission charges, and the net profit or loss on the transactions.

Par: The face value of a security. For example, a bond selling at par is worth the same dollar amount it was issued for or at which it will be redeemed at maturity.

Payment-In-Kind (PIK) Program: A government program in which farmers who comply with a voluntary acreage-control program and set aside an additional percentage of acreage specified by the government receive certificates that can be redeemed for government-owned stocks of grain.

Performance Bond Margin: The amount of money deposited by both a buyer and seller of a futures contract or an options seller to ensure performance of the term of the contract. Margin in commodities is not a payment of equity or down payment on the commodity itself, but rather it is a security deposit. See **Customer Margin** and **Clearing Margin.**

Pit: The area on the trading floor where futures and options on futures contracts are bought and sold. Pits are usually raised octagonal platforms with steps descending on the inside that permit buyers and sellers of contracts to see each other.

Point-and-Figure Charts: Charts that show price changes of a minimum amount regardless of the time period involved.

Position: A market commitment. A buyer of a futures contract is said to have a long position and, conversely, a seller of futures contracts is said to have a short position.

Position Day: According to the Chicago Board of Trade rules, the first day in the process of making or taking delivery of the actual commodity on a futures contract. The clearing firm representing the seller notifies the Board of Trade Clearing Corporation that its short customers want to deliver on a futures contract.

Position Limit: The maximum number of speculative futures contracts one can hold as determined by the Commodity Futures Trading Commission and/or the exchange upon which the contract is traded. Also referred to as **trading limit.**

Position Trader: An approach to trading in which the trader either buys or sells contracts and holds them for an extended period of time.

Positive Yield Curve: See **Yield Curve.**

Premium: (1) The additional payment allowed by exchange regulation for delivery of higher-than-required standards or grades of a commodity against a futures contract. (2) In speaking of price relationships between different delivery months of a given commodity, one is said to be "trading at a premium" over another when its price is greater than that of the other. (3) In financial instruments, the dollar amount by which a security trades above its principal value. See **Option Premium.**

Price Limit: The maximum advance or decline—from the previous day's settlement price—permitted for a contract in one trading session by the rules of the exchange. See also **Variable Limit.**

Price Limit Order: A customer order that specifies the price at which a trade can be executed.

Prime Rate: Interest rate charged by major banks to their most creditworthy customers.

Producer Price Index (PPI): An index that shows the cost of resources needed to produce manufactured goods during the previous month.

Pulpit: A raised structure adjacent to, or in the center of, the pit or ring at a futures exchange where market reporters, employed by the exchange, record price changes as they occur in the trading pit.

Purchasing Hedge (or Long Hedge): Buying futures contracts to protect against a possible price increase of cash commodities that will be purchased in the future. At the time the cash commodities are bought, the open futures position is closed by selling an equal number and type of futures contracts as those that were initially purchased. Also referred to as a **buying hedge.** See **Hedging.**

Put Option: An option that gives the option buyer the right but not the obligation to sell (go "short") the underlying futures contract at the strike price on or before the expiration date.

R

Range (Price): The price span during a given trading session, week, month, year, etc.

Repurchase Agreements (or Repo): An agreement between a seller and a buyer, usually in U.S. government securities, in which the seller agrees to buy back the security at a later date.

Reserve Requirements: The minimum amount of cash and liquid assets as a percentage of demand deposits and time deposits that member banks of the Federal Reserve are required to maintain.

Resistance: A level above which prices have had difficulty penetrating.

Resumption: The reopening the following day of specific futures and options markets that also trade during the evening session at the Chicago Board of Trade.

Ring Method: A method of settlement used by futures markets from the early 1900s until the 1920s, when the first formalized clearing operations were developed. Settlement clerks of brokerage houses maintained daily accounting records of customer transactions in ring notebooks.

Risk Disclosure Statement: A document enumerating some of the risks involved in trading futures and/or options on futures that a customer who wishes to trade futures and/or options on futures must sign before opening an account with a brokerage firm.

Runners: Messengers who rush orders received by phone clerks to brokers for execution in the pit.

S

Scalper: A trader who trades for small, short-term profits during the course of a trading session, rarely carrying a position overnight.

Security: Common or preferred stock; a bond of a corporation, government, or quasi-government body.

Selling Hedge (or Short Hedge): Selling futures contracts to protect against possible declining prices of commodities that will be sold in the future. At the time the cash commodities are sold, the open futures position is closed by purchasing an equal number and type of futures contracts as those that were initially sold. See **Hedging.**

Settle: See **Settlement Price.**

Settlement Price: The last price paid for a commodity on any trading day. The exchange clearinghouse determines a firm's net gains or losses, margin requirements, and the next day's price limits, based on each futures and options contract settlement price. If there is a closing range of prices, the settlement price is determined by averaging those prices. Also referred to as **settle** or **closing price.**

Short: *(noun)* One who has sold futures contracts or plans to purchase a cash commodity. *(verb)* Selling futures contracts or initiating a cash forward contract sale without offsetting a particular market position.

Short Hedge: See **Selling Hedge.**

Simulation Analysis of Financial Exposure (SAFE): A sophisticated computer risk-analysis program that monitors the risk of clearing members and large-volume traders at the Chicago Board of Trade. It calculates the risk of change in market prices or volatility to a firm carrying open positions.

Speculator: A market participant who tries to profit from buying and selling futures and options contracts by anticipating future price movements. Speculators assume market price risk and add liquidity and capital to the futures markets.

Spot: Usually refers to a cash market price for a physical commodity that is available for immediate delivery.

Spot Month: See **Nearby (Delivery) Month**

Spread: The price difference between two related markets or commodities.

Spreading: The simultaneous buying and selling of two related markets in the expectation that a profit will be made when the position is offset. Examples include: buying one futures contract and selling another futures contract of the same commodity but different delivery month; buying and selling the same delivery month of the same commodity on different futures exchanges; buying a given delivery month of one futures market and selling the same delivery month of a different, but related, futures market.

Steer/Corn Ratio: The relationship of cattle prices to feeding costs. It is measured by dividing the price of cattle ($/hundredweight) by the price of corn ($/bushel). When corn prices are high relative to cattle prices, fewer units of corn equal the dollar value of 100 pounds of cattle. Conversely, when corn prices are low in relation to cattle prices, more units of corn are required to equal the value of 100 pounds of beef. See **Feed Ratio.**

Stock Index: An indicator used to measure and report value changes in a selected group of stocks. How a particular stock index tracks the market depends on its composition—the sampling of stocks, the weighting of individual stocks, and the method of averaging used to establish an index.

Stop-Limit Order: A variation of a stop order in which a trade must be executed at the exact price or better. If the order cannot be executed, it is held until the stated price or better is reached again.

Stop Order: An order to buy or sell when the market reaches a specified point. A stop order to buy becomes a market order when the commodity or security trades (or is bid) at or above the stop price. A stop order to sell becomes a market order when the commodity or security trades (or is offered) at or below the stop price.

Strike Price: The price at which the futures contract underlying a call or put option can be purchased (if a call) or sold (if a put). Also referred to as **exercise price.**

Supply, Law of: The relationship between product supply and its price.

Support: The place on a chart where the buying of futures contracts is sufficient to halt a price decline.

Suspension: The end of the evening session for specific futures and options markets traded at the Chicago Board of Trade.

T

Technical Analysis: Anticipating future price movement using historical prices, trading volume, open interest, and other trading data to study price patterns.

Tick: The smallest allowable increment of price movement for a contract. Also referred to as **minimum price fluctuation.**

Time Limit Order: A customer order that designates the time during which it can be executed.

Time Value: The amount of money option buyers are willing to pay for an option in the anticipation that, over time, a change in the underlying futures price will cause the option to increase in value. In general, an option premium is the sum of time value and intrinsic value. Any amount by which an option premium exceeds the option's intrinsic value can be considered time value. Also referred to as **extrinsic value.**

Trade Balance: The difference between a nation's imports and exports of merchandise.

Trading Limit: See **Position Limit.**

Treasury Bill: See **U.S. Treasury Bill.**

Treasury Bond: See **U.S. Treasury Bond.**

Treasury Note: See **U.S. Treasury Note.**

U

Underlying Futures Contract: The specific futures contract that is bought or sold by exercising an option.

U.S. Treasury Bill: A short-term U.S. government debt instrument with a maturity of one year or less. Bills are sold at a discount from par with the interest earned being the difference between the face value received at maturity and the price paid.

U.S. Treasury Bond: Government-debt security with a coupon maturity of more than 10 years. Interest is paid semiannually.

U.S. Treasury Note: Government-debt security with a coupon maturity of one to 10 years.

Variable Limit: According to the Chicago Board of Trade rules, an expanded allowable price range set during volatile markets.
Variation Margin: During periods of great market volatility or in the case of high-risk accounts, additional margin deposited by a clearing member firm to an exchange clearinghouse.
Versus Cash: See **Exchange For Physicals.**
Vertical Spread: Buying and selling puts or calls of the same expiration month but different strike prices.
Volatility: A measurement of the change in price over a given time period. It is often expressed as a percentage and computed as the annualized standard deviation of percentage change in daily price.
Volume: The number of purchases or sales of a commodity futures contract made during a specified period of time, often the total transactions for one trading day.

Warehouse Receipt: Document guaranteeing the existence and availability of a given quantity and quality of a commodity in storage; commonly used as the instrument of transfer of ownership in both cash and futures transactions.
Wire House: See **Futures Commission Merchant (FCM).**
Writer: See **Option Seller.**

Yield: A measure of the annual return on an investment.
Yield Curve: A chart in which the yield level is plotted on the vertical axis and the term to maturity of debt instruments of similar creditworthiness is plotted on the horizontal axis. The yield curve is positive when long-term rates are higher than short-term rates. However, when short-term rates are higher than yields on long-term investments, the yield curve is negative or inverted.
Yield to Maturity: The rate of interest an investor would have to earn if an investment equal to the price of a debt instrument was capable of generating the coupon payments and the principal of the instrument in exactly the yearly pattern promised by the issuer.

INDEX